Brigadier General Tyree H. Bell, C.S.A.

★ TYREE H. BELL, COLONEL, BELL'S BRIGADE, FORREST'S CAVALRY. TENNESSEE STATE LIBRARY AND ARCHIVES.

Brigadier General Tyree H. Bell, C.S.A.
FORREST'S FIGHTING LIEUTENANT

Nathaniel Cheairs Hughes, Jr.

with

Connie Walton Moretti

and

James Michael Browne

THE UNIVERSITY OF TENNESSEE PRESS / KNOXVILLE

Copyright © 2004 by The University of Tennessee Press / Knoxville.
All Rights Reserved.
Cloth: 1st printing, 2004.
Paper: 1st printing, 2016.

Library of Congress Cataloging-in-Publication Data

Hughes, Nathaniel Cheairs, Jr.
    Brigadier General Tyree H. Bell, C.S.A.:
Forrest's fighting lieutenant / Nathaniel Cheairs Hughes, Jr.
with Connie Walton Moretti and James Michael Browne.— 1st ed.

    p. cm.

Includes bibliographical references (p.) and index.
ISBN 978-1-62190-194-5

  1. Bell, Tyree Harris, 1815–1902.
  2. Generals—Confederate States of America—Biography.
  3. Confederate States of America. Army—Biography.
  4. Forrest, Nathan Bedford, 1821–1877—Friends and associates.
  5. United States—History—Civil War, 1861–1865—
    Cavalry operations.
  I. Moretti, Connie Walton.
  II. Browne, James Michael.
  III. Title.

E467.1.B395H84 2004
973.7'3'092—dc22   2003026433

Contents

Preface		ix
1.	Excitement Reigned Supreme	1
2.	Belmont	11
3.	Shiloh	29
4.	Banners to the Breeze	49
5.	My Old Kentucky Home	63
6.	Shelbyville	73
7.	Slipping Back to West Tennessee	85
8.	Bell's Brigade	99
9.	A Dash into Kentucky	107
10.	Fort Pillow	115
11.	Brice's Crossroads	131
12.	Harrisburg	151
13.	Cheer Up	165
14.	Johnsonville	179
15.	Hood's Invasion of Tennessee	189
16.	Hood's Retreat from Tennessee	205
17.	All Was Gloom	219
18.	Disappointment in Dyer County	231
19.	South to West	239
Notes		261
Bibliography		315
Index		333

Illustrations

Figures

Tyree H. Bell	frontispiece
Bell Home in Cottontown, Tennessee	8
Col. Tyree H. Bell, 12th Tennessee Infantry	20
Brig. Gen. Gideon J. Pillow	23
Maj. Gen. Benjamin Franklin Cheatham	45
Capt. Alfred T. Fielder	50
Brig. Gen. Preston Smith	56
Brig. Gen. Abraham Buford	66
Brig. Gen. Daniel S. Donelson	70
Maj. Gen. Stephen D. Lee	92
Brig. Gen. James R. Chalmers	93
Robert "Black Bob" McCulloch	102
Maj. Charles A. Anderson	104
Fort Pillow Massacre	129
Maj. Gen. Nathan Bedford Forrest	133
Brig. Gen. Hylan B. Lyon	135
Col. William A. Johnson	141
Maj. Gen. Andrew J. Smith	152
Brig. Gen. James H. Wilson	220
Brig. Gen. William H. Jackson	224
Tyree H. Bell, about 1870	235
Bell Home on Goshen Avenue in Visalia, California	248
Bell-Cole Family Reunion, 1899–1901	248

Maps

West Tennessee, 1861–1862	34
Advance and Retreat in Kentucky, 1862	54
West Tennessee Raids, 1863–1864	109
Defense of North Mississippi, 1864	146
Attack on Athens, Alabama, September 1864	171
Johnsonville Expedition, October and November 1864	181
Hood's Tennessee Campaign, November and December 1864	191
Fighting against Wilson in Alabama, March–May 1865	228
Central California, 1876–1902	251

Preface

Thousands of Southerners rode with Nathan Bedford Forrest, that "Dread Warrior" of Tennessee. For generations his story has been told and retold by worshipful soldiers and admiring historians, North and South. Indeed, Forrest has become not only a folk hero but a military figure of international renown. The principal subordinates of this legendary Confederate cavalry leader, however, remain blurry background figures: William H. "Red" Jackson, Abraham "Abe" Buford, James R. Chalmers, Frank Armstrong, and Tyree Bell. Like most of the division and brigade commanders of the Army of Tennessee, Jackson, Buford, Armstrong, and Chalmers had received college educations and, prior to the Civil War, had become either professional soldiers or attorney-politicians. The other lieutenant, Tyree Harris Bell, was cut from different cloth—he was a farmer with no military experience whatsoever, a prototype citizen-soldier.

Connie Moretti and Jim Browne have a special reason to explore Tyree Bell's life and military career: they are his great-great-grandchildren. Early on they came to realize that Bell's story—indeed, the family story—had been largely lost as a result of the family's migration to California. Moreover, the general himself appears to have been neglected by historians. Moretti and Browne felt this imbalance can and should be redressed, but accomplished with the objectivity worthy of their ancestor.

These two cousins met for the first time in 1994 at a memorial gathering in California honoring General Bell. This event, for which Moretti was the keynote speaker, rekindled Browne's interest in Bell's life. Coincidentally, Browne and his family relocated to the Nashville, Tennessee, area two years later. Browne's business turned out to be located a few blocks away from the

Tennessee State Library and Archives, and thus he found at his fingertips superb raw material for the study of Tennesseans. He recontacted Moretti and let her know that he had begun research on General Bell. Browne discovered a lengthy 1901 newspaper interview of Bell when the general was visiting Nashville. Bell stated in this interview that he was in town to work on a history of his service with Forrest's cavalry. Another article at the time of his death and a family book written somewhat later also indicated that such a work was being written at the time he died. Browne's subsequent search for this manuscript was not successful, but he believed nevertheless that sufficient material existed for a biography. Moretti had decided to write such a book herself, and she readily agreed to collaborate with her cousin.

Browne's home south of Nashville in Brentwood fortuitously turned out to be a short walk from the site of a skirmish in which Bell's Brigade was involved the day after the battle of Franklin. This event served as Browne's starting point. He would examine Bell's participation in Hood's Tennessee Campaign.

Nat Hughes first encountered Tyree Bell while doing a study of the Battle of Belmont, the opening operation for what would become the Confederate Army of Tennessee. There in the bottomland of the Mississippi River, this well-respected West Tennessee farmer Tyree Bell commanded one of the proud West Tennessee infantry regiments: the Twelfth. Apparently Bell had gained the confidence of the regiment's original colonel, Robert Milton Russell, a West Pointer and an infantry officer in the Old Army. When Milton Russell moved up to brigade command at Belmont, it fell to the lieutenant colonel—Tyree Bell—to lead the regiment, and this overnight soldier performed with conspicuous and surprising competence during the Twelfth Tennessee's first combat.

Subsequently Hughes had found, quite by chance, a manuscript by Tyree Bell in the Rare Book, Manuscript, and Special Collections Library of Duke University. It was not identified as such, however, and was mixed in with a collection of old articles believed to have been submitted to the *Confederate Veteran*. Once he had verified the authorship of the document, Hughes immediately turned to the Battle of Belmont portion of the memoir and found information that Bell had not mentioned in his official after-action report. Hughes read on. It was an autobiographical sketch. Most of the memoir dealt with his service with Forrest, although Bell devoted a significant number of pages to the organization and early campaigns of the Twelfth Tennessee. Hughes determined to edit the manuscript, encouraged by Duke's senior reference librarian, William R. Erwin, Jr.

Meanwhile, Connie Moretti, two thousand miles away, had published a biographical sketch of Bell. This article came to the attention of Hughes, and he contacted Mrs. Moretti, asking if she would have an interest in collaborating. Connie Moretti agreed, explaining that she and her cousin Jim Browne had been collecting material about their ancestor for several years.

Thus the three joined forces, committing themselves to preparing Tyree Bell's story. They would use Bell's Autobiography as the spine of the study, allowing the subject, so to speak, to represent himself. They were intrigued. How did Bell, the farmer and stock raiser, adapt to the challenges war presented? How did this novice, this summertime soldier, measure up against the West Pointers, the Seminole and Mexican War veterans? Why had he been entrusted with a significant leadership position?

There is no previous biography of Tyree Bell, and no articles in historical journals other than Connie Moretti's. Bell has been overlooked by historians, as have Forrest's other principal subordinates largely, it seems, because of the powerful magnetism of their chief. Yet, how can one understand Forrest and his importance in the American Civil War without knowledge of those lieutenants entrusted with carrying out his designs? Forrest never won a battle by himself.

To follow Tyree Bell is to see Bragg's 1862 Kentucky Campaign from a different vantage point. This may also be said of Fort Pillow, Brice's Crossroads, and Hood's Tennessee Campaign, not to mention the confused state of affairs in Alabama and Mississippi during the winter and spring of 1865.

We like to think that we are completing what Tyree Bell set out to do himself when he was a very old man. He wanted to tell the story of his participation in the Civil War, and we try to do so for him, using his own words whenever advantageous to the narrative. Our account differs from what appears in his autobiography, however. He tended to keep the spotlight off himself; we change the focus and concentrate on his role. Bell accomplished many things in his life, but he also demonstrated deficiencies and made mistakes. He risked much to fight for the Confederacy and would wear to his grave the scars of his disappointments and deadly encounters.

Many people have helped us in our quest, generously providing guidance, encouragement, and resources: librarians, historians, and Bell family members. This spirit of sharing invigorated us and gave us new friends.

Our thanks are due to Earl Willoughby of Dyersburg, Tennessee, who read the chapters on the Twelfth Tennessee and contributed important documents and ideas. Brent A. Cox of Milan, Tennessee, also provided helpful material, particularly about Robert M. Russell and the Twentieth Tennessee Cavalry. Gordon D. Johnson of Wonewoc, Wisconsin, graciously shared the memoirs of one of Bell's escort. Timothy D. Johnson of Nashville and Roy Morris and Sam Elliott of Chattanooga read portions of the manuscript and offered valuable suggestions. Dr. Michael B. Ballard, an authority on the Civil War in Mississippi, patiently read and criticized the Brice's Crossroads and Harrisburg chapters. Thomas Y. Cartwright, curator of the Carter House in Franklin, Tennessee, kindly agreed to critique the Tennessee Campaign portion of the manuscript. To all of these readers and friends we are grateful.

Jim Ogden deserves special mention. As historian of the Chickamauga-Chattanooga National Military Park, he shared valuable material with us, gave us helpful insights, and provided invaluable encouragement.

Others we must thank include the following: Bruce S. Allardice of Des Plaines, Illinois; Margaret Alley of Montebello, California; James Bell of Tucson, Arizona; Marlon D. Bell of Luling, Louisiana; Marjeanne Blinn, interlibrary loan librarian at Palos Verdes Public Library, Palos Verdes, California; Paul V. Breazeale of Jackson, Mississippi; Walter T. Durham of Gallatin, Tennessee; Pat Elder of Memphis, Tennessee; Ed Frank at the University of Memphis Library; Susan Gordon of the Tennessee State Library, Nashville; Roberta and Carl Hancock of Gallatin, Tennessee; Ellen Harding and the staff at the California History Section, California State Library, Sacramento, California; Marylin Bell Hughes at the Tennessee State Library, Nashville; Gerald G. Jones of Anderson, Indiana; Bruce Kosmin of Wheeling, Illinois; Rick Kubiack of Fresno, California; Morgan V. Merrill of Sewanee, Tennessee; Randel M. Price at the University of Mississippi, Oxford, Mississippi; Julia Rather at the Tennessee State Library; Larry Reneau of Chattanooga, Tennessee; Ann Ross, assistant director, and the staff at the Sumner County Archives, Gallatin, Tennessee; Melissa Scroggins, Bill Secrest, and Ray Silva at the California History Room, Fresno, California, Public Library; Patricia M. Van Skaik at the Public Library of Cincinnati and Hamilton County; Don Stone of Cottonwood, Tennessee; David H. Wallace at the National Archives; and John E. White at the Southern Historical Collection, University of North Carolina.

1

Excitement Reigned Supreme

A young man, twenty-five at the most, harangued the crowd of Dyer County citizens assembled at Albert Harris's store. Hardly had the impassioned orator finished when another jumped up on the porch to take his place. "Tennessee must stand by her rights!" he shouted. "We must support Governor Isham G. Harris and resist aggression!"

Tyree Harris Bell stood there, watching, saying nothing. Excitement must have been welling up within him. Indeed, as he would remember, "excitement reigned supreme" that spring of 1861, not only here in the little Tennessee village of Newbern, but throughout the South. Bell had ridden into town every day that week and stayed till dark—business was suspended, school was closed. He had been quiet, listening to the speeches, but hardly immune to the excitement, the entrancement, that engulfed the little community.[1]

As the sun fell that pretty April day, Bell untied his horse and stepped into the saddle. It was time to go home. Just as he mounted, however, a group of men, delegates of the good citizens of Newbern, approached him and asked if he might meet with them. And there, just off the dusty road, they carefully paid their respects to this stocky, middle-aged man with the short, grizzled beard. Then the deputation offered him command of the men of Newbern, his neighbors and relatives, who had recently formed themselves into an organization resembling an old-fashioned militia company, quasi-political, quasi-military. Lead us to war, they asked, lead us to help Tennessee. Bell listened attentively to their offer, then thanked the committee for their compliment. "I must have more time," he said, "a little while to think over the matter." He wanted to go home, he added, and talk it over with his wife.[2]

One might imagine the dilemma confronting this forty-five-year-old farmer. Conflicting thoughts doubtless ripped through his mind—heritage and honor doing battle against experience and common sense. Where lay his duty? So Tyree Bell rode very slowly into the dusk, surrounded by faces from the past.

Borne on the breeze was the image of Tyree Rodes Harris, his maternal grandfather, the man for whom he had been named, the man who had taught him so much. Young Tyree and his mother, Susannah Harris Bell, had often traveled the 150 miles from Sumner County, Tennessee, back to the old brick home place just northeast of Lancaster, in Garrard County, Kentucky. Tyree always felt welcome during these extended visits and fit easily into the sprawling Harris family, with several of his mother's half-brothers and sisters close to his own age. His uncle, Russell Harris, just six years older, was a special boyhood friend.

It was there in Old Sumner, as he was wont to call it, that Tyree had the opportunity to observe his grandfather's manner and practical knowledge not only on the farm but in public matters. The family and the community thought Squire Harris a wise man, a man of judgment, a man to be trusted. He had done about everything in Garrard County, it seemed—justice of the peace, sheriff, and representative to the Thirty-eighth and Thirty-ninth sessions of the Kentucky General Assembly. Grandfather Harris's sense of obligation and honor had made a lasting impression on Tyree. What would be the old man's advice now?[3]

Then Bell may have seen, perhaps for an instant, the face of his old schoolmaster among the dark branches. He smiled to himself, for he knew what William Price Thomas would have said. Mr. Thomas's views, like his speech, were clear, emphatic. Bell had attended Thomas's "English School," a little one-room log structure, near Douglass Chapel in the Station Camp Creek valley. Along with the rules of grammar, memorized though constant drill, exemplary selections of English and classical literature formed the heart of the curriculum. The students learned to cipher, of course, and Thomas offered practical, experience-stretching exercises, advertising proudly in the *Gallatin Union:* "I have Globes, Maps and Surveying Instruments for the use of my Students." For thirty years this Virginia scholar taught and counseled not only Sumner County students like young Tyree, but other Tennesseans and Kentuckians who would board in homes in nearby Gallatin. Bell prized his education under William Price Thomas, and he admitted feeling the schoolmaster's influence throughout his life. Mr. Thomas's counsel, certainly, would have been to determine the right course, the just course, and to follow it wherever it might lead.[4]

This advice would have been echoed by his father-in-law, Josiah Walton, who took pride in having put service to God and country in the forefront of his life. Squire Walton had warmly welcomed Tyree into the family and given him land on which to build a home for his bride. He treated Bell as a son and as a good friend until the day he died.

Born at Mansker's Station in 1788, Josiah Walton and Sumner County had grown to maturity together. The squire was still a toddler when his father, Isaac Walton, became county coroner, lieutenant in the local militia, and then justice of the peace. At seven, Josiah, the eldest son of the family, proudly watched his father ride off to represent Sumner County at the first Tennessee Constitutional Convention in Knoxville. Later Isaac Walton would take his seat in the Third and Eighth Tennessee General Assemblies. Although only eleven when his father and his uncle began construction of the Walton Road leading from the Caney Fork to Knoxville, Josiah was still big enough to help with the construction of the wagon road, which travelers would later praise as being "broad and commodious as those in the environs of Philadelphia." He was an impressionable youth of thirteen when Bishop Francis Asbury convened the first annual Tennessee Methodist Conference at Strother's Meeting House on Station Camp Creek. The Waltons had become devout Methodists, and Walton's Campground, according to Sumner County historian Walter Durham, "became a familiar name throughout the Cumberland country." There was little doubt therefore that Tyree and Mary Ann Walton Bell would become active Methodists as well.[5]

Hardly a stereotypical backwoods settler, Josiah Walton was described as a man of "great amenity of manners . . . punctual, dutiful, steadfast and faithful in friendship." The squire had fought beside Andrew Jackson in the first Seminole War and served as the future president's private secretary. By the time Tyree Bell married Walton's twenty-one-year-old daughter, Mary Ann, in 1841, the prosperous and influential Walton had followed in his father's footsteps as justice of the peace and Methodist Church leader. Although Josiah had passed away four years before Tennessee's secession, his son-in-law, Tyree Bell, still missed his friendship and guidance.[6]

The Bell family military tradition also may have passed through his reverie—names from childhood, some a little larger than life—Captain Robert Harris, John Heard, Absalom Beddo, Thomas Allen Beall—direct forebears from Virginia and Maryland who had set aside personal interests and become Revolutionary War heroes. There were tales, too, of the famous Scotsman, red-haired, seven-foot-tall Ninian Beall, Tyree's distant ancestor who was transported to the colonies for standing against Cromwell.

Other legends whispered down through the centuries: stories of constant fighting between Bell ancestors and the English, even other Scottish clans. The Bells had belonged to the notorious Border Reivers, labeled by their detractors as outlaws, cattle rustlers, blackmailers, thieves. A fierce people who lived in the disputed stretch of land between Scotland and England, their story was one of seemingly endless raids and reprisals against the English, and against one another. This narrow belt of Scotland featured burned-out homes and castles—markers of doomed dreams and bloody surprises. It contained secret places of sanctuary, lairs to which one could flee when pursued, hidden valleys where one could hide cattle, irregular terrain, and suddenly twisting streams where enemies might be caught at distinct disadvantage. *You have the fighting instincts of a Reiver,* breathed those faint voices from the past.[7]

This lore of the elusive Reivers, Captain Harris, Absalom Beddo, and Ninian Beall made up the fabric of Tyree's early years as surely as the gentle breeze carried their memory, their sayings, to him. How proud he was that the blood of warriors, of patriots, coursed though his veins. Without a doubt, this present conflict was one they would have understood.

Riding on through the gathering twilight, Bell's thoughts must have turned to family men of the present—distant only in miles rather than time. Drawn like moths to the incandescence of booming Nashville, members of the extended Harris clan had come down from Kentucky in search of work in the building trades. Uncle Brightberry Harris, his mother's eldest brother, was among the first to make the journey. People sometimes commented on the resemblance between Tyree and his dynamic uncle. Tyree himself was about five feet, ten inches tall, a handsome man who appreciated his appearance. He was of stocky build and had a thick, unruly thatch of curly hair that had been black in youth, but now, past forty, was rapidly graying.[8] Uncle Brightberry, Tyree recalled, was also a man "of tremendous nervous energy, and always rode, walked and talked in a hurry. I have a mental picture of him as he used to come up the road to our house, on a big powerful horse, his arms and legs flying up and down. His voice was loud and sonorous, and when he talked reminded one of a rapid firing gun. He was a man of courage and determination. Once when he had a persistently aching tooth he arose from his bed at night and pulled it out himself with a pair of shoe-pincers."[9]

Uncle Bright excelled as a farmer. He specialized in raising fine stock—horses, cattle, sheep, and hogs, all of which he proudly exhibited at county agricultural fairs. This exuberant uncle, whom Bell admired, was married to Mary Ann Walton, Bell's quiet, sensible, kindhearted Aunt Sallie. Their long two-story house just across PeeDee Creek from Josiah Walton's had been a family gathering place, one where Tyree and Mary Ann had first become acquainted. What would Uncle Bright and Aunt Sallie have said? Doubtlessly they would have reminded him of his family responsibilities, especially his younger children—the three girls ranging from nine to thirteen and the three little boys aged three to seven. Abandon them to lead his neighbors to war?[10]

More of the Harris clan had followed Uncle Bright south. Tyree's uncle, John Wesley Harris, and his half-uncle, Greenberry Harris, journeyed down the rutted road from Lancaster, Kentucky, to Nashville and Cairo, Tennessee, a Sumner County town located strategically at the point where Bledsoe's Creek empties into the Cumberland River. Uncle John Wesley stayed around just long enough to find himself a wife, then moved on. Tyree's half-uncle Greenberry and step-uncle, John Branham, on the other hand, followed the example of Uncle Bright. Both came to the Nashville-Cairo area as apprentice stonemasons and looked to expand their opportunities. Uncle John Branham soon acquired a sixteen-acre farm on Bledsoe's Creek where he established a brickyard and built a saw mill. He quickly added to his holdings and eventually became one of the most prosperous farmers in Sumner County, owning fine tracts totaling twenty-five hundred acres. From Uncles Greenberry Harris and John Branham, Tyree learned construction skills and contracting techniques. From Uncle Brightberry Harris, he learned farming, particularly stock raising. What would be his uncles' counsel now, in April 1861: the caution of economic self-interest?[11]

When Tyree dwelled on his kinsmen, as he often did, he could not help but contrast their accomplishments and prominence, particularly Uncle John's rise from lowly apprenticeship to a condition of affluence, to his own father's unsuccessful life.

Absalom B. Bell, a native of Montgomery County, Maryland, had been brought over the Alleghenies in 1794 when he was three years old. His parents settled in Mason County, Kentucky, and there Absalom remained, probably until the time he made his appearance in Garrard County at age twenty-one, paying taxes on himself and a horse. While Josiah Walton was marching with Andrew Jackson, Absalom Bell hired Francis Brown to take his place in the Second Kentucky Infantry Regiment.

On November 9, 1812, Absalom Bell married twenty-year-old Susannah Harris, with her father, Tyree Rodes Harris, as bondsman. Absalom and Susannah Bell disappeared from Garrard County records for a time, and even their son Tyree's 1815 birthplace is clouded in speculation, being given variously as Cincinnati, Ohio; Covington, Kentucky; or Garrard County, Kentucky. Possibly Absalom, who described himself as a plasterer, went to the newly platted town of Covington in search of work. By June 1816, however, the Bells were back in Garrard County, where Absalom spent $400 on land with an unwarranted title and paid his taxes. Late the following year he sold that property and went to Tennessee. In 1819, Absalom's father, Thomas Allen Beall (pronounced Bell, hence the spelling change), wrote his will and entrusted $100 for his grandson, John Burroughs, to Absalom's care. Absalom probably received his share of the estate on coming of age, as no separate bequest was made to him. There is no evidence, however, that he ever delivered the $100 to his nephew, John Burroughs, nor does he appear to have been present when the estate was finally settled in 1831, although he and Susannah are listed as parties to the proceedings.[12]

In 1820 and 1830 the Absalom Bell family was living in the Bledsoe's Creek area of Sumner County, and it is recorded that in 1838 Absalom paid Elijah Busby $275 for 115 acres across the county on the main fork of Station Camp Creek. Just six short years later, Absalom mortgaged not only his land, but also all the family's household goods in order to satisfy oppressive debts. His second son, Thomas, redeemed the mortgage, and for the rest of his life, this son provided a home for his parents. After Thomas died in 1869, Absalom and Susannah went to live in the household of their daughter, Sarah Ann Douglass. Although Absalom was the eldest of twelve children, he does not appear to have maintained contact with his brothers and sisters. No letters from them appear to have been waiting for him at the various Sumner County post offices; few of his descendants are even aware of their names. None of his many grandsons and great-grandsons bear his name in a family that still names their sons Tyree. Although the Bell family connections appear to have been neglected, Absalom and Susannah's three children all married well, into old, prosperous, highly respected Sumner County families—Thomas and Sarah marrying into the Douglass clan, Tyree into the Walton family. Nevertheless, a proud man like Tyree Bell must have been motivated to prove himself, to succeed, perhaps to compensate for his father's obscurity.[13]

Perhaps Tyree's thoughts turned back to Kentucky. His Uncle Russell Harris had bought out the other heirs when Grandfather Harris died and now lived in a frame house he had attached to the original brick home. How well Tyree remembered the time he had spent with his friend Russell after finishing his schooling, when he was about twenty and Russell twenty-six. The two young men worked together, raising and trading livestock and learning the building trade. When Tyree left the old Harris place for home in December 1838, Samuel Lusk still owed him $46.75 for lathing and rough coating four rooms, but Tyree also had a note due to William Adams for $40.00. His carelessness about these bills generated a lawsuit that was not resolved until 1842 with the decision that

Lusk pay Adams. Thoughts of his old friend Uncle Russell reminded Tyree that he had not received a letter from the family for some time. He knew the secessionist sentiment in Kentucky was far more divided than in West Tennessee and wondered where Russell stood in this great debate? Russell was too old to fight, being fifty-one, but he had never been a fence straddler, especially when Tyree was involved. He would support his nephew, the issues and odds being beside the point.[14]

As he rode on, Tyree Bell may have recalled Miss Mary Ann Walton, the girl who had drawn him back to Sumner County in 1838. Tiny, lively, with dark hair and bright eyes, she was the perfect complement to his more reserved nature. Finally, he had asked her to marry him, and she accepted. The wedding was set for Thursday, December 2, 1841.[15] It proved a grand social event, being held at Squire Walton's with friends and relatives flocking in from all around. The entertainment included a sumptuous wedding supper at the Waltons' followed the next evening by another banquet and reception or "infair" at the home of the groom's parents.[16]

Squire Walton set aside a 180-acre parcel for the young couple's use, and on January 1, 1842, Tyree and a number of hands commenced building. On March 1, the young couple "moved home." Tyree farmed and raised stock, while Miss Mary (as he was wont to call her) tended to their ever-growing family. James William, born in 1842, was followed at two-year intervals by Isaac Thomas, Russell, Susan, and Sarah Catherine. Not long after Sarah's birth, the old Cotton family homestead adjoining Bell's land on the Red River Turnpike came on the market. Tyree purchased this property and set to work building the beautiful brick house that still stands in Cottontown. The family soon moved to this new home where Cynthia Ann, Josiah Walton, and Tyree Alexander were born.[17] Tyree continued to add to his holdings, purchasing tracts of 34 and 135 acres in 1850 for cotton cultivation. For crop diversification and investment purposes, he purchased an additional 44 acres in 1855, 44 in 1856, and 5 in 1857.[18]

How quickly the years had passed, in the typical country manner of the time. Long monotonous stretches of hard work were enlivened by visits with friends and family. Relatives lived all across Sumner County and in the Nashville area, while others had scattered into Kentucky, Mississippi, and Alabama. The sudden death of President James K. Polk would have led to condolence calls on his widow, Miss Mary's cousin, Sarah Childress Polk, even if the family could not attend his funeral, and extended visits with other family members were a regular occurrence. Raising stock, educating children, supporting the church, and opening their home to family and friends—the passage of time condensed these years into a fond memory.[19]

Life had taken another abrupt turn in 1857. Josiah Walton died in August, and about this time Tyree and Mary Ann lost their young son, Russell. Tyree grew restless; for him Sumner County had lost its enchantment. West Tennessee summoned. Tyree and Mary's cousins, Allen and Albert Harris, had moved west, past Nashville, beyond the Tennessee River to a Mississippi River county—Dyer County, Tennessee—and prospered. They invited Cousin Tyree to come out and investigate, join in the scramble for new land. Tyree went. He liked what he found; it smelled of opportunity. He probably thought, too, that a change of scene would benefit Miss Mary. Therefore, that winter of 1857, he sold his Sumner County property and bought two tracts "nearly entirely in the woods" in Dyer County. He decided to concentrate his efforts on the 160-acre tract located a mile and a quarter from Newbern, "a little town built up for school purposes." Thus, while Mary and the younger children went to stay with her mother, Tyree took one if not both of the older boys and "my family of negros, with the exception of a boy and a woman," out to the new place "and made a home of it." There, with his little contingent, he would undertake the hardship and privation of clearing virgin land and establishing a large farm in a new country.[20]

For two years Bell and his "second family" worked to improve the land and establish themselves "in the woods." He traveled "backwards and forwards"

★ BELL HOME IN COTTONTOWN, TENNESSEE. COLLECTION OF CONNIE MORETTI.

the 150 miles between Newbern and Cottontown many times until November 1859, when he brought Miss Mary and the children to their new home, "a very nice little farm" with two "negro houses and a comfortable residence."[21]

Mary Ann Bell found Newbern a little village of about ten families, "a fine school and two stores" in a raw, rapidly developing agricultural county of some ten thousand people. Nearly all the farmers in Dyer County grew oats, producing about twenty bushels an acre. Many, like Bell, also raised wheat, corn, and tobacco. Tyree and Mary Ann Bell in 1860 ranked (of 148 families) among the top ten property owners and slaveholders in the 6th Civil District of Dyer. They owned 350 acres (100 acres of improved farmland) valued at $8,250 and personal property of $22,560. They possessed $325 worth of farm implements and $2,435 worth of livestock—8 horses, 3 mules, 7 milch cows, 4 working oxen, 6 other cattle, 10 sheep, and 30 hogs. In 1860 they produced 60 bushels of wheat, 150 bushels of corn, 24,000 pounds of tobacco, 40 pounds of wool, 75 bushels of Irish potatoes, 50 bushels of sweet potatoes, and 365 pounds of butter. In addition, they made most of what they wore, and besides candles and soap, produced for sale orchard products, hay, clover seed, grass seed, beeswax, and honey. Through enterprise and energy the farm bountifully supported Tyree and Mary Ann's family of eleven as well as sixteen slaves: three men aged sixty-five, twenty-nine, and twenty-eight; three women aged twenty-nine, twenty-five, and twenty-five; and ten children.

Adjoining the Bell farm was that of Edward and Harriet Haskins, wealthy Virginians—slaveholders who had preceded the Bells to Newbern. They had four older sons at home, all of whom eventually would serve under Bell as soldiers, two in his escort. Also close by were the families of Albert G. Harris and his brother, Dr. Allen Harris, first cousins to both Tyree and Mary Ann Bell. Indeed, within the vicinity were a score of relatives, recent arrivals from Middle Tennessee—Douglasses, Wynnes, Harrises, Enochs, among them.

From 1859 to 1861, life settled once more into a familiar routine for the Bells as they established themselves in the Newbern community. Tyree helped found the Methodist church at Church Grove (on land purchased from Presbyterian Ed Haskins) and served as one of its original trustees. He also interested himself in the development of Church Grove Cemetery. Family and friends turned to him for assistance with their affairs, and he was involved in settling several estates. The younger Bell children were enrolled in school, while the oldest boys—James and Isaac, although continuing their education—served as farm laborers whenever possible, learning from a taskmaster father the business of operating a farm and breeding and raising livestock.[22]

Belmont

Doubtless many things whirled through the mind of Tyree Bell as he rode past Cousin Albert Harris's home, on beyond Ed Haskins's place, on down Haskins Lane, then turned his horse down the long drive leading up to his own house. The gloom of gathering evening must have distorted everything—the green shutters above the front porch at home appearing as elongated smudges against the quiet white backdrop.[1]

Later that night when Mary Ann Bell had finished with child minding, she and Tyree sat down together in their bedroom. She sat on one side of the fireplace, he on the other. Now and then Tyree would get up from his chair and pace the floor. "I tried to get her to decide the matter for me," he remembered, but that night Miss Mary just shook her head. She was a proud, determined woman and no doubt had strong ideas about what Tyree might do, should do, about what might be at stake, but she kept her peace.[2]

Who could have known better than Miss Mary? The very day Mary Ann Walton was born her own father had left home, marching down the road, off with General Jackson's troops for Florida. Her father had been gone for months. She had heard the story so many times—his leaving, the consequent hardships it placed upon her mother. But that night Mary Walton Bell refused to speak her mind. She told Tyree she wanted him "to do what was right about it and nothing else."[3]

Tyree Bell never volunteered his own thoughts. He was sufficiently independent-minded, of course, not to be swept away by popular sentiment. He had faced that before when he chose to remain on his farm in Sumner County in 1846 and watch his friends start out for Mexico. Perhaps that experience fifteen years ago weighed heavily, influencing him. Did he have regrets? This was a second chance. Yet Tyree still had young children under his roof and a farm to manage, not to speak of his age. Turn soldier at forty-seven? He was strong, exceptionally strong, and in good health, and he knew he could ride and march and shoot with the best of them, but for how long? Tyree Bell was no fool.

So, after they had sat together and Tyree had reviewed their situation and their options, then reviewed them all over again, they went to bed without coming to a decision.[4]

Events had been moving so fast: South Carolina's secession, the special session of the Tennessee Assembly early in January 1861, the secession of six other Southern states, Tennessee's vote against secession on February 9, the surrender of Fort Sumter on April 14, President Lincoln's call for seventy-five thousand volunteers, Tennessee Governor Isham G. Harris's angry response that "in such an unholy crusade no gallant son of Tennessee will ever draw his sword." Tennesseans had begun to gather much in the manner of Bell and his neighbors, ordinary citizens, by the dozens, by the hundreds. They organized militarily, forming a company in Dyersburg, and on April 24 the citizens of Newbern raised the "Secession pole."[5]

"The next morning we had another talk," Bell recalled, and as Miss Mary "walked down to the gate with me, I told her she had better make me some army clothes for I had made up my mind to take the captaincy of the company." So, when Tyree rode off to town, Mary turned back to the house and once inside began gathering material to fashion her husband a handsome, durable uniform. Meanwhile, Tyree rode into Newbern and met with his neighbors, telling them that he would become their captain. Thus the Newbern Blues were born. They began drilling in the dusty streets of town and in no time this makeshift military organization with the mellifluous name began to sound like, if not march like, a company of men going off to war.[6]

Two weeks after the secession pole went up in Newbern, Governor Harris and the Tennessee legislature transformed the state's militia organization into the Provisional Army of Tennessee and entered into an alliance or military league with the Confederacy. The Blues formally elected Bell captain, but Bell believed his company was only the beginning.[7] Surely there would be more, many more. He knew married men by the dozen who had hung back; then there were others hesitant of joining companies such as the Newbern Blues because of financial commitments, or because they continued to cling, albeit tenuously, to their almost religious faith in the Union.

While the Newbern Blues continued to organize, Captain Bell traveled down to Memphis to meet with Maj. Gen. Gideon J. Pillow, Tennessee's Mexican War hero, who commanded the state's provisional army. Pillow had been busy building a military organization since before Fort Sumter, for that matter since March 1861. Already Pillow had sent John C. Burch and Nathan B. Forrest deep into Kentucky to buy horses and supplies and to gather intelligence. It appears Pillow summoned Bell to offer him command of a regiment of West Tennesseans, yet to be recruited. Actively readying Tennessee for war, General Pillow had listened eagerly to Bell's report that with a little more time he felt he could raise "the other nine companies to complete the regiment that I was to command." Pillow granted Bell that time, and the persuasive and influential general made a mental note to remember this Dyer County farmer who knew the value of horseflesh and could rally men to his standard.[8]

So, on May 26 the Blues left Newbern and marched south to enter state service.[9] Upon their departure the young ladies of the village, represented by Miss Sue Williams, presented their gallants with a splendid silk flag. Two days later, in Jackson, Tennessee, Tyree H. Bell, farmer, officially became Captain Bell, Company G, Twelfth Tennessee Volunteer Infantry. A week later, on June 3, a regimental election was held, and Bell's comrades chose him lieutenant colonel of the Twelfth. Until the arrival of the regimental commander (a former professional soldier named Robert Milton Russell), Bell would lead the regiment.[10]

The Twelfth had developed differently than Bell anticipated. The men of Dyer surprised him, and probably disappointed him. Two companies, instead of joining the Twelfth, had opted to become part of the Thirteenth Tennessee Infantry. Two others had joined the Twenty-second Tennessee, and still another the Fourth Tennessee.[11] So the Twelfth, despite the presence of the Newbern Blues, turned out to be predominantly a Gibson County regiment—eight of the ten companies.

Bell was no stranger to the men of Gibson. He had traded with them and had made acquaintances and friends through Methodist district conferences and camp meetings. A good many of the Gibson soldiers were from Trenton or near about. Company E, Colonel Russell's own company, was composed of Trenton townsfolk who referred to themselves as "The Gibson Stars." Company I lacked such an exalted name and was led, at least initially, by the energetic, popular Robert Porter Caldwell, a forty-year-old Kentuckian who had been practicing law in Trenton for fifteen years and representing Gibson, Dyer, Carroll, and Obion Counties in the Tennessee General Assembly and Senate off and on since Mexican War days. Caldwell, with elegant self-assurance, had served as attorney general for the Sixteenth Judicial Circuit of Tennessee for the past three years. Moreover, his law partner in Trenton was the well-positioned Thomas J. Freeman, newly elected colonel of the Twenty-second Tennessee Infantry. This practiced politician, Bob Caldwell, was the best-known man in the Twelfth, better known certainly than Tyree Bell. It is a testimony to Bell's natural leadership, nevertheless, that the men of the Twelfth decided that the farmer from Newbern should be their lieutenant colonel; let Caldwell be major.[12]

Among the other officers in camp at Trenton was Bell's friend, Lt. William M. Harrell, whose younger brother Reuben several years later would marry Bell's oldest daughter Susan; another was Bell's first cousin and neighbor, Lt. Albert Gallatin Harris. Among the company commanders, Josiah N. Wyatt stood out as a leader. Captain of Company H, "Nick" Wyatt was thirty-three, a Mexican War veteran who loved telling stories of the California Gold Rush and of his adventures as a merchant in Sacramento. In addition to these nine companies of West Tennesseans, there was a singular company from across the state line: Kentuckians under Capt. Drew A. Outlaw. These Bluegrass Country boys called themselves Company K.[13]

Also joining Bell in Trenton were his two oldest sons—nineteen-year-old James W. Bell and seventeen year-old Isaac T., both privates. In addition the Twelfth Tennessee contained cousins other than previously mentioned Albert Harris: 1st Sgt. Conquest C. Harris, 2d Cpl. Tyree H. Walton, and 3d Cpl. Andrew S. Parks among them. The Dyer-Gibson regiment also included four "Free Men of Color"—two in Company D, one in Company F, and another, Charley Hill of Gibson County, listed as a musician on the regimental staff.[14]

No sooner had the Twelfth been assembled in Jackson and sworn into state service than they had to squeeze themselves into boxcars and onto flatcars and head back toward home by rail. They detrained at Trenton and made camp, many of them on Colonel Russell's land. Russell, until he was called away to assume brigade command, would drill the regiment himself. Pvt. Charlie B. Harwood remembered Colonel Russell "out under a large white oak," "northeast of the depot," "drilling the first young men of Trenton, who were preparing to go to war."[15]

Russell's election as colonel had come about largely because of Bell's support. "I used my influence," Bell would later write, "to have R. M. Russell elected Colonel of the regiment from the fact that he was educated at West Point and had seen service in the regular army."[16]

Robert Milton Russell, or "Milton" as he was called by his friends, was a gentleman of substance, one of the wealthiest property owners in Trenton, and all of Gibson County. He had not lived in Trenton long, however. A native of Fayetteville, Tennessee, the son of a Revolutionary War officer, Russell had been appointed to the United States Military Academy soon after his father's death in 1842.[17] Upon his graduation from West Point as a member of the illustrious Class of '48, Lieutenant Russell had been assigned to the Fifth U.S. Infantry and had seen garrison duty at East Pascagoula, Mississippi, before being given frontier assignments at Fort Towson in the Indian Territory and at Benica Barracks, California. There in California, in 1850, young Lieutenant Russell supposedly made his contribution to American place-names by suggesting to a superior that a mountain in the distance be named in honor of Josiah D. Whitney, a mining geologist and certainly an acquaintance, if not a good friend, of Russell's. Army life apparently proved tedious for Russell; certainly it could not match the allure, the opportunities, offered by gold-rush California. So in August 1850, within a matter of weeks after arriving in California, twenty-two-year-old Russell resigned from the army to become a merchant and miner near Mariposa, California, joining his brother John Cowan Russell. When Milton Russell had accumulated sufficient capital, he left California and purchased a farm in central Texas, then journeyed to Kentucky, where in 1852 he married Fannie I. January. The young couple returned to Texas and made their home on Russell's land near Austin, remaining there from 1853 to 1855. In the latter year Russell and his family (he had two children by now) moved to West Tennessee, where he purchased a farm at Trenton. Despite this outlay in capital, Robert and Fannie Russell held on to their valuable farmland in Texas and in California.[18]

Having a professional soldier as colonel of the regiment gave confidence to many of the citizen soldiers of the Twelfth Tennessee. They elected R. M. Russell colonel without opposition and, probably to balance his youth, paired him with Lt. Col. Tyree Bell, whom they also elected without opposition. Life at Trenton would prove pleasant as the men of the Twelfth entertained flocks of visitors. Some training was done, of course, and these men of Dyer and Gibson came to know each other much better, but largely it was a near-carnival atmosphere, much like an old-time militia rendezvous.

Governor Harris and General Pillow had done the job. By the end of May, Tennessee had twenty-one regiments organized with three others already mustered into the Confederate Army and dispatched to Virginia.[19] Ten days later Russell, Bell, and the men of the Twelfth climbed aboard the cars once again and moved north along the Mississippi and Ohio Railroad to Union City, Tennessee, where a large camp for instruction, Camp Brown, had been established. There 737 of them reported, most armed with flintlocks and shotguns, some just with large knives. Changes were inevitable as they attempted to transform themselves into soldiers. At Union City, a village located strategically on the Mobile and Ohio Railroad, Bell's Newbern Blues, Company G, had their unit redesignated as Company A, Twelfth Tennessee Volunteer Infantry. The regiment became part of a West Tennessee brigade, along with two other infantry regiments—the Thirteenth and the Twenty-first Tennessee (Tom Freeman's Twenty-second Tennessee would join Russell's Brigade on October 24, 1861, at Columbus, Kentucky, replacing the Thirteenth Tennessee).[20] Col. Robert M. Russell became brigade commander of this, the Second Brigade, Brig. Gen. Gideon J. Pillow's Division, which left Lt. Col. Tyree H. Bell, farmer turned soldier, in command of the Twelfth Tennessee Volunteer Infantry Regiment, an office he would hold for the following nine months.[21]

June quickly passed into July. With Tennessee having adopted its Ordinance of Secession, the Twelfth and her sister regiments at Union City were transferred to the Confederate Army. July 29, the day before they were to become the property of Jefferson Davis's government, Brig. Gen. Frank Cheatham reviewed them. Cheatham was a great favorite with the rank and file, and the men tried to march their best to make him proud. It was Cheatham's final day in his role as Gideon Pillow's chief subordinate, in charge of the recruits of upper West Tennessee. Prior to coming up to Union City, Cheatham had served as acting quartermaster general for Tennessee's Provisional Army. His thankless and limitless task required him to shuttle him back and forth from Nashville to Memphis, from the Military and Financial Board and Harris to Provisional Army headquarters and Pillow. Cheatham observed and undoubtedly assisted in the training of Tennesseans above Memphis, at Fort Randolph, and at another newly established post—just to the north of Randolph, on the highest of three Chickasaw bluffs at the confluence of the Hatchie River and the Mississippi, just south of Coal Creek. It was a good defensive location where the channel tightened, running under the bluff within easy musket range. They called the place Fort Pillow.[22]

Drill intensified in August 1861 as did "talking of war." The adjustment from civilian to soldier was not easy. A man had to give up his independence and place his welfare in the hands of others. Men died. Camp life itself killed them—diseases against which they had developed no immunity—measles, diarrhea, even mumps; they died from accidents incidental to military life. Responsibility for this costly transition belonged to Tyree Bell. Not only did he have to keep seven hundred men healthy and happy, but he had to see that they were disciplined and well trained. Colonel Russell aided Bell enormously in this regard. Bell absolutely depended upon his friend, and Milton Russell in turn displayed great patience as Lieutenant Colonel Bell did his best to internalize the maddening regimental and battalion evolutions required by *Hardee's Tactics*. The men of the Twelfth noticed that Russell and Bell got along famously, seemingly complementing each other. Apparently a warm friendship and a sense of trust between the two men developed at Camp Brown.[23]

Bell did not fare as well with the Confederate Quartermaster Department. It appears that he looked upon these bureaucrats with their multitude of forms and requisitions and reports as a nuisance and was careless or cavalier, not only in his attitude, but his actions, reminiscent of avoidable problems incurred during his sloppy Sumner County days. Bell would pay for his sins the following January, discovering that, as regimental commander, he was being held strictly accountable for the equipment, property, and clothing of the regiment. He would plead ignorance of these "forms of business" and have to ask humbly to be "released from my accountability."[24]

With September came a dramatic turn of events. Deeply concerned lest the Federal army seize the commanding bluffs at Columbus, Kentucky, Maj. Gen. Leonidas Polk, pressed by General Pillow, ordered the Tennesseans gathered at Union City to preempt the enemy movement. Control of the Mississippi River was at stake. Polk's action proved highly controversial, even to fellow Confederates. Years later, Tyree Bell himself would record open disapproval contending that he and his men "broke Kentucky Neutrality Laws" once they crossed the state line in force.[25]

Two of Bell's companies left Union City by train on September 2, the remainder on September 5.[26] Upon their arrival at Columbus the Twelfth encamped initially on the banks of the Mississippi just outside the little river town, down below the great chalk bluffs that dominated the river at this point.[27] On every side, it seemed, the streets ran towards the river; the river and the chalk bluffs defined life at Columbus. The high ground above and behind them bristled with big guns, and a huge iron chain had been stretched across the river supported by a series of rafts. This floating obstruction, backed by the massed heavy batteries on the bluffs, effectively blocked the Mississippi. Even privates knew the enemy must soon strike at this advanced Confederate stronghold.

With the approach of Yankee gunboats on September 8, the troops of Polk and Pillow "were at work as for life and death" strengthening Columbus's massive fortifications. The Federals continued their probes, nevertheless, and on September 14, they landed on the Missouri bank of the river. This "caused Considerable stir in our Camp," observed a Dyer County private. Bell's regiment, along with several others, formed into line of battle on the riverbank and remained on high alert until nearly sundown.[28] Then once again quiet set in; somewhere down the shore a drum was beating. Four days later Pvt. William W. House, Twelfth Tennessee, wrote his girlfriend Mollie: "Well, Mollie, the

Yankees have not gotten me yet, but we have 18 of them, and if they do not stop we will get some more. They have not troubled us for two or three days. We are fixing for them every day that we can. We are chopping down timber on the hill. They are going to blockade the road with timber. They are clearing 2000 acres of land and are digging down the bluff and building breastworks on the hill and in town."[29]

Summer now turned into fall with days marked by continuous alarms, rushes to formation, marches, and countermarches. When the excitement subsided Bell and his men would go back to the monotonous drilling, digging, chopping. Presently earthworks, fieldworks, artillery redoubts, and water batteries appeared. They seemed to be endless. Indeed, by late October, Columbus was probably the most heavily fortified point in North America. One hundred and forty cannon, including the "Lady Polk," the largest gun in the Confederacy, commanded the river at this point.

An uneasy Southern public, however, squirmed with dissatisfaction. The important river port of Paducah was Polk's for the taking, was it not? Polk seemed to be letting opportunity slip through his fingers. Why then had the South invaded Kentucky? Leonidas Polk, sensitive to such criticism though he might be, would not budge. His primary mission, he believed, was to defend the Mississippi River Valley, not widen the war by engaging in dubious military adventures. He also knew how thinly the Confederate forces were stretched from the Mississippi to the Alleghenies. His subordinate, Brig. Gen. Gideon Pillow, on the other hand, let it be known that he disagreed totally with the timid strategy of his superior.[30]

So they waited, these impatient Confederates, ready for action, ready to get on with the war and hurry back home. They had not volunteered to dig miles of trenches. Ditchdiggers they might be, but the boys of the Twelfth were not forgotten. Each train and steamboat brought not only more Confederate regiments, heavy guns and munitions, but gaily dressed visitors, family and friends, male and female, each, it seemed, carrying a large basket of delectables. Columbus with its splendid heights promised "a front row attraction" if one could be so fortunate as to arrive at the right time. Small West Tennessee boys would remember even after their eyes dimmed with age being brought up to the Confederate camps "to see a battle that was brewing."[31]

Indeed, a battle was brewing. Albert Sidney Johnston, newly arrived Confederate commander in the West, worried about the defense of the Tennessee and Cumberland Rivers and asked Polk to dispatch five thousand troops from Columbus to Clarksville, Tennessee. Polk chose Pillow's Division (Russell's and Col. J. Knox Walker's brigades) to move to the threatened area. The division broke camp on November 6, and early on the morning of November 7 they began their march up the chalk bluffs and off to the east toward Clarksville. The Twelfth and their comrades carried only essentials and a minimum of cartridges, their mess gear and camp equipage following along in wagons. Suddenly the column halted. A staff officer appeared on horseback and ordered Russell's Brigade to reverse itself and make for the river. The Federals had appeared across the Mississippi "in great number and their Gun Boats were then in sight." Bell's regiment reached the riverbank first, and he had his men board "as quick as the steam Boats at our landing (there being several present) were in readiness to receive us." Bell's men were the first of four regiments dispatched by Polk to support the Confederate camp on the Missouri shore. The Bishop-General retained the bulk of his forces on the east bank to meet the main body of the enemy reported to be advancing down that side of the Mississippi to attack Columbus itself. As the Twelfth loaded on the small steamers, Lieutenant Colonel Bell had an extra mount brought to him and placed aboard, just in case.[32]

The Twelfth (633 strong) came ashore on the Missouri side about 9:00 A.M., no later than 9:15, and immediately formed just beyond the steamboat landing at Belmont. They quickly learned that the Confederate force on the western shore consisted of only one infantry regiment (Thirteenth Arkansas) and one light field battery (the Louisiana Watson Battery). Bell noted these two units already had formed in line of battle, "but upon our arrival they advanced taking a new position near a half mile distance from the former."

General Pillow had crossed over with Bell and upon landing he ordered Bell and his regiment to form on the right of the Thirteenth Arkansas. This, of course, meant separating Bell from Russell's Brigade and from Milton Russell himself. "I remonstrated very much against it," Bell later wrote, "not having any experience in military affairs," but Pillow was adamant, his orders preemptory. He had no intention of fighting in brigade formation, which would have allowed Russell, who had no battle experience, a senior leadership role. He, Gideon Pillow, a division commander at Chapultepec, would handle the task himself. Thus Bell, under verbal orders from Pillow, marched out to the new line and deployed his ten companies on the right of Col. James C. Tappan's Arkansas soldiers (Bell, the military novice, would refer to their consequent dispersed line of battle as "the column that Pillow had formed to receive Grant.")[33]

Although on the extreme right of the Confederate line, Bell held a naturally strong position, certainly stronger than Russell's other regiments, which stood in line of battle badly exposed in an open field. Bell had the advantage of cover, not only from the heavy woods of the river bottom, but also from a ravine

COL. TYREE H. BELL, 12TH TENNESSEE INFANTRY. LIBRARY OF CONGRESS.

or slough to his front. There was also rising ground in his sector, forming a slight ridge that gave most of his men a somewhat elevated position. Bell, revealing his inexperience, did not seem overly concerned, or concerned at all, with the small opening between his right flank and the river.[34]

On came the Federals under the command of the untested Brig. Gen. Ulysses S. Grant, an officer who had overreached his orders in the first place by proceeding downstream from Cairo, Illinois, to attack the Rebel encampment at Belmont. Grant wanted a fight badly and once ashore pushed his five infantry regiments, augmented by a company of cavalry and a superb field battery, hard against Pillow's clumsily deployed line of battle.[35]

To his front Bell could hear "the firing of our pickets and the enemy and every minute or so a runner would come in telling us the enemy were steadily advancing . . . in great numbers and every moment the firing was plainer . . . and soon our pickets were in sight and run in and formed for battle." The Twelfth waited and listened as the Yankees struck the center and left of Pillow's line. "The enemy advanced within about 125 or 150 steps of our line," Bell reported, and then, "not having fired a gun," "I received orders to charge." The resulting bayonet charge was poorly coordinated, not only on the Twelfth's front, but all along the line. Forward raced Bell's men, penetrating into the woods fifty, perhaps seventy-five, yards. "Owing to the great quantity of fallen timber, brush and unevenness of the ground they did not keep as good a line as I wished," Bell lamented. The line slowed, halted, and the men began to fire. The enemy returned their ragged fire with good effect and Bell's men, realizing they confronted a superior force, recoiled. They pulled back and reestablished their line "somewhat sheltered behind a hill" and held it. Their musketry improved, fortunately, for Bell's left and left center companies had become engaged in a dangerous exchange of fire. They faced the left wing of Grant's biggest regiment, Col. John Logan's Thirty-first Illinois, with Grant himself up close behind his riflemen. Checked by Bell's effective musket fire, the Federals countered by shifting the Thirty-first Illinois farther to the left, lapping around Bell's right. This maneuver was given additional weight by committing a section of artillery to the fight against the Confederate right flank.[36]

Pvt. James N. Rosser, Company G, Twelfth Tennessee, had had enough of the ubiquitous Yankee artillery—"cannon balls, bomb shells, grape & canister shot playing all around thick as hail in a storm." Despite the terrible noise and the flying missiles, the enemy's main effort did not come here—against Bell's front—but came with continued probes against and around his right flank. Down went Bell's horse, killed by rifle fire or by canister from the Federal fieldpieces. Bell fought on foot now, his mobility as regimental commander sharply limited, until his extra horse could be brought up. After that, he noted, "I got through my suffering."[37] Sorely threatened and apparently not supported by Tappan, Bell twice repulsed these Yankee envelopments, but being informed that the regiment's ammunition was all but depleted, Bell pulled Company B, the Friendship Volunteers, off line and sent them back to the ammunition wagon at the riverbank for more cartridges. They returned, but, to the dismay of all, the cartridges were the wrong size, thus useless. Bell sent Company B back again. On this trip "the bullets whistled about our heads and about our feet," a private would enter in his diary, but the detail did succeed in reaching the riverbank and returning with the boxes. To Bell's dismay, the cartridges again were found to be "too small for the muskets used by my men." "When the minie cartridges gave out," Bell reported, "we had to retreat to the bank of the river."[38]

The retreat of the Twelfth Tennessee was dangerous and disorderly, all ten companies being under fire much of the way. "Just before the last order was given," Pvt. Alfred Fielder, of Company B, recorded:

Wm Parrish was wounded immediately at my left side dropped his gun[.] Clasping his hand to his right shoulder said to me "I am wounded in the shoulder" and shortly I felt the wind from a ball brush my left lock or whisker after we had retreated but a short distance. A man whom I did not recognize was shot through the shoulders angling and fell at my feet, the blood spouting from both sides[,] some friends picking him up and carrying him off when he soon expired. Just in front of me James Jackson of our company fell, being shot through the right Breast and was taken up by some of our boys and Carried off.[39]

The impressive abatis that Tappan's men had constructed to deflect any attack upon "Camp Johnston" only proved more of an obstacle for fleeing Confederates, blocking their escape and channeling them into Yankee musket fire. Having made it through the obstructions and the galling small-arms fire, Bell attempted to make a stand in the camp itself, but "the fast-moving Yankee field artillery would unlimber and blast away at any organized body of men." It was a hair-raising experience, Bell would remember. He told his granddaughter long after that "he had to reach up several times and pull his cap down over his head and that one's hair actually did stand on end" in this, "his first engagement in battle."

So they fled, these men of the Twelfth, to the river itself. There Bell managed to reorganize a portion of his men on the thin shelf of mud and sand beneath the banks of the Mississippi River. In the meantime Grant's troops had completely collapsed the Confederate left and center, capturing Camp Johnston and Pillow's precious battery, the guns of which they turned on the Rebel reinforcements as they began to arrive from Columbus. Knox Walker's Second Tennessee, which had come to Pillow's rescue, counterattacked through Camp Johnston, but was smashed.[40]

This bloody repulse of Walker seemed to take the energy out of the Federal pursuit, however, and the Confederates made excellent use of the resulting lull in the fighting. Under orders from Pillow, Bell's men (they could hardly be described as a regiment) began to work their way up the side of the river, concealed from the terrible fire of the Federals, most of whom now seemed preoccupied with looting Camp Johnston.

After watching Walker's large Second Tennessee being swallowed up in the fighting on the Missouri shore, General Polk boldly, but "with great reluctance," decided to commit Col. Samuel Marks and two additional regiments to the Missouri side, ordering Marks to land upriver from Camp Johnston, near

★ Brig. Gen. Gideon J. Pillow. Library of Congress.

Belmont Point. From there, using the cover of the woods, they were to strike the enemy in the flank and attempt to cut him off from his boats.[41]

As they landed, Marks's troops were met by Pillow and the leading elements of Bell's Twelfth. Being guided through the forest by battery commander Capt. William H. "Red" Jackson, this blocking and enveloping force of Confederates took position on Grant's left flank, Marks's Eleventh Louisiana forming on Bell's right, directly astride the Yankees' likely route of retreat. Bell immediately attacked. Under heavy fire the Twelfth charged with a yell across an open field and managed to close to within "75 or 80 steps of the enemy." At this point Bell's men instinctively became individual riflemen, abandoning "Fire by rank" and "Fire by file." "Down we fell," Private Fielder would record that evening, "and at it we went shooting as fast as we could load and fire, one not waiting for another." Then Marks's Louisianans opened on the Federals, subjecting them to a deadly cross fire. The enemy counterattacked, however, punching a hole through Marks's line and driving both Marks and Bell back to the cover of the woods. Then Grant's leading elements conducted a rather orderly "advance to the rear" toward their transports, with the last of the Federal units having to run for their lives through a gauntlet of fire from concealed Confederate riflemen. As the minutes wore on, the withdrawal degenerated into a rout as fragments of the Twelfth joined Frank Cheatham's fresh brigade and two regiments under Col. Preston Smith in giving pursuit. For two miles they chased the Federals, "strewing the way with dead and wounded."

"We pursued him," Bell remembered, "until we got near enough for the Gun-Boats to scare us badly and then we were ordered back." The enemy, under cover of the heavy fire of their gunboats, reembarked and steamed upriver. Bell turned his exhausted regiment over to Major Caldwell, who assembled the Twelfth once again at the Belmont landing and recrossed the Mississippi.[42]

Bell himself remained on the battlefield. According to Assistant Surgeon J. P. McGee and Surgeon Samuel H. Caldwell, Bell had been slightly wounded as had his second-in-command, Maj. Bob Caldwell, and the young regimental quartermaster, Capt. James L. "Jo" Lea. In addition to several company-grade officers who had been wounded (two seriously), Bell's adjutant, Capt. Tom M. Hutcherson, had become lost during the confusion of the fighting, as had cousin Albert Harris, who was serving temporarily as Colonel Russell's brigade adjutant. Bell, thinking Hutcherson and Harris might be wounded and helpless, determined to find them, so he set out late that afternoon, guiding his horse carefully across the battlefield. He found neither Harris nor Hutcherson, but came across a "badly shot" Yankee colonel. Two Confederate Irish stood over the Federal officer "tantalizing him." Bell dismounted immediately and "went to his relief." He found a litter and "made these two Irishmen carry him to our boat landing. I got off of my horse and walked along beside him."[43]

Col. Henry Dougherty, whom Bell had rescued from almost certain death, was perhaps the ablest combat officer on the field that day, Union or Confederate; certainly, with the exception of Pillow, he was the most experienced. An enlisted man in the Old Army, Dougherty had won attention for his heroism in the Mexican War. During the summer of 1861, in a fight with the Rebels at Charleston, Missouri, he had displayed courage and leadership as colonel of the Twenty-second Illinois Infantry. Dougherty commanded Grant's Bird's Point Brigade at Belmont, and during that long November day he and his men had carried the brunt of the attack. Dougherty coordinated infantry and artillery fire and had succeeded in capturing the Watson Battery. He and his men were the last two regiments out, however, and as a result had suffered dreadfully as they tried to make their way back to the transports past Cheatham's and Bell's Confederates lying in ambush.

Dougherty survived the retreat with his Twenty-second Illinois, then made the responsible but disastrous decision to return to the field and help his other regiment, the Seventh Iowa Infantry, extricate itself. His leg was shattered by Rebel musket fire in the process, and he was abandoned to the enemy.[44]

Bell believed Dougherty would "have died that night, if I had not found him. When I got [Dougherty] to the boat, it was good dusk, and there were so many soldiers waiting to get across, wild with excitement, it seemed like a mob." Dougherty, in great pain, became "very much excited and I had him laid on the ground." Bell happened to see his Sumner County friend Capt. John W. Lauderdale, Fourth Tennessee Infantry, who had come across the river to help. He asked Lauderdale to stand over Dougherty and protect him while he went aboard one of the crowded transports and made arrangements to have Dougherty cared for. Fortunately Bell encountered Surgeon William S. Bell (no relation), recently mayor of Chattanooga, now unofficial medical director of Pillow's Division, and managed to persuade him to have the badly wounded Yankee placed aboard a transport and given medical attention. The following day, in Columbus, a Confederate surgeon amputated Dougherty's leg. Bell remained attentive and, probably with the good offices of General Polk, secured rooms for Dougherty in the house of Mr. Owens, the local bank president.[45]

Mrs. Sallie G. Law, a Confederate mother who happened to be visiting her son in Columbus, now made Henry Dougherty her special project. With one leg amputated and compound fractures of his shoulder and forearm, Dougherty was near death. She nursed him and fed him lemonade with a spoon. Then Sallie Law went to General Polk and convinced him to agree to a special flag of truce so that Mrs. Dougherty might be brought through the lines from Bird's Point. Dougherty would eventually gain sufficient strength to be exchanged and would become post commander at Paducah, but his active military career was over and he would ultimately die in 1868 of his Belmont wounds.[46]

Early on November 8, 1861, the day following the Battle of Belmont, Bell took care to distribute forty cartridges to each man, warning his regiment to hold themselves in readiness for whatever might develop. Never again, he promised himself, would his men be caught short of ammunition at the beginning of a fight; never again would his men be found so unprepared for action by a sudden reversal of orders. The morning wore on quietly; fortunately, there was to be no follow-up battle. The Yankees had withdrawn. Instead, details from each company of the Twelfth were sent to the Missouri shore to tend the wounded and to bury the dead. Meanwhile, baggage wagons previously heavily loaded for the transfer to Clarksville were emptied, and once again the tents of the Twelfth were pitched at Columbus.[47]

Tyree Bell would write two after-action reports of Belmont. The first he prepared at Columbus two days after the battle, submitting it to brigade commander Russell. Neglecting to retain a copy, however, Bell would have to produce a second while at Tupelo, Mississippi, eight months later. This subsequent report he submitted directly to Gen. Leonidas Polk. The two versions do not differ substantively. Both are quite short, emphasizing the miserable ammunition situation and understating Bell's role. Bell was quick to brag, however, on the men of his regiment. They had "conducted themselves most gallantly," he reported. "Of which I take great pleasure in bearing testimony."[48]

The Twelfth had been bloodied. A dozen of Bell's men had been killed, forty-six wounded. Thus the regiment had been tested by battle and some leaders, like Capt. W. M. Walker of Company B, found wanting. Petitions for the removal of unfit officers sprang up on the Mississippi riverbank like bright winter flowers. Finger-pointing and faultfinding, however, occurred not just on the regimental level. Pillow blamed Polk for not supporting him promptly and fully on the Missouri shore, and he determined to embarrass his commander. Without notifying Polk, he zealously carried his case to the corridors of Richmond, much as he had attempted to undermine his commanding officer, Gen. Winfield Scott, fifteen years earlier in Mexico. Polk found out about Pillow's duplicity, of course, and responded in a fury. Charges, countercharges, and evidence gathering would continue deep into the summer of 1862.[49]

It should be noted that Bell and Russell carefully refrained from officially criticizing Pillow as a field commander, although both, in answer to specific inquiries from Polk, confirmed the ammunition shortage and agreed that the bayonet charge ordered by Pillow had failed miserably. Bell's criticism of Pillow (stripping him away from his brigade) would come much, much later, in a memoir written twenty years after Pillow's death. Other commanders, however, made plain that Pillow had bungled the battle. Col. Thomas J. Freeman wrote, "I think the charge was ill-judged and almost impossible to have been executed with success"; "there was a total failure to take advantage of any protection . . . abundantly furnished by the nature of the ground." Colonel Tappan criticized Pillow's artillery deployment and the bayonet charge as well.[50]

Belmont had been a hard experience for Tyree Bell. "I assure you I suffered more that day," he would later write, "than I ever did on any battle field during the whole war."[51] He and his men, beginning a long overland trek, had been countermarched back to the river at the double-quick, loaded aboard any boat that happened to have steam up, and thrust onto the opposite bank of the river without opportunity for reconnaissance or coordination with adjacent commanders. Bell, over his protest, was separated from his brigade and given a position on the flank, a post usually assigned to the most experienced officer. He had fought hard, beating back attacks of the enemy and their efforts to envelop his position. Even his immediate commander, the razor-tongued, micromanaging Pillow, complimented the stand at Bell's end of the line, although Pillow neglected officially to mention Bell by name. Of course, one did not earn his way into Pillow's effusive after-action reports by disagreeing with him. It is not easy to imagine a more difficult superior for such a totally inexperienced regimental commander. Of course, in perspective, the Confederate force on the west bank of the Mississippi was as green as Tyree Bell.

Bell had learned that beautiful day in November the humiliation of broken formations, the impossibility of rallying panicked men, the burning sting of an enemy bullet meant to maim or kill, the price of a failed charge, the fearful effectiveness of heavy guns. Belmont may have been fought on the anniversary of the glorious American victory at Tippecanoe during the War of 1812, but for Tyree Bell and the Twelfth Tennessee there was little glory at Belmont, only a nasty, bloody fight deep in the woods. True, Bell had displayed bravery, tenacity, and leadership, and on the whole offered promise as a field commander, but hardly could one claim that he had distinguished himself.

3

Shiloh

Belmont taught Tyree Bell and his Twelfth Tennessee Volunteer Infantry costly lessons: how to fight, how not to fight. Drills, reviews, military courtesies, tactics manuals, once grudgingly tolerated, now became consequential. The bitter struggle in the Mississippi River bottoms had convinced these citizen soldiers of Dyer and Gibson that they confronted a strong, determined enemy. The future loomed before them, uncertain now, save for the knowledge that more desperate, costly struggles lay ahead. Sacrifice would be required.

The fatalists saw an omen four days later. Their pride, the Lady Polk, blew up, killing and injuring a score of officers, General Polk among them. Polk, his uniform shredded, his nerves shattered, his hearing impaired, relinquished command to General Pillow. Indeed, before the fateful blast, before Belmont, Polk seemed to have lost heart in his work. Unknown to Tyree Bell and his men, the major general commanding had submitted his resignation to President Davis, explaining that he wished to return to Louisiana and resume his ecclesiastical duties, "far more congenial to my feelings and tastes." Davis pocketed the resignation.[1]

While Polk convalesced, Pillow seized his opportunity. He transformed Columbus into a beehive of activity and rang the alarm bell. "I anticipate being entirely surrounded," he dispatched the governors of Tennessee, Mississippi, and Alabama. So, Sidney Johnston's transfer of Bell—in fact, all of Pillow's Division—to Clarksville to meet the perceived threat against the river forts was canceled. Instead of traipsing across the countryside to confront imaginary Yankees, they set to work strengthening Columbus—feverishly cutting timber and lanes of fire, building breastworks, and relocating regimental camps. On

November 18, Bell and the men of the Twelfth moved from the Mississippi riverbank up on the bluffs near the Mobile and Ohio Railroad.[2] Here they drilled and dug in the clay hour after hour, and sometimes they played human mules, dragging heavy guns into specially constructed redoubts. Breaking this monotonous garrison duty was at least one noisy but uneventful excursion upriver by a wing (five companies) of the Twelfth "to protect our men at work upon submarine batteries."[3] Once, in anticipation of a major Yankee thrust, ten thousand Confederates turned out, grimly arranging themselves in a line of battle to receive an overland attack that never materialized.

Bad weather did come, however. In the northern sky the lightning cracked and reached for them, accompanied by soaking rain and biting wind. Then it turned cold, very cold, and the wind, up there on top of the bluffs, blew even harder, shaking the canvas tents and cutting at exposed skin. "Ground hard frozen—wind high" became a standard journal entry. The troops had to be moved indoors, so details went out to cut cypress logs and fashion them into cabins for the winter. Inevitably, boredom set in. Men quarreled and fought with each other over nothing; they drank destructively despite the vigilance of Bell, Pillow, and Polk, who bordered on being prohibitionist agents. One of the very few surviving letters of Robert M. Russell reveals deep concern about the liquor being smuggled into camp. "Unless this growing evil can be checked," he wrote to Polk, "it will finally result in the defeat and ruin of the Army and of the Country."[4] The volunteers chafed under military discipline; men had to be arrested and court-martialed, humiliated and disciplined publicly. Then there was disease, with measles reaching epidemic proportions. "So many were down at one time," remembered Col. Alfred J. Vaughan, Thirteenth Tennessee, "that there were scarcely enough well ones to wait on the sick."[5] Included among these unfortunates succumbing to common camp diseases was Bell's oldest son James William, Company A, Twelfth Tennessee, who apparently died in camp on December 5, 1861. Bell's reaction is unrecorded. The loss of their nineteen-year-old son, who had helped them carve out their home place in Dyer County, was doubtlessly a cruel blow for Mary Ann and Tyree and the family.[6]

On December 30 the army at Columbus was startled by the resignation of General Pillow. Most of those privy to the relationship between Pillow and Polk, and those with an objective mind-set, viewed the situation as an act of arrogant willfulness and malignant insubordination on Pillow's part.[7] Bell and his regiment, however, tended to support their fellow Tennessean against Polk. Pillow, whatever his shortcomings and despite his "blows," remained a favorite. He had been the driving force behind the creation of the Tennessee army, even using his own funds to help feed and equip the troops. Pillow knew how to talk to the volunteer soldier, how to empathize with his hopes, win his trust. This old Mexican War hero was enthusiastic and appealing and, contrary to his reputation, generally maintained the confidence of those he commanded. The conscientious and scrupulously honest Alfred Fielder recorded in his diary that "the Officers of our Reg. . . . and also of other Regiments and perhaps all the officers of Pillow's division paid him a visit Complimentary and so far as I have heard them express themselves they Justify him in offering his resignation." The following day the Twelfth Tennessee and other regiments marched down to the river and formed a hollow square around Pillow so that he might address them. He "pulled off his cap and saluted each [regimental] flag present," Fielder noted, "then rode off to the cars."[8]

Morning brought a new year and new orders. The dashing Gideon Pillow was all but forgotten. Early on January 1, Bell's Twelfth Tennessee formed along the Mobile and Ohio Railroad tracks, then boarded trains for Moscow, Kentucky, along with the two other regiments in their brigade: Freeman's Twenty-second and Ed Pickett's Twentieth. Off-loading near Moscow (midway between Columbus and Hickman, tucked in behind an extension of the Chalk Bluffs), Russell's Brigade (apparently commanded by Bell) made a sixteen-mile forced march lasting eight hours to Camp Beauregard, on the Kentucky-Tennessee border. Bell's Tennesseans represented General Polk's response to a plea of distress from Brig. Gen. James L. Alcorn, commanding three regiments of Mississippi "sixty-days men." Weary and hungry, Bell's men waited in formation while their colonel went into Alcorn's headquarters and conferred. Unfortunately, it appeared the Mississippian had made no preparations to feed or quarter the Tennesseans, so, after a short conference, the disgusted Bell, "ascertaining that no real danger threatened," returned from Alcorn's headquarters and had the brigade encamp along the road. Mirroring the attitude of their commander, the Tennesseans scoffed at the raw Mississippi infantry "whom we found in mortal terror." The next morning Bell again formed his three regiments in column and marched back to Moscow. His troops, softened by garrison life, broke down under the rigors of the march that left "a number of the boys hobbling about." Seeing the plight of his men, but determined to reach the railroad siding, Bell himself dismounted and gave his horse to a private. The stocky, middle-aged colonel would walk the remaining five miles. The brigade remained near Moscow overnight, then a train arrived the following afternoon to return them to their camp in Columbus. Fruitless and foolish, Bell's relief expedition nevertheless exposed the incompetence of Alcorn. Never again would this planter-politician command troops in the field. Leonidas Polk would disband his Mississippi brigade at Columbus within the month and Alcorn would proceed to wander about until his capture in Arkansas later in 1862.[9]

Other than the breakup of Alcorn's Brigade, January 1862 proved routine. Bell and a number of Tennessee officers, friends of Pillow, met at the general's former headquarters and signed a request for his reinstatement, which was promptly quashed by General Polk. Although Pillow would never return to the army at Columbus, he would reappear at Bowling Green, Kentucky, in early February 1862, to offer his services to Sidney Johnston.[10]

At Columbus "a thousand lies" were afloat—even more false alarms than in the fall, but on the whole the army, some fourteen thousand strong, remained calm and reasonably content as they attempted to adjust to soldier life. Happily, the train from Union City brought up relatives for visits, and soldiers who had become incapacitated by illness could be shipped home. Other ailing members of the Twelfth might receive attention in camp from Surgeon J. P. McGee and Methodist Chaplain Robert Byrnes. Bell and his staff also took great care to tend to the men's family concerns back home in Gibson and Dyer. Encouraging news had come from both counties. Excited by the tales of Belmont, men had flocked to the colors and by December 1861 a new regiment, the Forty-seventh Tennessee, had been organized. The Forty-seventh would be closely associated with Bell's Twelfth throughout the rest of the war.[11]

As 1862 opened, the Federals seemed to be preparing to attack in every section of Kentucky. Don Carlos Buell confronted Sidney Johnston's Green River line in heavy force; Henry W. Halleck threatened Polk at Columbus; and George H. Thomas menaced Felix Zollicoffer in eastern Kentucky. Everything blew apart on January 19. Thomas crushed Zollicoffer's little army at Mill Springs, and three weeks later Grant audaciously steamed up the Tennessee River and captured Fort Henry, a decisive offensive blow that cleaned the river of Confederate traffic, destroyed irreplaceable shipbuilding facilities, deprived Johnston of great stockpiles of provisions and equipment, and within days planted Union soldiers in northern Alabama. An elated Grant now turned on Fort Donelson, capturing it and its important garrison handily on February 16. With the fall of Forts Henry and Donelson, Nashville and Middle Tennessee lay open; the great bastion at Columbus had been turned.

Polk tardily attempted to assist the river forts, but by the time Cheatham's Division received its marching orders it was too late. The surrender of Fort Donelson and its twelve thousand defenders "has spread a gloom over many of our soldiers here," Alfred Fielder observed, but "most of them appear more than ever determined to have their rights or die in the attempt."[12]

Polk went to meet with Gen. Pierre G. T. Beauregard in Jackson, Tennessee, to decide what to do. How would they react to the disaster that had befallen the cause? Would it be possible to transform misfortune into opportunity? While their generals conferred, Bell and his men endured rain, sleet, and cold which transformed the company streets of the Twelfth Tennessee's camp into a freezing quagmire, "the mud in places being half leg deep."[13]

Reluctantly, Polk and Beauregard decided to abandon Columbus and unite with Johnston's army, somewhere farther south—deep in West Tennessee, perhaps in North Mississippi. In the meantime, they had to salvage what they could of the valuable war materiel stockpiled at Columbus. Polk raced back to headquarters and overnight had all Columbus astir. One hundred and forty guns had to be shipped south; cabins and buildings had to be burned. Heavy details of troops feverishly began packing and loading quartermaster, ordnance, and commissary treasures. The army worked quickly and for the most part efficiently, and, by the night of February 26, the time had come to evacuate the troops. Whole regiments began leaving Columbus, some by boat, some by rail. The Twelfth's turn came on February 27. Once alerted, Bell had his men carry their baggage to the railroad. The next day they were permitted to put their equipment and belongings aboard the cars, and at 8 P.M. they climbed on themselves, only to wait four hours in the gloom, before they finally left Columbus at midnight.[14]

Early the next morning, March 1, they passed Trenton, Tennessee, arriving in Humboldt (also in Gibson County) about 8 A.M. Humboldt was important militarily because it was a rail junction—where the Mobile and Ohio intersected with the Memphis and Ohio. Here they hoped to remain; they had heard rumors to that effect, but after a short time they climbed aboard again and continued south, arriving in Jackson late that morning. After a short wait they were ordered to unload and bivouac. Bell and his men slept fitfully that first night in Jackson, sharply aware, as Private Fielder noted, that "my family and all my earthly possessions being between me and Lincoln's army. I pray God," he continued, "it may not long be the case, but that the time may be near at hand when the soil of Tennessee shall not be polluted by the tread of an enemy of the Southern cause." The Twelfth Tennessee remained at Jackson four days, and Colonel Bell had the opportunity to see, if not meet, Generals Beauregard and Braxton Bragg, who were in town.[15]

Welcome orders came on March 5. The Twelfth was to retrace its steps up the line and make camp at Humboldt. Arriving at the railroad junction about midnight, cold and hungry, they unloaded from the cars and hurried to get their tents up and take shelter under the canvas. The regiment would stay in Gibson County about ten days. Many privates received short furloughs, and

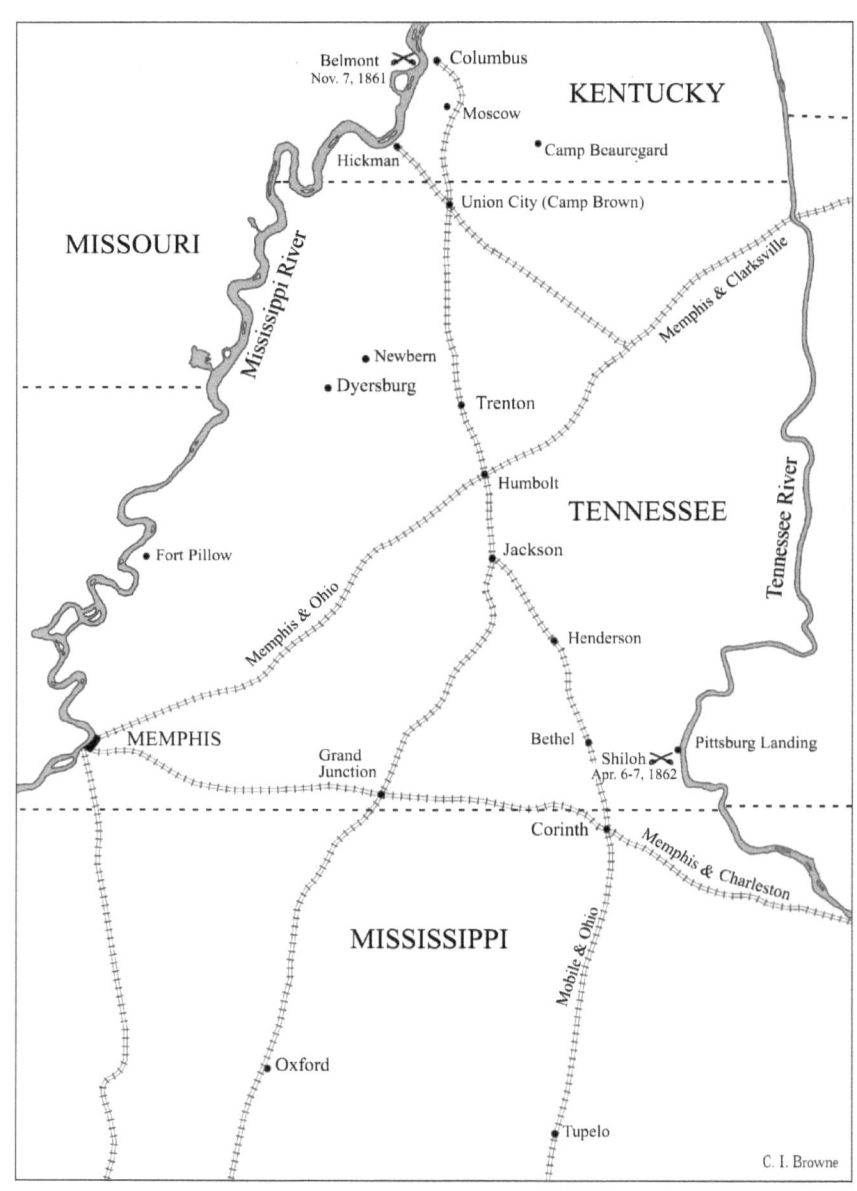

★ WEST TENNESSEE, 1861–1862. COURTESY OF C. I. BROWNE.

Bell kept those remaining in camp busy with inspections and battalion drill. It always helped to have spectators, and into camp at Humboldt came family and friends. March 11, for instance, proved a beautiful day, and Bell's battalion and regimental drill was attended by "quite a number of spectators," the larger portion being ladies. The following day, March 12, came a brigade dress parade in which they were reviewed by Gen. Charles Clark of Mississippi, their new division commander.[16]

Clark sparked enthusiasm and had every appearance of being competent. He had led the Second Mississippi infantry during the war with Mexico and did not seem awed by the professionals Beauregard and Bragg. Clark, like the highly political Gideon Pillow, knew how to talk to privates and appeared to care about the troops' welfare—their rations and clothing, the efficiency of their commissaries, their weapons. Tyree Bell had Clark's ear and expressed growing concern about the miserable status of his regiment's weapons. Some men were still armed with shotguns, some with the cumbersome Austrian muskets captured from the Yankees at Belmont, and some had no arms at all. Whatever assurances Clark may have given him, Bell knew he needed a good regimental ordnance sergeant—an efficient, conscientious man to monitor this critical situation and work with him—so he appealed to the well-respected and deeply religious Pvt. Alfred T. Fielder of Company B, a former member of the General Assembly who had represented Dyer and Lauderdale Counties from 1855 to 1857. "At the strong solicitation of Col. Bell," Fielder wrote in his diary, "I agreed to accept the appointment." It would prove a wise choice. While at Humboldt Fielder succeeded in swapping the Ordnance Department a number of obsolete weapons and accoutrements for serviceable muskets with bayonets, cartridge boxes, and cap boxes.[17]

On March 19 the regiment set out again, through Jackson this time, past Henderson Station and Bethel, heading south toward the Mississippi border. They would have to stop, sometimes back up, for wood or water for the engines, or to wait on a siding while the clumsy trains "sorted themselves out." Usually they were permitted to hop out of the boxcars and amuse themselves sitting on the bank playing cards or stretching their legs and arms by tossing baseballs. Finally, on March 21, they reached the outskirts of Corinth, Mississippi, and, at a point within walking distance, north of town, they began clearing off a campsite and putting up tents. What a welcome to Mississippi; almost the entire first week they endured rain and snow and cold, in late March! In Mississippi![18]

There at Corinth they saw more human beings than they had ever seen in their lives—troops, civilian soldiers like themselves—thousands upon thousands, from Louisiana and Alabama, Florida and Arkansas, from all across the South it seemed. One did not need a gold sash about his waist to know that something big was at hand. It was a time obviously to stock up on ammunition, so Bell had Sergeant Fielder take a detail and two wagons back to the railroad and fetch fixed cartridges and plenty of percussion caps. To protect the precious ammunition, Fielder and Bell did more than stretch a tarp over the boxes; they erected a tent and put the ammunition inside. There would be no more repeats of Belmont. Bell and Fielder also negotiated for more cartridges, muskets, and cap boxes—that is, when they could spare time from drill, for Bell had intensified the daily routine at Corinth, particularly battalion and skirmish line drill. There were inspections and reviews aplenty, and on March 29, Bell assembled the Twelfth in a square and had Maj. Bob Caldwell appeal to the men about reenlisting (the twelve months for which they had volunteered were just about up). Once Caldwell finished his speech, the men called out the popular Capt. Drew A. Outlaw, Company E, and then, when the officers were done, they asked for Sergeant Fielder. All the while Bell—who never considered himself a speaker, nor was he so considered, stood by, resolute, supportive, totally engaged. The speech making almost took the form of a camp-meeting profession of faith. They would fight together now, they would fight together later.[19]

As his new army assembled at Corinth, Sidney Johnston and his key subordinates—Beauregard, Polk, Hardee, Bragg, and John C. Breckinridge—agreed they must strike Grant's army encamped around Pittsburg Landing on the banks of the Tennessee River before Grant could be reinforced by the army of Gen. Don Carlos Buell, which was known to be moving south toward Corinth from Nashville. Time must be made the ally of the Confederates, not the enemy.

First Johnston saw to the organization of this mass of citizen soldiery, designating the whole as the Army of the Mississippi. In the process Russell's Brigade (Twelfth, Thirteenth, and Twenty-second Tennessee) was assigned another regiment—the Eleventh Louisiana (Col. Marks's men, beside whom they had fought at Belmont), and two sections of field guns (Capt. Smith P. Bankhead's Tennessee Battery). Clark's First Division thus consisted of Russell's First Brigade and Brig. Gen. Alexander P. Stewart's Second Brigade. The Second Division was commanded by Cheatham and consisted of the brigades of Brig. Gen. Bushrod R. Johnson and Col. William H. Stephens, plus two light batteries. Accompanying the two infantry divisions of Clark and Cheatham would be a battalion of cavalry. Collectively these troops constituted Polk's First Army Corps, Army of the Mississippi.[20]

On April 1, 1862, Polk's Corps was put on alert to move within twenty-four hours. Very early Thursday, April 3, came the long-awaited march order—cook three days' rations and be ready to move out at 6 A.M. that day. Clark's Division was to advance on the Ridge Road toward Pittsburg Landing, closely following the corps of Maj. Gen. William J. Hardee. Confusion abounded, however. Maps were wrong or incomplete, guides were poor, orders were misunderstood or never arrived, and, as a consequence, Johnston's giant, inexperienced army frittered away valuable hours, indeed, an entire day, laboring just to get out of Corinth itself and onto the road. April 4 saw little improvement. There was some motion toward Pittsburg Landing, which was good, but heavy rain, hail, thunder, and lightning played havoc with the columns and threatened to reduce the army to a milling mob. Nightfall brought an end to this chaotic madness, thankfully, and Russell's Brigade halted and encamped beside the Ridge Road. There, in the miserable rain, they set about trying to cook rations and attempting to sleep.[21]

Sleep or no sleep, they assembled for roll call in early-morning darkness of April 5, then formed their march column at 6 A.M. Off "through the wind and water" they went, moving forward until about 8 A.M. when they halted and stood on the roadside, arms stacked, waiting and continuing to wait while the slogging troops of Daniel Ruggles and John C. Breckinridge passed. About nightfall the Twelfth started again, made a short distance, then deployed from column into line of battle. Bell's hopes to bring on a battle were dashed, however, as darkness closed in once again. The boys from Dyer and Gibson stacked arms and tried to get something to eat. Then they lay shivering in the dark, wet woods, listening to Yankee music, coming from somewhere, not too far ahead.[22]

About 6 A.M. Sunday, April 6, Bell and his men were ordered into line of battle although they were about two miles from "the scene of action." The Twelfth, serving as the right regiment of the brigade, was tucked behind, and in support of, a wing of General Stewart's brigade. They advanced steadily this bright, beautiful morning up the Pittsburg-Corinth road until less than a mile from the enemy. When they reached Rea Field they encountered wounded men, soldiers with terror in their eyes. "Half of Cleburne's Brigade had been wrecked" in that field, according to Shiloh historian Larry Daniel, "and half of [Bushrod] Johnson's Brigade stopped cold." Russell's Brigade now came under enemy artillery fire. Nevertheless, "we continued to move on steadily," Bell reported, "losing a few men." General Bragg intervened at this point, riding up and ordering division commander Clark to knock out the Yankee battery (Capt. Allen Waterhouse's Battery E, First Illinois Light Artillery) enfilading his troops.

Clark proceeded to split Russell's Brigade, sending Russell and the left wing (Eleventh Louisiana and Twenty-second Tennessee) directly against the battery while he himself led the right wing (Bell's Twelfth and Vaughan's Thirteenth Tennessee) and veered to the right, coordinating with Stewart.[23]

As directed, Milton Russell advanced and launched his attack to the west of the Rea cabin. Devastating fire from Waterhouse's Battery and the Fifty-third Ohio Infantry, however, threw Russell's assault back in disorder. Meanwhile Bell and Vaughan pushed on to the camp of the Eleventh Illinois Cavalry. Shortly after passing through this abandoned camp, the Twelfth "found the enemy in large force, taking shelter behind logs, trees, and tents." Simultaneously they saw Marks's shattered Eleventh Louisiana to their left fleeing Rea Field. Smoke hampered visibility and seemed to cling to the trees and bushes—dense, whitish-gray fog, man-made smoke—unnaturally filling the woods in which they fought. It seemed to sting their eyes and obstruct their breathing, this slowly dissipating evidence of hasty volleys and solitary shots. A sequence of short advances and retreats followed with no advantage to either side. The fire continued heavy and vicious, and in this initial struggle Bell's mount was killed. Having foreseen this possibility, as at Belmont, he had another horse in reserve. He had it brought up and quickly remounted only to have this second horse "shot under me." The consequent fall shocked Bell and injured his leg. Nevertheless, he remained forward with his line of battle and retained command. Casualties mounted. Down went Adjutant Tom Hutcherson, along with several other company-grade officers and a score of enlisted men.

The Tennesseans could not seem to come to grips with the obstinate Yankees. Frustrated, Bell next took a leaf from Gideon Pillow's book and ordered, *Charge Bayonets!* The Twelfth leaped forward with a shout and closed on the enemy line of battle. Col. Jesse J. Appler, Fifty-third Ohio, commanding the defenders, realized the desperateness of his situation and called out to his men to fall back and save themselves. "This is no place for us," said Appler, pulling his men back. So Bell and Vaughan drove on triumphantly, forcing the enemy to the rear two hundred, five hundred yards, probably to within sight of Shiloh Church. The stubborn Appler succeeded in reforming his men, however, posting them in a strong position in thick woods laced with fallen timbers. Now a prolonged exchange of rifle fire ensued, in which General Clark received a dangerous shoulder wound and had to relinquish command of the wing to General Stewart.[24]

Bullets flew everywhere. The Dyer and Gibson County boys could not see their enemies through the heavy spring foliage and smoke; they could not see their friends. At this point a terrifying volley rang out. Totally unexpected, the fire had come from the Thirty-third Tennessee Infantry having mistaken them for bluecoats. Bell's men, confused and panicky, broke and fled to the rear, where Bell and Maj. Bob Caldwell managed to halt them and reform.[25]

Once again Bell and the men of the Twelfth pushed forward through the woods and shortly made contact with the left wing of Gen. Thomas C. Hindman's brigade. Hindman, happy that the Tennesseans had come up, immediately ordered Bell to charge and seize McAllister's Battery in the northwest corner of Review Field. Hindman would lead the assault himself. The Twelfth, acting in concert with the Fourth Tennessee and supported by Capt. Thomas J. Stanford's Mississippi Battery, surged forward. A cannon shot, however, crashed into Hindman's mount, pitching the brigadier general high in the air. Hindman struggled to his feet, turned to the Tennesseans, and shouted, "Take that battery." Then he collapsed. Under heavy fire, Bell, in concert with Vaughan's Thirteenth Tennessee, pressed on irresistibly. The Illinois battery, realizing its peril, attempted to displace to the rear and, in the rush and confusion, managed to evacuate three guns, leaving their fourth howitzer as Bell's trophy. McAllister had chosen well—a fine position with good fields of fire—so Capt. Tom Stanford limbered up and soon had his guns in battery occupying the same ground. Bell deployed his men in support of Stanford. A. P. Stewart, who was up with the advancing infantry, took command.[26]

The Yankees counterattacked, then fell back, regrouped, and counterattacked again, furiously. Bell and his Tennesseans managed to beat them back twice, but Bell was hit. Union sharpshooters had been targeting the conspicuous regimental commander all day, but until now had only had succeeded in killing his horses and clipping the edges of his uniform. This bullet entered the upper left portion of Bell's chest, and he sagged in his saddle, suffering from a "slight wound in the breast." Finally the counterattacks subsided and Bell, still mounted but riding slowly and tentatively, pulled his men off the line, leading them back to a branch for water.

There had to be reorganization, indeed consolidation. Sergeant Fielder reported that all the officers in Company B were either wounded or missing. When Bell learned Company G also "had no officer with them," he directed the former postmaster and legislator Fielder to combine the companies and take command of both himself. After filling their canteens and repacking their cartridge boxes, the Twelfth returned to Stewart's position only to be ordered off to the support of General Bragg. It was now late in the afternoon; the battered West Tennessee regiment moved forward once again, but with sharply reduced numbers.[27]

The Yankees were in full retreat toward the Tennessee River, but there they managed to establish pockets of resistance, backed by powerful concentrations of field artillery. They also enjoyed deep support from the massive firepower of the gunboats. Bell and what remained of the Twelfth Tennessee continued on toward the river, despite the increasing resistance. Frank Cheatham himself led the West Tennesseans. During this rather haphazard, uncoordinated, understrength pursuit, Bell and the men of the Twelfth happily reunited with Colonel Russell and what remained of Clark's Left Wing (Twenty-second Tennessee and Eleventh Louisiana). The injured Bell (the seriousness of his wounds and injuries apparently had not been determined) found his friend Col. Milton Russell elated. Russell believed he had distinguished himself that afternoon in the final attacks against the Federals at the Hornets' Nest. Indeed, it was Russell who had received Gen. Benjamin M. Prentiss's sword, which he properly sent on to General Polk. It seems one of Russell's young privates, T. M. Simms, Twenty-second Tennessee, had entered the enemy camp first and brought out a large number of prisoners, among whom was General Prentiss himself. Simms promptly delivered Prentiss to Russell.[28]

The Twelfth Tennessee Infantry and Russell's Brigade remained in this no-man's-land until sunset, yet with each passing minute they grew more uncomfortable and uneasy, vulnerable to counterattack and exposed to the lobbing shells of the Yankee gunboats. Finally orders came from General Bragg to break off contact with the enemy, and Russell led the brigade back to a captured Union camp near the south end of Jones' Field. Bell, physically exhausted and weakened from loss of blood, had grown faint. Russell, realizing his friend might be dismissing the danger of his wound, had him carried to the rear, probably in an ambulance.[29] Evidently the stubborn Bell believed he could be "patched up" and after a night's rest return to the field, for he refused to relinquish command of the Twelfth to the gallant Bob Caldwell.[30]

Tyree Bell, however, would suffer greatly that night, not only from the puncture wound in his chest, but from the effects of the hard fall when his second mount went down. Nevertheless, he escaped the terrible fate that befell others of the regiment who had been wounded. Lt. George Rice, Company B, survived only because a friend stretched a piece of canvas over him and sat with him throughout the night simply keeping the "blood out of his mouth. He would have drowned had I not," recorded Pvt. William F. Mays, "for I have never seen such a rain that fell. There were a great many of the wounded that were drowned." More depleted, disoriented men drifted into camp as the night wore on. Most occupied themselves by rummaging through Yankee rations and belongings, and by lantern light reading the private letters of their enemies. Then it was that Pvt. James Hammons opened his Bible and read from the Seventy-first Psalm. "In thee, O Lord, have I put my trust; let me never be put to confusion, but rid me and deliver me in thy righteousness; incline thine ear unto me, and save me. . . ." When Hammons had finished, these soldiers of the Twelfth Tennessee sang a few verses from a hymn, then knelt and "tried to return Thanksgiving and prayer to God," Fielder penciled into his diary. Then they tried to sleep, "but the enemy kept up such a bombardment from their gunboats we slept but little."

Nevertheless, they rested confidently. That terrible Sunday night these worshipers, these simple farmers and tradespeople of Dyer and Gibson, believed "the battle was won, that the victory was ours." So did Tyree Bell. Eventually, probably at the urging of the Ordnance Sergeant Fielder or of Bell himself, a handful of the enterprising would turn from gorging themselves with delectables and fondling Yankee personal treasures to collect some of the rifles that lay all about.[31]

The next morning, the regiment fell into line at dawn, forming on the road near the open parade ground that once belonged to the Eleventh Illinois. Bell had donned his coat, fastened on his sash and sword belt, and come out as the troops formed, but realizing he could not "perform my duty," he surrendered to the demands of his body, turning over command to Major Caldwell, and returned to his tent. Bob Caldwell then explained to the men of the Twelfth Tennessee that their commander's wound was more serious than previously thought and that he had assumed command of the regiment. Caldwell would remember that morning, recalling specifically and unhappily how depressed the men were to hear that Bell would not be with them. They trusted their rumpled, grizzled old lieutenant colonel.

A difficult, brutal day lay ahead. Russell's Brigade would fight all morning and into the afternoon, again suffering heavy loss. At one point (along the northern edge of Review Field), with both flanks turned, they found themselves caught in a murderous cross fire and broke. Caldwell managed to reform them, and Governor Harris and even General Beauregard, the army commander, made patriotic appeals to restore them, but the Twelfth, after a temporary, halfhearted rear-guard stand that afternoon, would melt into the mob that had been the Army of the Mississippi and stagger back toward Corinth.[32]

While his comrades endured their ordeal, good fortune shone on Tyree Bell. His capable quartermaster and friend, Capt. James L. "Jo" Lea, secured an ambulance and personally escorted his colonel off the field. They found the road almost impassable, deep with water and sucking sludge. "Men, mules and horses stuck fast in the mire," recorded Pvt. William Mays, "everything retreating, thoroughly demoralized." The air rang with the curses of teamsters, the groans and screams of the wounded, the roar of the merciless rain. It took all day for the ambulance to traverse the few miles back to Corinth, but when Bell arrived he found "my camp was just like I left it and my servant there with it."[33]

All the next day (April 8) the straggling stream of dispirited-looking men drifted into the camps about Corinth, while at the depot chaos reigned as officers and family members fought to secure room on the cars in which to place the wounded. Rolling stock was short, the casualties many. General Polk, ever solicitous, came by to visit Bell "and said if I would just remain in my camp and be treated there until they could get the wounded off, he would give me a car and send me home and send Parson [William J. 'Jack'] Mahon with me."[34] So Bell complied, staying in his tent until April 12. All the while he received reports about his wounded boys being carried down to the Corinth depot by litter and left there near the platform until they could be loaded aboard a train and evacuated to a hospital. The Twelfth had lost heavily. The exact figure is unknown, but Russell's Brigade itself lost over 25 percent of its effectives, ninety-seven of them killed.[35]

Tyree Bell could take pride in the performance of his regiment at Shiloh. During the first day's fight on Sunday, the Twelfth had remained on the offensive throughout the day, meeting with notable success in the repeated assaults on the batteries of Waterhouse and McAllister. Although separated from their parent brigade, these troops of Dyer and Gibson had fought well under the direct supervision of Generals Clark, Hindman, and Stewart. It should be noted especially that the Twelfth's long, sweeping flank attack (in conjunction with the Thirteenth Tennessee) against the Waterhouse-Nispel-Barrett artillery concentration proved highly effective. Indeed, they turned Sherman's left and forced him to abandon his excellent position on the commanding Meetinghouse Ridge.[36] Once again Bell had shown himself to be a fighter—brave, resourceful, persistent, and capable of tough, sustained offensive action. He also took good care of his troops, his men agreed, in camp and in battle—happily combining the best qualities of commissary and combat leader. Lieutenant Colonel Bell, however, would receive only one official compliment for his service at Shiloh, that of regimental and brigade commander Colonel Russell in his after-action report. Russell would write to corps commander Polk that his friend Bell had "distinguished" himself by his "courage and energy."[37]

Colonel Russell wanted so badly to succeed as a commanding officer. With Tyree Bell gone, maybe never to return, Milton Russell attempted to keep spirits up. While the men of the Twelfth languished at Corinth, "blue as the proverbial lump of indigo" reliving the agony of Shiloh, Russell did his best to encourage them, saying, "Cheer up! Never despond! . . . We will come out all right yet."[38]

Russell needed some cheer himself, for that matter. In the reports of his superiors, Clark and Polk, he had been mentioned only routinely, almost incidentally. Was he to be damned by the omitted, the unsaid? Russell had failed, one must remember, in the initial attack on Waterhouse's Battery. Granted his brigade had been halved by Clark, but Russell's wing fled demoralized and had to be regrouped with the help of other commanders. It seems the brigade remained fragmented throughout Sunday's fighting, at least until late afternoon when Cheatham reassembled them. The second day of Shiloh brought the same result, at least in the minds of the troops. For leadership they had looked to Tyree Bell. It was, it seemed, Russell's fate to be eclipsed by such men. His frustration, however, if it existed, has not appeared in surviving documents and letters. Moreover, he did not seem through his subsequent actions to hold his misfortune against Bell. Perhaps the man, oddly, existed without a will to be bitter. Russell, with his excellent professional credentials, had had the opportunity as brigade commander for six months to distinguish himself, to rise in rank, to become an important figure in the western Confederate army.

So the state of the Twelfth, psychologically and physically, eroded at Corinth despite Russell's upbeat efforts. Indeed, two weeks after Shiloh, illness and battle casualties had reduced the regiment to 310 privates.[39] Another two weeks passed and orders that would prove disastrous to Russell came down: Reorganize the regiment. Elections were held on May 8, and Robert M. Russell was supplanted as colonel of the Twelfth by the absent Tyree H. Bell. Captain Outlaw jumped over Caldwell, becoming lieutenant colonel, and Company Commander Nick Wyatt became regimental major. Ordnance Sergeant Alfred T. Fielder officially became captain of Company B.[40] Consequently, Russell's tenure as brigade commander also ended that June, and he was replaced by the charismatic regimental commander, Col. Preston Smith of Bushrod Johnson's brigade.

Thus Russell and Caldwell became casualties of the Confederate democratic process. As officers they were "dropped" from the rolls and became supernumeraries.[41] After their performances at Belmont and Shiloh, it appears a cruel reward. The fiercely patriotic Bob Caldwell seems to have stayed close to the army, nevertheless, serving as voluntary aide de camp until 1863, when he returned home and began recruiting for Forrest and Bell. Russell, on the other hand, was sent back to Gibson County by Polk, apparently, with instructions to raise a regiment of cavalry and report to Forrest. As Russell moved about in West Tennessee, dodging Union patrols and attempting to recruit, he was captured, reportedly on a Mobile & Ohio flatcar chaperoning a howitzer. This led to "house arrest" in Trenton under the supervision of Col. Jacob Fry, U.S.A., until the Battle of Trenton when, after observing the fighting from his home, Russell apparently broke his parole and rode off to join Forrest.[42]

True to his word, Gen. Leonidas Polk had found a railroad car for Bell. The severely wounded colonel, heavily bandaged, with the left side of his chest badly swollen, was carried to Trenton and thence transported painfully by crude ambulance to Newbern. "While at home," Bell recalled, "I was treated by Drs. [Allen] Harris, [John R.] Westbrook, and Richardson. During the time they met at my house and decided that I was compelled to die within forty-eight hours, but they were mistaken as you now know."[43]

Mistaken, indeed. Bell took their fatalism as a challenge and began "right then to mend." Miss Mary and the good doctors gave him close attention. "It was nearly a week before I could swallow anything solid, they fed me with a spoon," Bell recalled. "From then I mended slowly for six weeks." Almost as soon as he could get out of bed and stand alone, Bell began chafing to return to the army. After six weeks convalescence, Bell, worried about marauding Yankees who might capture him, managed to climb into a carriage and ride to Grand Junction on the Memphis & Charleston Railroad. He arrived in Grand Junction about May 28 accompanied by four friends from Dyer going to see their sons and friends in the army, which incidentally was preparing to evacuate Corinth that very night.[44]

From Grand Junction, Bell continued south to Oxford, Mississippi. There he would remain a week as the guest of General Pillow's family, who were refugeeing in Oxford from their home just west of Columbia, Tennessee. The abandonment of Corinth, however, required that Bell continue south by rail through Grenada to Jackson, Mississippi, then east to Meridian, then back north in order to reach Tupelo, where the Army of the Mississippi had established itself.

When Bell arrived in Tupelo he had a man drive him in a buggy out to the camp of Preston "Pres" Smith's brigade, formerly Russell's. This was now the home of "his" Twelfth Tennessee Infantry. He also made the pleasant discovery that on June 17, 1862, the Twelfth and Twenty-second Tennessee "both being below the minimum [manpower] requirements" had been consolidated into the new Twelfth Tennessee Volunteer Infantry. Moreover, Bell—with the blessing of Braxton Bragg, recently appointed commander of the "Army of the West" replacing the discouraged Beauregard—would be colonel of the combined regiment. Lipscomb P. McMurry (formerly colonel of the Twenty-second Tennessee) would become lieutenant colonel, and Nick Wyatt, major. Company E, Bell's orphan Kentucky company, however, had been transferred out, becoming Company L, Third Kentucky Infantry.[45]

★ Maj. Gen. Benjamin Franklin Cheatham. Tennessee State Library and Archives.

Pres Smith proved quite a different man and brigade commander from Milton Russell. He was older for one thing, almost forty. Whereas Russell was a West Pointer and an officer in the Old Army, Smith had seen fighting in Mexico as a volunteer. A native Tennessean, Smith had been educated at Jackson College near Spring Hill, Tennessee, then studied law, practicing first in Waynesboro, then in Memphis. Before war broke out, the popular and forceful Pres Smith had been elected colonel of the 154th Senior Tennessee Infantry, a large and socially prestigious West Tennessee militia organization, which had been founded on the eve of the Mexican War. Smith and his regiment had fought conspicuously well at Belmont, spearheading the pursuit that chased Grant's Yankees back to their transports. Pres Smith and Frank Cheatham were very close, and both had sided with Polk against the popular Gideon Pillow at Columbus. Indeed, Colonel Smith held old resentments against Pillow, for Pillow had made an example of him as a young man in Mexico, having him arbitrarily arrested as the general went about establishing iron discipline over his free-spirited Tennessee volunteers. In the recent Shiloh engagement the thirty-eight-year-old Smith had commanded not only his own regiment but Bushrod Johnson's brigade with distinction for much of the battle. Cheatham, who was never given to overstatement, would characterize Pres Smith as "active, energetic, and brave, with a rare fitness to command." Thus Smith inherited a fine brigade consisting of his 154th, Bell's consolidated 12/22d, the 13th, 47th, Bankhead's Battery, and Capt. James H. Edmondson's Company of sharpshooters. The 154th, 12/22d, 13th, and 47th would remain together for the balance of the war.[46]

Bell had a new division commander as well. Gen. Charles Clark had been ordered to Vicksburg, and Preston Smith's brigade had been assigned to Frank Cheatham's Division.[47] Cheatham was the prototype volunteer—the type of man and officer of whom an exacting Braxton Bragg despaired—"a curious combination of brawler and conscientious commander," but remarkably popular with the rank-and-file Tennesseans, truly "one of the boys." Bell probably kept his distance, for he and his division commander had their differences, although they had known each other since they were boys. Cheatham could not abide Bell's friend Pillow. Moreover Cheatham's religious apathy and his bent for "frolicking," horse racing, and cursing did little to endear him to the strict Methodist warrior. Time would draw them closer, however. They both knew horses, which would prove a great bond. Both had spent much of their lives, Cheatham particularly, raising and selling bloodstock—for riding, for the plow, and for the harness.[48]

So Bell returned to the army at Tupelo, and as the buggy drove down the regimental streets, word spread rapidly to the men of the Twelfth Tennessee. Many believed Bell had died of his wounds in Newbern. His arrival in camp produced a sensation, in Bell's terms, "a wonderful hurrah."[49]

The tone of the army had changed. Braxton Bragg, now a full general and in command of the Western Department, had set about sifting his command of the unfit and incompetent. There would be no more repeats of the clumsy maneuvers and fragmentation of command witnessed at Shiloh. Bragg put the quintessential professional Hardee in charge of the Army of the Mississippi—the troops who had fought at Shiloh—and named Leonidas Polk second in command of the department, in effect an administrative shelving, which gave Hardee immediate supervision of the training of the army. Bragg and Hardee established a rigorous routine for the thirty-one thousand men. Drilling, on the company regimental, brigade, and division levels, occupied the troops every day.[50]

Bell, "slowly improving, but still an invalid," joined in. By June 28 he was not only present, observing his troops drill under McMurry and Wyatt, but conducting battalion and regimental drill himself. The very act of shouting commands must have hurt the large, heavy-framed colonel with the light gray eyes. No matter, the men worked hard and took pride in their development as soldiers. The camp at Tupelo was healthy and well-ordered, and the men's spirits soared. Tyree Bell was proud of his strong West Tennessee regiment and worked hard to guarantee that the merger of the 12th and 22nd succeeded. One of the steps he took to ensure proper blending was to appoint his trusted Methodist friend, Jack Mahon of the 22nd, chaplain of the combined regiment. Henceforth he and Chaplain Jack would stand together at Armageddon and battle for the Lord! As Bell set out to impress his will, his personality, his beliefs, upon the 12/22d Tennessee Volunteer Infantry, so Bragg and Hardee worked to infuse the Army of the Mississippi with their determination and confidence. Col. William Preston Johnston, acting as a special inspector, reported to President Davis that recruits were coming in, discipline had been established and "seemed excellent," and added, "the certain evidences of improvement everywhere manifest give assurances that the Confederacy will soon possess there a disciplined and effective army."[51]

By mid-July Bragg had made the bold decision to invade Tennessee by way of Chattanooga, thereby hoping to gain the rear of Buell's army (now stalled in its advance upon Chattanooga and temptingly dispersed across North Alabama and along the two Middle Tennessee railroads). Bragg intended to interpose the Army of the Mississippi between these Federals of Buell's and the great Union logistical base at Nashville. All would depend upon cooperation with Edmund Kirby Smith's force, currently defending Chattanooga, and upon the timely and efficient shifting of troops from Tupelo to Chattanooga. If the maneuver met with success, if Buell fell back upon his base, the offensive possibly could be extended to Kentucky.[52]

The infantry of the Army of the Mississippi began their movement to Chattanooga by rail on July 21, heading south to Mobile. The Tupelo camp emptied rapidly. When it came time for Polk's Wing to leave (for operational purposes, Bragg's Army of the Mississippi had been divided into two wings of two divisions each), Polk turned the task over to Cheatham and departed by train for Mobile. Cheatham passed the responsibility to Bell. "Gen. Cheatham came over to me," Bell recalled, "and asked me if I would take charge of the moving and remain there until every thing was moved and come up with the last train." Bell believed he understood his commander perfectly: "I agreed to do what he wanted me to do, as I knew he wanted to do some frolicking and I was in no humor to frolick."[53]

So off they went, these western Confederates, bound for adventures and perils unknown. By 3:30 A.M., July 25, the 12th Tennessee had had breakfast and formed. Then, at dawn, they marched to the depot. There, as the army's last regiment, Bell's 12/22d would wait, ultimately watching the sun set. Finally, at 8 P.M., this patient rear guard would board the last train and depart Tupelo.[54]

4

Banners to the Breeze

On Saturday, July 26, 1862, Bell and his men reached Mobile. It was almost dark when they climbed down from the cars, then set off on foot, marching with spirit through the city to the riverfront. Immediately they went aboard the steamboat *Dick Keys* and presently found themselves steaming up the Tensas River "riding the waves triumphantly." After a short, exhilarating voyage of thirty miles, the regiment reached Tensas Station. There they disembarked and climbed on another train, journeying farther east, through long-leaf pine country, to Pollard, Alabama, the point at which the Mobile and Great Northern intersected the Alabama and Florida Railroad. Bell and the Twelfth changed trains at Pollard. Then they continued their journey using the Alabama and Florida line, passing depot after depot and small places no one could remember. Arriving at Greenville, Alabama, about 6 p.m., "quite a number of ladies" turned out at the depot. Captain Fielder and his men were pleased and humbled by the women who cheered them on "by throwing boquets [sic] waving handkerchiefs &c." The Twelfth, accompanied by General Cheatham and Col. Pres Smith, arrived in Montgomery shortly before midnight. They remained there most of July 28, many of them enjoying a swim in the "clear beautiful" Alabama River. The train whistle sounded and once again they set out by rail, heading east for Georgia, passing through West Point and LaGrange before arriving in Atlanta. "Ladies thronged the road," Captain Fielder again noted, "waving flags, handkerchiefs, throwing us apples, peaches and giving every token of their approbation." When the troops reached Atlanta, however, they were ordered to remain aboard. Finally, when it was almost morning, Bell and his men felt the engine strain as it pulled out of the depot bound for Chattanooga. On they journeyed, "crowded together and all sleepy,"

CAPT. ALFRED T. FIELDER. TENNESSEE STATE LIBRARY AND ARCHIVES.

complained Captain Fielder of Company B, "we being in open top Cars and it having rained pretty hard yesterday evening." Happily Fielder watched the train pass "two large stone pillars, one on each side of the road." These great stones marked the Georgia-Tennessee line. "The boys yelled at the top of their voices and shouted they were in Tennessee once more." Late that Wednesday afternoon, July 30, Bell and his men arrived at the station in downtown Chattanooga. The following morning they marched out of town, south along the Tennessee River to the base of Lookout Mountain. There, at last, the wet and tired 12/22d Tennessee Volunteer Infantry established their camp.[1]

The long trip had taken its toll. A number of men had bad colds, some were running fevers, and many had heavy coughs. As for Bell himself, some thought the colonel had reached the limit of his endurance. "At that time I was considered a great invalid," Bell remembered. "I had been sick for a year but had been in the army all the time and my lower limbs had swollen so that I had to be bandaged from my waist to my toes every morning before I could get into my saddle." His solicitous wing commander, Leonidas Polk, urged Bell to take sick leave. Remain until you are well, Polk told him. Not Bell. "I had made up my own mind that I was going with my army into Kentucky even if I was relieved of my command." Polk, Cheatham, and Pres Smith quickly reassured him. "If I was determined to go, they would give me every advantage they possibly could."[2]

Up to the end of July no one really knew what lay ahead—perhaps Kentucky, perhaps Middle Tennessee. Bragg and the commander of the Department of East Tennessee, Maj. Gen. Edmund Kirby Smith, had met on July 31 in Chattanooga and arrived at a hazy agreement that Bragg's Army of the Mississippi should strike into Middle Tennessee while Kirby Smith's small force, reinforced by the division of Maj. Gen. John P. McCown and the brigades of Brig. Gen. Patrick R. Cleburne and Col. Preston Smith (an ad hoc division under Cleburne's command) from Bragg's army, would attempt to recapture Cumberland Gap, presently held in strong force by Union Brig. Gen. George W. Morgan. If Kirby Smith succeeded in taking the gap, the two Rebel armies would unite and force their way back into Middle Tennessee, cut Buell off from his base in Nashville, and crush him.[3]

By August 9, certainly, Kirby Smith had shifted his eyes from Middle Tennessee to central Kentucky, specifically Lexington.[4] First Cumberland Gap had to be cleared or bypassed, so Pres Smith's brigade, after a stay of only a few days, left their comfortable camp at the foot of Lookout Mountain and on August 7–8 took a train north to Knoxville. Smith himself was absent, so Bell, as senior colonel, took command of the strong Tennessee Brigade (12th, 13th, 47th, and 154th Senior Infantry) and led them north.[5]

"When I got to Knoxville," Bell recalled, "it was my first duty to report to Gen. Kirby Smith, one of our officers I had never made the acquaintance of. . . . When I reported to Gen. Smith's headquarters, I was wearing overshoes, the smallest shoes I could get on my feet and walking with a cane."[6]

Bell was in pain and irritable. He immediately appealed to Kirby Smith to permit him to choose a better campsite. The one chosen by Kirby Smith's staff—three miles from Knoxville—"displeased him." Bell got his new campsite, only a mile from town, and he returned to his "boys." Before dark the Twelfth had their tents up. The next morning, a beautiful Sunday, many of the regiment gathered to hear a lengthy sermon by Chaplain Jack Mahon. The good chaplain struck hard at the "pernicious practice of profane swearing." That night Bell's regiment had more preaching, this time from the Rev. J. J. Brooks of their sister unit, the Forty-seventh Tennessee.[7]

By this time Kirby Smith's plans had crystallized. Despite Bragg's worries, Kirby Smith would attempt to bypass Morgan in Cumberland Gap, move to his rear, and cut his communications. If Morgan evacuated the gap, Kirby

Smith would pursue. If Morgan stood fast (which Kirby Smith discounted), he must soon "starve or surrender." Boldly, Kirby Smith divided his command and assumed the offensive. His sizeable cavalry force swept to Morgan's rear and broke his supply line. The infantry—Cleburne's and Brig. Gen. Thomas J. Churchill's divisions (four brigades)—crossed the Cumberland Mountain at Rogers' Gap, about ten miles south of Morgan's main position, while Smith's trains and artillery, another ten miles south, advanced through Big Creek Gap toward Barboursville. Smith's strongest division, however, under Brig. Gen. Carter L. Stevenson, remained behind, monitoring Morgan's force at Cumberland Gap.[8]

Despite his infirmities, Bell participated in this flanking march, the Twelfth Tennessee and Pres Smith's brigade moving with Cleburne's column. They left their Knoxville campsite on August 13 and took the road toward Clinton, Tennessee, reaching that point the following day, and crossed the Clinch River. As they prepared to enter Rogers' Gap, Kirby Smith halted his infantry and sent for Bell, informing him that he did not intend "to go up until dark to keep from being discovered." He told him to take half of his escort and lead the light army headquarters train through the gap to the south, the one used by the ammunition trains and the artillery. Bell was pleased. "I very willingly accepted as [Gen. Kirby Smith] said they would have to walk through the Gap . . . , and he thought I was not able to make the trip up the hill."[9]

Bell and his small train passed through the mountain quietly enough, but the trail, once they reached relatively level terrain, turned into a long, ominous lane bordered on the left for a considerable distance by thick woods. Just as they were about to clear these woods, the little column was ambushed by "East Tennessee Mountain Bushwhackers," Bell recalled. "Fortunately no one was hurt and we sent the little escort we had with us after them in a charge through the woods . . . and we were not bushwhacked any more."[10]

When Bell and the headquarters train arrived at Barboursville on August 21, he reported to Kirby Smith, who ordered him on another mission, this time to Manchester, Kentucky, about twenty miles northeast of Barboursville.[11] Kirby Smith had heard that there might be an enemy force in Manchester. If correct, these Federals would be perched dangerously on the right flank of the invading column, thus jeopardizing the entire operation. Bell was to investigate. As he later recalled:

> I got to Manchester in the evening, and found [the enemy] had evacuated. Manchester is a small town in the woods . . . and I assure you that the people we found there were very rare

specimens of mountaineers; there were a few that were very strong Confederates, but most of them were Federals.

One long, lank fellow, looked to be about 25 or 26 years old, came up to me where I was sitting on my horse and interviewed me. He wanted to know "If youenses were regular soldiers and if youenses had come to stay, and if youenses wuz huntin' for any thing." I told him that we were regular soldiers and that we had come to stay only a short time, and if there was any thing good to be found, we would like to see it. He said "Over thar in that hollow 'tween them two hills is an Old Baptist Church, which is as crammed full of good things as it can be." He said the soldiers had piled the things in as fast as they could when they heard we were coming, and took off to the mountains. I asked him if he would be willing to go over and show us the house and he said he would willingly go. When we got there the door was securely fastened and I wanted to know of him how we were going to get in and he said "O if youenses want to get in, I can get the door open." He picked up a billet of wood and very soon had the door down and we found that every thing was just as he had said.

The capture was really worth nothing to us [except] that we got 1400 pounds of tobacco, which we needed very badly. I ordered the regiment up and they all got what they wanted and they were all sick from the treat, but the tobacco was the best of the capture.[12]

The Twelfth Tennessee came up to Manchester on Sunday, August 24, and the following day, the regiment, with Bell in command, "turned square to the right and almost due west taking the road to London," which they reached the following day. Kirby Smith consolidated his column at this point, crossed Rockcastle Creek and continued north toward Richmond, Kentucky, Cleburne's Division in the advance. Actually they rushed toward Richmond, for Col. John S. Scott's cavalry screen was under great pressure and a dispatch had been captured showing strong enemy reinforcements were expected in Richmond on August 23. Kirby Smith had two divisions of infantry on hand, numbering somewhat less than six thousand effectives. To augment this small force he had about twelve hundred cavalry under Scott. Kirby Smith's other forces (over two divisions numbering about twenty-two thousand) were widely scattered to the south and east, employed primarily in neutralizing Morgan and protecting East Tennessee. Kirby Smith hurried north toward the Blue Grass region which lay

★ ADVANCE AND RETREAT IN KENTUCKY, 1862. COURTESY OF C. I. BROWNE.

beyond Big Hill, a high, difficult, T-shaped "mountain." Between Barboursville and Rockcastle Creek, Bell and his comrades found no stream except for the muddy creek itself. From there to Big Hill, Fielder recorded in his diary, they traversed a "barren desolate region, destitute of water for men or animals."[13]

One of the soldiers, stopping at a one-room cabin, asked for water. The woman of the house took one look at the ragged soldier with the "greasy wool hat" and recognized him for an invading Southerner. She responded "snappishly," "I guess you will find it in the Ohio River."[14]

Hungry and growing almost desperate for water, Kirby Smith's expedition pushed on to Big Hill, which they were pleased to find unoccupied, as it blocked any direct advance upon Richmond—indeed, upon the Blue Grass region itself. On August 28 they climbed it, "a verry [sic] rough high mountain." The weary troops found "what was not rocky and rough was shoe top deep in loose sand." A veteran of Cleburne's Arkansas brigade complained that crossing Big Hill "was the most dreary, desolate, and fatiguing day's march I ever remember making during my three years' soldier life."

That night atop the mountain they found themselves a place "among the rocks" and attempted to sleep. While his infantry struggled with Big Hill, Kirby Smith sent Scott's cavalry ahead. On August 29 Scott found the enemy at Kingston, five miles south of Richmond and about twelve miles north of Big Hill. Light skirmishing developed as the Federals seemed to be falling back toward Richmond. The nature of the resistance indicated to Cleburne (whose two brigades led the column) and to Kirby Smith that the enemy intended to dispute any further advance, probably at or near Richmond.[15]

Cleburne's Division encamped in a loose column along the splendid macadam road running from the base of Big Hill (from which they had just descended) through the village of Kingston and on to Richmond. They had entered Kentucky's Blue Grass region—"a land full of fat things," remembered a private in the Second Tennessee, "into which all seemed eager to rush as to a revel, and exchange the barrenness of foodless mountains for the abundance of fertile plains." Between Cleburne's lead infantry brigade (his own commanded by Col. B. J. Hill) and the enemy lay the fires and tents of Scott's cavalry, promising security against surprise. Apparently something seemed wrong to Cleburne. Perhaps it was inexperience or anxiety in his new role as division commander. In any event, Cleburne took additional precautions. He had Hill's Brigade form a line of battle, stack arms, then find a place to sleep just behind the rows of neatly stacked muskets. Hardly had the individual messes settled in around their campfires when suddenly to their front a sharp fight erupted and in no time at all Scott's cocky Louisiana cavalry fell back upon their infantry comrades. On their

★ Brig. Gen. Preston Smith.
Library of Congress.

heels thundered hundreds of hard-charging Yankee horsemen. Ben Hill's infantry had just enough warning to race forward to their stacked weapons and form in line of battle. When the audacious blue-coated cavalrymen appeared, flushed with success and expecting to make short work of what remained of the Rebel cavalry, they received a saddle-emptying volley from Hill's waiting infantry. The Yankee horsemen, confused and startled, momentarily thrashed about in the darkness, then hastily retreated, leaving behind "2 dead, 2 wounded, 30 prisoners and 100 much appreciated Sharps rifles."[16]

Well to the rear, encamped by a branch, the 12/22d Tennessee heard the roar of musketry. They stood to arms, ready to rush to Hill's support, when word came that the fight up ahead had ended almost as soon as it had begun. Moving forward about three miles Bell and his regiment encamped again, once more well to the rear of Hill's Brigade. The men from Gibson and Dyer put their weapons aside and tried to relax, knowing there would be more of them to fight over the next hill, across the next river.

In the darkness Tyree Bell and his close friend Chaplain Jack Mahon were hailed by Col. Edward Fitzgerald of Paris, Tennessee, Pres Smith's successor as commander of the 154th Tennessee Senior Infantry. The three talked a while and the young colonel told the two older men that he expected to be killed the following morning. "We tried to rally him," remembered Bell, "and get the notion out of his head, but to no effect. He asked me to give his watch and the other trinkets to his servant and tell him to carry them to his wife."[17]

The next day Bell and his men awoke at 3 A.M., moved forward about half a mile and formed a line of battle. There they rested until daylight. Nature seemed determined to mock Ed Fitzgerald's gloom as the world about them dawned "clear, warm and beautiful." Cleburne, true to his orders, pushed his column forward along the macadam road, Hill still ahead, Pres Smith following within easy supporting distance. Brushing back the Federal cavalry, Cleburne's advance soon found the enemy in force, some five hundred yards behind their forward elements. The Yankees, commanded by Brig. Gen. Mahlon Manson, waited for them in line of battle not far north of Kingston, near Mount Zion Church. Cleburne probed, bringing up his two batteries and placing them on a low hill running parallel to, and some five hundred yards from, this Federal position. In support of these guns he deployed Hill's infantry on the reverse slope of the ridge. Pres Smith's brigade he placed on the reverse slope of a second ridge in rear of Hill's line. Almost immediately an artillery duel commenced, and as soon as the Federal batteries had been unmasked, revealing themselves by their fire, Cleburne could deploy with confidence. He placed the bulk of Ben Hill's brigade to the right of the Richmond Road with just one company of skirmishers left of the road.[18]

Kirby Smith was up by this time and ordered Cleburne not to bring on a general engagement, but to wait for Churchill's Division. The first two hours of this little battle at Mount Zion Church consisted of brisk artillery firing and light skirmishing. Manson seemed to grow more confident by the hour. Observing the Confederate hesitation, he decided to take the initiative, attacking the extreme right of Cleburne's extended front with Brig. Gen. Charles Cruft's brigade fresh from Richmond. Cleburne countered by shifting more troops to the right, then called up Fitzgerald's 154th Senior Infantry from Pres Smith's brigade to further strengthen that flank.

On came the Federals, confident of turning the Confederate right. Cruft drove back the Confederate pickets easily, then clashed with Fitzgerald's skirmishers. Cleburne, realizing the danger, now directed Pres Smith to bring up the remaining three regiments of his brigade. They were to extend the right of the engaged line and, if Smith were to find his line overlapping that of the enemy, "to swing around their left flank," in effect attempting to envelop the large Yankee flanking force.[19]

Meanwhile, Fitzgerald's 154th had come up quickly and almost immediately began skirmishing heavily, then counterattacked the enveloping force of Kentuckians and Hoosiers, totally absorbed in feeling for the Rebel right flank. Leaping over a rail fence that offered temporary shelter, a Rebel shout was heard, "Mount the fence, lads; mount the fence, and at 'em; charge!" At the same time Pres Smith rushed forward with his remaining Tennesseans. Bell, at the head of the 12th Infantry's column, marched through a field which he, ever the farmer, noticed was brimming with "fresh, fine, thick corn." The Tennesseans made short work of the enemy skirmishers among the cornstalks, quickly capturing "a great many," and sent them to the rear as prisoners. Kirby Smith reported five hundred prisoners taken at this time. Just at this moment of triumph, however, stretcher bearers came up to Bell carrying the body of Ed Fitzgerald. He had been killed earlier in the skirmishing. Bell recovered Fitzgerald's watch and effects noting, "there was no written matter at all on his person," and in accordance with the wishes of this "gallant young man," told Fitzgerald's servant to carry the personal items home to his wife in Henry County. Colonel Fitzgerald had impressed Bell very much—"a very noble soldier . . . , one of the young officers in the army that was second to none."[20]

The crisis of the fighting at Mount Zion Church had arrived. Pres Smith's envelopment had succeeded famously—turning the Federal left. Bell approached the enemy (who held higher ground) with great deliberation. To prevent premature firing, he ordered the Twelfth "at a trail arms" and to keep their weapons down "until we got in good range of them." When within easy musket range, Bell halted his front line and ordered the first volley. "In about three minutes, I don't think it could have been longer, after I opened on them, [the Yankee's] front line broke," Bell noted. The enemy commander "tried to rally them but the second line broke so badly that they all went off together." Exposed to the Yankee musket fire, as at Shiloh, visible to all, Bell patently risked his life alongside his men. Doubtless his presence on the field at the height of the action must have greatly strengthened the resolve of his men and the bond they felt with their regimental commander. Old Tyree had courage and the willingness to share the fate of his boys.[21]

As Bell's regiment and Smith's Brigade smashed into the floating, vulnerable Federal left, Hill made a frontal attack upon the enemy center. Cleburne, with uncanny instinct, believed quite correctly that the Federals had weakened this portion of their line by shifting troops to strengthen their ill-fated flanking movement. Thus the Yankees at Mount Zion found themselves with their left turned and their center pierced. If that were not enough, Tom Churchill and a brigade of his Arkansas boys now appeared, advancing rapidly, threatening to envelop the Federal right. The result was sudden and total Confederate victory. The enemy abandoned the field and fled toward the security of Richmond.[22]

Victory, however, demanded her price—not only the life of Ed Fitzgerald, but at the climax of the battle, as Cleburne threw Hill forward in the frontal assault, he himself was painfully wounded. Pres Smith took command of the division. V.M.I. graduate Col. Alfred J. Vaughan, Thirteenth Tennessee—the senior colonel and a hero of Belmont—took over the Tennessee Brigade. Kirby Smith, determined to exploit the advantage he had won, directed Division Commander Pres Smith to continue his advance on the right side of the road while Churchill moved forward on the left. Time was precious, to maintain the initiative, imperative.[23]

Kirby Smith pushed down the Richmond Road—only to learn that the enemy had rallied some two miles back. They had established a new line near Rogersville, at a point called White's Farm. Pleased with the success of his envelopments, Kirby Smith ordered Churchill with one brigade to again turn the Federal right; meanwhile, Pres Smith would strike the other flank. Manson's green Indiana troops preempted this chessboard line of maneuver, however. They attacked Churchill's lead brigade in force, and this advance Rebel force (McCray's Arkansas-Texas brigade) found itself fighting for its life. By careful, disciplined volleying and a wild, ferocious counterattack, Col. T. H. McCray's troops routed the attacking Federals "just as the cheers of Pres Smith's division announced their arrival." Again the Yankees fled.[24]

The blue line of battle drifted in fragments from White's farm toward Richmond, with Churchill strong in pursuit on the left of the road. Pres Smith's division, however, came on much more slowly, as Smith would later explain: "The troops under my command were by this time almost famished for water, having only had about one canteen of muddy water to the man during the entire day. A scant supply of water having been obtained by the troops, we again pressed on." Capt. John Lavender, Fourth Arkansas Infantry, B. J. Hill's brigade, remembered the closing approach on Richmond more graphically: "Our march was nearly all through wheat stouble or heavy Corn Fields. The temperature must have been near 100 Degs in the shade. We had not water until about 2 P.M. We struck a large Stock Pond in a Field numbers of cattle standing in it. We rushed in like wild cattle, stopped and Drank the hot muddy water, was then pushed on in Double Quick time which means a trot."[25]

Soon they came in sight of the enemy massed to receive them, their line running along the south edge of Richmond itself. The Confederates could hear

Yankee cheering in the distance. Word had come back that they had been reinforced, perhaps heavily. Actually the cheers, Bell and his comrades were to learn, were for the arrival of Kentucky's hero of Shiloh—Maj. Gen. William "Bull" Nelson—after riding all night from Lexington. Nelson, beloved by privates but notorious for his arrogance and heavy-handed treatment of subordinate officers, immediately took command and attempted to breathe confidence into his two divisions of green Indiana, Kentucky, and Ohio troops. He would lead them personally to give Kirby Smith's cocky invaders a proper reception.[26]

Nelson completed his preparations, positioning many of his men on a ridge just south of Richmond. Some took cover behind the tombstones of a little cemetery on the edge of town. To reach Nelson's waiting Federals, the Confederates had to advance across a thick cornfield enclosed by a high rail fence. Once that had been passed, the attack needed to continue up a slope through a beautiful grove of trees. Kirby Smith halted his advance some two miles south of town. He carefully rested his men for an hour, allowing time for stragglers to rejoin their proper commands. Then he deployed. During this interval of preparation and reorganization, Kirby Smith once more sent Colonel Scott sweeping around the Union right and into their rear, this time beyond Richmond itself. Once Scott was on his way, Kirby Smith again ordered Churchill with one brigade to locate the enemy left and attack. Meanwhile Pres Smith came up and deployed his division on the right of the road—Ben Hill's brigade on line with the 13th and 154th Tennessee. Bell's 12/22d and Col. Munson R. Hill's 47th served as temporary reserve for Alfred Vaughan's brigade.[27]

Preceded by clouds of skirmishers to "feel the enemy's strongest positions," Vaughan's Brigade attacked. The conflict, according to Vaughan, was short and decisive—Nelson's troops "completely routed and demoralized." "With volley after volley and shout after shout," Col. Ben Hill reported, we "routed them from their stronghold and pursued them through the streets of Richmond." For Bell, it was his "hardest fight" of the day, but "there was little damage done." Nelson's and Manson's green troops fought as well as could be expected, but they were no match for the Rebel veterans of Belmont and Shiloh. Bull Nelson would report that he took "a strong position, where I was confident I could hold them in check until night, and then resume the retreat. The enemy attacked in front and on both flanks simultaneously with vigor. Our troops stood about three rounds when, struck by a panic, they fled in disorder. I was left with my staff almost alone."[28]

The Federals "struck out from the cemetery," Bell recalled, "and went right down the hill, pell mell, and we after them and they never halted until they run right into the trap we set for them." The trap, of course, was Scott's cavalry, who ambushed the fleeing Yankees, striking them suddenly in the flank and scattering them across the countryside. The Confederate infantry pursued up to three miles, but, conceded Preston Smith, it was ineffectual. Too tired to chase farther, the Twelfth Tennessee and its sister units turned about and returned to Richmond where they hurriedly encamped.[29]

Kirby Smith's Army of Kentucky, in this series of small battles on August 30, had captured a great deal of useful supplies and equipment: "All the enemy's artillery, their artillery horses, their transportation, quartermaster and commissary supplies, together with all their camp equipage," Col. Alfred Vaughan proudly recalled. Richmond proved a treasure house. Capt. Frank T. Ryan remembered, new blue uniforms, "canned fruits of all kinds, condensed milk (the first I ever saw), cheese, and other edibles." In Tyree Bell's words, "We captured everything." This included General Manson and 4,300 Union troops. Nelson managed to escape, however, despite being wounded in the thigh.[30] Casualties ran high for the Federals, who had 206 killed and 844 wounded. The Confederates lost far less: 78 killed, 372 wounded and 1 captured. Among the Rebel casualties were 5 killed and 25 wounded in the Twelfth Tennessee, one of whom was L. P. McMurry, onetime colonel of the Twenty-second Tennessee who had been serving faithfully as Bell's second in command, although retaining his rank as colonel.[31]

One must evaluate Bell's August 1862 performance with caution, for the sources are unusually limited. Bell made no after-action report, neither did his brigade commander, Alfred Vaughan, nor the other regimental commanders of the brigade. Neither Kirby Smith nor Pres Smith mentioned him in their reports. Indeed, as goes the chaotic reporting system of Kirby Smith's force, Bell might as well have been in Richmond, Virginia. This compels a great reliance on Bell's Autobiography. Bell proudly remembered his role in the Cumberland Mountains, at Manchester and at Richmond. As for the latter, he doubtless would have agreed with Alfred Vaughan, who observed years later that Richmond was "the most complete victory gained during the war in which the Thirteen participated."[32]

In the opening battle at Mount Zion Church, Pres Smith and his entire brigade played a crucial role. In the words of Alfred Fielder, they were "the principal actors." In the second fight at White's farm (Rogersville), Smith's Tennessee Brigade was slow to come up and of far less importance. Their contribution to the singular victory in the final fight for Richmond itself is undeniable. Although they suffered less than B. J. Hill's brigade, their attack on Nelson's left was essential to Kirby Smith's success. Their performance in the pursuit of the routed Federals, however, was criticized by their own commander—Pres Smith—as "ineffectual," surely one of the more candid admissions recorded during the entire war.[33]

Bell doubtlessly slept well that August night in Richmond. He and his boys had performed admirably in the strenuous, all-day, running fight. Fortunes were changing, he must have been tempted to believe. Watering their horses in the Ohio River? Perhaps not such a far-fetched idea, after all.

5

My Old Kentucky Home

Sunday, August 31, was cloudy but pleasant. Despite the misgivings of the devout, the 12th and 47th were marched out Sunday morning to the battlefields of yesterday "to gather up the trophies." They loaded many wagons with supplies, equipment, and weapons and hauled it all back to Richmond, turning over their booty to the quartermaster. Truly, the Blue Grass region was a bounty of riches. More and more, it appeared, these sister regiments, the 12th and 47th, were considered by brigade and division headquarters as one large regiment divided into two wings for administrative and tactical purposes. Of course, the 13th Tennessee and the 154th Tennessee Senior regiments also tended to maneuver together and share details. Now, with the death of Col. Ed Fitzgerald, they too were being considered as a unit. Both were West Tennessee regiments and the 13th, although containing men from Gibson and Dyer Counties, was primarily a Hardeman and Fayette unit, thus next-door neighbors of Shelby County, the home of the 154th.[1]

While the Twelfth Tennessee harvested the fruits of war, Bell divided his time between supervising the troops and helping his officers with the paperwork necessary to parole the thousands of Union prisoners. Kirby Smith could not allow his army to remain stationary at Richmond, enjoying their triumph. Time was precious. So September 1, 1862, Bell awoke his men at 2 A.M., fed them a light breakfast, and within an hour the Twelfth and its sister regiments marched away from the luxurious life of Richmond, heading down Tate's Creek Turnpike, straight for Lexington.[2]

Presently the column came to the Kentucky River, and there on the bluffs crowning the opposite side was the enemy, who greeted them with artillery fire.

The Confederates, not to be denied, found a ford and forced a crossing. "When we got across the river they were gone, pell mell," Bell recounted. "We rushed our men up the bank out on the level plain and pursued them rapidly, but never got in sight of them." On marched Kirby Smith's little Army of Kentucky. "The citizens male & female show us every sign of a warm & cordial reception," Alfred Fielder observed. "The ladies in places thronged the road and could frequently be heard to say hurrah for Jef. Davis and Southern rights all of which is encouraging to a poor weary soldier." The tramp continued. Mile after mile they marched. About eight miles from the river the column sagged and began to come apart, stragglers abounded. At 3 P.M., after a march of eighteen miles from Richmond, Kirby Smith had the good sense to halt at a little brick church. "Eat your rations and go into camp," he told his troops.[3]

About 11 o'clock that night, Kirby Smith sent for Bell. When the colonel reported to army headquarters, the general told him that the Twelfth Tennessee was to be honored. They were to march on Lexington and occupy the town. Bell was thrilled, of course, and decided to celebrate. He allowed his men to sleep until dawn and issued the order: "no command to form line or move forward until about 8 o'clock." The men of the Twelfth were "astonished" at their leisurely morning and delighted with the honor accorded them. They formed into column on the road and marched a few miles until Bell halted them at "old Mrs. Morgan's, mother of Col. John Morgan, about six miles from Lexington."[4]

Mrs. Morgan, alert to their approach, had stationed a "picket" out on the road watching for the head of the column. "She had a number of ladies with her when we got there," and as Bell recalled:

> She received us quite royally, had a fine lunch over on the road, mixed with all kinds of drinks, not necessary to mention whiskey or brandy.
>
> We staid there as long as we dared stay. When I told her I had to go on, she said she had a special request to make of me. She said that she wanted her carriage to go at the rear of my column to Lexington. I very promptly declined to allow her carriage to go at the rear of my column as she desired and I waited some time without making an explanation. She and the balance of the ladies seemed crestfallen. I said "Mrs. Morgan, your carriage can go at the extreme head of my column, me and my staff will follow and I have a fine Brass Band that will follow me and we will go into Lexington with as fine a display as you have ever seen." Gen. Kirby Smith had ordered me to go through all the streets of Lexington and rendezvous at the Court House.

The ladies seemed delighted and in a very few minutes, we were moving on rapidly and when we began to get into the suburbs of Lexington, the dust was intolerable. You never saw such a storm of dust, it was perfectly black. I moved up to her carriage and told her my orders and that she had better go straight to the Court House Park. She said "If you order me to do so, I will go, but I know the streets of the city better than you and I will go at the head of your column as I have done if you will allow me."

I told her that the column would follow her carriage and make all the streets and rendezvous at the Court House. When we got to the Court House, all the ladies were there and the men were all hid, with a few exceptions and such another dinner as we had set before us, no soldiers had ever seen. . . .[5]

That afternoon they congregated, civilians and soldiers. "The ladies crowded in among us, . . . the old men rushing forward grasping our hands like old friends," Captain Fielder reported, "bidding us welcome, declaring that they felt free once more . . . I never saw so many glad faces at once before." Soon the bell atop the courthouse rang and the crowd moved in closer. The Confederate flag was raised, and Kirby Smith among others spoke briefly. "He is no orator," lamented Fielder. Then the Twelfth ended their glorious visit and "moved out some half mile to where there was plenty of yanky tents already stretched."[6]

The remainder of Kirby Smith's army began to come up, receiving a similar "ovation" from Lexington; then appeared the hometown hero, Col. John Hunt Morgan, who arrived September 4 with a small force consisting of the Second Kentucky Cavalry and Lt. Col. Richard M. Gano's squadron of Texas horsemen. "Of all the parades that you ever saw," remembered Bell, "this was one. They actually pulled him [Morgan] off of his horse, took him in their arms and carried him upstairs to the second floor of the hotel. He was the 'Pet of Lexington.'" And the bells rang—"church-bells, town-bells, dinner-bells, sheep-bells, cow bells, blacksmiths anvils, and triangles, and old clevises—everything that had a ring to it."[7]

The next day, September 5, Bell and the Twelfth Tennessee broke camp and "started out on a pleasure trip." The Yankees were gone, at least gone from their front.[8] From Lexington the Confederates marched northeast to Paris "where they make so much Bourbon Whiskey," Bell noted. "We marched about 7 miles through the finest Country I ever saw," he added, "finely improved and inhabited by an intelligent people who thronged the road showing us every demonstration of respect." After one night in Paris, the column continued north,

★ BRIG. GEN. ABRAHAM BUFORD. NATIONAL ARCHIVES.

following the Kentucky and Central Railroad, through Ruddles Mills to Cynthiana. Then Bell turned his infantry about and marched southwest through "the beautiful town Georgetown" and encamped on the Frankfort Road at Johnson's Spring, near "Old Man Ward's" place. Ward happened to be a relative and political ally of the John C. Breckinridge family. Bell had dinner with the Wards and Mary Cyrene (Mrs. John C.) Breckinridge and her daughter Mary Desha. During the meal and afterward they discussed what would be involved in having the ladies travel with Bell's column if the time were to come to leave Kentucky.[9]

Bell marched toward Frankfort September 9, passing a camp of Kentuckians who had volunteered for the Confederate Army. Unfortunately most "who joined at this time," according to Gen. Basil Duke, "wanted to ride. As a people, [Kentuckians] are fond of horses, and if they went to war at all, they thought it a great tax upon them to make them walk." Chief among these locals was Abraham Buford, forty-two-year-old resident and stock farm owner of Versailles. Buford and Bell probably met at this time, thus beginning a long and important relationship.[10]

Abe Buford, mirroring the sentiments of his native state, had sat out the war up to this point, despite his military background. He had graduated from West Point in the Class of 1841 and won distinction in Mexico, but army life soon lost its attraction, so in 1854 he resigned and returned to Kentucky to raise cattle and horses. Many Kentuckians now appealed to Abe Buford to take up the fight, and President Davis even offered him a commission as brigadier general. The popular Buford finally agreed and began gathering Kentucky volunteers. Soon he had three regiments of them, but all cavalry.[11]

Bell and his men continued on toward Frankfort, passing within sight of the Capitol. They crossed the Kentucky River and bivouacked near enough so that the soldiers might bathe in the river. The next morning Bell and his men broke camp and marched back through Frankfort and to the north, retracing their steps through Georgetown and Leesburg, reaching Cynthiana on September 12. Their objective was to post themselves within supporting distance of Brig. Gen. Henry Heth's division demonstrating outside Covington, just across the Ohio from Cincinnati. Bell and most of Pres Smith's brigade continued further north, halting at the village of Crittenden, about twenty miles south of Covington. "There we remained for a couple of days," Bell recalled, "all the time living off the fat of the land. The ladies of Kentucky, God bless them, wherever we stopped or wherever we travelled, always furnished us with the best the land afforded."[12]

When Heth's anticipated attack against Covington was canceled, the Twelfth turned about and marched south. Bell must have felt some twinge of disappointment. To have liberated Covington, the place of his birth, to have seen a shell splash into the Ohio, would have gone far to justify the personal cost of the past five months.

Bell did not dwell in the land of could-have-beens, however. He had his hands full moving the Twelfth in orderly, expeditious fashion. They halted and rested at Big Pond, a place that impressed Bell: "It is a magnificent pond, covers several acres of land, clear, deep water, and we stopped there for the purpose of giving our soldiers a chance to wash their clothes and bathe."

On south they tramped, back to Georgetown where "the whole country came to see us." The citizens had learned Tyree Bell had a fine preacher traveling with him, and they implored the colonel to let him preach to them and to the soldiers that night, Sunday, September 21. As Bell assured them:

> there was no trouble about the preaching, that my preacher,
> the Rev. W. J. Mahon, was always charged and ready, but the
> difficulty was, we could not seat an audience. We decided that
> we would have preaching though, and the visitors circulated it.

> There was no way to establish a place to preach but at my ambulance, that was headquarters. We had a fine crowd and Parson Mahon did justice to himself fully. The crowd was delighted and they left at my ambulance some dozen or two bottles of Kentucky Fair Water. I suppose they intended that as tithes for the sermon.[13]

Bell neglected to mention in his Autobiography, however, that he felt encouraged by the reception given Parson Jack Mahon and, as a result, the men of Pres Smith's brigade and the local citizenry were treated to four straight nights of handsome sermonizing.[14]

On September 23, the wounded Cleburne returned to his makeshift division and resumed command. While the rest of the Army of Kentucky remained in the vicinity of Georgetown, Cleburne and his troops, including Smith's Brigade, marched off to Frankfort, encamped, and at 4:00 the next morning set out to the west with large elements of cavalry toward Shelbyville, from which they could unite with General Bragg's advancing army and attack Louisville.

All depended upon Bragg, who now commanded Kirby Smith's army as well as his own. So Bell and his men waited for orders at Shelbyville, all the while enjoying themselves. Large, enthusiastic crowds of citizens, men and women, visited the camps. Cleburne, having learned well from his mentor Hardee, arranged colorful reviews for the guests. Continuous drill, good food, and plentiful preaching were the order of the day. Then came disappointing news: General Bragg had chosen not to give battle to Buell's army. Rather, stepping aside, he had allowed what he deemed a superior force of Federals to continue on to Louisville. Thus the initiative passed to Buell.[15]

The Union forces at Louisville, emboldened by Buell's arrival, now marched forth. Therefore on October 1, under orders from Bragg, Cleburne's Division pulled back and returned to Frankfort where they remained three days. An enemy force, believed to be quite large, closed in. Actually, only one division threatened Frankfort, but the Confederates seemed mesmerized by the advancing columns of Yankees and declined to offer battle. Cleburne's Division was ordered to retreat again, this time almost due south to Harrodsburg, the county seat of Mercer County, Kentucky. Hardly had they arrived than "Gen Bragg's army commenced pouring in," reported Capt. Alfred Fielder. It was Polk's Corps, and Division Commander Frank Cheatham came out to Bell's encampment for a visit. "A general shout went up from our boys at seeing him." Cheatham reclaimed Pres Smith's brigade and Cleburne, relegated once again to brigade command, marched away with his Arkansas boys to fight in other parts. "We may look for stirring events soon," the men of the Twelfth believed. On all sides one could hear martial music and "one continual yell has been the consequence."[16]

During the afternoon of October 7 cannon fire could be heard, and about dusk Bell's regiment marched smartly out of Harrodsburg about four miles toward Perryville, then countermarched and returned to camp about 11 P.M. All seemed confusion as to purpose. The following morning the cannon fire intensified, and men recognized the noise of battle. About 8 A.M. Pres Smith ordered his brigade into line, and they marched off again toward the little town of Perryville, some nine miles to the southwest. The brigade was larger now, having been strengthened by the addition of the Ninth Texas Infantry. Pres Smith's Tennessee-Texas brigade looked forward confidently to meeting the National Army once again.[17]

Bell's regiment, indeed the entire brigade, would see no action at Perryville, however. Maj. Gen. Polk ordered Pres Smith to "have all the trains belonging to this army collected and moved out on the road to Bryantsville, and to be ready to move . . . on that place." In effect, the brigade would be guarding the wagon train during the battle, although close enough to the battlefield for use as a ready reserve. So Tyree Bell and the Twelfth Tennessee and Smith's brigade would miss the vicious combat at Perryville, where Bragg's understrength Confederates threw themselves repeatedly against the ever-growing enemy host. Although they met with a few tactical successes, Bragg's Army of the Mississippi would suffer frightful losses. The night of October 8, following this violent test of strength, an uneasy Bragg and his disheartened wing commanders decided it would be folly to remain in their broken condition facing a foe far superior in numbers. Orders were given to retreat northeast to Harrodsburg, and by 3 A.M., October 9, the last of Bragg's army had withdrawn safely across the Chaplin River.[18]

Remaining a day at Harrodsburg, Bragg's army fell back farther east to their logistical base at Bryantsville, placing the formidable barrier of Dick's River between them and the slowly pursuing Yankees. After pausing briefly at Bryantsville, Bragg retreated a short distance south to Camp Dick Robinson. There he united finally with Kirby Smith's Army of Kentucky, but the sometimes aggressive Bragg now had second thoughts about giving battle at all, even after being strongly reinforced. He could not afford defeat. Citing scarcity of provisions and the Federals' superior numbers, Bragg decided to withdraw from Kentucky before the onset of winter. It was agreed that Kirby Smith would retreat through

★ BRIG. GEN. DANIEL S. DONELSON. LIBRARY OF CONGRESS.

Big Hill, while Bragg, with Polk's and Hardee's corps, would fall back farther south to Lancaster, then swing east along the line of the Lebanon Railroad through Crab Orchard and Mount Vernon, and on east to Cumberland Gap.[19]

As the Confederate high command deliberated, Pres Smith and his disappointed Tennesseans remained on the west side of Dick's River serving as either an advance/bridgehead force or as a rear guard, contingent to the outcome of the council of war at Camp Dick Robinson. Apparently they managed this assignment effectively and without a serious encounter; the enemy seemed content not to bring the Rebel army to bay. The brigade, including Bell's Twelfth, would cross the river and rejoin the army at Camp Dick Robinson October 13.

It was time to leave Kentucky and prepare for new adventures. Bragg hurried on to Knoxville with his staff, turning the army over to Polk, who in turn abandoned the plodding column, leaving Brig. Gen. Daniel S. Donelson in charge. Donelson, a resident of Sumner County and a prominent state political leader, was an old friend of Bell's and the Harris clan. So the morning of October 13, when the Twelfth reached Lancaster, Bell went to see Donelson. He explained that they were only four miles from the Harris homestead, and that he wanted to use the opportunity to visit the family home and relatives. He particularly wanted to see his old friend (and uncle) Russell A. Harris. Russell, who now owned the home place, continued to be important in Bell's life. Not only had they worked together as young men, but Russell had taught Tyree a great deal, not only about construction, but about profitable methods to raise and trade livestock. Bell was, and considered himself, Russell's protégé, acknowledging their special lifelong relationship by naming a son for his kinsman.

Initially Donelson refused the request. The army was on the march and there was great risk of Bell being captured; Col. Frank Wolford's Yankee Kentucky cavalry were "pecking away at our rear."[20] Bell persisted, however, telling the old general that "unless he ordered me not to go, that I would go." So Donelson yielded and Bell, accompanied by Capt. Tal Craig, rode over that afternoon while Donelson and the long infantry column continued down the road through Lancaster toward Crab Orchard. The two Confederate officers found Uncle Russell without trouble and were greeted warmly. Indeed, their risky visit would last all that afternoon, Bell remembered, and well into the night.[21]

> A great many of the citizens found out that I was there and came in to see me. When I left, they loaded me and Craig down with such things as we needed in the army. In the first place, we took a large bucket holding twenty lbs. of fine yellow Blue Grass Butter. They gave me four dozen pairs of yarn socks for the soldiers, and they gave me a full bolt, forty yards of Kentucky jeans and last but not least, they put up a dozen bottles of old peach brandy.
>
> They furnished me a guide to take me into the big road at the foot of the hill at Crab Orchard. The country was all fenced in and had many gateways, and roads leading in all directions. He went with me until I got in sight of Gen. Donelson's camp fires. The little fellow's name was Bettis; he had to ride about twenty five miles and try to get in before day, for if caught, he would go to the Federal prison. The little fellow made the trip and was never captured.
>
> I rode along the line, not going to my own camp until I came up to Gen. Donelson's camp. Day was just making its appearance. Gen. Donelson's servant had gotten up and built a little fire in front of the camp and when I rode up, the General heard me and called to me to get down that he would be out in a few minutes.
>
> When he came out, he seemed very much pleased to see that I had gotten back safely, and after chatting a while, I related to him

the foraging that I had done. The first thing that I told him was that I had brought a large bucket of fine yellow Blue Grass Butter and to have his servant get something to put part of it in and I gave him half of it. The next thing, I asked him how he was off for socks. He said that he did not have a pair that had either heel or toe in them. I gave him one dozen pairs. I then gave him enough of the Kentucky jeans to have him some pantaloons made to ride in. We talked a little while and as if I had forgotten to mention it, I said "O yes, General, I have a dozen bottles of Peach Brandy too"; and he said "Why in the name of God didn't you mention that first?" I gave him 1/2 dozen bottles.[22]

Grateful though Donelson may have been, he did not give Bell time to rest from his strenuous night ride. The column moved out early that morning headed through Crab Orchard for Mt. Vernon and London. Initially they made good time, but by October 17, the tramp grew much more difficult. Although they were no longer pursued by Wolford's Yankee cavalry, "there is great Complaint among the boys feeling weary and unwell," reported Captain Fielder. "This poor mountainous County is being left desolate. [There] not being forage enough near the road to half feed the stock belonging to the army."

"We have marched from Dick Robertson," Fielder continued, "on half rations because the roads run through such a mountainous Country full rations could not be hauled." Finally, on October 20, 1862, the Twelfth Tennessee reached Cumberland Gap, passed through and, for the most part, put behind them the "mountainous and rough" road. Bragg's army had paid a high price for their safe passage—in loss of morale and physical suffering. The veteran Col. Alfred Vaughan of the Thirteenth Tennessee considered this retreat from Kentucky "one of greater trial and hardship than any march made during the war." On Friday, October 25, Bell and Pres Smith's brigade approached Knoxville and encamped four miles outside the town. They procured their baggage, which had been left behind, and for the first time in over two months slept under their tents. Knoxville had a nasty surprise for them, however. It grew very cold that first night, then snowed and continued to snow all the next day. Some welcome to Tennessee. On this note, the disappointing, bitterly disillusioning Kentucky Campaign ended.[23]

6

Shelbyville

Almost immediately upon their arrival at Knoxville, Bell and the Twelfth Tennessee received a new assignment, and once again the regiment would act independently. General Bragg's newly styled Confederate Army of Tennessee was moving to Middle Tennessee. Murfreesboro would be its forward position; Tullahoma, its logistical base. Nearly all of the army had executed the transfer from Knoxville to Middle Tennessee by rail, but because of a shortage of rolling stock, the wagon train of Cheatham's Division and the ordnance and artillery of Polk's Right Wing needed to travel overland, so Bell and his men were chosen to escort the valuable train, with Bell in general command. All was ready on October 31, 1862, and Bell set out at daylight, riding at the head of the cumbersome column that extended almost three miles. General Polk, as the column moved off, admonished Bell, "You must by all means make the trip through in sixteen days, you cannot possibly be longer than that time."[1]

Bell made it in eleven days. The wagon train crossed the Clinch River above Kingston, then followed the Tennessee River down to Smith's Crossroads. From this point they climbed over Walden's Ridge into the Sequatchie Valley and proceeded to Jasper and Pelham, reaching Tullahoma on November 10. There Bell's regiment encamped, reuniting with Pres Smith's brigade and Cheatham's Division. They would remain in Tullahoma almost two weeks. A number of conscripts arrived during this time, and some were assigned to the 12th, thus modestly patching the great rips and tears in the regiment's ranks resulting from Shiloh and the Kentucky Campaign. These days at Tullahoma provided Bell with the opportunity to continue the 12/22d's training (company and battalion drill primarily) and to integrate the new recruits and conscripts.

The boys also received their pay and drew blankets and shoes, all of which improved regimental morale.[2]

On the night of November 21, Bell's troops, as part of Smith's Brigade, received orders to move to Manchester, Tennessee, some dozen miles northeast. They awoke to "a white frost and a good ice" and presently set out with three days' rations, but without their tents. It was an easy tramp over good roads, and they passed through Manchester soon after dark and encamped. The following day they marched northwest through Beechgrove and Hoover's Gap toward Murfreesboro, making about sixteen miles; the following day, at 5:30 P.M. on the courthouse clock, they marched into and through Murfreesboro itself, bivouacking about a mile and a half outside town. There they would remain until December 5, when they moved with the division to LaVergne, Tennessee, about halfway between Murfreesboro and Nashville. They encamped along Stewart's Creek, remaining in this advanced position several weeks, employed in picketing and supporting Brig. Gen. Joseph Wheeler's cavalry screen.[3]

On December 9, 1862, they had their first fight in over two months. Wheeler's cavalry had attempted to attack and capture a large Yankee foraging party, but soon found themselves confronting a strong force of infantry. The Twelfth, acting as Wheeler's support, came up at the double-quick as some of the cavalrymen "had become alarmed and fled." Bell deployed the regiment in line of battle and advanced about a mile through a heavy cedar forest until within fifty yards of an unidentified body of troops. "Each party commenced calling to each other," Captain Fielder reported, "not to shoot, halt, dont shoot, &c when we heard their officer give the command fire." A volley struck the Twelfth, and Bell ordered his line of battle to return the fire. They had "warm work" for about thirty minutes, then the enemy line crumbled. Bell pursued about a mile, his troops finding the bodies of half a dozen Federals (Fielder reported fifty-seven) as they passed over the ground where their volleys had struck. The regiment lost two killed and six wounded in this little fight at LaVergne. One of the dead, Sam Trigg, had come from Middle Tennessee, so regimental commander Bell had the body taken to the old home place and buried him in the family cemetery. Bell was careful, and always would be careful, of the disposition of his dead.[4]

The Twelfth Tennessee and Smith's Brigade returned to their camp near Murfreesboro on December 17. It was here that the men heard upsetting talk of officially consolidating the Twelfth and Forty-seventh Infantry, but in this merger, unlike that with the Twenty-second, the Twelfth would be formally reduced to a battalion. Half of its officers and noncommissioned officers would be left without a command, thus becoming supernumeraries and subject to discharge.

Tyree Bell himself would remain as colonel of the combined regiment, but he quickly became "pestered and somewhat fretful" because so many good men—Chaplain Jack Mahon and Alfred Fielder for instance—were "being left off the list."[5] Some officers, like Mahon, simply resigned, left camp, and headed for home. Bell may have had command of a regiment, but the Twelfth as he knew it was gone. Frank Cheatham knew his faithful subordinate was unhappy and probably could use a diversion. Opportunely, word came of Bedford Forrest's successes in West Tennessee—at Lexington and Jackson and Trenton, in Bell's words, "making a big parade in West Tenn. and it looked as if he was making a grand success, that was cleaning out the entire country of the Federal soldiers." Generals Cheatham and Polk capitalized on the occasion. They decided to get the discontented Bell out of camp, granting him an extended furlough to go home and "gather up all the troops that could be gathered up." With him would go Lieutenant Colonel McMurry and twenty other officers. This small but important party of West Tennesseans left camp on Christmas Eve. They traveled cautiously, heading south to Columbia, then west to Clifton (where Forrest had crossed the Tennessee River into West Tennessee), then north to Perryville, Tennessee, on the east bank of the river. There, on the morning of December 31, they heard the sound of fighting from far across the Tennessee. Undoubtedly it was Forrest. Perhaps he needed their assistance, but Bell would not allow any of his band to cross the river until he knew "the result of the fight." By dusk word came that Forrest had been defeated at the Battle of Parker's Crossroads and "had commenced retreating out of West Tennessee."[6]

It may have been there on the Tennessee at Perryville that Bell was reunited with his friend Milton Russell. Russell, apparently a paroled prisoner of war, had been at home in Trenton when Forrest attacked on the afternoon of December 20. Russell seems to have taken no part in the fighting, but after the Federal garrison surrendered, Russell is believed to have presented Forrest with a heavy, finely balanced, dragoon sword in appreciation for his victory and thereupon decided to ride off with him. In time Milton Russell would win Forrest's complete confidence, just as he had Bell's.[7]

Whether Russell was the messenger or not, Bell and his party believed that recruiting openly in West Tennessee was out of the question with Forrest having gone back to Mississippi, so the little band turned east and retraced their steps to Murfreesboro. Nearing Columbia, they learned of the Army of Tennessee's terrible battle at Stones River. Bloody victory on December 31 had turned to bitter defeat on January 2, 1863. When Bell and his party reached Murfreesboro, they found the army in motion, retreating south toward Tullahoma. Because of the confusion and jammed roads consequent to such a massive withdrawal in the presence of the enemy, Bell could not rejoin his regiment until January 7. To his dismay he found that the 12/47th Tennessee, commanded by Maj. Nick Wyatt, had been chopped to pieces at Murfreesboro: 56 percent of the troops dead or wounded. They had fallen in windrows, it was said.[8]

The 12/47th Tennessee and the bulk of Polk's Corps had encamped near Shelbyville, Tennessee, and there General Polk established his headquarters. He sent for Bell soon after his return and gave him the news that he was naming him post commander of the town. Bell would serve in this capacity at Shelbyville about five months—a quiet assignment during a quiet period for the Army of Tennessee as it attempted to recuperate from the ordeal of Murfreesboro or Stones River.[9]

At this time Bell's officers stepped forward on his behalf. Fourteen officers of the Twelfth Tennessee led by Lt. Col. L. P. McMurry, Maj. Nick Wyatt, and Surgeon Benjamin F. Dickinson petitioned the secretary of war that Col. Tyree H. Bell be promoted to brigadier general. This document was accompanied by a similar appeal signed by Maj. Thomas R. Shearon and fourteen other officers of the Forty-seventh Tennessee. "Col. Bell," they wrote, "was among the first to respond to his country's call, and on the fields of Shiloh, Richmond Ky and Lavergne he has exhibited the utmost courage and gallantry, combined with the greatest tact and Military Skill, of unblemished character and great Morals." All in all, they asserted, Colonel Bell has "shown himself possessed in an eminent degree of the qualities requisite for a safe and skillful commander." Division commander Frank Cheatham endorsed the application wholeheartedly. He had known Bell "since early youth, and from my knowledge of him as a man & gentleman, there is no man his superior." Cheatham noted particularly Bell's quiet nature, his strict sobriety, and his gallantry and skill on the battlefield.[10]

Doubtlessly quite pleased by this action of his comrades, Bell took up his duties as post commander. Within days everything seemed routine, slow and sleepy, "every morning the same." His responsibilities included the procurement of whiskey and brandy to be sent south for "hospital purposes," so the 12/47th pickets remained alert to "anything in the way of liquor." They were under strict orders to confiscate it and bring it to post headquarters immediately. Delicate business, and as might have been anticipated, they soon ran afoul of libations intended for higher bodies. Presently a sentry brought in a bottle of brandy, a gift from a Col. John T. Abernathy to Maj. Gen. Jones M. Withers, commander of the Second Division, Polk's Corps, a veteran officer, particularly esteemed by General Bragg. Before Bell could inform Withers of the confiscation, a "very insulting letter" arrived from that general demanding the return of the brandy. This angered Bell and he not only refused, but had his adjutant, Capt. Thomas E. Richardson,[11] rather than himself, sign the letter responding to Withers. Bell knew this act constituted "a great breach of propriety, me being only a colonel, it was my duty to sign it myself." Withers immediately took the matter to Polk and "threatened to prefer charges" against Bell. Polk, being Bell's "warm friend" and knowledgeable in the ways of men, called Withers in for a talk, intending to soothe him, explaining that the gaff in protocol was unintentional on Bell's part. Withers, however, was still not satisfied and left headquarters angry, "but I suppose the general [Withers] went home and thought the matter over," Bell remembered, "as it was dropped right there and nothing more was heard of it; but he did not get his demijohn."[12]

Despite Bell's heavy-handed efforts, whiskey leaked through the security wall of the 12/47th Tennessee in alarming fashion; even the guard details "were frequently drunk." Polk, as he had at Columbus, became exasperated. Find it, find it, he demanded of his post commander. At this point Bell's resourcefulness at last came into play. He called in Pvt. Franc G. Sampson of Dyersburg, formerly captain of Company E, Forty-seventh Tennessee.

> Frank was a noble fellow, a young lawyer, but loved whiskey better than a fish loves water. . . . Frank came in, I took him into a back room; told him what I wanted to know and what I wanted him to do. He told me that "I could not possibly do it, colonel, could not think of such a thing as all the soldiers, should they find it out, would kill me." I talked with him and told him that no one would ever know if he could find it out where they procured it and that I would give him a bottle of whiskey every Monday morning, while I stayed in office.[13]

Some might deem it preying on human frailty, others artful persuasiveness, but the stratagem worked. Sampson finally acquiesced. He confided to the colonel that one of the army's secure warehouses had a basement ventilated by small windows with iron bars. There was a trapdoor into this basement, and now and then a shipment of provisions would come in. Mixed among the barrels and boxes of supplies would be a barrel of liquor. As the wagon was unloaded the culprits would see that the valuable barrel was rolled to the trapdoor and lowered into the basement. After the unloading was completed one man would remain behind locked in the basement. All night long, through the iron bars, he would slip canteen after canteen, each carefully filled with the precious liquid. This trusted soul would remain on duty all night until morning brought someone to unlock or hoist the trapdoor that kept him imprisoned with the liquid gold. Then he would wait for his opportunity and leap out.

Bell took a detail to investigate one morning, opened up the trapdoor, and seized a man from the 154th Tennessee who had been "drawing whiskey for the soldiers the whole night." Having solved the mystery and having a transgressor in hand, Bell turned the matter over to General Polk, who called in the officers of the proud 154th and ordered them to move their camp eight miles out of town. The regiment, officers and men, were not to show their faces in Shelbyville as long as the Army of Tennessee remained. That ended the liquor trouble.[14]

A post commander, it seemed, always knew trouble, especially the post commander at Shelbyville. Soldiers would escape from the guardhouse and Bell would have to apprehend them. On February 23, in cold weather, he had to order Shelbyville's comfortable garrison, his West Tennessee boys, "to move out of town" and encamp to prevent the spread of smallpox. With them Bell sent a small army of frightened and disgruntled citizens. Soon a tent city of the discontented arose on a high bluff overlooking Duck River. Although the new encampment promised good water and plenty of wood, the men of Bell's 12/47th Tennessee Infantry were harassed by thunder, lightning, and two days of ceaseless rain, a deluge so heavy that Duck River overflowed its banks. A month later, after everyone had returned to the "suburbs" of Shelbyville, the fire bell rang out in the night: The courthouse was ablaze. Despite the best efforts of Bell and his men, in a few hours the building was reduced to a hollow rim of brick. Then, as if to insult them, March brought not spring, but more rain and hail and snow. Indeed, the last day of March a "pretty smart little snow storm" blew into town. Inspections held that month found the regiment in fair condition. The inspecting officer reported, "Their Minie Muskets and Enfield Rifles, being found to be not in as good condition as they should be, the attention of the commanding officer has been called to this, and the neglect has been ordered to be remedied." Their equipment and clothing were found to be in "not very good" condition, and they were "tolerably well supplied with cooking utensils, axes, hatches & spades."[15]

The weather, fortunately, changed with the calendar. April in Middle Tennessee meant soft, beautiful mornings and fine days, "the birds are twittering and everything looks lovely." Citizens from across the Tennessee, from distant Dyer County, appeared like jonquils of spring, bringing happy news from home: "all was quiet; no yankees from Jackson to Columbus." Then on April 15, Miss Mary arrived in Shelbyville, accompanied by her cousin, Mrs. Martha Harris Douglas, whose husband, Guy, was a private in Company D of the 12/47th. Mary had traveled some three hundred miles to see her husband, but happily "without any difficulty at all." Very soon after Mary arrived an elated Bell went to see General

Polk. He requested a leave not to exceed thirty days so that the couple might visit "very particular friends" in Maury County, Tennessee. His friend Polk said he would approve the request, but Bell knew what that entailed. The procedure, the paperwork, "would take weeks to get back," so he asked Polk to personally present the application to General Bragg who had come to Shelbyville to review Polk's Corps. General Polk declined, however, saying that "the relations between him and Gen. Bragg were such that he could not afford to do it." Instead, he promised to prepare the way. He would inform General Bragg of Mary Ann's arrival and of Bell's desire for "an indefinite leave of absence."

The following afternoon, April 16, as the 12/47th marched in review past the commander of the Army of Tennessee, Col. Tyree H. Bell was at their head. When Bell passed and saluted Bragg, the general asked Bell to join him. Having moved aside a staff officer to make room for Colonel Bell, Bragg turned to Bell and asked about Mary Ann's trip through the lines, then asked him about the application for leave. When the colonel told the general about the proposed Maury County visit, Bragg responded, "Have you the application with you?" Bell said he had it in his pocket. He pulled it out and handed the form to Bragg who looked it over "and then something happened," Bell said, "that had never happened before." General Bragg "laid the application on the pummel of his saddle and took out his pencil and approved it and handed it back to me."[16]

The subsequent Maury County vacation from the war proved to be not only "a very pleasant time" but an important time for Tyree and Mary Walton Bell. Traveling with them from Shelbyville to Columbia was their friend, Congressman John D. C. Atkins, and several other members of the Confederate Congress (which happened to be in recess). Also appearing in Columbia at this time was Governor Isham G. Harris. In all probability the host for this informal political convocation in Columbia was the sociable and highly political Gen. Gideon Pillow, with whom Bell had spent a week a year earlier in Oxford, Mississippi, and who, as Head of the Volunteer and Conscript Bureau of the Army of Tennessee, was deeply involved in—indeed, responsible for—recruiting troops and chasing deserters throughout West Tennessee. Bell thought of himself as Pillow's friend and openly expressed that "I entertain the highest regard for General Pillow, both as a man and an officer."[17]

Pillow's powerful and highly effective network of subordinates functioned throughout Mississippi, Tennessee, and Alabama, and even into the Carolinas. Also enthusiastically assisting Pillow gather manpower for the Army of Tennessee were Brigadier General Forrest and Brig. Gen. William H. "Red" Jackson, a division commander under Maj. Gen. Earl Van Dorn. Both Forrest and Jackson, active subordinates of Pillow's in the 1861 Provisional Army of Tennessee, now indicated their willingness to serve under the old Mexican War hero if he were to be given command of the cavalry of Bragg's army. In fact, according to Dr. John A. Wyeth, Forrest's surgeon and biographer, "Forrest never for a moment neglected to show his appreciation and friendship for General Pillow."[18]

While Bell and Miss Mary relaxed in Columbia, Bedford Forrest, stationed in Spring Hill, received orders from Bragg to give chase to a strong Union raiding party under Col. Abel D. Streight, which had started east from the Mississippi-Alabama line headed for Tuscumbia and ultimately, it was feared, the Western and Atlantic Railroad, the principal supply line for the Army of Tennessee. Forrest pursued Straight relentlessly and made a spectacular capture of the raider and his entire force. This stunning victory made Forrest the toast of the western Confederacy, indeed the Confederacy itself. Bragg, after congratulating him and offering promotion to major general, ordered Forrest back to Spring Hill. Maj. Gen. Earl Van Dorn had been murdered in a private quarrel May 7, 1863, and the important cavalry command was vacant—all the cavalry of the western wing of the Army of Tennessee. Bragg asked Forrest to assume this task. Whether Bell and Forrest talked during the former's extended visit to Columbia is unknown, but probable. Most likely Bell made the easy ride up the handsome pike to Spring Hill at least once.[19]

Bell returned to Shelbyville from his extended leave about May 25 "very much refreshed and rested" and quickly became involved in the heavy drill routine of the 12/47th.[20] The emphasis had changed in the past few months. Target practice was much more frequent, with the standard marksmanship distance usually set at four hundred to six hundred yards. Skirmish drill took place almost daily now, certainly more frequently than the accustomed company and battalion drill. Bell, as regimental commander, did not simply observe these exercises, but conducted many of the drills himself. Moreover, he held a special school (two sections, divided according to rank) in tactics for the officers of the regiment. As evidence of his developing technical proficiency, Colonel Bell also conducted brigade drill.[21]

An old friend now joined Bell in camp: Lt. Col. William Azariah "Bill" Dawson, sometime flatboat operator, farmer, and the former sheriff of Dyer County. As an junior officer in the Twenty-second Tennessee, Dawson had fought beside Bell at Belmont and Shiloh, but had been wounded three times and sent home in April 1862 with a surgeon's discharge. That summer, however, Bill Dawson received orders from Braxton Bragg authorizing him to recruit a cavalry battalion behind enemy lines. By November 1862, Dawson had five companies of West Tennesseans operating over a wide area from the Forked Deer River south to Shelby County. Primarily, Dawson's battalion of partisans enforced the

Confederate conscript law and attempted to resist any Federal raiding or foraging parties venturing forth from Fort Pillow, the new powerful Federal base on the east bank of the Mississippi above Memphis. Dawson's force, one of several operating in West Tennessee at that time, caught the attention of Federal commanders in Memphis and Union City, and the decision was made to suppress these guerrillas. Dawson was captured in Dyer County in February 1863 and his battalion broken up. Imprisoned several months, he had been exchanged just before coming to Shelbyville. He and Bell had a happy reunion, and Bell took a deep interest in Dawson's report of his activities in West Tennessee.[22]

Several field-grade officers such as Bill Dawson hung around Tyree Bell's headquarters at this time. Some were waiting for authority to go behind enemy lines and raise cavalry or mounted infantry units. Others, most of them supernumeraries, hoped for a command or staff assignment in the Army of Tennessee or in John C. Pemberton's Department of Mississippi and Eastern Louisiana.[23] Elated over Forrest's successes and having visited with his old friend Bill Dawson, Bell himself must have been attracted by the talk—the opportunities offered by returning to West Tennessee. He believed he could recruit troops, many troops, for the army—men he knew well, men formerly associated with the Twelfth, the Twenty-second, the Forty-seventh, and a host of others whose political convictions had changed once Union troops had begun to occupy West Tennessee. For that matter, Bell knew where to look for the stragglers, the deserters, those who had managed to evade the conscript officers. If he could reorganize the fragments of units in Dyer, Obion, and Gibson Counties alone, he would have almost a brigade of cavalry that he could bring back across the Tennessee and phase into Forrest's command, or he could, like Dawson, remain west of the river and operate as a partisan force.

As he faced Pres Smith's Brigade on Monday, May 25, and proceeded to put the four infantry regiments through their evolutions, such thoughts could well have been tracing through Tyree Bell's mind. He must have been considering where his duty lay: with Pres Smith and Cheatham and Polk and the infantry, or back home as a partisan leader like Dawson or Forrest. What if he could mount his 12/47th Tennessee?

Fueling these desires was the knowledge that West Tennessee, from Memphis to Union City to Paducah, was alive with guerrilla activity. Even control of the rivers was in dispute, with gunboats and transports being fired upon constantly. Gen. William T. Sherman, in utter frustration and echoing the sentiments of Union commanders and Unionists generally, declared, "I will expel every secession family from Memphis if this mode of warfare is to be continued, and will, moreover, land troops on unexpected points and devastate the country into the interior." By the spring of 1863, when Bill Dawson was suppressed, the attitudes of Union officials in West Tennessee had hardened. Many simply looked upon partisans, men like Dawson, as "highway robbers." They would be dealt with accordingly.[24]

Historian Benjamin F. Cooling has pointed out that these guerrillas had succeeded in tying down over 60,000 Federals. "A separate cavalry division of 3,873 officers and men operated out of Memphis solely against West Tennessee partisans." These Federal or National troops included West Tennessee Unionists under leaders such as Col. Fielding Hurst of McNairy County, commanding the Sixth Tennessee Cavalry, U.S.A., and Maj. W. F. Bradford, a former lawyer in Dyersburg, who had organized the Fourteenth Tennessee Cavalry, U.S.A. All manner of atrocities were attributed to Hurst's and Bradford's commands as they wandered and raided throughout West Tennessee. Hurst, who resigned from the Union army in late 1864, would be charged with "exacting large sums of money from citizens of Jackson, Madison County, and Purdy, McNairy County."[25] Another regiment of Tennesseans operating in the area in similar fashion was the Seventh Tennessee Cavalry, U.S.A., commanded by the controversial Col. Isaac R. Hawkins. These Tennessee Unionist regiments augmented a far heavier body of Midwestern occupation troops. These Federal units included the Sixty-second Illinois Infantry, Third Michigan Cavalry, Second, Fourth, Seventh, Eleventh, and Fifteenth Illinois Cavalry; and Twenty-second Ohio. They all operated in the West Tennessee area, searching out, attacking, and often smashing partisan bands such as Dawson's or William W. Faulkner's Kentuckians. They also could recruit. An enterprising Federal commander could swell his ranks and certainly obtain guides and informers with U.S. "hard money." Union officials coveted the manpower pool of the politically ambivalent and of slaves, Rebel deserters, and men eluding the grasp of Pillow's Conscript Bureau. They wanted these men as much as Tyree Bell.[26]

Another factor influencing Bell, Gideon Pillow, and the Confederate War Department was the defeat and dispersal of Col. Robert V. Richardson's command, the largest organized Confederate partisan unit operating in West Tennessee. The debacle had occurred in March 1863. Richardson had partially succeeded in reconstituting his regiment, but in the meantime had run afoul of Confederate authorities who charged him with "great oppression" and "exercising authority not intended to be given." This resulted in an order for his arrest being issued April 15, 1863. Trusted and experienced leadership was needed badly in West Tennessee.[27]

Indeed, it had become a no-man's land, with citizens victimized by the occupying Federals and by poorly disciplined, paramilitary Rebel forces.

"Witnesses were struck not only by the intense suffering," observes historian Stephen V. Ash, "but also by the awful devastation and the eerie lifelessness. . . . Ravage and desolation everywhere." And fear.[28]

On the morning of June 11, 1863, the men of Dyer County present in the Army of Tennessee gathered at Shelbyville to elect delegates to a state convention to be held at Winchester, Tennessee. This political convention would nominate candidates for Congress and also for governor. The preference, at least as far as Dyer Countians were concerned, was clear: John D. C. Atkins for Congress representing the Ninth District. Among those chosen to speak for Dyer in the convention and to vote were Col. Tyree H. Bell, Capt. Alfred T. Fielder, and Col. Otho F. Strahl.

The delegates traveled to Winchester by train on June 16 and the following day listened to speeches from the congressional and gubernatorial candidates. The convention nominated Robert L. Caruthers to serve as governor. Bell, Fielder, and the other army delegates returned to camp the night of June 18 confident that they had fulfilled their assignment as delegates.[29]

Following this quiet interlude in Bell's military career, everything changed. By noon, June 21, all was ready. Bell rode out of camp headed back to West Tennessee, his saddlebags brimming with letters for the folks at home. With him rode his staff and several other officers "for the purpose of recruiting our Army." Although Bell would return briefly to Bragg's headquarters on July 14, 1863, and again that fall, his service as an infantry officer, his association with the 12/47th Tennessee Infantry and the Army of Tennessee, had ended. He had become a subordinate of Gideon J. Pillow.[30]

7

Slipping Back to West Tennessee

Tyree Bell's timing was propitious. As he ventured toward home, the overall Federal commander in the Mississippi Valley, Ulysses S. Grant, was drastically reducing manpower in West Tennessee to support his campaign against Vicksburg. In mid-June the Federals abandoned Jackson, Tennessee, to concentrate on control of the rivers, the railroads, and peripheral strong points in West Tennessee: Union City, Columbus, Memphis, and Corinth. Soon thereafter the commander of the Columbus, Kentucky, District, Brig. Gen. Alexander S. Asboth, complained to the War Department that Grant's directive had left "the whole country between the Tennessee and Mississippi Rivers—from Paducah to Corinth . . . where secessionism prevails and guerrillas are constantly organizing—guarded by only a part of my former force, now not over 4,000 men."[1]

As Union strength and authority diminished, more partisans entered Tennessee, coming across the Tennessee River from the east and south, and from Kentucky to the north. Some were Confederate patriots intent on redeeming the country from Yankee invaders, others dangerous criminals ready to prey not only on the weakened Union occupation forces, but on civilians, Confederate and Union alike. In mid-July the guerrillas and desperados would be joined by a number of paroled soldiers, angry, despondent human wreckage from the Vicksburg disaster. It was a time of revenge and reprisal.[2]

At this time, the summer of 1863, reestablishment of Confederate presence, much less control, in this chaotic area depended more on Gideon Pillow's Conscript Bureau operatives than any other agency or command. Pillow himself was quite active (as Union reports verify), appearing throughout West Tennessee in early and mid-summer. The Army of Tennessee could be of no help; it was in full retreat from Middle Tennessee to Chattanooga. Nor could anything be expected from John C. Pemberton or Joseph E. Johnston in Mississippi. Bell, it should be emphasized, may have come to West Tennessee in June as the agent of Corps Commander Leonidas Polk, but by mid-July he willingly had become one of Gideon Pillow's chief subordinates, though nominally remaining the senior colonel of Pres Smith's Brigade, Cheatham's Division.

It was fair to admire General Pillow. Forrest did. So did Bragg, Polk, and Joe Johnston. He held the secret, they believed, to the desperate Confederate manpower problem. Pillow had been quite successful in the spring of 1863, astonishing the Army of Tennessee and the Confederate War Department by forwarding so many troops to Shelbyville and Tullahoma. He could find them in the swamps, it seemed, in the hospitals, in the "great houses," and in the indispensable factories. The success of his efforts greatly encouraged Confederate patriots like Tyree Bell. As always, however, Pillow tended to overreach and alienate, and the authorities in Richmond in their wisdom soon decided to curtail his operations. When disaster at Vicksburg turned the Western Theater upside down, nevertheless, Jefferson Davis and the War Department wrung their hands. In a flash, Pillow became the center of activity again, this time working directly under Gen. Joseph E. Johnston in the Department of the West, being vested with "complete control over conscription in Alabama, Mississippi, Tennessee, and Florida."[3]

Gideon Pillow had high ambitions for Bell. His orders to the Dyer County colonel read: "proceed into West Tennessee and raise a regiment, and, if practicable a Brigade of Cavalry for the defense of the country. As soon as the troops are raised, they will be armed and mustered into the service of the Confederate States. He [Bell] is authorized to receive all organized companies and organize them into Regiments."[4]

Pillow also gave Bell, as though the latter were some general officer, a staff of seven, not to speak of "control and direction of all the officers of the [Volunteer and Conscript] Bureau operating in West Tennessee." Pillow cautioned Bell to "enforce order and discipline from the beginning, and not allow them to plunder the citizens of the country."[5]

Pillow specifically authorized Bell to take charge of the commands of Lt. Col. Henry C. Greer in the vicinity of Tuscumbia, Alabama, and those of Col. John F. Newsom, Lt. Col. Andrew N. Wilson, and Capt. Thomas N. Kizer in West Tennessee. Regarding the latter three, Bell was "to assist these organizations in their efforts [to recruit and conscript] and as far as practicable to protect them and provide for their wants."[6] Among these partisan leaders was Henry Clay Greer, a young and energetic citizen of Henry County, who had begun his Confederate service as a lieutenant in the Fifth Tennessee Infantry. After seeing action at Shiloh, Greer was discharged in the consolidation that followed. He returned to Henry County and began organizing a cavalry company. By the fall of 1862, his band had grown to battalion size and had come to the attention of Union authorities for its annoying operations along the Tennessee River. Greer's Battalion would eventually become the nucleus of Bell's command.[7]

Another West Tennessean dispossessed of command when his Sixth Tennessee regiment merged with the Ninth Tennessee was Capt. John F. Newsom. His company of guerrillas had linked up temporarily with Col. R. V. Richardson's regiment in the winter of 1862–1863 and, in a running fight that February, Newsom had been "dangerously wounded and paroled." Somewhat later he had been authorized by Pillow to raise a regiment within Federal lines and had succeeded famously. Newsom's cavalry regiment was sworn in at Jackson, Tennessee, July 27, 1863.[8]

Col. Andrew Neal Wilson had pulled together a small regiment in Lake County, Tennessee, by July 1863. Originally a company commander in the Fifty-second Tennessee Infantry, Wilson also had become a supernumerary following Shiloh. He returned home to West Tennessee taking with him many disaffected men and officers of the Fifty-second. Together they recruited a partisan cavalry command under authorization from Pillow. Brig. Gen. James T. Chalmers, commanding all cavalry in North Mississippi, appreciated Wilson. He had seen this native Mississippian in action at Shiloh and had commended the colonel for his leadership and gallantry.[9]

Originally a private in the Fifty-fifth Tennessee, Capt. Thomas N. Kizer had come to West Tennessee and organized about two hundred men into a guerrilla band in 1863 under orders from Pillow's Volunteer and Conscript Bureau. This small regiment would be absorbed into Andrew Wilson's Twenty-first (Sixteenth) Tennessee Cavalry the following February, the dispossessed Kizer moving on to become the trusted and capable leader of Kizer's Scouts operating directly under General Forrest, and "active with him until the end."[10]

These men of Greer's and Newsom's and Wilson's were sometime Confederates "who fought when they pleased—went home when they could—and did mischief generally," according to Leroy M. Nutt, later Forrest's chief of scouts. They were duly ordered to report to Colonel Bell, and while adding modestly to his numbers, Nutt noted they also added "infinitely to his trouble—for they were under no discipline and were a reckless set in the main—men who preferred to fight around home—make a dash—at scouting parties of Yankees—get horses and clothes &c. and now and then get back—and live a free life generally."[11]

Bell's mission was to gather these irregular units and two dozen others and attempt to knead them into a cohesive whole. Perhaps the best chronicle of his activities may be found in the dispatches and reports of the Federals in West

Tennessee. If Yankee forces approached, Bell had little choice but to evade, hide, disperse. He put out as many scouts and pickets as possible, frustrating the attempts of sizeable raiding parties sent out from Fort Pillow, Union City, and Memphis to smash his recruiting activities. It was impossible, complained one Union commander in mid-September, to surprise these Confederate collecting points ("rendezvouses") despite movements "made as rapidly and quietly as possible." From these enemy reports it appears that once Bell had gathered one hundred to three hundred recruits, he would cross the Tennessee with these men, put them in camp, and picket nearby river crossings to guard against surprise and to prevent his reluctant conscripts from slipping away. Greer and Bell were particularly active in the Paris-Huntington area, with Faulkner, Wilson, and Newsom appearing from LaGrange to Henderson.[12]

To counter such recruiting and conscripting operations, Union commanders sent out regimental-sized scouting parties east toward Jackson from Fort Pillow, north from Moscow and Corinth toward Henderson, and south from Union City to Camden, in effect crisscrossing the country, picking up likely suspects and forwarding them to Columbus, Kentucky, for confinement. Orders to Yankee subordinates were simple: "clean out what guerrillas [one] might find." Important elements in these raids and suppression operations were mounted infantry such as the Seventh Illinois and former slaves armed and organized into the Second West Tennessee Infantry (African Descent).[13]

For the most part, Bell managed to hide himself and his recruits successfully from the enemy (and from historians attempting to reconstruct his activities). During the early fall of 1863, Union authorities reported him everywhere, it seemed, in West Tennessee and North Mississippi, even in western Kentucky. He did travel widely, establishing and maintaining contact with Greer, Wilson, Newsom, and the others. Indeed, Braxton Bragg, never one to lavish praise, credited Bell with having been instrumental in raising R. V. Richardson's cavalry brigade.[14] It is known that in September Bell brought back over the Tennessee River and down to Florence, Alabama, two hundred men, well mounted but unarmed. General Bragg happily assisted him by providing rifles, and Bell returned to West Tennessee accompanied by two companies of John Uriah Green's battalion of partisans, each man carrying an extra rifle and as much ammunition as he dared strap on his horse.[15] Bell established himself close to Trenton on property belonging to Colonel R. M. Russell and styled the rendezvous "Camp Bell." It was there that Captain Nutt saw him: "I remember meeting him with some fifty or sixty men perhaps—lying in the woods, without anything necessary for a military organization except the few men and their horses—scarcely blankets to keep them warm—no shelter—save the customary

'Shebang' of the cavalry Soldier—two poles or rails placed in forks of Saplings and blankets spread over them—or occasionally a lucky fellow who had killed a Yankee—had an oil cloth."[16]

Good fortune, however, attended Bell. Federal authorities to the north in Obion and Weakley Counties had begun vigorously "conscripting" citizens and "the Boys who had stayed at home came rushing over Forked Deer & Obion Rivers," Captain Nutt remembered. "Being compelled to take side[s] one way or the other—they went for the South." Particularly encouraged was Russell, "who now determined again to take the field." Tyree Bell always could count on his friend Milton Russell.[17]

At the end of September 1863, Bell determined to "take out" the large body of troops he had gathered. He assembled his "recruits" at Jackson, some twenty-five hundred of them (twenty-two hundred unarmed). To avoid the Federal concentration at Corinth and along the Memphis and Charleston, they crossed the Tennessee by flatboat at Clifton, marched south and recrossed at Tuscumbia, Alabama, proceeding to Russellville (Russell's Valley), Alabama, about forty miles below Tuscumbia. There Bell left his little army of irregulars under command of Col. Milton Russell and set out with a small escort to find the Army of Tennessee and secure arms for his troops. Bell's personal army, his "Escort," was somewhat unusual; at least it had an unusual name: "Bell's Babies." Virtually all of these young men had been discharged as underage when the Twelfth and Twenty-second Tennessee had been consolidated following Shiloh. Under the experienced leadership of an older Capt. William W. McDowell, a Gibson County farmer-lawyer-editor, they had managed to stay together as a cavalry company in Col. John G. Ballentine's Second Mississippi Partisan Rangers. Later they would become Company K, Twentieth (Russell's) Tennessee Cavalry. On October 13 Bell and his "Babies" arrived at Missionary Ridge, where Bragg and the Army of Tennessee were attempting to besiege William S. Rosecrans's battered Army of the Cumberland. They would remain four days. They listened to the tales of the army's great victory at Chickamauga in September, but when they looked about on Missionary Ridge they saw sadly diminished units with drooping spirits. How could this hungry army—miserably supplied, exposed to the constant rain, and forced to live in a sea of mud—continue to hold Rosecrans's host in Chattanooga? It was as if a hunter had his arms clasped around a wounded bear, holding on, afraid to let go.[18]

President Davis also was in camp, attempting to understand and deal with the debilitating organizational and personnel problems of the Army of Tennessee. The president, as well as General Bragg, welcomed this "outsider" Tyree Bell, untarred by the command controversy. Bell could hardly have been in a better bargaining position. Bragg happily wrote out requisitions for the arms and equipment Bell requested for his "brigade" in Russell's Valley. He also allowed Bell to have Capt. Jo Lea, veteran quartermaster of the Twelfth Tennessee, and transferred to him his son Pvt. Isaac T. Bell and other carefully selected members of the Twelfth. Not only that, but Bragg agreed to supply Bell (because he now had a bonded quartermaster) with seventy-five thousand dollars in quartermaster funds and an equal amount in commissary funds.

Bell met with Forrest. Forrest, of course, had had his celebrated encounter with Bragg on the field of Chickamauga. Refusing to serve any longer under Bragg, Forrest resigned from the army. President Davis had pocketed the resignation, however, and agreed to transfer his tempestuous cavalry commander to North Mississippi. Although his assignment in Mississippi was vaguely defined, Forrest was assured he would have great latitude in building a cavalry force. At once he invited Colonel Bell to join him in the new enterprise, stating "that I would be of great benefit to him and that he could help me." Bell received Forrest's offer enthusiastically and went to President Davis, who immediately wrote out a formal transfer from the Twelfth Tennessee to Forrest's command. Bell then took the transfer to his friend Frank Cheatham, who had been present during his discussion with Forrest, and presented it. This act officially ended Tyree Bell's career as an infantryman and his association with the Army of Tennessee. The transfer was not done lightly, however, for "at that time I was senior colonel of Pres Smith's Brigade," Bell explained, Smith's death at Chickamauga having "placed me in command of the Brigade of Infantry, if I had asked for it." Thus Forrest, wrote Dr. John A. Wyeth, "enlisted the energy and loyalty of Tyree H. Bell, a man of great influence in [West] Tennessee, and a leader of dauntless courage and ability."[19]

An elated Tyree Bell left Missionary Ridge on October 17 and, in the company of Captain Lea, Isaac, and his escort hurried to Atlanta. There he drew down the funds Bragg had authorized and had the requisitioned ordnance and quartermaster equipment loaded aboard a train bound for Rome, Georgia. The weapons (five hundred muskets) were disappointing, however, mostly Austrian rifles captured at Belmont and Shiloh.[20] After the short run to Rome, Bell's men unloaded the cars and placed everything on a little steamboat that carried them down the Coosa River to Gadsden, Alabama, where again they offloaded the crates and barrels. Gadsden marked the end of rail transportation, however. Now they must use wagons, indeed a small wagon train, to reach the camp in Russell's Valley. Initially encouraged by the citizenry at every hand, Bell sent Jo Lea to procure the needed transportation. Lea spent a whole day searching and talking to people, but failed to get a single wagon. "I was non-plussed," Bell remembered, "for I was in a hurry." Bell met with several good citizens of Gadsden after supper and explained his problem; again he received assurances, but no wagons. Disgusted and angry, Bell and Lea went up to their rooms, where Bell paced the floor, dictating an order to his quartermaster:

> to start out next morning, taking a few men with him, and press into service every wagon he found until he got forty. At the same time, I dictated in that order that he must read them [the wagon owners], "If you will send your wagon and send your driver with it, when I get to Russell's Valley, I will furnish plenty of forage for your team and plenty of provisions for your teamster; if it is not convenient for you to send your driver, I will just leave your wagon and team in Russell's Valley and when you get time you can come over and get it."[21]

Tyree Bell got his wagons, more than he needed, and noted "every wagon had a driver." They made the journey west to Russell's Valley without incident, and Bell found Milton Russell and his men "in good condition and ready to move." Indeed, waiting for Bell was the new cavalry commander in North Mississippi, Maj. Gen. Stephen D. Lee. Lee presented him with five hundred more muskets. Bell had promised Forrest to meet him in Jackson, Tennessee, so, after distributing the arms and equipment to his troops, Bell marched off to West Tennessee, bringing with him, according to "sure" Union intelligence, one thousand Enfield rifles and sixty thousand rounds of ammunition, not to speak of about eleven hundred men: "a nucleus for three regiments."[22]

Keeping well south of Corinth, out of the way of nosy Union scouting parties, Bell passed through Tupelo, Mississippi, slipped across the Memphis and Charleston Railroad, then turned almost due north to Purdy, Tennessee. From there the wagon train wound northwest over good roads to Jackson. Having left a portion of his troops in Russellville, Bell left more in Jackson to be integrated into Forrest's command. Then, in obedience to Forrest's orders, he and his "staff" continued north to Trenton, Tennessee, where he established his headquarters at Camp Bell. He would range widely from Trenton, however, visiting at least half a dozen counties. Although diligently recruiting and conscripting, Bell and his men also took care to "spy out the land" and to make certain "to spread throughout all that quarter the information that Forrest was coming to occupy that section and hold it for the Confederacy."[23]

The news, according to Pvt. John Johnston, Fourteenth Tennessee Cavalry, "carried joy and hope and enthusiasm everywhere. The country now seemed

★ MAJ. GEN. STEPHEN D. LEE. UNITED STATES MILITARY HISTORY INSTITUTE.

thick with Confederate soldiers." Bell set up several rendezvous points besides Camp Bell in Trenton. There was also "Camp Bell" on his farm at Newbern where five companies of troops including Company I, Twentieth Tennessee Cavalry and Company G, Fifteenth Tennessee Cavalry, gathered on December 1 and took an oath to serve the Confederacy for three years. Bell and Col. Henry Greer enrolled them, and on December 6 Bell and Greer led the recruits out of Newbern on the road toward Jackson. Bell, moving from place to place, would repeat this process again and again, bringing in groups of men and herds of livestock until Christmas Eve, when he rejoined Forrest in Jackson to undertake the precarious task of extracting nearly four thousand troops, the vast majority unarmed, from West Tennessee.[24]

Meanwhile, Forrest had been quite busy. He had left Missionary Ridge and met formally with President Davis in Montgomery, Alabama, where Davis assured him not only of his support, but of arms and equipment. Forrest hurried back to the Army of Tennessee to bring his men to Rome, where they received equipment and transportation for the march across Alabama. As his tiny three-hundred-man force (all the troops Bragg would permit him to take from his old command) pushed west to Okolona, Mississippi, Forrest sought ordnance at Selma and visited the headquarters of Gen. Joseph E. Johnston in Meridian, Mississippi, where he received the following charge: "Under the

★ Brig. Gen. James R. Chalmers. Library of Congress.

orders of His Excellency the President, Brig. Gen. N. B. Forrest is assigned to the command of West Tennessee. He will, on arriving there, immediately proceed to raise and organize as many troops for the Confederate States service as he finds practicable." Having received his authority from Johnston, Forrest hurried north to rejoin his command at Okolona.[25]

The following day, November 15, 1863, Forrest met in Okolona with his new immediate superior, Maj. Gen. Stephen D. Lee, commander of the cavalry in Mississippi. Lee was thirty years old, a professional soldier, an Academy man. He openly admired his fiery, rough-cut subordinate and greeted him cordially, promising, "we shall not disagree, and you shall have all the assistance and support I can render you. I would feel proud either in commanding or co-operating with so gallant an officer as yourself and one with such an established reputation in the cavalry service." Lee quickly demonstrated his resolve by alerting James Chalmers in Oxford for a quick strike against the Memphis and Charleston Railroad in about eight days. Brig. Gen. Phillip D. Roddey's cavalry force in North Alabama was also asked to cooperate by threatening Corinth from the east. Additionally Col. R. V. Richardson, whose "brigade" had diminished to about 250 men, was assigned to Forrest, plus a Tennessee regiment of Chalmers's, Col. W. L. Duckworth's Seventh Tennessee Cavalry, and, most welcome of all, brother Jeffrey E. Forrest's Alabama regiment. Lee also showed General Forrest the order he had sent to his staff to fill Forrest's requisitions "as far as practicable and afford you every facility in your new assignment."[26]

Forrest's mission was take his small force of less than a thousand men, indifferently armed, across the Memphis and Charleston Railroad, a "fortified and garrisoned line," and find himself an army in the no-man's land that was West Tennessee. If that were not sufficient challenge, across his front marched William T. Sherman's Army of the Tennessee headed to Chattanooga to reinforce Grant's beleaguered army. Forrest learned, however, that as Sherman passed to the east, many of the railroad posts were being evacuated, thus weakening the Memphis and Charleston barrier. Forrest and Lee determined to take advantage of the situation. They assembled their troops at New Albany, Mississippi, forty miles northwest of Okolona, on November 29 and, as quickly as a bridge could be built across the flooded Tallahatchie, the Confederates effected their passage on December 2–3, Forrest's force shielded by the small brigades of Samuel W. Ferguson and Lawrence S. Ross.[27]

Ferguson, supported by Chalmers who had crossed at Rocky Ford with a "demi-brigade" under Col. Robert "Black Bob" McCulloch, broke up the enemy posted near Saulsbury, in effect forcing a passage for Forrest's troopers, his five ordnance wagons, and the two guns of Capt. John W. Morton's Battery. Young Captain Morton (twenty years old) would see a great deal of Tyree Bell in the coming eighteen months and would become an admirer, considering him "a man of unusual military and social qualities—genial, companionable and a shrewd judge of men and things." In action Morton and his gunners "always felt safe when supported by Bell's Brigade."[28]

To occupy the enemy, Stephen D. Lee had Chalmers's other demi-brigade threaten the railroad west of LaGrange. Thus Lee's troopers fanned out, making demonstrations at points along the railroad from Moscow to Pocahontas. They would continue these diversionary efforts for another two days, effectively screening Forrest's vulnerable force and allowing them to proceed northward virtually unnoticed. Once across the railroad, Forrest hastened to Jackson, arriving on the afternoon of December 6. There, according to plan, he met Bell and Russell with a force of recruits that outnumbered his own. Then he sent Bell and Russell back to fetch more.[29]

They needed to hurry, however. The Federals knew of Forrest's and Bell's presence and on December 15 the enemy put in motion a wide-flung operation to strangle in the cradle this new rebel West Tennessee army. The Federal district commander, Maj. Gen. Stephen A. Hurlbut, first dispersed strong elements of cavalry along the Memphis and Charleston. As that wall was being formed, infantry and cavalry columns set out toward Jackson from Columbus, Fort Pillow,

Corinth, Huntsville, and yet another from Middle Tennessee, in all five columns numbering about fifteen thousand troops. "I think we shall cure Forrest of his ambition to command West Tennessee," Hurlbut assured Grant.[30]

While Forrest organized the men at Jackson and sent recruiters into the countryside, attempting to collect the "much scattered" pieces of units, Bell returned to Trenton and gathered up even more men at Camp Bell and nearby points. He tried to incorporate into his command the many isolated "commands," consisting of a dozen, sometimes four dozen, men. He met with resistance from some of these fiercely independent groups, of course. Many had deserted the regular Confederate forces, or simply gone home on furlough or sick leave and never returned. While Bell attempted to persuade and sometimes intimidate, he had Russell and several hundred of the recruits round up the cattle and sheep, starting them for Jackson where they were turned over to Forrest's quartermaster, Middle Tennessean Maj. T. F. P. Allison, who later would become one of Bell's most valuable staff members and his friend. After delivering the livestock, Russell and his mounted but largely unarmed "regiment" left Jackson (before December 23), acting as escort for Allison and the great herd. The mission of this quasi-military force was to get Allison across the Hatchie River at the village of Estenaula and reunite him with Bell—well to the south— at Como, Mississippi, near Okolona. To facilitate the Hatchie crossing, Forrest had "ordered the ferryboat at Bolivar moved and sunk in shallow water near Estenaula." When they neared the Hatchie, the ferry was to pop up miraculously from its watery grave to facilitate Allison's crossing.[31]

Forrest ordered Bell to take the unarmed men (the regiments of Andrew Wilson and John Newsom) and proceed to the crossing at Estenaula. Bell left Jackson Christmas Eve morning. Richardson (his numbers now up to about one thousand) had been ordered to meet Bell at the riverbank with the sunken flatboat raised and "in good condition for crossing." Also converging on this site, however, were five hundred Union troops that Brig. Gen. Benjamin H. Grierson had dispatched from LaGrange under Col. Edward Prince, Seventh Illinois Cavalry, with orders to proceed to Bolivar and from there "to cover all crossings of the Hatchie . . . destroying all the boats as he proceeded."[32]

Richardson managed to reach Estenaula first, and crossed to the south side of the Hatchie on the afternoon of December 24. After his troops had raised the flatboat, Colonel Richardson ventured forth from the Hatchie bottoms to screen the crossing, but encountered the Seventh Illinois Cavalry four and a half miles out. The Federals attacked and scattered Richardson's force, driving Richardson himself back upon Col. James J. Neely and his newly formed Fourteenth Tennessee Cavalry, who guarded the crossing itself. The situation stabilized somewhat, but an anxious Richardson sent a courier back to Bell, who was approaching the crossing leading the main body of Forrest's command. It was a slow-moving and vulnerable host—about twenty-five hundred troops, many unarmed, with some forty commissary wagons, and a herd of beef cattle. Richardson asked Bell for support. Bell could provide but few, at best. Moreover, he was almost ten miles away and had responsibility for the safety of the main column. Then a second courier arrived and Bell realized he must go to Richardson's aid. Leaving the lumbering column under command of the trusty Col. John F. Newsom, Bell took Andrew Wilson's regiment and "went in a trot from there to the river and crossed it." Not more than a mile on the south side he found Richardson's wagon train under his old friend Capt. John Skifington.[33] Bell ordered Skifington off on a side road "double quick time," while he and Wilson's regiment rode forward through Richardson's retreating men. Bell deployed his small force and succeeded in blocking the advance of the Seventh Illinois. Then he counterattacked the Yankee horsemen, driving them back. He and Wilson would continue to drive them until sundown.[34]

Soon after dark, Forrest came up to Bell's position and the two discussed the likelihood of an attack by Grierson's troopers the next morning. Bell was worried. The long, ponderous column invited attack, and the troops at hand were too few to provide reliable defense. To add to their worries, Lt. Col. Dew W. Wisdom's and Maj. Charles McDonald's armed battalions of veterans, plus Lt. Col. William D. Lannom's band of Kentuckians (William W. Faulkner's regiment), in all about five hundred men, had been sent to strike at an enemy column advancing from Corinth toward Jack's Creek and were out of immediate supporting distance.[35] There was, however, the rear guard of Bell's column. It was armed. Bell told Forrest that he believed it should be brought up to Estenaula and pushed over the river. "I will go back to the ferry," Bell told Forrest, "cross the river and go to see Colonel Newsom and give him his orders." So Bell turned his horse about and went back, taking with him Capt. Reuben D. Clark, who was acting as his adjutant. By now there were many unarmed men on both banks of the Hatchie, and Bell passed through them, dismounted, boarded the ferry, and recrossed the river. When he reached the other bank he walked about half a mile to the point where Newsom had halted with his regiment. Bell told Newsom he wanted the entire regiment across before daybreak, and he so instructed Capt. Jo Lea who was superintending the crossing, making certain that Lea understood that Newsom's armed men were to be given priority. The bitter cold weather complicated everything. Not only the water, but the mud was freezing.[36]

Bell walked back onto the small ferryboat to return to the west bank. The boat, however, was "so frail and unsteady" that it had not gone more than thirty yards into the Hatchie River before it capsized. "Wagons, teams, and a lot of soldiers were in the end of the boat where I was," Bell recalled, "and everything was big excitement." A couple of small mules banged into him and knocked him down. Forrest saw the desperation of the situation and the general plunged into the icy stream himself, grabbing for the harness that entrapped the mules. While Forrest attempted to cut the animals loose, Bell managed to free himself from the struggling animals. Believing "it would overtax my strength to try to swim across the river," he tried floating and swimming downstream, aiming for a bend where he could see some shrubs sticking out of the water. "Finally I got to where I could touch bottom with my feet."

Captain Clark came to Bell's rescue at this point and pulled him out of the icy water. Once up on the bank, Bell looked at himself—soaked from head to foot and caked with creekbank mud. "I thought I would freeze to death," Bell recalled, but Clark and others wrapped him with blankets and built fires on either side of him. Capt. Drew Outlaw "who happened to be around and always had whiskey in his canteen, poured some down me." Meanwhile Clark hastened to get the nearly frozen Bell some dry clothes.[37]

Early the next morning Bell and Forrest took all the armed men and moved out from the Hatchie River bottoms against the Seventh Illinois. The enemy retreated, however, "and we never got close enough to them to have a standing fight," Bell wrote. "After running them all day, we turned our course towards Lafayette [just east of Collierville], a station on the Memphis and Charleston Road."[38]

With the Hatchie to their rear, there still remained the barrier of the Wolf River to the southwest. This must be crossed before they could reach the Memphis and Charleston Railroad. Forrest wanted to cross the Wolf River at LaFayette. There was a bridge there presenting the possibility of a rapid crossing. Forrest directed Bell to take three hundred men and seize the bridge. Repair it if necessary, Forrest told Bell. The following morning (December 27, 1863), thanks to a careful reconnaissance by Col. Thomas H. Logwood and Lt. John A. Williamson, Bell approached the bridge well concealed by heavy woods on the north bank. Immediately he reconnoitered, then gathered his officers. Although the bridge was protected by a "closed work," the enemy had not destroyed it, just taken off the planks, leaving the string timbers. Bell, "without parley or hesitancy," charged across these timbers, so quickly that the enemy guards only had time for one ineffective volley before fleeing their fortified position. Bell sent Col. John Newsom and about fifty men in a sham pursuit, the real purpose being to keep up "the appearance of vigorous aggressive purposes." Meanwhile Bell quickly had the bridge flooring replaced. He and his men were startled in their work, however, by the approach of a Yankee troop-train. Bell again decided on bold action. He deployed his troops along the tracks and fired a volley into the passing train. Soon Forrest appeared with the balance of the command and before moving on they set to work destroying the LaFayette station, burning the water tank, and ripping up track.[39]

Once again they were interrupted, this time not by a train, but by the appearance of a strong force of Yankees advancing from Collierville. Forrest ordered up Morton's Battery and opened fire, then he and Bell deployed their fifteen hundred to two thousand men in the line of battle "in fair view of Collierville but out of reach of their shells," Bell remembered. "We skirmished around and about there the balance of the day until night came." While Bell and Forrest continued this noisy demonstration against Collierville, the last of the main column of unarmed men, cattle, and wagons pushed further south. Crossing the Wolf River at LaFayette by nightfall, December 27, they were over the Memphis and Charleston Railroad, bound for Holly Springs, Mississippi. Once the main body had passed to their rear, Forrest and Bell withdrew and followed as rapidly as they could through the darkness and heavy rain. Pursued by converging heavy columns of Federal cavalry, they continued their remarkable escape through this dangerous land between the Wolf River and the Coldwater. Once across Coldwater River they were safe. It had been a remarkable military feat. Even the enemy recognized this. Two weeks later a report, laced with disgust, appeared in the *Cincinnati Commercial:* "Forrest, with less than 4000 men, has moved *right through the Sixteenth Army Corps,* has passed within *nine* miles of Memphis, carried off over 100 wagons, 200 beef cattle, 3000 conscripts, and innumerable stores . . . and all too in the face of 10,000 men."[40]

The fatigued column slowed their march once they had put the Coldwater to their backs, and continued on at a leisurely pace to Como, Mississippi, on the north-south Mississippi and Tennessee Railroad. There, tucked behind Coldwater River and Senatobia Creek, forty-three miles below Memphis and twenty-five miles northwest of Oxford, Forrest established his headquarters on January 1, 1864. Later that day Chalmers came into camp, bringing with him Faulkner's Kentucky contingent. Groups of men, ranging in size from half a dozen to one hundred, would continue to drift into camp at Como throughout January, men from West Tennessee and Kentucky. One welcome addition was the former colonel of the Thirty-first Tennessee Infantry, Egbert E. Tansil of Weakley County, who brought with him one hundred recruits. At last Forrest, aided by Bell, could assemble in relative safety the army they had come west to build.[41]

8

Bell's Brigade

Upon his return from West Tennessee, Forrest learned that Joseph E. Johnston had been replaced by Leonidas Polk as head of the Department of Alabama, Mississippi, and East Louisiana. Forrest reported dutifully to his new commander and in return General Polk, whose admiration for Forrest never wavered, telegraphed him the happy news that he had been promoted to major general on December 4, 1863. Very soon, Polk promised Forrest, you will "be assigned a proper district, embracing all the Confederate forces in north Mississippi and West Tennessee." Forrest's district eventually would be known as the Northern Cavalry Department and also, even officially, as Forrest's Cavalry Department. While Forrest was to control cavalry operations in North Mississippi, Forrest's former commander, Stephen D. Lee, would be in charge of the Southern Cavalry Department.[1]

Forrest immediately set about organizing his force with the enthusiastic support of Polk, who provided not only encouragement, but vital logistical assistance, including two thousand rifles and a howitzer battery. Col. R. M. Russell, who had been sent ahead to Meridian by Forrest, would play a key role as middleman in the transfer of the ordnance and quartermaster stores from Polk. He would do more. Department Commander Forrest wanted and needed an officer with impeccable credentials on hand at his camp at Como for the critical task of helping him select the best company and field-grade officers from the dozens who had been brought out of West Tennessee.[2] Not that this was a new idea. Forrest had known that he ought to have an experienced officer (with proper Old Army credentials) for such an assignment. Appreciating Russell's background and abilities, Forrest, as early as December 13, 1863, had sent regimental commander Milton Russell to army headquarters in Meridian requesting that

Gen. Joseph E. Johnston examine him for fitness to lead a cavalry brigade. No record of this examination of Russell appears to have survived, but Forrest, no doubt influenced by Bell, would continue to promote Russell's fortunes with the Confederate War Department.[3]

Certainly the task confronting Major General Forrest was daunting. Almost overnight he needed to create an effective operational strike force that required not only rigorous training and discipline, but the unwelcome consolidation and discontinuation of proud skeleton commands and roaming Robin Hood bands. Thus units must be merged. Many officers consequently became supernumeraries. It was the same, familiar, sad story: Field officers who had succeeded in raising companies instead of battalions or regiments were in effect demoted. The competition for office was fierce and disheartening, breeding "a state of discontent and disorganization." But Bedford Forrest was resolute. Having smashed many of the old organizations, he proceeded to rebuild his command structure from junior officer to brigade commander. Forrest divided his troops into four small cavalry brigades under Brig. Gen. Robert V. Richardson, Col. Robert C. McCulloch, Col. Jeffrey E. Forrest, and Col. Tyree Bell. Richardson's and Jeff Forrest's brigades were organized into a division under Chalmers, while McCulloch's and Bell's temporarily remained as independent brigades. Bell's Third Brigade was the largest by far—two thousand men. Richardson's numbered fifteen hundred, McCulloch's sixteen hundred, and Jeff Forrest's one thousand.[4]

Bell's Brigade consisted of five regiments: Milton Russell's Twentieth (Fifteenth) Tennessee Cavalry; John F. Newsom's Nineteenth (Eighteenth) Tennessee Cavalry, Andrew N. Wilson's Twenty-first (Sixteenth) Tennessee Cavalry, and Clark R. Barteau's Twenty-second (Second) Tennessee Cavalry.[5]

To assist Bell in his capacity of brigade commander was a staff, about half of whom had served with him as he rode about West Tennessee the previous summer recruiting and conscripting. Bell named as his chief of staff Capt. Reuben D. Clark, the man who had saved him from the frozen waters of the Hatchie River. Thirty-year-old Clark was a native Tennessean and a neighbor of Tyree's brother and sister. He had served in Sumner County's Seventh Tennessee Infantry before becoming ordnance master under Gen. Daniel Donelson. Upon Donelson's death the previous April, Clark joined his friend Bell as adjutant general.[6]

For his inspector general, Forrest allowed Bell to choose from his own staff the highly competent Maj. T. F. P. Allison, an experienced cavalry officer. Tom Allison was unusually well educated (Jackson College, Western Reserve, and Cumberland Law School), but had given up a law career after having been captivated by the science and art of farming. Tyree Bell, lifetime farmer, viewed

Allison as an authority on agriculture, as did Allison's friends and casual acquaintances, and Bell also knew from observation Allison's effectiveness as a staff officer. They would become friends for life.[7]

To fill the office of brigade chaplain, Bell selected R. H. Mahon, sometime cavalryman in Milton Russell's Regiment and son of Bell's old friend and former chaplain, Jack Mahon.[8]

Other men named to Bell's inner circle were Capt. Jo Lea, quartermaster; Thomas E. Richardson, adjutant; and kinsmen Albert G. Harris, commissary, and Conquest Cross Harris, ordnance officer. William Porter, Robert P. Caldwell, and son Isaac T. Bell would serve as aides-de-camp. Others would join the staff later or ride along as aides on a temporary basis, but the core of Bell's staff came together in very early 1864.[9]

Bell and Forrest worked furiously to whip the brigade and the little army into shape. The fickle January weather cooperating, they drilled every day, primarily teaching the recruits (many of them veterans of the Twelfth, Forty-seventh, and Twenty-second Tennessee Infantry regiments) how to maneuver as mounted infantry, how to mass efficiently and suddenly. They learned (or relearned) to obey orders, they learned discipline. Most of the men understood the need for such, but having enjoyed "the habit of staying in the field very much at their own will and pleasure, the soldiery . . . became very restless under the restraints imposed in this respect." One should not overestimate the success of Bell's and Forrest's drill at Oxford, however. Training a force of that size required experienced instructors, many of them, and the time was so short. Bell and Forrest could only hope to transform this disorganized mass of civilians into a reasonably efficient volunteer force. One of Russell's men would remember "we had verry [sic] little training but we knew how to use guns." It must be on-the-job-training.[10]

Bell's fellow brigade commander, Col. Robert "Black Bob" McCulloch, was an interesting study. In his mid-forties, this Virginia-born Missourian had fought well in the Trans-Mississippi, then had crossed the Mississippi with Maj. Gen. Sterling Price at the time of Shiloh. While the other Missouri cavalry units were dismounted once east of the great river, McCulloch and his regiment continued as a cavalry unit, gathering Mississippians to fight beside them. They would see action at Vicksburg, then move on to northern Mississippi with Black Bob acting as a brigade commander under Chalmers. McCulloch and Milton Russell doubtlessly talked around the campfire about their years in California (1849–52) where they may have known each other. Certainly, together with Capt. Nick Wyatt, they were to lift the geographic horizons of Tyree Bell.[11]

Suddenly at 2 A.M., February 1, 1864, came the call to depart their "snug" encampment at Como. Bell ordered his brigade to mount, and they made an

★ ROBERT "BLACK BOB" MCCULLOCH. FROM JOHN A. WYETH, *LIFE OF GENERAL NATHAN BEDFORD FORREST* (1899).

easy march south fifteen miles to Panola. The next day, however, the column turned east "and after a heavy day's march we arrived at Oxford and camped." Once they had established themselves on a good site, Governor Isham G. Harris appeared and made a patriotic appeal to the West Tennesseans. The following day Forrest visited Bell's camp and gave a speech that, according to Capt. Elisha Hollis of Russell's Twentieth, "stirs greatly."[12]

Forrest was worried. Widespread unrest prevailed within his command, much of it resulting from the painful reorganization process. As he wrote President Davis on February 5, consolidations of "paper commands into full regiments have caused quite a number of disaffected officers and men to run away." He estimated about a hundred so far. He and Bell had had to depart West Tennessee "at very short notice and unexpectedly," he explained, creating shortages and hardships and uncertainty.[13] Now sunshine warriors were leaving camp, resisting all his efforts, and Bell's, to prevent their departure. The discontented could cite a roster of excuses: the formality of drill and discipline; the lack of uniforms, weapons, and blankets; but most of all being unable to return to their homes when "not needed." And, of course, among Bell's West Tennesseans there were the unwilling Rebels who wanted no part of the war, who had resisted conscription, the victims of Gideon Pillow's and Tyree Bell's press gangs. The integrity of Forrest's Cavalry Department was at stake. Consequently Forrest acted promptly and harshly when a group of nineteen men from Bell's Brigade left in a body. Forrest had them pursued, arrested, and brought back. "In consequence of their flagrant, defiant desertion," Forrest believed, "the whole detachment should be shot."[14] Forrest's Cavalry Command was deeply disturbed, believing the remedy not only cruel but ill-advised. Bell backed Forrest, but he understood if not sympathized with the prisoners—"they had been in little commands commanded by men that did not try to get them out of Tenn. and they went home when they pleased. . . . It was hard for them to submit to the strict discipline of the army." Forrest was risking everything by his peremptory action, and it seems probable that Bell joined the other senior officers in telling Forrest "of their serious apprehension of a mutinous resistance on the part of the soldiery, to the attempt to execute so many of their comrades."[15]

Forrest, quite justifiably one might argue, named Colonel Bell as the officer in charge of the executions to be held February 12, 1864. Coffins were made, graves dug, and Bell's Brigade, to whom the culprits belonged, was formed on three sides of a square, to witness the execution. That evening the nineteen doomed soldiers, seated on their coffins, were brought forward in wagons "to a skirt of woods just west of the university buildings, where the graves had been dug." After having the prisoners blindfolded and once again seated on their coffins, Bell stalled. He was dissatisfied, he said, with the demeanor and performance of the firing squad and had the detail go "through the manual of arms several times, omitting 'Fire.'" It must have been, of course, as agonizing emotionally for the executioners as those to be executed. Again and again they practiced, only the clicking of hammers and thudding of musket butts broke the stillness. And yet again the firing squad examined their pieces and went through the exercise, but this time, as they braced themselves for the command "Fire," a shout was heard and Maj. Charles W. Anderson of Forrest's staff came rushing through the woods "waving a whip and hollering 'Hold, hold.'" Anderson gripped in his hand a pardon from Forrest, which he presented to Bell. Bell asked Anderson to read the message aloud to the prisoners, loud enough for the gathered troops to hear as well. The prisoners were overcome at their deliverance; "some of them were almost crazy." The effect was electric, certainly salutary for the brigade as well as Forrest's entire command. It "put a great check to desertion," Bell admitted. Moreover, he added, if the situation had continued, "I have no doubt but what Forrest would have had whole companies shot."[16]

★ MAJ. CHARLES A. ANDERSON. FROM JOHN A. WYETH, *LIFE OF GENERAL NATHAN BEDFORD FORREST* (1899).

Was Tyree Bell privy to Forrest's plan, one wonders. Although the former's autobiography hints that Bell was just as startled as any private, the matter of Forrest's trusted lieutenant having the firing squad repeat and continue to repeat its manual of arms drill sounds suspiciously as if Bell knew of Forrest's ploy from the start—that Forrest, ever the calculator of advantage, knew better than to chance an accidental mass execution.

While this emotion-charged drama played out, the regimental commanders of Bell's Brigade initiated a campaign of their own at Oxford. They wanted Colonel Bell to enjoy the rank to which he was entitled: brigadier general. So once again, to the Confederate War Department went letters recommending his promotion, the most important from Forrest himself and from J. W. C. Atkins, congressman from Bell's district. "He is an experienced and meritorious officer," Forrest wrote, "and his appointment as Brig. Gen. is respectfully requested and recommended."[17]

Forrest had worries other than securing a deserved promotion for his able lieutenant, however. Heavy Yankee columns were on the march in a coordinated attempt to bring the remaining Confederates in Mississippi to bay. Sherman had forced his way to Meridian and destroyed that crucial rail center, inflicting widespread collateral damage along the line of march. Meanwhile, another force had gone up the Yazoo River threatening Greenwood, Mississippi; Brig. Gen. William Sooy Smith, with seven thousand cavalry and twenty pieces of artillery, after feinting at Panola, appeared to be headed for Okolona on the Mobile and Ohio Railroad en route to uniting with Sherman in Meridian. Forrest dispersed his command, initially skirmishing with Sooy Smith's troopers at the Tallahatchie River crossings. Bell's Brigade, accompanied by Forrest, Forrest's escort and the artillery, had sharp encounters at Wyatt and Abbeville, immediately north of Oxford, on February 13, and managed to prevent the Federals from crossing in force. The enemy, however, was moving laterally, across Forrest's front, to the east. Anticipating Smith would strike at Okolona, Forrest shifted Bell's Brigade south through Coffeeville to Grenada, then east toward Starkville. All the while it rained and grew colder. The farther Bell's troopers marched, more and more horses broke down. On February 18, an especially cold and unpleasant day, as they reached the village of Starkville, some forty miles south of Okolona, it began snowing. Men and horses gave out. All along the line of march, Forrest's command left men in houses sick and unable to keep up. Tyree Bell was one.[18]

"I had been feeling very badly," he recalled, "suffering intensely for two or three days. It was raining and the weather was bad and when we got to Starkville, I was compelled to go to my bed. I remained at Starkville at Mrs. Stark's where I was nobly attended by her and her daughter. I saw no more of the campaign against [Sooy] Smith. He was entirely done up before I got off of the bed."[19]

While Bell recovered at Mrs. Stark's, Colonel Barteau took command of the brigade. Barteau and the Second Tennessee Cavalry were new to Bell, having been transferred from Gen. Samuel W. Ferguson's brigade. Clark Barteau was a popular twenty-eight-year-old native of Ohio, with a wide range of experience, having demonstrated ability and energy in the roles of Middle Tennessee schoolmaster, newspaper editor, and orator. As a soldier he already had proven himself a natural leader, daring and resourceful. The ranks of the Second Tennessee Cavalry contained a number of Barteau's schoolboys of the Hartsville Academy, where he had been principal, as well as a goodly number of young men from Sumner County known to Bell and his son Isaac.[20]

At the Battle of Okolona, February 22, 1864, Forrest and Bell's Brigade (led by Barteau) crashed into the advancing troops of Sooy Smith, but were repulsed. Forrest resorted to a flanking movement, and being reinforced by Black Bob McCulloch's Brigade, charged again, this time breaking the enemy line of battle and forcing the Federals into a disorderly retreat that continued back to Memphis. Forrest was enormously pleased. In a letter to Polk on February 26 he praised "the fortitude and gallantry displayed by the troops engaged, especially the new troops from West Tennessee, who, considering their want of drill, discipline, and experience, behaved handsomely." During this running fight with Sooy Smith, Clark Barteau was knocked from his horse and injured. Once again Milton Russell, Twentieth Tennessee Cavalry, stepped forward and assumed brigade command. A far more serious casualty was the death of Forrest's younger brother, Brigade Commander Col. Jeffrey E. Forrest. All in all, however, the Confederate losses at the Battle of Okolona were not high, but the strategic results were significant. Forrest not only had won a splendid little battle with his raw, outnumbered command, but he had gained the initiative in North Mississippi. He could lift his eyes toward West Tennessee.[21]

9

A Dash into Kentucky

Having partially frustrated Sherman's hopes for a spectacular winter campaign in Mississippi, Forrest regathered his command at Starkville. Bell left his sickbed and resumed command of his brigade, then marched south with Forrest to Columbus. Bell and his men went into camp at Tibbee Station, where they remained about two weeks "recruiting our stock." "Our horses," noted one of Bell's troopers, "never needed rest before as they did just at this time."[1]

Also appearing in camp during this first week in March 1864 was a small Kentucky infantry brigade (three regiments) led by a Kentuckian—the tall and amply proportioned Brig. Gen. Abraham Buford, Bell's acquaintance from the 1862 Kentucky Campaign. Abe Buford's regiments unfortunately "were mere fragments," according to artillery chief Capt. John W. Morton, "decimated by battles, exposure, and illness, poorly clothed and only about one-third of them mounted." Buford and his Kentucky Brigade had left the Army of Tennessee following the Battle of Murfreesboro, being transferred to Mississippi as reinforcements. They had added little to their reputations during the sieges of Port Hudson and Vicksburg while serving as infantry, which led Department Commander Leonidas Polk, who had inherited them, to decide the best use for Buford's troops would be to assign them to Forrest as mounted infantry. Forrest fought his cavalry as infantry, anyway. A natural fit, it appeared. So it seemed to Buford and his men. Joining Forrest promised not only the opportunity to be in the saddle, but the hope of returning to Kentucky, John Hunt Morgan–style.[2]

Abe Buford and Tyree Bell had much in common and each day grew to be better friends. Of course, the huge Buford was easy to like—"a genial, jovial companion, full of war reminiscences," remembered Forrest's staff officer, Mercer Otey, "and generally his chief commissary kept a supply of good Nelson County Bourbon, which he always set before us when we returned the General's visit."[3]

Forrest welcomed Buford and his foot-weary veterans. Feeling quite comfortable with the convivial Buford, an acknowledged expert in regard to racehorses, Forrest was wise enough to recognize the value of this professional cavalryman's background, not only his Mexican War service, but his tour of duty at the Old Army's Cavalry School at Carlisle Barracks, Pennsylvania. He designated General Buford to lead the Second Division, to which Bell's Fourth Brigade belonged, as well as the Third Brigade, Jeffrey Forrest's old command, under the enthusiastic Col. Albert P. Thompson, Third Kentucky Infantry. The heart of Thompson's Brigade would be the three small Kentucky regiments plus Col. William W. Faulkner's Twelfth Kentucky Cavalry, which previously had been assigned to Jeff Forrest's brigade. Thompson's Kentucky Brigade also included the heart of Jeffrey Forrest's old Alabama regiment (four companies) under Lt. Col. Dew M. Wisdom.[4] Abe Buford brought Thompson's Kentucky Brigade to Tibbee, Mississippi, on the Mobile and Ohio Railroad, and there united with Bell and his troops. Buford's combined force at Tibbee, however, numbered only twenty-eight hundred effectives. Four miles south of them, at Mayhew Station, was Chalmers' Division.[5]

Forrest believed he must make another venture into West Tennessee. Bell's troopers still suffered from lack of clothing and blankets, while Albert Thompson's Kentuckians desperately needed not only clothing, but horses, at least one-third of them being without mounts. To capture these essential stores and animals was the primary justification for a West Tennessee expedition, a deep raid, ranging perhaps as far north as Paducah.[6]

Forrest's objectives, however, were limited: to reassert Confederate power in West Tennessee and the Jackson Purchase (western Kentucky). Being weak and hardly mobile, he would restrict his operations to the west side of the Tennessee River. Moreover, Forrest would limit his force on this far-reaching expedition, taking only one division with him—Buford's—reinforced by Duckworth's Seventh Tennessee Cavalry and McDonald's Battalion. Chalmers's troops would remain behind in North Mississippi "to sweep the area clean of absentees and deserters, and to act as police for the region."[7]

The expedition began March 14, 1864, for Bell's Brigade, as they moved without wagons, but with sixty rounds of ammunition for each man, from Tibbee Station, west across Tibbee Creek, then north toward Okolona. Continuing north, they rode through Tupelo, across the Memphis and Charleston Railroad at Corinth, and into Tennessee. Forrest broke up the command March 23

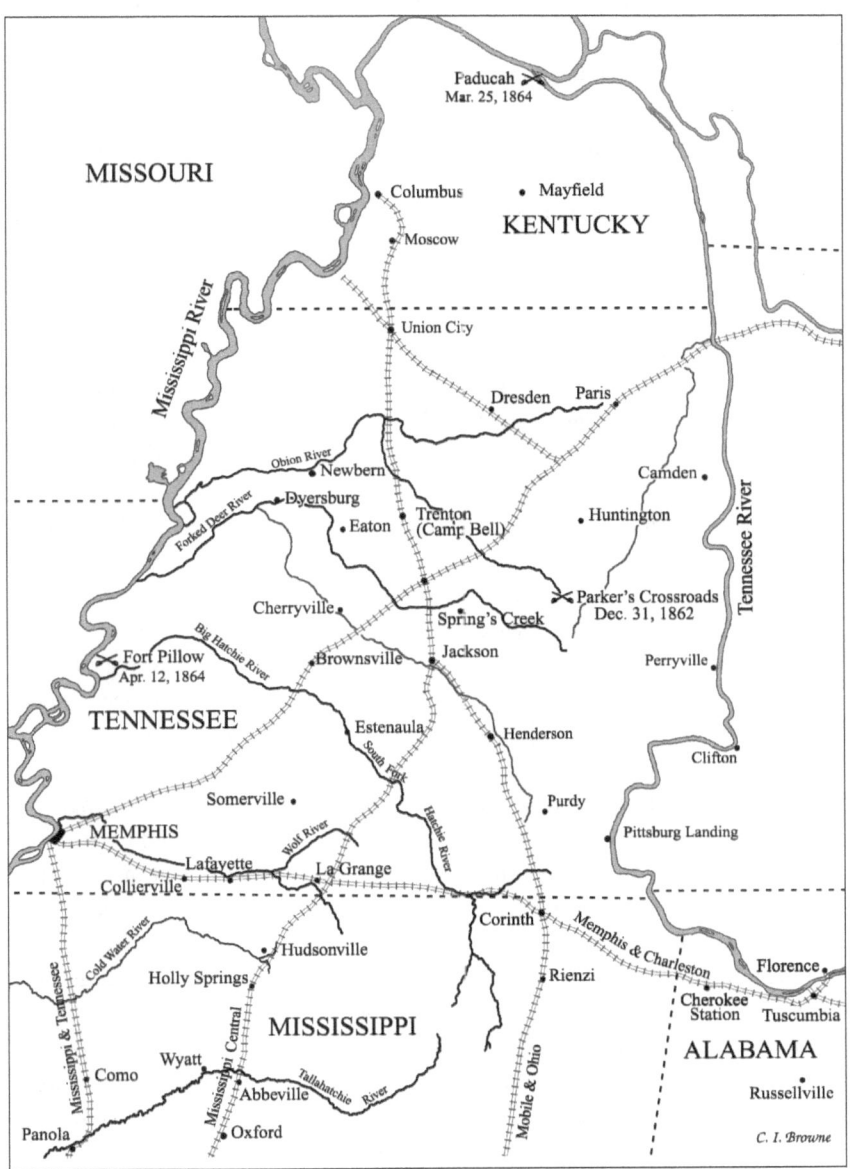

★ WEST TENNESSEE RAIDS, 1863–1864. COURTESY OF C. I. BROWNE.

as they passed Jackson. He left Col. Andrew Wilson with a battalion of cavalry and the dismounted Kentuckians to hold that town and directed a five-hundred-man force (Seventh Tennessee Cavalry, McDonald's Battalion, and Faulkner's regiment) under Col. William L. Duckworth to "move upon Union City and capture any Federal force there." Forrest himself would continue to march north with Bell and Buford, at the time encamped at Spring Creek, twelve miles northeast of Jackson.[8]

Forrest and Bell, particularly Bell, enjoyed Buford's company enormously. Of course, they had much in common, the Dyer County farmer and the one-time professional cavalryman. Forrest's adjutant, Mercer Otey, no stranger to whiskey nor to whist, rolled his eyes when contemplating Abe Buford's Falstaffian appearance: "He weighed something over three hundred pounds, of powerful frame, a round ruddy face covered with a short, stubby red beard, dressed in brown butternut Kentucky jeans, his pants invariably stuck in his boots, he was the Jack of Clubs, as displayed on the packs of cards made [during] those times." The man was brave, charming and amazingly light-footed. "With all the weight," Otey contended, "he was the most graceful dancer I ever saw swing a lady on the light and fantastic."[9]

Bell also admired very much, perhaps envied, Buford's eye for horseflesh. Years later, when the war had become a dark memory and Bell had moved off to California, he would continue to hear stories about his old friend and the triumphs of his fabled racehorses—Enquirer, Crossland, and Exchequer.[10]

Forrest received depressing news while in Jackson. The whole of West Tennessee, citizens reported, "is overrun by bands and squads of robbers, horse thieves and deserters, whose depredations and unlawful appropriation of private property are effectually depleting the country." West Tennesseans complained bitterly to their hero about the tyranny and cruelty of Union troop commanders in the area, specifically Col. Fielding Hurst. In response, an aroused Forrest sent strongly worded messages to Union authorities in Memphis about the depredations—intimidation, robbery, murder (seven incidents in the past sixty days, particularly the "death by torture" of Lt. William Dodds, a member of Newsom's regiment, and the execution of three other members of that command) and the "wanton extortion" from the citizens of Jackson of five thousand dollars under threat of burning the town. Forrest demanded that Hurst be turned over to Confederate authorities and threatened retaliation unless the Tennesseans who were being held against their will and without being charged were released, specifically mentioning the Rev. George W. D. Harris, whose brother, Governor Isham G. Harris, accompanied Forrest at this time. Should his demands be rejected or ignored, Forrest promised to "declare the aforesaid Fielding Hurst, and the officers and men of his command, outlaws, and not entitled to be treated as prisoners of war falling into the hands of the forces of the Confederate States."[11]

Forrest would reinforce his demands with a brazen show of strength and destruction. He and Buford, with the brigades of Bell and Thompson, marched thirty-seven miles north on March 23, and on March 24 they made forty-two miles, passing through Dresden, Tennessee, into Kentucky, heading straight for the river town of Paducah, the strategic point where the Tennessee River empties into the Ohio. It was hard riding. Not all of the command were mounted and some of the dismounted soldiers, including at least one in Bell's Brigade, "walked the whole route."[12]

On Friday, March 25, 1864, they rode twenty-six miles, arriving in sight of Paducah in the early afternoon. Sensing that he had the element of surprise, Forrest and his escort crashed into Paducah, compelling the astonished Federals to abandon the city streets and withdraw into their earthen strongpoint, Fort Anderson, close to the Tennessee riverbank, under the protective fire of two gunboats. While Bell's men advanced as skirmishers into town and Forrest and his escort drove the remaining pickets into the center of Paducah, Albert P. Thompson and his Kentuckians, without waiting for support and without explicit orders from Forrest, audaciously assaulted the garrison (about 650 troops) in their earthworks, only to meet with a sharp repulse. Colonel Thompson, a native of Paducah, was struck by a shell from one of the Yankee gunboats and killed instantly. Col. Edward Crossland, Seventh Kentucky, immediately succeeded Thompson in command of the badly shaken Kentucky Brigade. Ten years younger than Bell, Ed Crossland, former attorney and sheriff, would provide confident, practical leadership.[13]

Forrest immediately reacted to the setback. First he sent word to Buford: Do not attempt to storm the fort with Bell's troops. Then he sent a message to the Federal commander at Fort Anderson, demanding the surrender of the garrison. He had more than sufficient troops to reduce the fort, he wrote, but wished to avoid unnecessary bloodshed. "If you surrender," Forrest continued, "you shall be treated as prisoners of war; but if I have to storm your works, you may expect no quarter."[14]

The Union commander, Col. Stephen G. Hicks, refused. In the interval Confederate sharpshooters moved up close to the fort, taking cover in the town itself. From their magnificent vantage points they would keep up their fire upon the fort until 11:30 P.M.[15] Forrest held Paducah for almost ten hours, full time enough for his raiders to collect their booty and deliberately, carefully, withdraw. He was able to do this because his carefully positioned sharpshooters kept the Federals in the fort, and even those on the gunboats, pinned down.

While the riflemen held the enemy's attention, Bell led his brigade out of Paducah, marching about five miles south toward Mayfield, and bivouacking at a "Dutch Colony." "I arrived there about 12 o'clock at night," Bell recalled. "There I found plenty of forage for my stock and room a plenty for my men."[16]

The following day, Saturday, March 26, Forrest continued his withdrawal to Tennessee. He had fifty prisoners, several hundred mounts, and wagons loaded with supplies, equipment, and clothing. In effect, he had outfitted an entire cavalry division. Once they crossed into Tennessee, Forrest's expeditionary force fragmented, the Tennesseans taking different roads. Bell's men broke into small details, sweeping the country between the Obion and Tennessee Rivers for conscripts and deserters. They picked up additional horses and even weapons they found in the hands of Unionists. In the meantime, while Bell cast his wide net, most of Crossland's Kentucky Brigade had been "detached by squads" into Southwest Kentucky to visit their homes and to recruit.[17]

Forrest was ecstatic. Particularly pleased with the handsome flag of the Sixty-Second Illinois that Bell's men had captured, Forrest would forward the flag to President Davis to be presented as a gift to Mrs. Davis. It had been captured by Bell's newly organized Tennessee Brigade, Forrest explained proudly, a group of fighting men who have distinguished themselves in all of their encounters. It was good to be appreciated officially.[18]

The brigade, having completed its mission, rendezvoused in West Tennessee, and Bell established his headquarters at Eaton, ten miles west of Trenton, still in Gibson County, but considerably closer to Newbern. The entire brigade encamped there, and the majority, in compliance with Forrest's orders, were quickly furloughed. On April 3 Abe Buford arrived in the area, but chose to make Trenton headquarters for the cavalry division. Presently, footsore Kentuckians began to appear, rushing up from Jackson. These were the dismounted troopers who had trailed behind all the way from Tibbee while their comrades invaded Kentucky searching for horses. Into Trenton from the north came the Third and Seventh Kentucky, which had remained in the Jackson Purchase area visiting their homes, recruiting and refitting. Faulkner's Twelfth Kentucky Cavalry also arrived and encamped. While the Kentucky Brigade regrouped, Bell and his Tennesseans continued their recruiting and conscripting, meeting with great success, swelling the ranks of the brigade by almost one thousand men. Ed Crossland's Kentuckians had done almost as well, increasing their numbers from fourteen hundred to seventeen hundred.[19]

At Trenton Buford read in a northern newspaper a story of their expedition to Paducah. This account blamed the Confederates for carrying off the horses in the vicinity, but announced smugly that the important mounts—beautiful, strong artillery horses belonging to the U.S. government—"had escaped by their adroit concealment in the old foundry or rolling-mill, n the outskirts of the town." Buford was tempted. He immediately sought and secured permission from Forrest for a second Paducah raid, this time using just Crossland's Brigade. He vowed he would complete the remounting of the command with this sweep.[20]

So Buford boldly set out on April 8. Bell watched him and his eight hundred Kentuckians ride off' then he and his brigade, now almost two thousand strong, prepared to move in the opposite direction—toward Jackson, Tennessee. Bell's Brigade, it seems, had a mission of its own.[21]

10

Fort Pillow

Now that he had his command mounted and equipped, Forrest hungered to get even with the Tories. These West Tennessee Unionists had made war upon their neighbors and kinsmen, the "secesh" who had followed Isham G. Harris, Tyree H. Bell, and John D. C. Atkins. Forrest was to be their avenger. Already Col. Fielding Hurst had been defeated by Col. J. J. Neely's Brigade on March 29, 1864, and, for the moment, that "traitor," as Chalmers labeled Hurst, and his gang were scattered to the winds. The remaining enemy threat west of the Tennessee River, other than the troop concentration in Memphis and the garrison at Columbus, was from Fort Pillow.[1] This earthen fortress had been reoccupied by Maj. William F. Bradford and his Tennessee Unionist cavalry battalion in early February 1864, providing Major General Hurlbut in Memphis an important window into "Forrest Country" and a handy "recruiting rendezvous" for Unionists and fugitive slaves.

To Confederate sympathizers of West Tennessee, Fort Pillow represented something else: a nearby stronghold of Yankee authority, a menacing symbol of suppression and aggression.[2] Moreover, the very presence of Bradford promised intensification of the "hard pacification program" instituted by Sherman along the Mississippi. The river counties of Tennessee had suffered from these counterinsurgency measures, as had towns like Brownsville and Jackson. Citizens had been gathered up and taken to Fort Pillow as prisoners. Men in blue had ventured forth from that place repeatedly on "scouts" looking for horses, supplies, illegal whiskey, and contraband of all types. Some had taken advantage of their authority to plunder and terrorize. These Yankees also searched for partisans, hoping to break up Rebel guerrilla bands before they could form. To assist them in their despised efforts they had clusters of carefully cultivated informants.

Secesh citizens, however, sometimes managed to identify their turncoat neighbors and, as 1863 turned into 1864, murder of informants occurred with increasing frequency. Distrust, betrayal, vengeance, hatred, violence, and death tore asunder old and valued relationships. It was as though the people were reliving the Scottish Reiver experience—a world of distrust and discord many of their ancestors had fled. With Bradford at hand, Southern sympathizers were convinced widespread and even nastier retaliation would follow. The conventional war of 1861 had degenerated into a "people's war." The beast was loose.[3]

Bradford's troops, in actuality, were too few in number to be more than a mobile occupation strike force, and Forrest's startling Paducah raid had exposed Fort Pillow's vulnerability, not only to Forrest, but to Hurlbut as well. The latter quickly strengthened the garrison of the river fortress with a battalion of black artillerymen from Memphis, under command of Maj. Lionel F. Booth, a former enlisted man in the regular army. Booth, being senior to Bradford, would assume command.[4] By placing these black troops at Fort Pillow, Hurlbut, of course, exacerbated the fears of the Rebel citizenry.

Forrest knew all about it. Complaining, angry West Tennesseans had besieged his headquarters at Jackson demanding, begging, that he do something. He had written Leonidas Polk on April 4, 1864, that "there is a Federal force of five or six hundred at Fort Pillow, which I shall attend to in a day or so. . . ." Moreover, he plainly stated, the post and its defenders "have horses and supplies which we need."[5] And which they intended to take.

Forrest, Bell, and their troops did not respect the garrison of Fort Pillow or its ability to withstand attack. These were not soldiers. Bradford was a native Southerner, a Virginian by birth, who had practiced law in Dyersburg with his older brother, Theodorick, then moved on to Obion County. The brothers were known, not only to Bell and the men of Dyer County, but to many within the brigade, certainly to the men of Obion and Gibson. A passionate Unionist, the thirty-seven-year-old Bradford had organized others of similar conviction in Obion and, backed by the powerful Federal presence at Columbus and Island No. 10, had led them in suppressing guerrillas in 1862–1863. His activities, "his crimes against the citizenry," as Forrest put it, had made him and his band notorious in the eyes of the Confederate supporters of West Tennessee, not to speak of Rebel soldiers, far away across the Tennessee River, anxious men unable to protect their families and property. Bradford and his Tennessee Tories were regarded as terrorists and armed bandits, as evil in their way as Fielding Hurst.

As a military leader, however, Major Bradford was as green as the troops he commanded, lightly regarded as a soldier, not only by the Confederates but by his own commander, the experienced Stephen A. Hurlbut.[6] As for Bradford's

Battalion (277–295 men), recently organized at Union City and still accepting recruits at Fort Pillow, many of its members were known to Bell and his men as "renegade Southerners," Confederate deserters and conscription-dodgers. Their motivation was suspect, their fighting mettle highly questionable.[7]

As for the black soldiers being sent to support Bradford, many if not most of Forrest's command saw them as runaway slaves who had turned against their masters, willingly aiding and abetting those who would loot and destroy and terrorize. Bell probably agreed, thinking of these blacks as Forrest did, as most Southerners did: not as legitimate soldiers, unworthy of the same respect and consideration that a professional soldier would display toward a brave enemy. These rebellious slaves would not fight according to the rules of war; indeed, they had no rights according to the rules of war. This was a slave insurrection, incited and fueled by outsiders. The very existence of black troops infuriated Bell's men and undoubtedly Bell himself.

The black troops manning the post were believed to be even less experienced than their white comrades and were expected to bolt when confronted by determined Confederates. Actually Booth's troops (most of whom in 1862–63 had been slaves on farms in North Mississippi and Alabama between Corinth and Courtland) had been organized for more than a year and had seen garrison duty at Corinth and Memphis as the First Alabama Legion, Heavy Artillery (African Descent). Just a month before, on March 11, 1864, they had been reorganized as the Sixth U.S. Heavy Artillery (Colored). From this regiment Booth had brought upriver to Fort Pillow from Memphis the First Battalion (four companies: 221–270 men) and one section of Company D, Second U.S. Light Artillery (Colored) (35–41 men). Combined with Bradford's cavalrymen, this gave Booth a garrison of some 600 troops, about the same number that had successfully resisted Forrest at Fort Anderson in Paducah.[8] Major Booth gave his men no rest as he rushed to perfect the fort's defenses. The post surgeon, Dr. Charles Fitch, reported, "For the past 12 days nearly every man that was capable of doing two hours labor, was engaged in this work." Booth intended to fight. He knew Forrest was in the area with considerable manpower, but, to his mind, an assault on his works would be Fort Anderson all over again.[9]

To distract Hurlbut and the force at Columbus, Forrest had permitted Buford and half of his division to charge back into Kentucky to retrieve the horses they had missed rounding up on the Paducah raid. While Buford struck at Paducah, a special splinter force from Buford's command was to demonstrate before Fortress Columbus itself. To the south, almost simultaneously, half of Chalmers's Division would feint at Memphis, making threatening advances against that cotton town from the north and east. They also would pass along the misleading news that Stephen D. Lee was marching, or preparing to march, toward Memphis with his entire force.[10]

Forrest rode up from Jackson to Bell's headquarters at Eaton, Tennessee, on Friday, April 8. The time had come to seize Fort Pillow, he told his friend, and he intended for Bell's Brigade to play a prominent role. Forrest wanted Bell to leave Eaton early Monday morning, April 11, and lead his brigade southwest to a crossroads about thirty-five miles from the objective. There he would unite with Black Bob McCulloch's Brigade, which was presently encamped at Sharon's Ferry on Forked Deer River, about nine miles from Brownsville. This joint force, constituting a makeshift division of two brigades and commanded by Chalmers, would then push on west as a single column to Fort Pillow.[11]

Bell readied his brigade, ordering them to see to their ammunition, rations, and mounts. Meanwhile, he and three other members of the brigade who lived near Newbern left Eaton and went home for a short visit. When Bell returned to camp on Sunday evening, April 10, he found a sealed dispatch from Forrest, "changing the time for me to move up to Sunday morning." Realizing "Sunday was already gone," Bell scrambled to meet the deadline, but it was not until quite late Sunday evening that all was ready—the command on the road in column, their tents having been struck, rations cooked, campfires smothered.[12]

At midnight Bell's Brigade marched out of Eaton, in the general direction of Brownsville. The Forked Deer River proved an obstacle almost at once. A portion of the bridge at Cherryville had been destroyed. Fortunately, Bell's scouts found another crossing point, and a large detail of men dismounted and for about a half mile waded in knee-deep to waist-deep icy water, tugging and pulling two of Forrest's precious fieldpieces across the Forked Deer bottom. After crossing the river, the column took the Fort Pillow road. "From this time on," wrote Sgt. Achilles V. Clark of Russell's Twentieth Tennessee Cavalry, "we rightly supposed that we were going to attack that place." They marched all night, and Bell's Brigade arrived at the rendezvous a few hours ahead of Chalmers.[13]

After riding wearily into the night, Bell halted and permitted his men one hour's rest just before daylight, then they were back in the saddle, following Black Bob McCulloch's Brigade and Lt. Edwin S. Walton's Battery of mountain howitzers. The Confederates hurried, the forced march continuing all day and all night, over difficult roads and uncertain bridges, "thro' the darkest rain and mist I ever saw," recorded one of McCulloch's scouts. "Dark night, awful," commented a company commander of Bell's, but they pushed on, these drenched, gloomy troopers in a foul mood. Just before dawn, Tuesday, April 12, the two brigades arrived before Fort Pillow and dismounted. Bell and his men could be pleased with themselves. It had been a seventy-mile march from Eaton, and they had made it in thirty hours.[14]

Bell's tired and sleepy troopers confronted a very long line of field fortifications that had been erected by their fellow Confederates during the first year of the war, at a time when Fort Pillow boasted thousands of defenders. This outer line was about two miles long and lightly manned by enemy pickets. There were other earthworks and rifle pits to the rear, an unperfected second line, intended by Major Booth as a fallback position for his advanced guard. The heart of Fort Pillow's defensive network was even farther to the rear—a small, semicircular interior fort backed up against and overlooking the Mississippi. This extended redoubt held no heavy ordnance like Columbus, but it did have half-a-dozen fieldpieces; the muzzles of five showed through earthen embrasures, directed to the land side.[15] This inner fortress should not be considered to have been formidable, however. Once inside the outer defenses, Fort Pillow offered attackers covered avenues of approach, and if they happened to gain control of the outer line, then the fort itself, on lower ground, could be dominated. Fort Pillow, manned by six hundred men, was not meant to be defended from land attack.

Forrest knew the layout of the objective very well, thanks to complete reports from Capt. William J. Shaw, a Southern sympathizer who had been held prisoner at the fort as late as April 10. Shaw not only provided intelligence, but volunteered to serve as a guide. Forrest's plan was to attack the interior fort employing a double envelopment. A small distracting force would make a secondary attack, or demonstration, in front of the main works, while Bell's and McCulloch's brigades would slip around both flanks, concealed from enemy fire, and position themselves for the assault—the object being to advance the two main bodies as close to the river as possible, to the flanks and rear of the works. Both brigade commanders wanted the assault force close to the breastworks—the closer, the better—reducing the distance they must traverse in the open under fire.

After securing the horses (leaving every fourth man to hold the mounts), ambulances, and his few wagons, Bell motioned his troops forward toward the fort on foot, hoping to capture the "outside pickets." They were quite successful, picking up most of the enemy sentinels, apparently by surprise. Bell's and McCulloch's brigades pressed on, deploying as they advanced and rapidly seizing the high ground or ridge that commanded the fort. The investment was complete.

Actually Booth did not intend to hold this two-mile line with his few men. Instead the advanced Federal skirmishers and pickets retired about three hundred yards to a line of knolls, as expected, and then about 11 A.M. fell back into the fort itself. "The enemy did not attempt to hold the outer line," Chalmers reported, "but trained their artillery so as to play upon the only roads leading through it." Naval gunfire augmented the coverage of Fort Pillow's five fieldpieces.[16] It was the gunboat *New Era*, blasting away at targets of opportunity while standing offshore. With Capt. Theodorick F. Bradford as their forward observer on shore, the gunboat should have provided effective close-fire support for the garrison, but the shells appear to have done little damage to the advancing Rebels. For that matter, the noisy fieldpieces within the fort proved equally ineffective.[17]

Bell deployed his brigade to the right, or north, along the forward slope of the ridge, in sight of the interior fort but out of range for small arms. He anchored his right flank on Coal Creek with Barteau's Second Tennessee Cavalry. In accordance with Chalmers's orders, Bell initially attempted to move Russell's and Barteau's regiments down along Coal Creek until they reached the riverbank or bluff. There he intended for the two regiments to redeploy and open the attack from this supposedly choice flank position. Bell was to open the attack from the north and McCulloch would join in from the south once he heard rifle fire from the opposite side of the fort. While Barteau and Russell filed through the Coal Creek bottom or ravine, Bell directed his third regiment, Andrew N. Wilson's Sixteenth (Twenty-first) Tennessee Cavalry, to "deploy directly in front and occupy the close attention of the garrison by an immediate, vigorous skirmish."[18]

Wilson, together with some troops from the right of McCulloch's line, enjoyed great initial success. In a well-executed rush, they dislodged the enemy manning the middle redoubt and occupied it.[19] The main body of Bell's Brigade, on the other hand, had to abandon its enveloping movement down Coal Creek because of the swollen and unfordable stream. Bell decided to backtrack. He would slide to the left with a portion of his flanking force, leaving Barteau's regiment struggling to make its way across the creek. If successful, Barteau was to extend his lines from the creek mouth all along the ravine on the north face of the fort's defenses. This was an unwelcome change of plan, however. Bell (and Forrest) had wanted to mass troops at the north end of the earth fort, which they believed would be the weakest portion of the enemy's inner defenses. Now a new tactical plan had to be improvised.[20]

So Bell retraced his steps. He brought Milton Russell's Twentieth Tennessee Cavalry out of the bottom and had him extend his line left from the Coal Creek ravine until he touched the right of Wilson's regiment. With Russell in place, Bell's Brigade now manned a continuous and sheltered front running from below the bluff on the right, back along the low ground conforming to the semicircular face of the interior fort, and it connected with the right of McCulloch's line. The sudden change of plan, however, had consumed much more time than anticipated, and Bell clearly could see that it was not yet a tight investment, certainly not a compact position from which to launch an assault. He ordered Maj. Tom Allison and a handful of troopers to reconnoiter. The faithful Allison, who had an excellent eye for military terrain, worked his way through the rifle pits facing him and drew close enough to the Yankee parapets to report that "the fort could be taken by a charge."

This intelligence invigorated Bell. He now ordered Clark Barteau to press up closer to the enemy works, which Barteau did, although the regimental commander reported gloomily that he did not think the works on the north flank could be stormed "without great loss of life." The Yankee position, Barteau felt, needed to be softened up somehow, but no Rebel field guns were available on the right. Prompted by Barteau's report, Bell decided to deploy even more sharpshooters, within easy range of the works, on the high ground and knolls that constituted portions of the old 1861–1862 defenses. It seemed a magical solution. Once these troops were in place, "to all intents and purposes the fort was ours," reported Capt. Charles W. Anderson, Forrest's aide-de-camp.

The sharpshooters (most of them Bell's rank-and-file privates) became quite active, "crawling and getting behind every chunk as they went," Bell recalled; all the while the Yankees "were firing on them rapidly from the fort." Having taken advantage of the excellent cover, the sharpshooters soon "commanded the fort completely." In effect the defenders, having to duck behind their thick, high parapet, were pinned down, blind to the flanking movements on either side of the earthen fort. Meanwhile, sharpshooters (whether Bell's or McCulloch's has not been determined) had shot and killed Major Booth and his adjutant. Unknown to the Confederates, the command of the fort had devolved upon Major Bradford.[21]

Bell should have been pleased. By noon his men were in position and his sharpshooters could pick off any Yankee who peeked over the earthworks. Perhaps of greater importance, any Federal who attempted to take position behind the parapets facing McCulloch's men would be exposed to the careful aim of Bell's sharpshooters, shooting "from behind stumps and logs on all the neighboring hills," catching the works and their defenders in reverse. "We suffered pretty severely in the loss of commissioned officery by the unerring aim of the rebel sharpshooters," complained Lt. Mack J. Leaming, Bradford's adjutant. Better yet, as the lines tightened on Fort Pillow, Bell had not had a man killed and only two wounded slightly. The same tactic would benefit Barteau. In the rush forward to position themselves even closer to the enemy earthworks, Bell would have his sharpshooters open in "lively fashion," thereby providing close suppressing fire, essential to an assault against a fortified position.[22]

About noon, according to Bell, General Chalmers and his staff came around to the right and stopped. The general told Bell that Forrest had not yet arrived. "If he does not get here," said Chalmers, "we cannot take that place as it is too formidable."[23] Chalmers had seen at close hand the parapets in the interior fort: eight feet high, fronted by a ditch or moat twelve feet wide and six feet deep. Chalmers asked Bell's thoughts, and Bell replied that he "was not willing to leave, and leave the fort standing; that we had come nearly a thousand miles for the express purpose of taking that place." Chalmers did not respond to Bell's blunt assessment. He and his staff rode off, continuing to the right, taking their horses down into the Coal Creek bottom. There they turned their mounts loose to graze while they examined the terrain and waited for Forrest's arrival.[24]

When Forrest rode in early that afternoon, he came up to Bell. "Where is Chalmers?" he asked. Bell pointed toward Coal Creek and offered to bring the division commander to him. When Chalmers came up from Coal Creek and reported, Forrest sent him back to the left, to McCulloch's portion of the line.

Before committing his troops to an assault, Forrest conducted his own reconnaissance on horseback from the extreme left around to Coal Creek, and in the process had three mounts shot from under him and was "badly bruised" in one of these falls. According to Bell, his own brigade now "covered the entire fort, with the exception of a small space on the left," where McCulloch "with a small detachment" had taken position. Forrest directed Bell to find fifty volunteers for a special reconnaissance mission. Bell called together a group of his officers and explained that it must be "something pretty serious." When he asked for a volunteer company commander to lead the group, Capt. James Stinnett of Andrew Wilson's Sixteenth Tennessee Cavalry stepped forward. Sixty-five-year-old Stinnett was tough and brave and full of fire. Bell assigned the ancient captain two lieutenants and fifty men, then gave the little band their orders. They were to test the enemy's reactions, their defenses, on Bell's portion of the line, moving up within thirty feet of the enemy ramparts. Stinnett framed the mission realistically for his troopers. "Boys," he said, "it's a pretty tight pill, some of us will be hurt and some probably killed. But that is what we bargained for when we joined the army." Then Stinnett led the men in a rush toward the fort, halting so close to the works that the enemy could not see them or depress their weapons sufficiently to fire upon them. Snug under the fortification, the gleeful captain, frisky as a colt, proceeded to take his hat off and strut around for Bell and Forrest and his comrades to see.[25]

The fort could be taken by assault, the Confederates were now certain, and as soon as the ordnance train arrived (Bell and McCulloch appear to have exhausted their ammunition supply), Forrest sent in a flag of truce, demanding surrender. Major Bradford, pretending to be the dead Major Booth, responded that he needed an hour for "consultation and consideration with my officers and the officers of the gunboat." Forrest granted the request, but the Confederates "saw smoke from boats above and below in the Mississippi," Bell remembered, "and we felt certain that they were reinforcements and the commander was just delaying, expecting them to get there in time to reinforce him."[26]

Forrest reacted to this development by sending a strong detail (at least a squadron of McCulloch's men) through the "town" just south of the fort to a position under the bluff, facing and flanking the extreme right (south) of the Federal works. By occupying the several rows of log storehouses, barracks, stores, civilian shacks, and a hotel, McCulloch's troops gained protection from Yankee musket fire, and being in defilade they were also immune to the fire from the fort's fieldpieces. Forrest placed a section of Walton's Battery on the bluff on the Confederate extreme left, where plunging fire from the lieutenant's two little howitzers discouraged the *New Era* from maintaining her station at the landing.[27] The presence of this section also served as a precaution against enemy boats that might attempt to land reinforcements. Forrest, in effect, had interdicted the battlefield.

Moreover, Forrest's advanced wings, now under the river bluffs, were actually in rear of the fort. While three companies of McCulloch's men (led by the ever-present Captain Anderson) extended and consolidated the Confederate extreme left, Bell's entire brigade pushed up even closer, within fifty yards of the parapet. Enemy fire was fitful, poorly directed. Resistance seemed to be limited to the taunts of the black cannoneers on the ramparts. Rifle fire? There was none to speak of. The river fort, controlled by Rebel fire, with Forrest's troops pressing up against its ramparts and virtually encircled, was ripe for assault. The miserable marksmanship of the Yankee riflemen and cannoneers (not one Confederate was killed during the deployment) doubtless gave Bell and his men enormous confidence.[28]

When yet another demand to surrender was refused, Forrest determined to attack immediately—evening was rapidly approaching.[29] He rode up and down the lines, giving instructions: "At the sound of my bugle, I want the whole command to ride up on and over the breastworks of the fort, and I want the officers to go with them." Soon the bugle sounded. As Bell would relate, most of the brigade "almost as solid as if they were really a log," crowded up under the high parapets, then hoisted one another up and over "with their navy sixes and their guns loaded. They landed right amongst the enemy." To be successful the assault had to be "short, sharp and desperate."[30] It was. Bell led the way himself. He went down into the ditch, and by use of his strong back as a step and his clasped hands as a stirrup, he helped his boys pull themselves up over the earthen wall. In this dangerous, difficult effort to cross the ditch and clamber up the face of the parapet, one of Barteau's men, J. C. McAdoo, Company C, Second Tennessee Cavalry, was "*long* enough to jump into the ditch but *too short* to leap out until Colonel Bell came to his assistance." Although two of Bell's men were killed on top of the breastworks, the Yankee resistance was weak, disorganized.[31]

The assault in Bell's sector seemed particularly effective to the Federal adjutant, Lt. Mack J. Lemming. The first line of Rebels poured over the parapet, he reported, "as if rising from out the very earth on the center and north side."[32] Bell appears to have positioned himself almost exactly midway between the right of Russell and the left of Barteau. Although helping men like McAdoo cross the ditch, he still was among the first to make it to the top of the parapet. "Our troops never fired a gun until they landed inside the fort," Bell noted. "The firing lasted not exceeding three minutes, and there was no more firing from either side."[33] Bell jumped into the fort. "The first thing I saw was several barrels of whiskey with the heads knocked out and tin cups scattered about, and the first thing I did, was to turn those barrels over."[34] Then, Bell recalled, "General Forrest came in a gallop . . . , jumped off his horse and turned over one barrel at least."[35]

The proudest moment of the attack came when Bell's son, Isaac, acting as his aide-de-camp, yanked down the enemy colors and gave them to his father. "When General Forrest came into the fort," Bell recalled, he took the flag and handed it to Isaac.[36]

This startling successful assault, according to Chalmers, took only five minutes. The Yankees fled. "The enemy made no attempt to surrender," Chalmers reported, "no white flag was elevated, nor was the U.S. flag lowered until pulled down by our men." The Yankees "broke to the river, right over the bank, which made a part of the fort, and into the river," Bell remembered. "Our men emptied their guns and navy sixes," he continued, "and my opinion is that few were reloaded, but we killed a great many of them."[37]

"Our men came rushing down the Bluff next to the River," reported Federal surgeon Charles Fitch, "the greater portion of them throwing away their arms as they came." As the fleeing Federals plunged down the high steep bluff toward the river, toward what they believed might be safety, they were surprised by "an enfilading and deadly fire" at very close range from McCulloch's and Barteau's advanced parties waiting under the bluffs on either flank—a murderous crossfire. "The slaughter," reported Forrest, "was heavy." To compound the enemy's misery, Bell's men who had stormed the parapets now lined the top of the bluffs and at close range "poured a destructive fire into the rear of the retreating and now panic-stricken" Federals. A number of Yankees threw themselves into the Mississippi, Bell recalled, and "pretty nearly froze to death." As they finally came out of the water onto the bank, Bell's and McCulloch's men rounded them up. At this point, according to Forrest, firing ceased. It had been twenty minutes since the bugle sounded the attack.[38]

There remained the Yankee gunboats. One, ironically named the *Olive Branch,* stood off from the fort, dangerously close, and opened fire. This seemed to justify Major Bradford's promise, that plenty of help was on its way. "There is a thousand soldiers on the boat," he had told them.[39] Forrest was ready, however. He had one of the fort's Parrott rifles rolled up to the bluff and opened on the *Olive Branch,* sighting it himself. "We had good gunners," Bell remembered, "and we turned their own guns on them and in a very few minutes, the boat put out back up the river; consequently, we had no more trouble until we got things wound up."[40]

Bell remained inside the fort atop the bluff, and presently up from the Mississippi River came Major Bradford, dripping water and shivering. Previously, Bradford had attempted to surrender but "the Rebs fired volley after volley at him," according to Dr. Fitch. "He retreated backwards into the River, crying that he surrendered, until the water became so deep that he had to swim." Finally he felt it safe enough to come out, and the first man he met when he had climbed the bluff was his old acquaintance Tyree Bell. The major chose to ignore the Rebel colonel. Bradford "would not recognize me," Bell recalled, "just because he didn't want to." Instead Bradford asked to speak to Forrest, and Bell escorted him. "Here is Colonel Bradford," he told Forrest, explaining that Bradford commanded the fort. Forrest sent the major to get on some dry clothes, then ordered him "placed in the custody of Colonel McCulloch." McCullouch fed him supper and provided him with a bed in his own quarters.[41]

Dr. Fitch, the garrison surgeon, walked up the bluff and asked for General Forrest's protection. Fitch found him sighting one of the Parrotts at a riverboat.

"What do you want?" asked Forrest.

Fitch replied he "was the surgeon of the Post, and asked protection from him that was due a prisoner."

"You are surgeon of a damn nigger regiment," Forrest said.

Fitch said, "I was not."

"You are a damn Tenn. Yankee then."

"I told him I was from Iowa."

"What in hell are you down here for?" Forrest asked. "I have a great mind to have you killed for being down here."

Forrest did order a guard for Fitch, and other white Federals who had come up into the fort gathered around Fitch for protection, but soon, according to Fitch, "drunken Rebel soldiers came up and fired in among the Prisoners with their revolvers." "While here," Fitch continued, "I saw them kill every negro that made his appearance dressed in Federal uniform." Chalmers came on the scene about this time and, seeing the desperate situation, put a double file of Confederate troops around Dr. Fitch.[42]

Tyree Bell (who made no after-action report) offered two sentences of explanation thirty years later: "There was promiscuous shooting for some time at different places, whenever they saw a negro or a white man running. This was contrary to the commands of the commanding officer."[43]

Finally the shooting stopped. "The garrison," reported the correspondent for the *Memphis Appeal,* "never did surrender, but with guns in their hands, they huddled together at the lower side of the fort where they were shot down by our victorious troops who had risked so much in scaling their walls in the face of such danger, and who could not offer quarters while the enemy's flag still floated over them, and their arms were still held in their hands."[44]

Two of Bell's veteran soldiers, Sergeant and later Company Commander Achilles V. Clark, Twentieth Tennessee Cavalry, and Surgeon Samuel H. Caldwell, Wilson's Sixteenth Tennessee Cavalry, son of Maj. Bob Caldwell, wrote home two days after the battle. The fort "was garrisoned by 400 white men & 400 negroes & out of the 800 only 168 are now living," Sam Caldwell recounted to his wife. "So you can now guess how terrible was the slaughter. It was decidedly the most horrible sight that I have ever witnessed."[45]

Sergeant Clark wrote his two sisters April 14:

> The slaughter was awful—words cannot describe the scene. The poor deluded negroes would run up to our men, fall upon their knees and with uplifted hands scream for mercy but they were ordered to their feet and then shot down. The white men fared but little better. The fort turned out to be a slaughter pen. . . . I with several others tried to stop the butchery and at one time had partially succeeded but Gen. Forrest ordered them shot down like dogs and the carnage continued. Finally our men became sick of blood and the firing ceased.[46]

Pvt. William R. Dyer, Forrest's Escort, penciled in his diary: "We arrived at Fort Pillow and attacked the fort early in the day. The fort was defended by about 450 Blacks and 250 whites. We captured about 40 Blacks and 100 Whites and killed the remainder. We demolished the place."[47]

Bell had the prisoners "collect the dead and lay them in the ditch at the foot of the parapet. After they were collected and laid in, we then had them covered up about three feet deep." At the specific request of Major Bradford, the Union officers were buried separately from the enlisted men. Meanwhile, Bell had staff officers divide the brigade into two large work details—one hurrying and laboring to drag the six captured cannon out of the fort, the other shoving the unwounded prisoners into a sullen and frightened column. Then between sunset and dark, Bell marched the captured Yankees out of Fort Pillow and encamped about a mile and a half east, secure from any sudden strike inland by a Federal amphibious force. At last the men could sleep. It had been two days and almost three nights since they had left Eaton.[48]

Early on April 13, details from Bell's Brigade were sent back into Fort Pillow to retrieve small arms, commissary, and ordnance stores. Bell himself appears to have given his attention to organizing the column for the march to Jackson. Teams for the captured cannon had to be found, and if sufficient horses and mules were not available, oxen had to be secured from the countryside. Nevertheless, by late morning, elements of the brigade were in motion.[49] In the meantime, McCulloch's Brigade had encamped close to the fort and made good use of the buildings and tents overnight. While Bell struggled to get the heavy column under way to Jackson, McCulloch's Missourians and Texans had primary responsibility for destroying everything of use in the fort. Some set fire to the buildings and tents, while others attempted to level and demolish the earthworks.

The Yankees quickly put a stop to this. "The rebels could be seen moving about applying torches to the barracks, huts and stables," reported a naval observer, so the *Silver Cloud* moved in close to the bank and threw shell and shrapnel. Captain Anderson of Forrest's staff got the gunboat's attention with a flag of truce, however, and it was agreed to stop the firing while the Federal wounded were "brought down from the fort and battlefield and placed on board the *Platte Valley*. Details of rebel soldiers assisted us in this duty," Acting Master William Ferguson reported. About 4 P.M. Anderson withdrew his flag to the top of the bluff and burned all the houses and tents around the fort except for the hospital where the Federal wounded were gathered. Union soldiers with minor wounds were left behind to man the hospitals along with about a week's supply of food and medicine.[50] While Anderson finished up at the fort, Chalmers left Fort Pillow with McCulloch's Brigade and set out to catch up with Bell. The following morning, April 14, Chalmers reassembled his makeshift division and resumed the march toward Brownsville. Bell led, followed by McCulloch—a large, slow column burdened with prisoners, captured equipment and supplies, six Federal fieldpieces, and a small group of conscripts.[51]

In the vicinity of Brownsville another prisoner was brought in: Maj. William Bradford, commander of Fort Pillow. It seems that Bradford had left the quarters of Colonel McCulloch upon receiving the latter's permission to "superintend the burial of his brother," Capt. Theodorick Bradford, who had been killed in the fighting. Major Bradford, however, failed to return to McCulloch's quarters as he had promised, thereby, Confederate sources agree, violating "his parole of honor." Instead, Bradford attempted to escape only to be recaptured dressed in civilian clothes by a scout of Col. W. L. Duckworth's command at Covington, Tennessee. Duckworth brought the fugitive to Chalmers, who placed him in the column, but among the conscripts rather than with the Union prisoners. On April 14, about dusk, Bradford was marching with W. R. McLagan, a Confederate conscript from Covington, and some thirty other dispirited conscripts. According to McLagan, a few miles outside Brownsville, the "guards took Bradford a short distance from the road into a thicket of woods and shot him." McLagan seemed to think that Duckworth was responsible for giving the order.[52]

Even Forrest's biographer, Dr. John A. Wyeth, called it murder. Bell knew Bradford and doubtless he was aware of what had happened. It seems reasonable to believe that he would have had little if any sympathy for Bradford. "A great many of the soldiers in Forrest's command felt that they had a personal grievance against this man," Dr. Wyeth observed, and it was "not a matter of great surprise that opportunity was taken to exact private revenge upon him at this time." The evidence is sparse, vague, and contradictory, and McLagan certainly is not the most reliable source; nevertheless, Bell's silence, as well as that of Forrest, McCulloch, and Chalmers, regarding Bradford's death is deafening.[53] Perhaps they regarded Bradford's disappearance as did the correspondent for the *Memphis Appeal:* West Tennessee is now clear of deserters, conscripts, and tories . . . , about one thousand six hundred deserters and conscripts have been sent to the rear, and a large number of bad men have been sent back in irons, and some few outlaws have been lost in the woods."[54]

Bell's admission that "promiscuous shooting for some time" occurred at Fort Pillow invites examination. This is a strange, vague, and disappointing statement by a brigade commander. Recent authoritative studies have revealed that almost half of the 585 defenders died as a result of the attack. Of these, almost two-thirds were black soldiers. Confederate casualties, on the other hand, were relatively light. Bell lost five killed and thirty-two wounded; the entire assaulting force fourteen killed, eighty-six wounded. Bell's statement, when coupled with the accounts of Confederate participants Clark, Caldwell, Dyer, Fort, and southern newspaper correspondents "Marion" and "Memphis," is convincing. Union soldiers at Fort Pillow were killed as they attempted to surrender, when they posed no real threat to the Confederates who had them virtually encircled. Some retained their rifles; some fired at the Confederates, inviting retaliation. These presumably were killed out of hand. Others, however, who had thrown down their arms, were killed, their number undetermined. The door is opened for conjecture, however, by Forrest's shocking report: "the river was dyed with the blood of the slaughtered for 200 yards." The Confederates, in the words of Chalmers, had "taught the mongrel garrison of blacks and renegades a lesson long to be remembered."[55]

If one takes into consideration the inept defensive measures by Bradford; the drinking, if not drunkenness, of the garrison; the taunting of the Confederates by the black soldiers during the truce; the refusal to surrender, to haul down the national colors; and the fact that many Federals carried their weapons out of the fort and down the bluff—and that some continued to fire at the water's edge—the motive, if not the justification for reprisal, exists. An apologist might argue that such happens in war when an offer of surrender is refused. No matter, the issue persists. On April 12, 1864, at Fort Pillow, Confederate soldiers killed a number of their defenseless enemies, particularly black enemies, after they had ceased to resist.

Bell later would deny the deliberate killings in a sworn statement to Dr. Wyeth in 1899. Forrest ordered the firing to stop, Bell maintained. "The drunken condition of the garrison and the failure of Colonel Bradford to surrender, thus necessitating the assault, were the causes of the fatality," Bell declared. He also dismissed "the statements [of the Federal Congressional Committee

★ FORT PILLOW MASSACRE. COLLECTION OF JIM BROWNE.

investigating the incident] in relation to the alleged 'cruelty and barbarism' practised by Forrest's command." The testimony and conclusions of this body, according to Bell "are a tissue of lies from end to end." His denial was echoed by Chalmers, McCulloch, Barteau, Anderson, and many others who took oaths to that effect in 1898 and 1899.[56]

They insisted Forrest had attempted to stop the killing and failed, or intervened too late; the same is said about Chalmers. Perhaps Bell, too. No observer, however, mentions Bell's role in this regard. He probably remained atop the bluff, but based on his later comments, it would appear he knew, if not saw, what was happening on the bank below. Regardless of what action Forrest and Chalmers took or might have taken, Bell himself should have attempted to stop the executions, "the promiscuous firing." No matter how frenzied the attackers, no matter how drunk some defenders (or attackers) might have been, he might have ended it. He not only had the authority, but the force of his personality and reputation. He could have done more, should have done more, to control his troops. Once victory was at hand, once the attack on Fort Pillow reached the consolidation phase, it appears Tyree Bell let down, permitting at least some of his soldiers to run wild, to retaliate against a broken, virtually helpless enemy. And thus he failed in his responsibilities as a soldier and as a brigade commander.

Is this observation fair? Perhaps it is naive to hold Bell to such a standard 150 years later. In an all-out assault of a fortified position, in the short seconds when attackers' and defenders' lives dangle precariously, frenzy and fury drown the still voice of reason. Reflex governs a soldier's action, his inaction. No one may judge Tyree Bell's actions conclusively based on the thin, contradictory, prejudicial evidence available.

Otherwise Tyree Bell's performance at Fort Pillow had been commendable. He had moved his command, despite difficult weather and road conditions, from Eaton to Fort Pillow promptly and in good style. Bell and his men were proud of that forced march. He found splendid positions for his sharpshooters and posted them effectively. He appears to have encouraged Forrest to try a direct assault upon the fortified position; when the assault was ordered, he lodged men close in and led them in person over the breastworks in a dangerously wide but surprisingly well-coordinated charge. As at Belmont and Shiloh and Richmond, Bell proved a first-rate combat leader—energetic, brave, and resourceful.

Such an bright assessment remains incomplete, however, and inaccurate. Fort Pillow was not just another military engagement like Richmond or Belmont. Its name connotes a shameful episode in American history. Tyree Bell and his fellow Confederates at Fort Pillow can never shake loose from the ghosts below the riverbank, the ghosts who point their fingers and shout their names.

11

Brice's Crossroads

After reaching Brownsville, Chalmers's column, rather than continuing east, veered almost due south, crossing the Hatchie River, passing through Somerville, Tennessee, then across the Wolf River toward LaGrange. Sunday, April 17, following the line of the Mississippi Central Railroad, they marched on, now almost straight south, passing Hudsonville, Mississippi, and camping six miles from Holly Springs. Here Chalmers, acting on Forrest's orders, broke up the column. Clark Barteau's regiment, specifically charged with guarding the Fort Pillow prisoners, would move deeper into Mississippi, accompanying McCulloch's Brigade, while Bell with the balance of his own brigade was to retrace his steps up the railroad—back to Tennessee.[1]

Bell's mission had changed. Rather than sweep from Cherryville, Tennessee, east to Jackson for deserters and conscripts, Abe Buford had ordered him to march his brigade past Forrest's headquarters in Jackson, on north to Carroll County, Tennessee. There he was to "take up and send to Jackson every one subject to military duty and all absentees from the army," virtually "every man between the ages of eighteen and forty-five." Bell did so, establishing his headquarters at Huntington, the seat of Carroll County. He remained in the area several days, then moved west to Dyer County, "gathering considerable recruits at both places." It was stern, unrelenting duty, requiring firmness, an uncompromising man with an authoritative, threatening air. No one excelled Tyree Bell. Even Ed Rucker, a man much respected by Forrest for his bravery and determination in a fight, backed off from picking up conscripts and deserters. "Nasty duty," he called it. When his efforts in Dyer began to show diminishing returns, Bell turned back east and cast his nets in Gibson County—recruiting, conscripting, and rounding up deserters. He completed his work in a few days and reported to Buford in Jackson on April 28, "with my command strengthened by at least three hundred." His brigade, Bell proudly proclaimed, "now mustered over 1700 well-mounted horsemen." While the brigade awaited further orders, Bell took this opportunity, as he repeatedly had done in the past, to furlough a number of his men.[2] He had an understanding with his boys, it seems.

On May 1, 1864, Bell's Brigade marched south from Jackson as part of a large column of Forrest's Cavalry—all of Buford's Division plus Col. James J. Neely's brigade of Chalmers's command. The heart of the column that the cavalrymen escorted consisted of some three hundred prisoners of war and another long, heavy train of precious supplies and equipment, the wagons drawn by oxen. Their intermediate objective was Corinth, by way of Purdy, Tennessee (thus avoiding crossing the Hatchie River). Once they reached Corinth, Newsom's Nineteenth Tennessee Cavalry and Kizer's Scouts were dropped off to garrison that town and to picket the line of the Memphis and Charleston Railroad. Bell and the remainder of the brigade continued on, from Corinth down the Mobile and Ohio Railroad to the depot at Rienzi. Here the prisoners and supplies were dropped off to be moved further south by rail. Happily unencumbered, Bell and his remaining regiments made an easy march to Tupelo, arriving on May 6. They would remain there, largely inactive, almost a month.[3]

Late in May Brig. Gen. George B. Hodge, a well-connected Confederate congressman and sometime cavalry leader, made a careful, detailed inspection of Forrest's Cavalry. He found it poorly armed for the most part and "extremely deficient in cavalry equipment." Of the saddles on hand, for instance, many were "indifferent in quality and destructive of the horses backs." "Only one third of the men could be properly mounted," Hodge reported, "with even so much as a necessary item like a saddle or bridle." One fourth of Buford's Division was still unarmed, and almost half of the remainder were fighting with ancient Mississippi rifles. Only 17 percent of Buford's and Bell's troops had pistols, and many of these required special ammunition "good only as long as the cartridges last." One could doubt, with good reason, if Forrest's Cavalry, especially Buford's Division, was capable of meeting the enemy at all. Somehow they needed to be equipped.[4]

While Bell's men sat in their tents and looked in wonder at their cumbersome muskets and received instruction on firing their LeFauchaux pinfire pistols, the National forces under Grant and Sherman had opened momentous campaigns in Virginia and North Georgia. The Confederacy rushed to respond, hustling all the troops they could gather to support the Army of Northern Virginia and the Army of Tennessee. As a result, Forrest saw his command melt as the War Department (guided by General Bragg) sent officers to sift his cavalry

★ Maj. Gen. Nathan Bedford Forrest. Tennessee State Library and Archives.

for infantrymen belonging to the Army of Tennessee. Assisted by muster rolls voluntarily provided by Forrest, they found 654. When the first officers arrived to identify such men and return them to their proper commands, Forrest sent a strong protest to Stephen D. Lee, who had replaced Polk as department commander on May 9. "There are 1,000 men in my command who left the army at its reorganization in the spring of 1862," Forrest wrote. At the first attempt to reclaim men from his command by the Army of Tennessee, he anticipated losing 800 or 900, "for as soon as you commence arresting, the balance, anticipating a similar fate, will take to the woods with arms, equipment and horses."[5]

The War Department refused to yield, nonetheless, and Forrest sought to comply, not only by handing over the muster rolls, but also having his two divisions assembled for dress parades on Sunday, May 22. While the troopers stood by silently, Confederate officers went through the ranks of ten regiments, arresting over six hundred men and placing them under guard.[6]

Tyree Bell had to sit his horse as some of his old veterans of the Twelfth Tennessee went up and down the ranks identifying former comrades. When Bell had gone into West Tennessee in 1863, he had assured many of these men "who left the 12th Tenn. by desertions & Some who had left on furlough & leave of absence on account of sickness; all of whom were now absent without leave, furloughs having expired . . . that the old Regt. to which they belonged would be mounted" and remain mounted. This was welcome news. These veteran infantrymen wanted no part of drill-masters, Confederate rations, or "fire-by-file" and "Charge Bayonets!" They wanted very much to be mounted, and they wanted very much to stay within reach of home. In 1863 Bell and Pillow had gone so far as to assure former members of the Twelfth Tennessee that they "would never be in danger of being dismounted. They therefore enlisted anew and most of them mounted themselves."[7]

Bell sat in his saddle and watched as men from the Twelfth, Twenty-second, and Forty-seventh Tennessee, men he had known as neighbors and commanded in battle, men he had promised would fight henceforward as cavalrymen were put under arrest and marched off the parade ground as though they were a contingent of Fort Pillow prisoners. It was a terrible test of Bell's loyalty and a stunning rebuke by the War Department for his recruiting and conscripting efforts over the past year.[8]

As he and Forrest had warned, this act proved thoroughly disheartening to many of the freshly raised troops. West Tennesseans deserted by the dozens, fearing being locked in boxcars and carried back in disgrace to their old infantry units in distant Georgia, as did happen. Capt. Elisha Hollis, Twentieth Tennessee Cavalry, recorded in his diary on May 24, "Great many of our soldiers went home today and night."[9]

Forrest knew his command had been weakened, but he (perhaps advised by Leonidas Polk as he relinquished command of the department) wisely reacted constructively, using the quiet time at Tupelo to do his best to reequip, rearm, and reorganize. Forrest created an artillery battalion of four batteries (Morton's, Rice's, Thrall's, and Walton's) under Capt. John W. Morton and realigned some of his brigades. Chalmers's Division would contain McCulloch's, Neely's, and Edmund W. Rucker's brigades, while Buford would command Bell's Brigade and the Kentucky Brigade, now led by the unusually able Col. Hylan B. Lyon, who had superseded Ed Crossland.

Lyon was only twenty-eight, but was a West Point graduate and a professional artillery officer. He had become colonel of the Eighth Kentucky early on,

★ BRIG. GEN. HYLAN B. LYON. LIBRARY OF CONGRESS.

but had been captured with his men at Fort Donelson. Upon his exchange Lyon served at Vicksburg and somehow managed to avoid being swept up in the host of captives. Forrest did not possess a more professional, experienced brigade commander than this young, energetic Kentuckian.[10]

During May 1864, as Sherman's three armies forced Joseph E. Johnston's Army of Tennessee from its formidable natural defenses at Dalton, Georgia, and necessitated the recall of General Polk and his two infantry divisions from Mississippi, Forrest would remain stationary in North Mississippi. A raid into Middle Tennessee, which virtually every Confederate strategist advocated and William T. Sherman feared, was abandoned because a strong Federal cavalry force threatened what could prove a highly destructive raid into Mississippi.

When Brig. Gen. William H. "Red" Jackson was sent from Alabama to reinforce Johnston's army, Stephen D. Lee also felt compelled to detach Chalmers's Division and sent it east to shield Montgomery and Selma. This further depleted Forrest's command by about one-half. Nevertheless Forrest and Lee, seeking somehow to respond to the appeals of Joseph E. Johnston, sought an opportunity to strike against Sherman's vulnerable communications in Tennessee.

Conditions seemed promising as May closed, and on June 1 Lee authorized his cavalry commander to take two thousand men and two batteries and march for Russellville, Alabama, preparatory to crossing the Tennessee River "and destroying the railroad from Nashville." To assist Forrest were one thousand troops of Roddey's North Alabama command. Bell's Brigade (less the regiments of Newsom and Russell), with Morton's and Rice's batteries, made up the heart of this ambitious expedition, which rode out of Tupelo on June 1, 1864. Lee and Forrest were ambivalent, however. Both worried about leaving Mississippi dangerously exposed to sudden raids from Memphis. To guard against this, they detached Milton Russell and left him behind in general command of his own Twentieth Tennessee Cavalry at Tupelo and Newsom's Nineteenth Tennessee Cavalry at Corinth.[11]

No sooner had Forrest and Bell reached Russellville, after a three-day march in heavy rain, than they received a dispatch from Lee recalling the expedition. Information was sparse, but it was known that a heavy column of Federal infantry and cavalry, believed to be commanded by Maj. Gen. Andrew J. Smith, was heading southeast from Memphis. Perhaps it was the long-expected strike at Tupelo, but more likely it was corps-size reinforcement for Sherman in North Georgia. If so, the movement along the Memphis and Charleston Railroad could be harassed, perhaps impeded, by Forrest's cavalry.

On the other hand, the Yankee expedition might be aimed at the vital agricultural center in the Tupelo-Okolona area, a land the Confederates were wont to call "Egypt." Samuel A. Agnew, an attentive young pastor who lived near Brice's Crossroads, recorded in his diary, "Their object is supposed to be to destroy the Prairie corn. Others think their design is to hold Forrest here." To meet either of these threats, prudence dictated that Stephen D. Lee concentrate his cavalry quickly.[12]

While the Confederates had been dispersing their few cavalry forces thinly and defensively across Alabama and Mississippi, the Federals had gathered a small, mobile army of over three thousand cavalry, five thousand infantry, and twenty-two guns in Memphis, "the largest and best equipped force" ever sent down to "smash things in north Mississippi." It would be led not by A. J. Smith, however, but by Brig. Gen. Sam Sturgis, a veteran Federal cavalry commander. "I have sent Sturgis down to take command," Sherman notified Grant, "and whip Forrest."[13]

Forrest turned about promptly from Russellville and headed back west to Tupelo. Bell's Brigade, serving as his advance, reached the latter place on June 4. Lee came up from Meridian two days later and conferred with Forrest to determine how to deal with Sturgis. At this time the main Yankee column was reported to be at Salem, Mississippi, some fifty miles to the west. To assist Forrest in the fight that seemed certain to come, Brig. Gen. Philip D. Roddey, commander of Confederate cavalry in North Alabama, offered to reinforce him with a brigade under Col. William A. Johnson, currently stationed on the Memphis and Charleston Railroad at Cherokee Station. Colonel Johnson was directed to link up with Forrest at Baldwyn, north of Tupelo.

Lee and Forrest hastened to Baldwyn where they established their headquarters and ordered up Buford and his division from Tupelo. Initially Forrest had intended for Buford to join them at Baldwyn, but upon learning the main Yankee column was pressing southwest, attempting to cross the Hatchie River, he decided to move his base of operations even farther north to Booneville, some twenty-five miles above Tupelo, midway between that point and Corinth.

While Forrest hurried north, Lee took a train south to Okolona to rally more troops and convert Tupelo into a staging area for an anticipated battle just below, in the Okolona vicinity. Buford, however, was to come up to Booneville immediately bringing along Morton's and Rice's batteries. From there Forrest's cavalry could more easily discern Sturgis' intentions and react quickly if Sturgis struck east toward Rienzi and Corinth or southeast toward Baldwyn and Tupelo.[14]

Bell's Brigade pushed hard on June 7, reaching Baldwyn, then set out for Booneville. Considering the jaded condition of the horses having just returned from the aborted Alabama-Tennessee expedition, they made excellent time and displayed good march discipline. Heavy rains had swollen the creeks, unfortunately, and Twenty Mile Creek lay across their path. They found the creek out of its banks, water raging across the bottomland. To make matters worse, two miles beyond flooded Twenty Mile Creek lay yet another obstacle, Wolf Creek. Both needed to be bridged to reach Booneville. Buford demonstrated on-the-spot leadership as he personally supervised the construction work, rushing to defeat the rising, surging water in the bottoms. Even Buford's staff officers joined in the effort, up to their knees and waists in water. To the astonishment of Forrest, Abe Buford, using primarily details from Barteau's and Wilson's regiments, managed to rapidly complete both temporary bridges and cross his cavalry, wagons, and artillery before sunset on June 8.[15]

Buford could not control the rain, however. It poured and continued to pour, ruining the roads, rendering the streams brimful and unfordable, and making even routine marches laborious. Bell's Brigade, upon their arrival in Booneville, received fresh orders from Buford for a new march. It was eat and rest, then back in the saddle and off into the rain and darkness. Dutifully they made their way west about five miles, finally dismounting wearily at Blackland, a village west of Booneville, but strategically located to observe and intercept enemy movements in the direction of Booneville. They paused only long enough to feed and rest their horses, for discouraging word had reached them. A highly mobile enemy force had passed to the north two days earlier and struck Rienzi on the Mobile and Ohio Railroad. In reaction to this news Buford ordered Bell to divide his command. Clark Barteau would make a reconnaissance in force along the Ripley-Rienzi road, serving as a screen for Bell and the remainder of the brigade, who were to march on an interior road to the northeast and occupy Rienzi itself.[16]

In the saddle before dawn, Thursday, June 9, Bell proceeded about ten miles to Rienzi only to find the depot burned, ties piled and burned, and rails twisted like saplings. Village folk informed him the Yankees raiders had struck suddenly, destroyed the railroad for several miles outside town, then ridden off as quickly as they had come, heading north for Corinth along the roadbed of the Mobile and Ohio.

Trouble awaited the intruders, however. The four hundred Yankee raiders, led by Col. Joseph Kargé, encountered John F. Newsom's Nineteenth Tennessee, which deflected the raid away from Corinth by burning the bridge over the Tuscumbia River. Most of Newsom's regiment, which had been detached since May 23, crossed the Tuscumbia as soon as Kargé made off to the west to rejoin Sturgis. The Nineteenth Tennessee Cavalry would come on down the Mobile and Ohio to rejoin Bell at Rienzi. In command was the veteran Lt. Col. Dew M. Wisdom, formerly of the Thirteenth Tennessee Infantry, who had fought beside Bell at Belmont. Wounded twice at that bloody little battle, Wisdom had returned to the army from his home in Purdy as soon as possible. This former newspaperman—articulate, persuasive, and patriotic—would make a strong regimental commander, Bell believed. Clark Barteau and his Second Tennessee Cavalry also made a timely arrival. They had completed their scout along the Ripley-Rienzi road and found the way empty. However, they had learned the enemy was advancing in heavy force south toward Baldwyn and Tupelo.[17]

Bell found himself in no danger at Rienzi. He and his four regiments, some twenty-five hundred strong, were somewhat isolated as the northernmost element of Forrest's command, but Bell knew he was within an easy march of the main body at Booneville. At that little town, Buford and Forrest had concentrated the brigades of Lyon and Rucker, while ten miles below Booneville, at Baldwyn, was Col. William A. Johnson's brigade of Phil Roddey's North Alabama command, newly arrived from Cherokee, Alabama.[18]

Also coming to help was Black Bob McCulloch of Chalmers's Division, who was rushing west by forced marches from Montevallo, Alabama. Stephen D. Lee intended to fight Sturgis at Okolona once he and Forrest had been reinforced by Chalmers and a few troops from Mobile. But Forrest had other ideas. Rather than fall back through Tupelo upon Okolona, Forrest decided to exercise the discretionary authority given him by Lee and move west at dawn, June 10, toward Brice's Crossroads, six miles west of Baldwyn. From that point he might surprise Sturgis's advancing column or, if no advantage presented itself, continue south toward his rendezvous with Lee at some place between Tupelo and Okolona.[19]

Sturgis's cavalry, under Benjamin H. Grierson, a newly appointed brigadier, had halted and encamped at Stubbs's plantation, "on a fine high ridge" some fourteen miles southeast of Ripley and ten miles from Brice's Crossroads, the point where Forrest hoped to give battle with his inferior force of forty-eight hundred effectives. So Forrest moved via Old Carrollville toward Brice's Crossroads with the available cavalry at Booneville—Lyon's and Rucker's brigades—and from Baldwyn—Johnson's brigade. Buford with the two batteries would remain in Booneville awaiting the arrival of Bell.[20]

Back in Rienzi Bell had received orders directly from Forrest, who ordered him to "to have [his] brigade supplied with rations and ready to move at daybreak." At dawn on Friday, June 10, Bell "broke camp, went forward as rapidly as I could" south toward Booneville. "It having rained incessantly for days," Bell noted, "and my horses badly fatigued for the want of rest, and the roads for the first five miles uncommonly rough, it was difficult to make anything like speed."[21]

Bell arrived in Booneville in good time, nevertheless, and learned from Buford that Forrest had departed, taking with him Lyon's and Rucker's troops, and had marched toward Brice's Crossroads. Bell was to follow. Bell drew two days' rations and forage and set out at 7:30 A.M. Although the rain had turned to bright sunshine, the road west was even more miserable than that from Rienzi to Booneville—"saturated with water" and badly rutted. Captain Morton's artillery teams, guns, and caissons floundered in the mud. The gap separating Forrest's force and Bell's lumbering mass of cavalry and caissons began to widen.[22]

Meanwhile, Forrest had determined to strike the enemy column while it was in motion. He would do so with the troops on hand. From his headquarters in Old Carrollville, at the intersection of roads from Baldwyn and Booneville, he sent Lyon's Kentucky Brigade and his escort forward about 10 A.M. "to feel the enemy"—in effect, a feint to buy intelligence and time while his two other brigades came up. Having sent off Hylan Lyon to temporarily impede if not block Sturgis's advance, Forrest now dispatched Major Anderson back down the road toward Booneville. Hurry on, Buford and Bell, he told his conscientious aide-de-camp—"Tell Bell to move up fast and fetch all he's got."[23] Anderson set out at a gallop. When he caught sight of Bell, Anderson reined in his horse and said, "Come as fast as you possibly can." Anderson also handed Buford a dispatch directing him "to send one regiment of Bell's Brigade from Old Carrollville across to the Ripley and Guntown road (Sturgis's line of advance), with orders to gain the rear of the enemy or attack and annoy his rear or flank." This regiment, according to Captain Morton, was "to proceed across country through the woods and farm roads until it struck the road over which Sturgis would pass from Stubbs' plantation to the cross-roads."[24]

Bell eagerly did as ordered. As Major Anderson said, "He was always ready for a fight." His cavalrymen bypassed the two struggling batteries and rushed on "at a gallop."[25]

While Bell rushed to join Forrest, Lyon's Kentuckians had struck and driven back the forward elements of Sturgis's force. The Union line soon stiffened, however, as more and more of Grierson's troopers crossed the narrow bridge over Tishomingo Creek and deployed east of Brice's Crossroads. It was impossible terrain for cavalry, so the Yankees dismounted and spread out, trying to determine the location and strength of their foe. They knew their artillery and infantry would be up presently and, once concentrated, there would be no chance for any Rebel force known to be in North Mississippi to stop them.

Forrest came up just about the time it appeared Lyon's Kentuckians might be overwhelmed. He immediately deployed Johnson's and Rucker's brigades on either side of Lyon. The fighting intensified.[26]

About 11 A.M., but before the first Federal infantry arrived, Tyree Bell rode up and reported to Forrest. It was a most timely arrival, earning for Tyree Bell in Confederate lore the sobriquet "Blücher of Brice's Crossroads."[27]

By that time, the first phase of the battle was over. Forrest's three brigades had fought Grierson's cavalry to a standstill, then driven them back. When Buford arrived somewhat later, he and Forrest conferred about what course of action to take now that Bell's large brigade was on the field and the artillery was at hand. Should they give battle or should they pull off and maintain themselves "between the Federal column and Tupelo," as Lee had planned? According to Capt. F. G. Terry, a member of Buford's staff, Forrest told division commander

★ COL. WILLIAM A. JOHNSON. FROM JOHN A. WYETH, *LIFE OF GENERAL NATHAN BEDFORD FORREST* (1899). LIBRARY OF CONGRESS.

Buford that he intended to follow it, that is, "push his 'column past the crossroads and move on to Tupelo, where we will unite our forces and give the enemy battle.'" Buford answered, "Well, you have all your men on the ground, the enemy is moving rapidly up the Ripley road. It is very hot and . . . [Sturgis's] men will be badly blown when they get up, and I think now is the time to strike him before he gets his men in line." Forrest seized the idea, according to Terry, and ordered up both batteries, placing the eight guns and the brigades of Johnson and Lyon under Buford's command. He himself would take Bell's Brigade and proceed by a farm road to seek the enemy's right flank. While

Buford was to open with the artillery as soon as he and Morton had found the proper position to go into battery, he was to hold back Lyon's and Johnson's attack, Forrest directed, until "you hear me charge." Then Buford was to "press him heavily in the center."[28]

Following this conversation between Forrest and Buford, Forrest sat his mount with Bell, Capt. Tom Henderson (Forrest's chief of scouts), and Major Anderson by his side. Forrest turned to Bell and directed that he have his men mount and move out to the left.

Bell passed the march order to his regimental commanders, then, accompanied by Forrest and his escort, he led his three remaining regiments down a farm lane until they struck the Ripley-Guntown-Fulton road about a mile southeast of Brice's Crossroads. At this point Bell's column turned up the Ripley-Fulton road and proceeded north until they came abreast of Rucker's Eighteenth Mississippi Battalion off to the right (east) of the road. Once he made contact with Rucker's right, just before noon, Bell had his troopers dismount. He deployed Russell's regiment on the Eighteenth's left, then positioned Wilson's Sixteenth (Twenty-first); on Russell's left across the road. Somewhat to the left and rear in echelon formation, he placed Dew Wisdom's Nineteenth (Newsom's) Tennessee Cavalry. To protect Wisdom's (and the brigade's) left flank, Bell looked to Forrest's Escort, and Capt. H. A. Tyler's squadron from Lyon's Twelfth Kentucky Mounted Infantry and Col. William L. Duff's Eighth Mississippi Cavalry, which had been detached temporarily from Rucker's command.[29]

As his troopers dismounted and prepared to deploy into line, Bell realized, "the disparagement in numbers we had to fight, made the eighth man horseholder instead of the fourth." Then, instead of forming them in line, skirmisher-fashion, Bell decided to put them in line of battle—reminiscent of the Twelfth Tennessee Infantry days—which would concentrate their firepower and facilitate his control of their movements. So his troopers took their places in line with stray minie balls smacking into the bushes and trees around them. Soon all was in readiness, and about 1:30 P.M. they launched their assault along the Ripley-Fulton road.[30]

The Union infantry had now come up and also taken their places in the semicircular formation Sturgis established. Those immediately confronting Bell enjoyed the advantage of holding higher ground, while Bell's men would have to push forward over uneven ground thickly covered with tangled undergrowth and blackjack. The terrain, on the other hand, did offer Bell the advantage of concealment as his troops closed on the Yankee position. "Owing to the density of the undergrowth," Forrest reported, "Colonel Bell was compelled to advance within thirty yards of the enemy before assaulting him." Bell did not have his men charge wildly, but judiciously kept them in hand, aligned as well as possible. They advanced slowly and deliberately, firing as rapidly as they could.[31]

Upon reaching open ground, Bell ordered the three regiments to attack with a rush over the few acres immediately about the William Brice house. Once they emerged from the dense thicket, however, the Yankees spotted them and the blue line of infantry erupted in a blaze of musketry fire. A number of these enemy troops, unknown to Bell and to the dismay of his men, had been armed with repeating rifles. Bell and his staff made a conspicuous target. After going but a short distance, 1st. Lt. John L. Bell, brigade inspector general, was shot off his horse, mortally wounded.[32] Colonel Bell kept his brigade "firing and moving, moving and firing." He knew too well to order his men to "stand and fight" the blue infantry in line of battle. He would be asking too much. "I don't think there were any troops on earth that could have stood and felt the mortality without faltering."[33]

Slipping to the side, making short rushes, giving ground, advancing obliquely, Bell attempted to close the distance, aiming primarily at the big house in the distance. He could see the enemy now, quite clearly. They were lying down, "right in front of Brice's house," partially concealed behind temporary breastworks, piled fence rails, marked here and there with a crude bit of abatis fashioned from the "brushy-topped back-jacks." Immediately ahead of Bell, Capt. Joe Hibbitt went down, "dead right at his post." Hibbitt was one of Milton Russell's original company commanders and one of his most dependable. "Moving steadily forward but a short distance farther, my own horse was shot," Bell recorded. "And a little farther on, my son, Isaac T. Bell, my aide-de-camp at the time, was shot off his horse." Isaac was gravely wounded, being struck in the left arm and side.[34]

Bell knew he must act quickly, not only to save Isaac, but to save his command. He turned to his friend Maj. Bob Caldwell, "the only staff officer I had with me at the time," and told him to "take my son off the battlefield." After Caldwell had moved back into the woods with Isaac, Bell summoned "a little courier," one of Bell's Babies who was close by, a boy in his late teens known to be "sprightly and quick." He asked the young man if he remembered the spot "where we left General Forrest when we formed the line of battle." Can you find it, Bell asked. The young private said he could. "I told him to go as fast as his horse would carry him and tell General Forrest that if I did not get reinforcements I could not stay where I was."[35]

The situation had become desperate. Andrew Wilson's Sixteenth Tennessee Cavalry, guiding on the Ripley road, momentarily found themselves flanked and enfiladed. Struck by murderous volleys, with eleven of their officers wounded, Wilson's men broke to the rear. At this crucial moment, Dew Wisdom's regiment came up on the left side of the road with 250 men and attempted valiantly to stabilize Wilson's left. Aided by Wisdom's troops and attacks and demonstrations against the Union right from Forrest's Escort and Tyler's squadron, the two battered regiments were able to return to their place in line and fight on. They struggled to regain the initiative by renewing the advance down the Ripley-Fulton road, aiming straight at William Brice's two-story house.[36]

About this time Bell's young courier rode up, having made the circuit to Forrest's headquarters "in a wonderful short time." He told the colonel that General Forrest wanted the brigade to hold fast. He would "send a section of Morton's Battery to our relief as quick as they could move."[37]

A section of guns? With the two lines so close? Bell had wanted more troopers, musket-fire. "It sounded ridiculous to send a section of Morton's Battery to my relief," Bell thought, and "I made some very arch remark." Bell apparently turned about as he spoke and, to his astonishment, there was Forrest. "He had mounted his horse and followed the little courier so closely that he could hear what I said." Forrest said firmly, "Stay on the field. I am here and I will stay as long as you live." Up with Forrest came Morton, not with the section Bell had requested, but with his entire four-gun battery.[38]

The Yankees, sensing victory, seemed to be fighting with even greater determination. They counterattacked from behind their rail fence. On they came across one of the open fields to within thirty paces. Bell's cavalrymen put aside their muskets, drew their trusty Navy Colts, and finally repelled the enemy with "sheer valor and tenacity." We were "standing so close to them," Bell remembered, "that we almost made a fence with their wounded and dead and they arose to run." The issue seemed to have been settled, Bell's misgivings notwithstanding, by an "artillery attack." All of Morton's guns were up and went into action, firing at point-blank range against the Federals. The impact of the sudden appearance of Morton was aided dramatically by a highly effective, indeed disconcerting, counterattack by Johnson's brigade, on the extreme Confederate right against an enemy force that had wedged in between his own and Lyon's Brigade.[39]

The Federal line to Bell's front sagged, then broke, as Bell's and Rucker's men took advantage of the splendid artillery support and charged across the open ground, cheering at the top of their lungs. "We pressed forward after them," Bell noted, "and at the creek some three quarters of a mile or more from where they broke, they made a temporary stand, but as we rushed upon them, they broke again and made a rapid retreat."[40]

Capt. H. A. Tyler saw Bell and Rucker at this time, "both leading their brigades up to the cross-roads and General Forrest. It was but a few minutes when we all met at the cross-roads . . . , a happy and enthusiastic band." Many of the Yankees sought refuge in a ravine, west of the Brice house, which led into Tishomingo Creek, but this proved a death trap as Rice's and Morton's batteries continued their advance and poured canister into the confused, tangled mass of the enemy. Forrest added to their misery by reversing three of the guns captured at the Brice place and turning them on the retreating Federals. Many fled down the Ripley road toward the narrow wooden bridge across Tishomingo Creek, but found it clogged and blocked with wagons. Many tried jumping into the creekbed itself only to find themselves again targets for the guns of Morton and Rice when they emerged on the opposite bank. Capt. Mercer Otey of Forrest's staff, who had seen many battlefields, remarked, "I never saw since Bull Run such total confusion; they were terror-stricken."[41]

Helping dislodge the enemy at Brice's Crossroads was Clark Barteau and about 250 of his regiment. As directed, they had found the enemy rear and attacked while the battle raged on the south side of the creek.[42] Barteau's unexpected appearance caused consternation. The Federal teamsters panicked and pandemonium spread down the road, through the Union baggage train to the baggage-guard and even to the trailing artillery. Word reached the front that a Confederate brigade blocked the road. To meet this surprising and violent envelopment, nearly all of Sturgis's cavalry turned about, abandoning the main body fighting Forrest across Tishomingo Creek.[43]

Vigorous pursuit was imperative, but it was not easy to pry men loose from the captured wagons and spoils of war. In a few minutes the horse-holders brought forward Bell's horses, and many troopers gave them a rubdown and allowed them to "partake of the bountiful refreshments" by "gorging them on Federal forage."[44]

Most of the cavalry, led by those who had served as horse-holders, soon remounted and attempted to follow the enemy on the narrow road with thick woods pressing on either side. Even the artillery pushed down the road after the fleeing enemy, opening on them whenever they attempted to make a stand. When Sturgis's African American brigade sought to establish a blocking position across the Ripley road, Morton's gunners loaded their pieces with double-shotted canister and opened fire "with appalling effect." These black regiments broke and fled. As they did so, they ripped off their badges that read "Remember Fort Pillow" and threw them away.[45]

After fleeing two miles down the Ripley road, the retreating Federals pulled themselves together and made a strong stand, even launching a counterattack. This half-hour struggle ended, however, when Rice's battery came up, unlimbered, and went into battery, firing double-shotted charges of canister.[46]

★ Defense of North Mississippi, 1864. Courtesy of C. I. Browne.

At this point darkness fell. Forrest's pursuit faltered as the cavalry and artillery batteries became entangled and jumbled and exhausted. The pursuit stopped before midnight as the weary units pulled up and sought to reassemble. Forrest permitted most of the command to rest themselves and their animals for two hours, then he ordered the chase renewed. The troopers saddled up once more, happy to find that "the darkness had somewhat diminished." It was now 3 A.M., Saturday, June 11.[47]

The determined pursuit continued with Bell's Brigade replacing Rucker's in the advance. While the main force followed on the road to Ripley, Bell threw out a regiment on either side of the road to mop up enemy stragglers, many "stupidly indifferent to fate." The Federals attempted another stand about four miles east of Ripley, blocking the causeway leading across the Little Hatchie bottom, but were promptly flanked by Forrest personally leading two of Bell's regiments. The enemy now withdrew back upon Ripley itself where they sought to reorganize. Bell dismounted the brigade on a little creek south of Ripley and closed in. "I soon discovered that they had the advantage of me," Bell recounted, "being in the town and having the protection of the buildings to fight behind. I then mounted my brigade as quickly as possible and charged the town by fours. They at once retreated."[48]

Having driven the enemy from Ripley, Bell halted his brigade, allowing them to rest and eat. He saw to it that a wounded Federal colonel, George W. McKaig, 120th Illinois Infantry, was given medical attention, then he himself took the breakfast of "old ham and coffee a plenty" that had been prepared especially for Ben Grierson.[49]

Forrest ended this morning reverie and Bell's Brigade remounted and pressed on, capturing parties of Yankees here and there, until further organized pursuit became impractical. Forrest and Bell had been riding together and, as they neared Salem, Mississippi, the exhausted Forrest stopped. When his horse tripped, he fell off and lay by the roadside for a long while "in a stupor." He asked Bell to turn his brigade over to one of his regimental commanders and come with him to a friend's home where they could get something to eat and rest. Bell, preoccupied with thoughts of Isaac, declined, telling Forrest, "I could not afford to lie down anywhere, short of my hospital."[50]

Bell doggedly ordered his men to press on, and the main body continued on past Salem for twelve miles, then encamped at Davis's Mill on the Wolf River. Fragments of the brigade, almost squads now, would ride northward nearly to LaGrange, still in the hunt. The pursuit was over, nonetheless. Buford was heard to say, "Every damn man with me is sound asleep." Men and mounts had reached the limit of endurance. At this point Bell himself turned back, riding through the night until he reached the battlefield. At Mrs. Brice's house he found Lt. William H. Porter, his young staff officer, dead. Porter had been wounded very close to the house itself "after the victory had been won," according to Will's friend, Lt. Achilles Clark of the Twentieth. Porter was twenty years old and had been a Confederate cadet until joining Bell's staff. He was the youngest brother of Bell's friend Maj. James D. Porter, later governor of Tennessee. "A more gallant young man I never had with me," Bell remarked.

Close by was the field hospital. There he searched for his staff officer, John L. Bell, whom he found dying but "perfectly at himself." He remained with Bell until the end, then had a detail bury him and young Porter. Afterwards he had the badly wounded Isaac carried to the train and placed aboard. He asked Surgeon Tom Prince to stay with Isaac and take the boy to Bell's uncle's home near Macon, Mississippi. Then Bell rode back north, locating his brigade near Salem.[51]

He turned the four regiments about and headed south, passing through Ripley on June 12. Again he put out heavy flank details and succeeded in rounding up Union prisoners by the dozens. After remaining a short time at the battlefield, gazing in wonder and hunting for souvenirs, the brigade continued on, through Guntown to Saltillo, Mississippi, where they encamped, remaining until Tuesday, June 21. That day they faced south yet again and returned to their old campground in Tupelo.[52]

Brice's Crossroads is generally considered Forrest's outstanding battle. It is rare in warfare when cavalry drives infantry from the field, particularly when heavily outnumbered. Forrest brought all his strength to bear in timely combinations, pushing the attacks and the pursuit vigorously.

Tyree Bell's role in this signal victory has been underplayed generally. Perhaps labeling him "the Blücher of this hard-fought field," as Maj. Charles W. Anderson and others have done, indulges in overstatement, but one must acknowledge that Bell's Brigade, in the saddle before dawn, on June 10, made a difficult forced march of twenty-five miles to reach the battlefield. They fought for five hours, then aggressively pursued the enemy an additional fifty miles—all this in less than forty-eight hours. It was one of Bell's regiments that struck the enemy rear and threw a shiver of uncertainty and apprehension into Sturgis's army. The all-out assault of Bell's Brigade over open ground at the Brice house, struggling against well-posted dismounted Federal cavalry and infantry, drew the attention and the volleys from the enemy strong point. Yet they continued their attack and ultimately broke through. Bell, as usual, exposed himself boldly, perilously. Luckily, he escaped being struck down. For a general officer to have lost three members of his small staff (two killed, one seriously wounded) and his own mount attests to the severity and gravity of the situation.[53]

Forrest's reaction to Bell's call for help was magnificent, his use of a classic artillery attack audacious and decisive. Although enormous credit has been given John Morton and his "Bull Pups," one cannot but wonder what role Hylan Lyon played, what influence this highly trained and proficient artillery officer had in this Mexican War–style of attack.[54]

Forrest trusted Tyree Bell and knew how to employ him. In his report of battle (neither Bell nor Buford nor any of Bell's regimental commanders made reports), Forrest showed his appreciation of this most dependable officer, crediting him with displaying "great gallantry" and exhibiting "coolness, skill, courage, and ability."[55]

One must commend Bell's subordinate commanders as well. Clark Barteau proved once again not only capable of independent operations, but skillful and imaginative. Dew Wisdom handled the Nineteenth Tennessee splendidly. Andrew Wilson, although thrown back, rebounded, fought well, and displayed a resilience confounding to his opponents. The unassuming Milton Russell was simply reliable, conscientious, and effective.

The brigade had been hurt, however. Without counting Barteau's losses, Bell had suffered 40 percent of the Confederate casualties, particularly some company-grade officers he could not replace, leading one to wonder if Bell's Brigade would be able to perform as well next time.[56]

12

Harrisburg

While Tyree Bell and his brigade relaxed in camp above Tupelo, Bedford Forrest worried over intelligence obtained from Memphis. A fresh expedition was to be sent against him, it appeared, this time using portions, perhaps all, of two divisions of Federal infantry, tough veterans of the Red River Campaign. These men of the Sixteenth and Seventeenth Corps were commanded by Maj. Gen. Andrew J. Smith, an experienced and highly regarded lieutenant of Sherman's. It appeared Smith had wasted little time. Already Rebel scouts stationed in the Memphis vicinity reported the tracks of the Memphis and Charleston Railroad groaning from trainloads of troops, horses, and artillery rushing east. The Wolf River had been bridged; Federal General Ben Grierson and thirty-two hundred cavalry patrolled aggressively the Moscow-LaGrange-Saulsbury railroad corridor. By June 27, 1864, it was confirmed, A. J. Smith had arrived in LaGrange with almost his entire infantry contingent; Grierson and his troopers, from all reports, had begun a push further east—to Saulsbury—in great strength.[1]

These repeated Federal incursions into North Mississippi were quite clear in purpose. As Sherman advanced deeper and deeper into Georgia, he had grown even more apprehensive about his extended lines of communication, particularly the two railroads from Nashville to Stevenson, Alabama. Truly they represented Sherman's lifelines. The Confederates realized this also, of course. Forrest should be ordered to break these lines and disrupt Sherman's logistics, so Gen. Joseph E. Johnston and Georgia's Gov. Joseph E. Brown told President Jefferson Davis repeatedly. If an interruption of supply were to occur, even if it were only for ten days, they argued, Sherman's large army, which consumed

★ MAJ. GEN. ANDREW J. SMITH. LIBRARY OF CONGRESS.

supplies at a tremendous rate, would be embarrassed, perhaps compelled to break off the campaign against Atlanta.[2]

Sherman had taken measures, however, to preempt any such course of action. He sought to protect these Tennessee railroads by stationing troops along the tracks at critical spots, constructing a line of blockhouses, and keeping strong mobile reaction forces in the general area. To engage Stephen D. Lee's attention, to throw him off balance, Sherman put five widely spread expeditions in motion against Lee's Department of Alabama, Mississippi, and East Louisiana. The fifth such invasion he aimed directly at Forrest with the intent of keeping the raider fully occupied in Mississippi and thus neutralized. "I have two officers at Memphis that will fight all the time—A. J. Smith and [Joseph A.] Mower," Sherman wrote the War Department. "I will order them to make up a force and go out and follow Forrest to the death if it costs 10,000 lives and breaks the Treasury. There will never be peace in Tennessee till Forrest is dead."[3]

It was the responsibility of Stephen Dill Lee, newly appointed lieutenant general and commander of this huge, virtually indefensible, geographic department, to frustrate Sherman's strategy. He believed the best way was to meet and defeat A. J. Smith's invaders with concentrated and strengthened forces. Once Smith had been finished off in the manner of Sturgis at Brice's Crossroads, opportunities for different strategic combinations would multiply. To effect this concentration, Lee ordered Chalmers to move up from Columbus to Verona, Mississippi (immediately south of Tupelo), and McCulloch's Brigade to push out to Ripley. Lee took Roddey's Division from Alabama and stationed it in North Mississippi at Corinth, and he brought up a brigade from the Yazoo area and assigned it to Buford's Division, thus adding almost six thousand men to Forrest's command.[4]

This brigade of Arkansas and Mississippi troopers from the Yazoo country was commanded by Col. Hinchie P. Mabry, former Texas lawyer and politician, a man who had gained wide combat experience in the Trans-Mississippi campaigns and who had now exercised cavalry brigade responsibility for over a year. Recognized as "absolutely fearless and a strong disciplinarian," Mabry would prove a reliable partner for Bell.[5]

Forrest also had anticipated A. J. Smith's plunge into North Mississippi, and had initiated measures of his own. Scouting intensified throughout the area from Memphis to Pocahontas, and he established a strong outpost to the west at Abbeville and another of brigade strength to the northwest at Ripley. On Wednesday, July 6, 1864, scouts reported Smith had marched out of LaGrange moving toward Ripley, apparently an intermediate objective on the way to Tupelo. Forrest ordered Buford to send one of his brigades to Ellistown, midway between Ripley and Tupelo, astride Smith's most likely route of advance.[6]

Buford assigned Bell the mission of establishing himself at Ellistown and watching for Smith's approach from Ripley. Bell set out from his camp near Tupelo at 5 A.M., July 8, 1864, and upon his arrival at Ellistown later that day, he dropped off two regiments, Second and Sixteenth Tennessee, in the town itself while he rode north to Kelly's Mill on the Tallahatchie River. There he stationed

Russell's Twentieth and Newsom's Nineteenth (once again led by Dew Wisdom) to watch the road and the river crossings. They only remained in this advanced position one day, however, as Bell received orders to return to Ellistown where he found Abe Buford and Lyon's Kentucky Brigade. All had changed. The Federals had broken off their advance toward Ellistown and switched roads—west to the Ripley-Pontotoc road. In the meantime, Clark Barteau had been sent ahead on an independent mission west toward New Albany, Mississippi, to observe the Ripley-Pontotoc road and to oppose A. J. Smith's advancing Federals. Buford and Bell followed, but, learning Smith had seized New Albany, they made a night march to the south of that point—toward Pontotoc, hoping to reach that town in force before the Yankees. They were joined in this night march by Hinchie Mabry's Brigade, fresh from Saltillo. This would be Mabry's first operation with Buford's Division. Forrest directed Buford to close in on Smith's column, "to hang on his flanks, and to develop his strength, but to avoid a general engagement."[7]

A. J. Smith had shoved Barteau out of a strong position by force of numbers and kept pushing him south toward Pontotoc. Barteau would be joined on the Pontotoc-Okolona road by Black Bob McCulloch's Brigade on July 10, and both units would continue skirmishing with the forward elements of Smith's column. Slapping at the head of Smith's column did not satisfy Forrest, however. He wanted more, so he ordered Barteau on yet another independent "find and strike the enemy rear" mission, but while Barteau rode off with high expectations of repeating his Brice's Crossroads success, nothing appears to have come of his little expedition and Barteau was ordered to rejoin Bell.[8]

Bell's horses were worn out by the time he and Buford passed through Pontotoc. Buford decided that if the coming fight developed into a battle of maneuver, the brigade would be in questionable condition, "having no forage nor any prospect of getting any." Buford wanted Bell's Brigade fit for a ranging operation, so he ordered Bell to turn about and march his brigade south and feed his animals at the supply center in Okolona. Thus Bell continued on, welcoming Barteau's roaming regiment back to the fold as the brigade rode through Prairie Mound. They reached Okolona on the evening of the July 10 and would remain encamped there until the night of July 12.[9]

That evening Forrest ordered Bell to move out on the Pontotoc-Okolona road (Okolona Stage Road) the following morning. He and Lee planned to block that route at Pinson's Hill, a strong point overlooking Chiwapa Creek, a fine spot in which to offer battle. Bell and his men dutifully rode out Wednesday morning, July 13, 1864, and about five miles below Pontotoc they moved off left of the road "some distance," dismounted, and formed in line of battle. Bell, like Forrest, admired this promising terrain at Pinson's Hill, and his brigade set to work chopping down trees to obstruct passage through a creek bottom and setting up log breastworks. They worried in vain, however. The strength of the Rebel defensive position had so impressed Smith that he suddenly broke off his advance on Okolona, moving by the left flank to the east, over to the Pontotoc-Tupelo road. Meanwhile his cavalry remained in position, demonstrating before the Confederates on the Okolona Stage Road.[10]

In a short time, new orders arrived for Bell; the bulk of the enemy force had withdrawn to Pontotoc with the purpose, it appeared, of striking directly at Tupelo. Mabry's Brigade was to closely follow the enemy's movement and press their rear, while Bell's Brigade was to remount and turn north toward the Pontotoc-Tupelo road. Before they had proceeded but a short distance, however, they learned definitely that the Federals were moving east on that road. Tupelo not only seemed to be in their sights, but within their grasp. "It was determined at once," Bell reported, "to strike the enemy a severe blow, if possible," to hit their right flank while in motion, to intercept the Yankees at Verona. To accomplish this, Abe Buford led his division onto the Birmingham road, which offered the possibility of a flank attack against Smith's column advancing on the Pontotoc-Tupelo road. Buford, who was riding with Bell at the head of the brigade (the advance of the division), directed his friend and his troops to move forward quickly across Coonewah Creek and strike Smith's Federals at Coonewah Crossroads, some five miles west of Tupelo.[11]

Bell had his men dismount, cross the muddy creek, and move up close to the Pontotoc-Tupelo road, at a point designated as Coonewah Crossroads. "The weather was exceedingly hot," remembered Sgt. Gabriel J. Puryear, "and a great many of our men got overheated." Division commander Buford took charge at this point, deploying Barteau parallel, but quite close to the road, with Russell's Twentieth on his left. As Russell moved into position, however, Bell's short and incompletely formed line became heavily engaged with the strong flank guards of Smith's compact infantry column. Volleys were fired. Losses mounted, particularly in the Second Tennessee. Before Wilson and Wisdom could arrive in support, the two lead regiments broke, having been assailed from the front and flank by heavy numbers of blue infantry and cavalry. At this critical moment Ed Crossland and his Kentuckians came up. There had been another of those sudden command switches, with Col. Crossland replacing Hylan B. Lyon in command of the brigade. The able Lyon, newly appointed brigadier general, had been given an ad hoc infantry "division" that had been thrown together hurriedly in Tupelo by Forrest in early July.[12] Lyon would be missed as a field commander in the division, but Edward Crossland and Bell had worked together for six months, which was reassuring. Of course, Crossland lacked the experience and professionalism of Lyon, but this thirty-seven-year-old ex-sheriff and politician matched Lyon's combativeness, which pleased Forrest. He could lead and enthuse citizen soldiers, a throwback to the ill-fated Albert P. Thompson, although Crossland was known as a more deliberate commander.[13]

"When I arrived," Crossland would later report, "Bell's brigade was falling back in some confusion." Crossland reacted promptly, dismounting and forming a line of battle shielding Bell's fleeing troopers. An irritated Bell would later report, "No blame can certainly be attached to the men for falling back, as they were completely overpowered and forced to retire. . . . The attack [led by Buford] was made, doubtless, thinking the other brigade of the division [Crossland's] was near enough to come up to my assistance." Bell's men fled to the rear almost a mile and began to reform under Crossland's protection on the Birmingham Road. Joseph Mower's Federals, having smashed Bell's Brigade at Coonewah Crossroads, did not pursue, however. They had a fixed purpose: to station themselves within striking distance of the Mobile and Ohio Railroad at Tupelo. So Smith's victorious infantrymen returned to the Pontotoc-Tupelo road, reformed into column, and continued their march.

Meanwhile Bell reorganized, no doubt grateful that the fight had been broken off. "Our loss in killed and wounded for the time the brigade was engaged was quite heavy," he reported, "each regiment sacrificing some of its best officers and bravest men." Bell and his brigade encamped close to the place where they had fought and tried to rest and recover from their failed attack. They enjoyed precious little time, however, for not long after dark orders came to be "saddled and ready to move at 2 o'clock the next morning."[14]

Thus Buford's ambitious flank attack against Smith's tight, disciplined column had proved ineffective, as had a similar attack a few miles to the west by Chalmers. Standard Forrest tactics were no longer a surprise. The enemy, having handily beaten off Forrest's two harassing attacks, pushed steadily toward Harrisburg, just west of Tupelo. Harrisburg in July 1864 consisted of a hamlet at a crossroads, a few houses "scattered at wide intervals over a somewhat commanding ridge." In actuality, the village had been absorbed by Tupelo with the coming of the Mobile and Ohio Railroad.

As Smith's infantry approached Harrisburg, Grierson's cavalry continued on to Tupelo and began destroying the railroad, with wrecking details ranging north and south along the Mobile and Ohio. The Federal infantry, pestered, but not dangerously threatened by Forrest's attacks, marched into the night. Knowing they were virtually surrounded by Confederates of undetermined strength, but well-documented aggressiveness, the Union soldiers halted in Harrisburg. Smith and Mower set to work furiously throwing up a defensive line. Down came houses and up went breastworks. On top of these strong timbers they piled dirt, and by morning on July 14 they had constructed a formidable position nearly two miles long, facing west. Smith's left flank was refused (thrown back), shielding the wagon train which was guarded, as at Brice's Crossroads, by Col. Edward Bouton's First Brigade U.S. Colored Troops (four infantry regiments and two batteries). Grierson's cavalry took position on either flank and secured the rear. These Federal dispositions, however, were known to the Confederates, to Forrest himself, for, as usual, he had made a daring personal reconnaissance, riding entirely around the army of A. J. Smith during the night.[15]

Forrest would later declare the enemy position to have been "impregnable," yet when Stephen D. Lee determined to attack, the fiercely independent Forrest, for reasons unknown and debated to this day, "acquiesced" in the decision. As though it had been fated, that terrible Thursday, July 14, 1864, Forrest and Lee would violate military principle and common sense with disturbing and disheartening results.[16]

Smith held the higher ground with superior numbers and splendid cover. Forrest's men, on the other hand, needed to advance over open, rising ground, in Bell's case three hundred yards. Thus eleven thousand "well-entrenched" Yankees awaited attack by about six thousand Rebels. Stephen D. Lee, a trained artillery officer, had seen fit to disperse his five field batteries among his brigades of dismounted cavalry; A. J. Smith, on the other hand, had his six batteries well in hand, capable of concentrated fire, anchoring his contracted line. At least one of Smith's batteries, if not attacked frontally, could shift its trails to the south, enabling it to enfilade almost the entire open space over which the Confederates must charge. Abe Buford offered an unsolicited opinion to his commanders: "I modestly expressed the opinion that the attack should not be a direct one," but Buford drank too much and talked too much. His desire for a flank attack was but a whisper on the wind.[17]

Buford's Division would attack the right or north end of Smith's line, charging down the Pontotoc-Tupelo road, Mabry on the left of the road, Crossland on the right. Bell, with his battered brigade, would advance immediately behind Mabry in close support. In reserve, standing to Buford's rear was Chalmers's division, and in deep reserve on the left stood Lyon's shadow division of infantry. These three divisions (and four batteries) on the Rebel left would be commanded by Lee. To the right of Crossland was Phil Roddey's Division with Hudson's Battery, the Alabama cavalrymen widely dispersed in the woods south of Harrisburg. Forrest, for reasons known only to him and Lee, would command Roddey's sector, not the men to whom he was accustomed.[18]

Things went wrong from the outset. To establish a connection with Roddey's line, Crossland had his men oblique to the right; Mabry, rather than dress on Crossland's left, obliqued to the left through a cornfield, attempting, it is supposed, to hook around the enemy's right. These maneuvers opened up the center of Buford's line, and when Buford reported the resulting interval, Lieutenant General Lee ordered him to bring up Bell and fill it.[19]

Tyree Bell had been waiting, under orders to be "ready to move at 2 o'clock" that morning, but it was after dawn when the attack order finally reached him. After moving a short distance by horseback, the brigade occupied its assigned position behind Mabry, left of the Harrisburg road. They dismounted and placed their horses in the hands of the horse-holders. Then these West Tennesseans began to move forward in support of Mabry—Barteau's Second on the left flank (and ultimately on the left flank of the army), Wilson's Sixteenth and Newsom's Nineteenth in the center, with Russell's Twentieth on the right of the extended brigade front. Off to his right Bell could hear Crossland's men raise the Rebel Yell and see them rush forward. But the Kentuckians were too early—Mabry was still forming in the woods. When Mabry did emerge from the woodline, Crossland's attack was spent, his brigade beginning to stream to the rear, badly broken. It was now Mabry's turn and across a large open field he charged, rapidly driving in the skirmishers who opposed him. Once the Yankee skirmishers had filed back into their supporting breastworks, the enemy fortifications belched fire, striking Mabry's approaching line of battle with "a terrific fire of small-arms." And when he approached even closer, the Federal fieldpieces opened on him and the musket fire grew even heavier. If this were not bad enough, the Yankee riflemen had the advantage of the sun at their backs; the Rebels had to squint into the low morning glare. Nothing seemed right. Crossland's Kentucky Brigade to Mabry's right had been blown apart, but Roddey had not yet attacked, enabling the Federals to concentrate their fire first on Crossland, then on Mabry. It was devastating.[20]

Buford had watched in agony as Crossland and his boys, so hasty in their attack as to charge unsupported and clumped together in reckless disregard of elementary infantry tactics, buckled and fell back into the timberline.[21] Then he watched the fire of A. J. Smith's infantry and artillery shift to Mabry's Mississippi brigade. Their firepower was terribly effective, and in a few minutes the Yankee riflemen, as Mabry would report, "left my line almost like a line of skirmishers." To save what remained of his brigade, Mabry ordered the survivors to lie "down in a hollow and behind a low fence which covered a part of my front." From there he and his Mississippians would observe while Bell came up and went into position, resting his right on the Tupelo-Pontotoc road. Ahead, Bell saw about three hundred yards of open ground between the woodline where he had formed his line of battle and the Yankee fortifications. The space was daunting, but for that matter, his position in the woods offered less protection than might be expected—being so open as to provide visibility to Mower's waiting and watching infantry.[22]

Unlike the Kentuckians, who broke formation early in their enthusiastic charge, Bell's men had fired at least one volley from the edge of the woods before advancing deliberately and in good order across the open cornfield. Bell felt confident, despite the calamity that had befallen the Kentuckians. The breastworks ahead, while formidable, could not compare in strength to those at Fort Pillow. Furthermore, General Lee, who was up with him, had promised, "Sir, I hold in reserve reinforcements for you, and I will see that you are relieved at the proper time." With that assurance, Bell stepped out of the woodline toward the enemy breastworks. His dismounted troopers would advance, stop, fire a volley, then advance again. Accompanying them was Lt. Tully Brown's section of Morton's battery in a risky two-gun artillery attack, the same device that had worked so effectively at Brice's Crossroads. The Yankees' fire grew heavier as they came closer. Muskets and cannon shifted toward them from left and right, and Mower's defenders enjoyed direct frontal fire and enfilade fire. The concentrated fire was lethal. When Bell's Brigade approached within seventy-five yards of the enemy, Mower had his infantry rise in their works and fire a volley in the faces of the Tennesseans' attacking line. The Yankee volleys were disciplined, accurate, "a most galling fire." Tully Brown's section was put out of action with a high percentage of his gunners wounded and every horse of one piece disabled and a wheel of another destroyed by enemy artillery solid shot. Despite the active fire of Morton's other section (Sale's) and Rice's Battery in support of Bell and Mabry, the opposing infantry's musketry and cannon fire had not been suppressed. Indeed, one of Barteau's privates would confide to his diary, "Never had such an appalling fire of musketry and artillery blazed and gushed in the face of the Second Tennessee before."

"The place was truly a hot one," Bell would write a week later. "The enemy's position strong and commanding, well selected, and well fortified." The Union troops also enjoyed the exceptionally fine combat leadership of Joseph Mower. The loss of Bell's brigade in killed and wounded, both officers and men, was "immense." Struck by almost point-blank frontal fire as well as by oblique and even enfilade fire from the right, Bell's men could suffer no more and abandoned the open field, fleeing back to the cover of the trees. Bell's Brigade was wrecked, and it was only with the greatest effort that Bell could rally them even deep in the woods. If there had been a determined counterattack at this time, Bell's Brigade, bloodied, disorganized, and "fainting from exhaustion," could hardly have maintained itself, even had they been able to establish an emergency line of battle. Indeed, Buford's Division itself was badly broken and quite vulnerable. Mercifully, these brigades were allowed to withdraw from the field, their retreat covered by Chalmers's Division. As feared, the Federals under Joseph Mower soon did come out of their prepared defenses and advanced over the field strewn with Buford's dead and wounded, but the "vicious southern sun" and prudence halted Mower's counterattack. The Yankees would content themselves that night with the burning of Harrisburg.[23]

Under cover of darkness the Confederates pulled back a few miles below Tupelo and licked their wounds. Forrest, doubtless puzzled and dismayed by the stinging repulse of his Tennessee-Kentucky division, came upon Abe Buford and asked about his men. Buford, an emotional man, reportedly covered his face with his arm and replied, "I have no command. They were all killed."[24]

General Lee made a point to seek out Bell and said, "Sir, I owe you a great apology. I regret that through the excitement of the day I did not have you relieved earlier than I did." Years later Bell would write Morton, "It is known to everybody acquainted with the history of Harrisburg that we had on the first day over 2,000 infantrymen [Lyon's 'Division'] sent from Mobile who never fired a gun." Apologies or not, there was to be little rest for Bell and his men that awful night.[25]

Apparently concerned about a sudden swing to the south by A. J. Smith, Forrest ordered Buford to have Bell's Brigade remount. They were to move to the south themselves and take a position at the crossroads at Dr. Calhoun's house, thus enabling them to resist any enemy advance from Harrisburg to Verona. To give depth to the defense, Buford had Colonel Crossland place the Kentucky Brigade midway between Bell and the enemy at Harrisburg.[26]

The next morning surprising word came to the defeated and badly weakened Confederates. Smith appeared to be readying his army not for attack, but for a return to Memphis. Once Lee and Forrest had satisfied themselves that the Federals did not intend to press "with resolution" their advantage won July 14, they determined to seize the initiative, assume the tactical offensive. Bell, under orders from Buford, moved up the Tupelo-Verona road and united with Crossland. Together the two diminished brigades would "feel for" and attack A. J. Smith's left. Bell and Crossland formed an extended front and advanced, driving the Union skirmishers back almost a mile to Smith's main line. Perhaps because of the terrible leadership vacuum in Bell's brigade, as they closed with the enemy the four regiments fell under the immediate command of Bell, Buford, and even Forrest himself. They were in no condition to launch an assault, however, and Forrest and Buford wisely halted Bell's and Crossland's brigades before they struck the Union main line of resistance. Instead, a heavy protective skirmish screen was thrown out. Buford and Bell could see the troops were not capable of immediate offensive action. Thirst, the oppressive heat, and memory of yesterday had almost taken the fight out of them. "I had eighty men carried off the field that morning," reported Buford. In the early afternoon, however, came the welcome news that the enemy was withdrawing toward Ellistown. "Pursue him vigorously," Forrest told Buford. The man seemed to be living a dream.[27]

Tyree Bell and his men again led the advance, with Andrew Wilson and his Sixteenth Tennessee as the point regiment for the brigade. Newsom's regiment left the column, swinging wide into Tupelo itself and then back seeking the enemy left flank. Barteau and Russell, having taken a position in support of Wilson's Sixteenth, temporarily moved off the Verona road to allow Rice's Battery to pass through so it could work with the Sixteenth Tennessee.

Wilson pressed the pursuit to Old Town Creek, five miles northwest of Tupelo. There he confronted the Yankees drawn up in "a strong position on the crest of a hill." The firing grew brisk as Wilson deployed and continued forward. When Russell and Barteau came on line, the attack gathered greater momentum. It seemed a miracle: Bell's boys succeeded in driving the enemy rear guard off the hill and into the creek bottom. The velocity of the attack could not be sustained, however, and grew feeble as the enemy poured in infantry and cavalry reinforcements. Again it was Mower who reacted quickly and forcefully, and who, according to Dr. Wyeth, "handled his troops with his usual skill and courage." Once the front had been stabilized, the Union cavalry counterattacked, driving Bell's Brigade before them. Fortunately for Bell, elements of Crossland's Brigade came up in support at the critical moment, providing cover for Bell's troopers fleeing "in great disorder." The Kentuckians poured a volley into the pursuing enemy cavalry, stunning them and inflicting "very heavy" loss, but soon they too found themselves thrown back and were saved only by the arrival of Forrest with Rice's Battery and McCulloch's Brigade of Chalmers's Division. The Confederates had to fight desperately simply to disengage. This fight, usually referred to as "Old Town Creek," proved costly. Crossland fell seriously wounded and Forrest sustained a disabling wound in the foot.[28]

Saturday morning, July 16, Chalmers's Division took up the pursuit of the deliberately retiring A. J. Smith. His cavalry nipped at the rear and flanks of Smith's column as it moved north toward Memphis through New Albany and Salem, but once again the Rebel cavalrymen found no openings to exploit. Smith, as usual, had "his column well closed up," observed one of Ed Rucker's privates, "his wagon train well protected, and his flanks covered in an admirable manner." No matter. As one of Forrest's privates would observe later, "Clearly our men were in no condition to make anything more than a spiritless pursuit."[29]

Thus A. J. Smith returned to Memphis, having inflicting severe losses upon Forrest, and having fulfilled his primary mission of keeping the dreaded raider occupied and far away from Sherman's precious line of communications. The battles that Smith fought at Harrisburg and Old Town Creek reflected well upon him and his command, as did their smart approach march and careful withdrawal.[30]

Harrisburg, on the other hand, brought little credit to Bedford Forrest, Stephen D. Lee, or Tyree Bell. Roddey was hardly used in the fighting, and Lyon's reserve "division" never made its appearance. It was an amateurish, bungled battle replete with wrongheaded, confusing, even contradictory orders and poorly coordinated attacks against a superior enemy possessing commanding terrain and prepared defenses. Harrisburg, even in the words of Forrest's admirer and apologist, Robert Selph Henry, was "badly planned and worse executed." The same should be said for the botched ambush at Coonewah Crossroads and Bell's reckless assault at Old Town Creek.[31]

Of Forrest's casualties (210 killed, 1,116 wounded, 49 missing), almost a third belonged to one of his seven brigades—Tyree Bell's Fourth Brigade. Bell lost 5 officers and 42 enlisted killed, 54 officers and 209 wounded and 28 missing—400 men in all—a third of his brigade—over 10 percent of the Confederates engaged. For that matter, Bell's parent unit, Buford's Division, lost over 900 of Forrest's 1,300 casualties.[32]

Although Bell was officially recognized by Forrest and Buford for his "coolness under a most galling fire," his "ready appreciation of positions and full obedience to all orders," his performance at Tupelo is not so easy to assess. He made three frontal attacks, overmatched numerically in all three. Two of these attacks failed outright with heavy loss; the other—at Old Town Creek—after initial success—degenerated rapidly into a stalemate, then, with the arrival of strong enemy reinforcements, a rout.

Five of his regimental commanders fell wounded: Russell, Newsom, Dew Wisdom, Wilson, and Barteau. Indeed, Barteau's Second Tennessee Cavalry ended up on the night of July 14 commanded by a lieutenant—George E. Seay, "his superiors having been killed, wounded, or disabled." Bell's Brigade in the three engagements of July 13–15 had been mangled. "Brave men never marched more fearlessly to death," Chalmers would assert, "than did Forrest's cavalry on that occasion. . . . We were badly defeated, and in a very short time." Ed Bearss, historian of the Battle of Harrisburg and the Tupelo Campaign, contends that these losses suffered by Bell deprived his brigade of its capability "of mounting an effective assault on a Union position. Their combat effectiveness had been destroyed."[33]

Bell, nevertheless, would always be proud of his men at Harrisburg. As an old man, six months before his death, he would write his young friend Morton, "In all the battles that I was engaged in during the time I served under General Forrest, my brigade never was as thoroughly tested in the same length of time of fighting . . . , and I can say to you with great pleasure that there was not a part of the line, from one end to the other, but acquitted itself with the greatest honor that could be attached to a body of soldiers."[34]

13

Cheer Up

Bell's battered brigade spent the remainder of July 1864 in the vicinity of Pikeville, Mississippi, recuperating from the Harrisburg ordeal. It proved a most pleasant interlude. This prairie country below Okolona, this land called Egypt, was rich in corn and watermelons and hogs. The terms "half-rations" and "scant rations" were like bad memories from the past.[1]

Stephen D. Lee was gone, departing Mississippi to assume command of John Bell Hood's Corps in the Army of Tennessee, Hood having relieved Joseph E. Johnston as army commander. Lee's Department of Alabama, Mississippi, and East Louisiana was to be commanded temporarily by Maj. Gen. Dabney H. Maury, an experienced, professional soldier. Maury had been most recently in charge of Mobile and its defenses, an area designated in Confederate officialdom as the District of the Gulf. Maury, discreet, refined, would wisely rely on Forrest and tell him so: "You are accustomed to accomplish the very greatest results with small means when left to your own untrammeled judgment. . . . I intrust to you the operations against the enemy threatening an invasion of north Mississippi."[2]

Appreciative of Maury's confidence, Forrest responded that being too weak to risk a general engagement with the invading enemy, he nevertheless would do all within his power "to harass, annoy, and force the enemy back." He reminded Maury that the battles at Brice's Crossroads and Harrisburg had reduced the effectives of his command to little over five thousand. The capable Hylan B. Lyon had been promoted to brigadier and left the department, Rucker and McCulloch were wounded, leaving Colonel Bell as his only experienced brigade commander, and even in Bell's Brigade, Forrest pointed out, "the greater number of field officers are wounded or killed."[3]

When the Federals, again led by A. J. Smith, once more began an advance south from Grand Junction, Tennessee, early in August 1864, Forrest deployed his forces to meet his challenger. He kept Buford's Division at Okolona to await developments, while Chalmers, with McCulloch's Brigade, had the unenviable task of manning the Tallahatchie line, "a river front of ten miles," against Smith's strong force.

On August 8, A. J. Smith committed himself. He left his new base at Holly Springs, broke across the Tallahatchie and began probing toward Oxford. Forrest countered by pushing out Bell's Brigade northwest to Pontotoc in Smith's general direction. Then on the evening of August 9, Forrest made a forced march across Smith's front, but farther to the west, to Oxford, with Bell's Brigade and James J. Neely's Brigade of Chalmers's Division. Accompanying Bell and Neely was John Morton with his battery of four three-inch Rodman rifles. Bell and his bone-weary brigade arrived in Oxford late Monday night, August 10. There Forrest established his forward base, having Bell's Brigade fan out along Hurricane Creek northeast of town.[4]

Fortunately for Forrest, supply considerations compelled A. J. Smith's advance to halt south of the Tallahatchie, but short of Hurricane Creek. Three days of continuous but light skirmishing followed, principally by Bell's Brigade. As a result Forrest was able to determine Smith's strength—sixteen thousand infantry and four thousand cavalry, an even greater army than the one that had whipped Forrest's and Lee's combined force at Tupelo. Knowing he lacked the requisite strength to confront Smith, Forrest resorted to an imaginative expedient.[5]

Originally Forrest had thought of sending Bell even farther west to Panola, then turning sharply north to menace Memphis, hoping that this diversion might cause A. J. Smith to draw back from his position across the Tallahatchie. Chalmers had his doubts, however. Bell's Brigade, even strengthened with a battery, seemed insufficient to "accomplish much." Rather, why not station Bell at Panola, Chalmers suggested. From there he "would threaten Memphis without running any risks and may draw the enemy back from here." Dabney Maury agreed, and noted when the Union commander "finds Forrest in his rear he will not be apt to advance, and the weather is unfavorable to him."[6]

Bell pulled back from the Tallahatchie line on August 15 and gave his troopers three days of glorious rest in Oxford while Forrest decided what to do and how to do it. To Chalmers he replied, "If you can hold them back two days [along Hurricane Creek], I will be in Memphis." From the force assembled at Oxford, Forrest carefully chose some two thousand men and on August 18 he set out through heavy rain toward Panola in what proved to be an exhausting forty-mile march. The rain, although it made the roads muddy and slippery, the streams brimming, actually assisted Forrest by keeping the curious off the roads and off front porches. To occupy Smith's forces, Chalmers with another two thousand troops demonstrated all along the Tallahatchie front. Meanwhile, Bell and J. J. Neely rode on through Grenada and Senatobia, having to bridge swollen Hickahala Creek and Coldwater River as they progressed still farther north. Bridging the latter stream was finally completed "about one hour before sundown," Pvt. H. R. A. McCorkle, of Russell's regiment, entered in his diary. "We then had 32 miles to travel to get to Memphis which we did before daylight next morning."[7]

After a short rest stop at Hernando on Sunday, August 20, in which Forrest again had Bell and Neely winnow out their weak horses and sick troopers, the little expedition, now reduced to fifteen hundred men and two guns, pushed on. Quietly they rode into the outskirts of Memphis, a city overconfident in its security. Forrest's primary object was the recall of A. J. Smith. He hoped to do this by displaying the vulnerability of Memphis and by the capture of Major Generals Cadwallader C. Washburn, commander of the District of West Tennessee, and the former commander of that district, Stephen A. Hurlbut. Entering the city with three columns, Forrest ordered Bell with Lt. T. Saunders Sale's artillery section and portions of three of his regiments—Russell's, Newsom's, and Barteau's—to hang back, but remain concentrated as a ready reserve.[8]

This bold Memphis raid, of course, passed into legend even as it transpired. The daring Capt. Bill Forrest rode into the lobby of the Gayoso Hotel, terrifying its guests, civilian and military alike, but narrowly missed capturing General Washburn. The Confederates subsequently attacked the notorious Irving Block unsuccessfully, and later, when Colonel Neely became sorely pressed by Union infantry, Forrest committed his reserve, sending Bell to Neely's support. Forrest, with Bell riding at his side, now threw the brigade against the Third Illinois Cavalry and their camp. It was a quick, incisive attack. The Federals broke, leaving in Bell's hands twenty-eight prisoners and most of the regiment's horses.[9]

Many of the Federals fled into the central brick building at the State Female College, and it became the next point of attack for Bell's dismounted cavalry and Lieutenant Sale's two-gun section. They threw themselves into this fight with mock ferociousness ("bluff," Bell would have called it). They knew they needed time to reduce such a strong position; a demonstration would have to suffice. Neely remembered all too well the disastrous consequences of his and Gideon Pillow's attack against such a strong brick building during their June 1864 Lafayette, Georgia, raid, and may have shared his misgivings with

Bell and Forrest. In any event, Forrest, despite having Sale's guns doing good execution on the building, decided to heed Neely's admonition and bear off. It was a raid, after all, not a siege.[10]

It appears to have been a wise decision. The Federals recovered rapidly and Yankee infantry, cavalry, and artillery began swarming into the streets, then joined in attacking the Confederates as they withdrew. Once they had disengaged, however, the Rebel horsemen succeeded in getting away safely and after a four-hour march reached Hernando where they halted for the night. The next day the entire command rode on farther south to Panola, where they dispersed, returning to their parent units. Bell and his men moved across the Zacona River and encamped near Springdale, about twelve miles south of Oxford on August 25, then moved up to Oxford on August 28, remaining "where Oxford *had been*" for about nine days.[11]

Meanwhile, A. J. Smith, having broken through Chalmers' resistance and pushed on to Oxford, was astonished by the news that Forrest had slipped past him and attacked Memphis. Unofficially, General Washburn, Smith's department commander, was led to observe that Forrest had succeeded in "leaving his [Smith's] immediate front at Oxford and making a dash at Memphis without Smith knowing it, tho he had 4500 Cavalry with him." Although the material results of Forrest's Memphis raid were insignificant, its strategic results proved highly effective. Smith's large force turned about, retreated across the Tallahatchie, and on back to Memphis with Forrest's troopers snapping at their heels.[12]

Bell's tired cavalry received a welcome respite the last week in August 1864 while they encamped with J. J. Neely's brigade at Oxford. As Bell and Neely rested and fed their horses, Forrest set about reassembling and reorganizing his command. On August 30, 1864, he announced that Forrest's Cavalry would be composed of two divisions, led by Chalmers and Buford. Each division would contain two brigades, the Kentucky Brigade continuing under the command of Col. Ed Crossland and the Tennessee Brigade (Bell's) would serve under Buford, while McCulloch's Missouri-Texas-Mississippi Brigade (commanded by Col. William B. Wade, Eighth Confederate Cavalry) would remain under Chalmers along with Rucker's Tennessee troops. Hinchie P. Mabry's brigade, which had fought alongside Bell during the Tupelo Campaign, was returned to Brig. Gen. Wirt Adams's command in central Mississippi. Tyree Bell's brigade would retain its four familiar regiments: Barteau's Second Tennessee Cavalry, Newsom's Nineteenth (Eighteenth), Russell's Twentieth (Fifteenth), and Andrew Wilson's Twenty-first (Sixteenth). Forrest's artillery battalion remained unchanged, composed of Hudson's, Morton's, Rice's, and Thrall's batteries.[13]

The opportunity to heal from the rigors of late summer ended on August 30 with a call for help from General Maury in Mobile. Maury confronted an overwhelming Federal amphibious force and appealed to Forrest for aid. "Come and help Mobile," he requested rather than directed. "We are very weak." Forrest promptly responded to Maury's urgent summons by ordering Chalmers's Division south. Black Bob McCulloch's brigade hurried to Mobile, but before any more of Chalmers's men could enter Maury's domain, President Davis scotched the transfer, at least of the remainder of the command.

"Forrest's troops are better suited to their present duty than that of the trenches," Davis wrote. "If the enemy to his front should be withdrawn he [Forrest] would, I think, contribute most to the public defense by going into Tennessee to destroy the communications of Sherman's army, and, probably, to obtain a large accession of troops." Strange words from the president who consistently all summer had resisted the same suggestion from Governor Brown and General Johnston. Thus, on September 4, the movement was suspended, much to Forrest's delight. "Cheer up," he wired Chalmers, "and be prepared for a move in the direction of Memphis." Unfortunately McCulloch, despite Forrest's appeals, would not be returned to Forrest's command in 1864, being sent to West Florida to protect against the large and occasionally aggressive Federal garrison at Pensacola.[14]

Forrest wanted action; the Confederacy needed action. Buoyed by the success of the Memphis raid and knowing that he had the full backing of Maury, he made a bold offer directly to President Davis on September 5. He proposed to chop Sherman's supply lines—without being reinforced. "If permitted to do so with 4,000 picked men and six pieces of artillery of my present command," he wrote, "I believe I can proceed to Middle and West Tennessee, destroy the enemy's communication or cripple it, and add 2,000 to my command." What a welcome tonic this telegram must have been for the discouraged Davis, beset on all sides by department and army commanders pleading for additional troops.[15]

In the meantime Lt. Gen. Richard Taylor, who had superseded his friend Dabney H. Maury as department commander on August 15, had arrived in Meridian September 6 and taken charge. Taylor believed Mobile to be "safe for the present" and concurred wholeheartedly with Forrest's proposal of September 5, agreeing that such an expedition into Tennessee could well relieve the pressure on Hood's bloodied and beleaguered army. "This will be productive of more benefit," Taylor wrote, "than the detachment of a portion of it [Forrest's command] for the defense of Mobile."[16]

Forrest could proceed. Having established his headquarters at Verona, just south of Tupelo, Forrest readied his command for the Middle Tennessee expedition. First, he set his house in order, designating Chalmers to take command in North Mississippi during his absence. Chalmers, however, would have only Mabry's Brigade (borrowed from Wirt Adams) and a mixed bag of state reserves of highly questionable fighting quality. Forrest's expedition thus would consist of Buford's Division, with its brigades of Bell and Crossland, in addition to Rucker's Brigade of Chalmers's Division. These troops began moving east from Oxford through Pontotoc to Verona on September 7.[17]

For over a week the cavalrymen assembled at Verona and readied themselves. Then, on the evening of September 16, Bell led his brigade out of their encampment. They and most of the cavalry (including the artillery horses) rode cross-country to the northeast, passing through Fulton, Mississippi, intending to strike the Memphis and Charleston Railroad at Cherokee Station, some ten miles east of Iuka, just inside the Alabama state line. Bell and his command were eager to attempt this venture, and Bell himself felt good. Clark Barteau, the splendid young schoolmaster-editor in command of the Second Tennessee, had recovered from his wounds and returned, promising reliable, energetic leadership.

Another portion of the expedition, led by Forrest himself—450 dismounted troopers, the artillery (two batteries), and at least a boxcar full of supplies—moved on a parallel route by rail. This auxiliary column came up the Mobile and Ohio to Corinth, then changed cars and turned east on the Memphis and Charleston, halting at the eastern terminus of the latter railroad: Cherokee Station, Alabama, just below the Tennessee River, sixteen miles short of Tuscumbia. There the command, 3,542 strong, reassembled on September 19. They spent the day leisurely cooking rations and shoeing horses. While they encamped and rested their mounts for the push north, Forrest rode to Tuscumbia and conferred with Maj. Gen. Joe Wheeler, leaving Bell to put all in readiness.[18]

Forrest hoped for significant help from Wheeler, but he was to be badly disappointed. Wheeler's Cavalry had been smashed as a result of a disastrous raid on Sherman's supply lines, and the residue of Wheeler's once-proud force had been chased across Middle Tennessee, barely escaping over the Tennessee River into Alabama. The disheartened Wheeler gave Forrest little encouragement, but he did return to Forrest his old brigade, at one time two thousand strong, but now numbering only sixty effectives. As for Phil Roddey's command, Forrest had hoped for another two thousand men and Roddey himself. But Roddey was indisposed and the three regiments he was to loan Forrest would total fewer than one thousand men. There was good news, however. William A. Johnson, the veteran brigade commander of Brice's Crossroads, would lead Roddey's troops participating in the raid.[19]

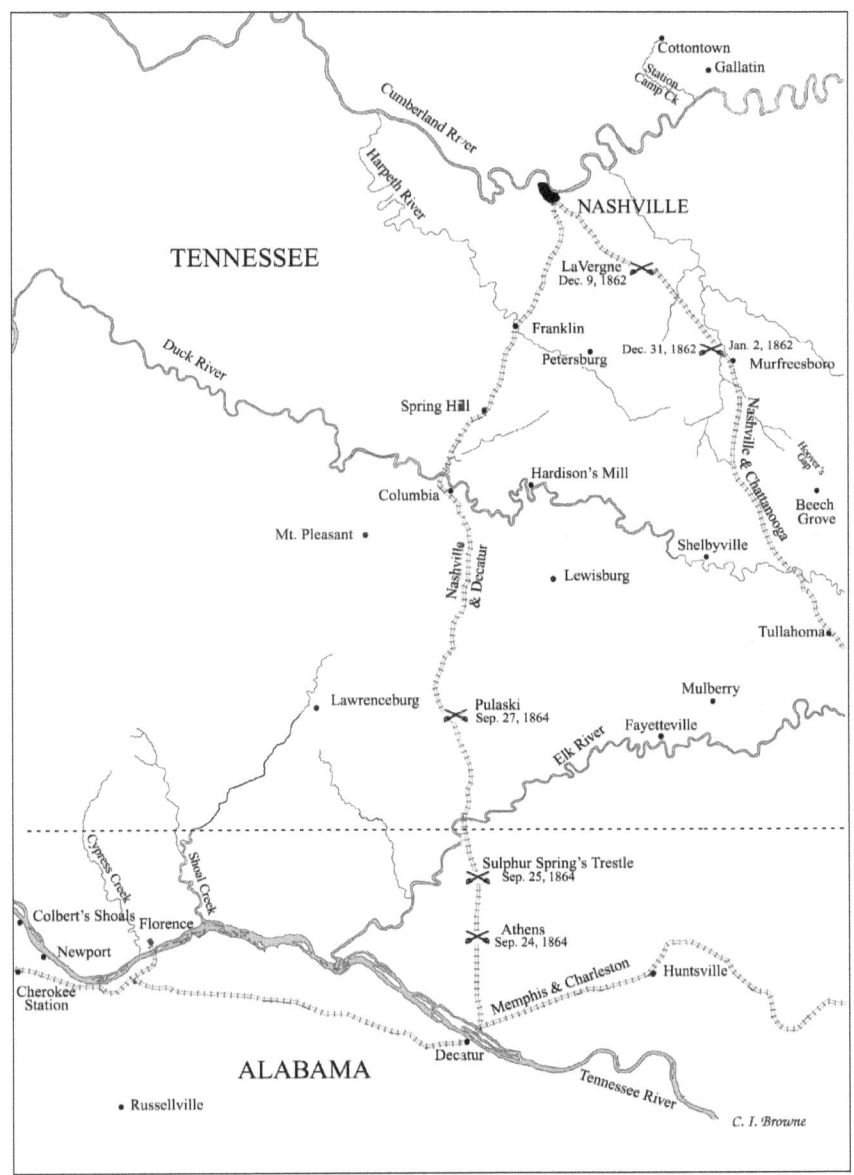

★ ATTACK ON ATHENS, ALABAMA, SEPTEMBER 1864. COURTESY OF C. I. BROWNE.

Forrest wanted to strike before the Federals could be alerted, so he forded the Tennessee River early on September 21 at Colbert's Shoals with the mounted men. Bell was pleased to accomplish this without loss, for the Tennessee River at this point was "wide and extremely dangerous," noted one of Bell's privates. "The path along the ledges of the shoals being very high and narrow in some places, to have strayed from it would have been almost certain destruction. The winding of the path made the ford about two miles in length." Bell carefully kept the column closed up. "At one time the whole ford from side to side was filled with horsemen," one of Barteau's troopers recorded in his diary, "presenting the appearance of a huge, sinuous, tawny serpent stretched across the river among the breakers." Meanwhile, the ubiquitous Maj. Charles W. Anderson supervised the ferrying of the artillery, trains, and unmounted troops at Newport (located about six miles northeast of Cherokee Station). Once across the Tennessee they hastened north to join Forrest just west of Florence, Alabama.[20]

The next morning, September 22, these troops of Forrest's main body proceeded down the north bank of the Tennessee River to unite with Colonel Johnson's brigade at Shoal Creek. The addition of Johnson's men increased the expeditionary force to forty-five hundred troops, although four hundred of these marched on foot "with the expectation of being able to mount them on horses captured from the enemy." It would be, Bell and Buford hoped, the Paducah campaign all over again.[21]

Forrest struck quickly. To isolate his objective—Athens, Alabama—he dispatched units south of the town to cut telegraph lines and damage the railroad connecting Athens with the Federal garrison at Decatur. The following day, September 23, Forrest's entire command moved on Athens, a march of almost thirty miles. They arrived after dark, and in a downpour his troops encircled the objective. Forrest directed Bell's Brigade to seal off the town from the east and assigned Barteau's Second Tennessee the semi-independent task of snapping railroad communications with Pulaski, Tennessee, to the north. So Bell deployed his brigade, less Barteau's command. The extended skirmish line advanced steadily and, despite some sharp resistance, pushed the Federals back into Athens. Having established his line within easy assault range, Bell threw out a protective screen of skirmishers and had the brigade rest in place the remainder of the night.[22]

Aiding Bell in this opening attack on Athens, in effect protecting his rear from Federals approaching from Decatur, was a newly recruited regiment of Tennesseans operating along the Tennessee River: Nixon's Regiment.[23] Under the eyes of Forrest himself, Col. George H. Nixon and his men dismounted, threw back the advance of an enemy infantry regiment, reported to be five hundred strong. Forrest admired this performance and quietly tucked Nixon's command into the fold of Forrest's Cavalry, assigning the onetime infantry commander and his men to Bell's Brigade. Bell and Nixon would get along famously.[24]

Early the next morning, September 24, Bell formed a double line of battle with his dismounted cavalry and advanced across the Tennessee and Alabama Railroad (commonly called the Nashville and Decatur Railroad). The firing from inside the Athens defenses was intense for a while, until suppressed by Captain Morton's two batteries: his own and the Hudson Battery, Lt. Ed S. Walton commanding. While Bell and Morton moved in from the east, Buford with Lyon's Kentuckians under Col. Ed Crossland closed in from the west. Once he had all his men positioned for the assault, Forrest stopped the firing and sent in a flag of truce calling for surrender of the garrison. He had to send in another flag, and while he waited for the response, he had to beat back a relief column advancing from the south. In this fight against the Yankee reinforcements, Andrew Wilson's Sixteenth (Twenty-first) Tennessee played a decisive role, not only in defeating the enemy, but in capturing most of the four-hundred-man force. The surrender of the fort at Athens followed soon thereafter, and in short order two nearby blockhouses fell, giving the raiders a haul of thirteen hundred prisoners, three hundred precious horses, two guns, and a wagon train–load of supplies and equipment.[25]

Having sent the captured Federals and wagonloads of booty back to Cherokee under the watchful eye of Colonel Nixon and his 150-man Twenty-second (Twentieth) Tennessee Cavalry (one of Wheeler's regiments "on loan"), Forrest hurried north along the tracks of the Tennessee and Alabama Railroad, capturing and burning more blockhouses. Further up the line was the important Sulphur Springs trestle, seventy-two feet high, three hundred feet long, over a deep ravine. It was guarded, however, by 1,000 men manning two blockhouses and a fort. After the dismounted cavalry moved in close and pinned down the Union defenders with accurate small-arms fire, Morton and his gunners opened fire with splendid execution, neutralizing the fort's guns and ultimately compelling its surrender. Thus the raiders had captured another garrison and another large group of horses, enabling Forrest to mount his entire command. Indeed, the haul had become embarrassing. More than 800 additional prisoners, along with the captured cannon, wagons, and a great number of small arms were started back across the Tennessee, guarded by Col. Thomas H. Logwood and his Fifteenth Tennessee Cavalry. Each victory, however, reduced Forrest's numbers. To add to his problems, Hudson's Battery had been crippled by a large number of broken-down horses. Forrest decided to send these guns to the rear also. This meant, however, the sacrifice of firepower.[26] As security for Hudson's Battery, the prisoners, and prizes, and in expectation of having Nixon and Logwood return, Forrest wired Richard Taylor to forward sufficient troops to Cherokee Station to meet these columns and relieve them of their charges.[27]

Forrest regrouped his diminished force and pushed even faster to the north along the Tennessee and Alabama Railroad on September 26, reducing strong points protecting the Elk River bridge and destroying another long bridge across Richland Creek, six miles south of Pulaski. The Yankee force at Pulaski, however, was formidable, gaining strength by the hour, and when the Confederates approached, the enemy opened the action by attacking Forrest's advance, driving it back upon the column. "The enemy was most obstinate," Forrest would report. "He contested every inch of ground and grew more stubborn the nearer we approached the town." A general engagement followed, and although Forrest succeeded in pressing the Federals into their fortifications, he realized "the enemy was strongly posted with a large force," and "therefore determined to make no further assault." So the Confederates pulled off, having lost about one hundred men wounded. First Forrest had campfires built along his lines to deceive the enemy, then after destroying the railroad and telegraph north of town, the Rebel cavalry broke contact, making a short, miserable march in the direction of Fayetteville, Tennessee. The elements seemed to dispute his retreat as the rain poured, the roads turned to deep mud, and it became pitch dark. The artillery and wagons bogged down completely, and a frustrated Forrest ordered a halt, allowing his men to set up their little city of shebangs in an attempt to keep dry.[28]

Forrest entertained thoughts of attacking the post at Tullahoma, Tennessee. Upon reaching the vicinity of Fayetteville, however, word reached him of troops, large numbers of troops, rushing toward Fayetteville by rail, so he halted the main column at Mulberry, Tennessee, sending out small parties to the east to cut the Nashville and Chattanooga Railroad, Sherman's primary line of supply. More intelligence flowed in from reliable sources on September 28 and 29 of extremely heavy Union forces converging upon him. Thousands were said to be approaching from Memphis, Nashville, and Chattanooga, even two veteran infantry divisions being sent north from Sherman's army at Atlanta. Rumor had it that the highly praised commander of the Army of the Cumberland, George H. Thomas, had been sent north by Sherman to take care of the situation. Moreover the raiders' horses were foot-sore and almost worn out.[29]

In the face of such danger, Forrest divided his forces. He sent Abe Buford back to Alabama. With him would go a portion of Crossland's Brigade, in addition to Rucker's (commanded by Col. D. C. Kelly) and Johnson's brigades and Morton's artillery. En route to the base at Cherokee, they were to menace Huntsville, Alabama, and seek to cut or destroy the Memphis and Charleston

Railroad between Decatur and Huntsville. As Buford rode off, a Tennessee private, full of curiosity, attempted to describe him: "a notably large man, making his way that night on a very fine mule. He was one type of ye jolly Kentuckian, popular with his men, and perfectly reliable in a fight."[30]

Meanwhile, Forrest, with Bell's Brigade and an assortment of smaller commands, changed course. They would swing sharply north rather than continue eastward; they would again attack and break the Tennessee and Alabama road rather than the Nashville and Chattanooga.[31]

Marching down the Duck River valley, Forrest and his severely reduced expedition passed west of Tullahoma, through Lewisburg, and crossed the Duck River at Hardison's Ford. Continuing north, Forrest snapped the Tennessee and Alabama Railroad near Spring Hill, his old 1863 headquarters, on October 1. The column now turned south, marching easily along the splendid Columbia-Nashville macadam pike. Four miles below Spring Hill they passed a large Union saw mill and close by Bell observed "large piles of wood collected for the locomotives." Bell used the wood for another purpose, Forrest proudly remembered: "This wood was piled and burned upon the railroad, by Colonel Bell, who had previously and ingeniously caused the rails to be firmly fastened at each extremity by spikes. In this way, longitudinal expansion, under the heat of fire, being prevented, the rails were warped into short curves, which rendered them useless for three miles of the road."[32]

While Bell supervised the destruction of the rails, Forrest, being without artillery, used deception and ingenuity to capture and burn four blockhouses, four bridges, and a large amount of supplies One blockhouse held out, however, and Forrest called for Bell. He had the colonel, under cover of darkness, attack and burn the bridge commanded by the blockhouse. "In the face of murderous fire," Forrest reported, details of Bell's horsemen "applied the torch, which burned the bridge enough to make it useless, and to make the construction of a new one indispensable."

The following day, October 2, Bell with his entire brigade moved down to the Duck River and demonstrated for several hours, threatening an attack on Columbia itself. But, as with Pulaski, the carefully prepared defenses banished any serious thought of assault, particularly in light of Forrest's reduced numbers and lack of artillery.[33]

With the enemy closing in rapidly, Forrest paused only long enough in the vicinity of Columbia to burn railroad trestles south of town, while parties of Bell's troopers scouted about for "fat beeves and supplies in the rich country roundabout." Then the command reassembled and hurried southwest, recrossing Duck River west of Columbia, passing through Mount Pleasant and on toward

Lawrenceburg, which they carefully bypassed, not wishing to become entangled with the Federal garrison, which might slow or jeopardize their escape over the Tennessee. Continuing west they forded Shoal Creek and encamped eighteen miles north of Florence on October 4, planning to recross the Tennessee River at that point.[34]

When the cavalrymen reached the riverbank, however, they found that two weeks had made a great difference. The Tennessee River, "already very high, was still rising," according to Forrest, "and so full of driftwood as to be dangerous to the swimming horses." Furthermore, Forrest would report, "the winds had made the river so rough that it was hazardous to ferry it." There was no choice, however, so the small, fragile ferries loaded with men, saddles, weapons, and equipment ran day and night on October 5 and 6, the flatboats losing fully "half a mile down-stream at each crossing." Compounding the hazard of crossing the Tennessee was the approach of the persistent Brig. Gen. James Dada Morgan and his Yankee infantry, reputed to be one of Sherman's finest combat divisions. Although slow moving, Morgan and his men quickened their step, itching to come to grips with Forrest's rear guard, which included Bell's Second and Sixteenth Tennessee Cavalry.[35]

Joining Morgan for the kill were three thousand Federal cavalry coming from the west down and along the Tennessee. To save his little army, Forrest decided to have his men remaining on the north bank swim their mounts some one hundred yards out to an island in the river. From there, safe from the Federal infantry, they could be ferried across the Tennessee River. To protect these vulnerable cavalrymen as they swam out to the island, Forrest designated Andrew Wilson's Sixteenth Tennessee and Clark Barteau's Second Tennessee. The two little regiments somehow must engage and temporarily hold back the approaching Yankees, then disengage and find a way across the river themselves. Barteau's and Wilson's troopers immediately deployed as skirmishers and showed fight. This tactic, of course, compelled the enemy to deploy, thus slowing his advance and diverting his attention, providing time for the other troops to reach the island. Once across the Tennessee, Forrest and his expedition made their way safely to Cherokee Station, where they encamped, being welcomed back by Abe Buford and his boys.[36]

Bell and his men awaited news of Wilson and Barteau, the expendable rearguard on left behind on the north bank. Fighting plucky, unsupported rearguard actions at Cypress Creek against fearful odds, they had been attacked in front and rear by Federals furious that the Confederate main body had managed to escape. For days the running fight between Barteau and the Federal bloodhounds continued, but finally, on the night of October 13, Barteau, Morton,

Andrew Wilson, and the handfuls who had been fighting alongside them managed to sneak back across the Tennessee at Newport, the little task force pretty much intact. Bell and Forrest, who had given them up as captured, welcomed them back into camp at Cherokee with open arms.[37]

Measured by usual standards, Forrest's spectacular two-week Middle Tennessee campaign had proven highly successful. Not only had the rebels created havoc and consternation behind Federal lines, from Memphis to Washington, from Nashville to Atlanta, but at the cost of 47 killed and 293 wounded, the raiders had captured well over 2,000 Federals and inflicted about 1,000 casualties. Forrest also brought back to his base at Cherokee eight hundred horses, seven guns, two thousand stand of small arms, fifty wagons, and a large quantity of quartermaster, commissary, and ordnance stores. Of equal if not greater importance, the Tennessee and Alabama Railroad had suffered major damage, requiring months to repair. It "may possibly be the means of forcing the evacuation of Pulaski and Columbia," or so Forrest wished to believe, "and thus relieve the people from further oppression."[38]

To the contrary, this most recent gallop about the countryside by Bedford Forrest and Tyree Bell helped entice George Thomas and many thousands of bluecoats into Tennessee. It can be argued, when viewed strategically, that the Confederate cavalrymen had encouraged, if not caused, Sherman to abandon his vulnerable, well-nigh indefensible line of communications and to divide his massive army of invasion. In any event, this spectacular gobbling of garrisons and burning of bridges had come too late to help Johnston and Hood in their struggles to defend Atlanta.

14

Johnsonville

Forrest dared not linger at Cherokee Station. The enemy had landed infantry and artillery at Eastport, Mississippi, threatening to cut communications with Corinth, so Forrest reacted immediately, engaging the Federals with a portion of his command while he moved west with his wagon train to safety at Corinth, or so it was meant to appear. He alerted General Chalmers on October 9, 1864, however, that the command was shifting to Corinth, not to evade the enemy river force, but in preparation for a general movement north to Paris, Tennessee. He planned to reach Corinth by the October 12 and start immediately for West Tennessee, intending to arrive in Jackson by October 16.[1]

Forrest outlined his intentions to Richard Taylor three days later in a letter from Corinth. After reaching Jackson he planned to continue up to Paris, then move east from that place to seize what remained of the old Confederate fort—Fort Heiman—on the west bank of the Tennessee River, close to where the Big Sandy River empties into it. Fort Heiman was located just north of, or "downriver" from, Johnsonville, Tennessee. "The enemy derives much of his supplies from the Northwestern Railroad," Forrest reminded Taylor. Goods and ordnance were being shipped up the Tennessee River, off-loaded at the depot at Johnsonville (on the east bank), then transported by rail to Nashville. Once he gained possession of Fort Heiman, Forrest believed he could "prevent all communication with Johnsonville by transports." If such could be accomplished, this important logistical Federal artery would be severed. "It was by this route," Forrest emphasized, "that the enemy received most of his supplies at Atlanta"; thus the Tennessee River route was crucial to Sherman's designs.[2]

The Cumberland River, on the other hand, was so low during the fall of 1864 that river commerce had ceased; as for the Louisville and Nashville Railroad, raiders had repeatedly put it out of service until Federal transportation officials in Nashville had ceased to depend on it. Thus successful continuation of the campaign in Georgia and supplying Nashville largely depended upon the Nashville & Northwestern Railroad, which linked Nashville with Johnsonville and its large river docks and warehouses. It was a new seventy-eight-mile stretch of track, much easier to defend that the winding, vulnerable L&N.[3]

With the enthusiastic endorsement and support of Taylor, Forrest began moving troops north on October 16, Tyree Bell's brigade leading the way. Generally following the path of the ruined railroad from Corinth to Jackson, Bell passed through Purdy, then marched on past what once had been Henderson Station, effecting a rendezvous there with elements of the tiny commands of Chalmers and Rucker.[4] Indeed, Chalmers's "Division" seemed but a shadow of itself. Mabry's Brigade, for instance, had dwindled to 350 men. The remainder of the division would not exceed 750. In all, Forrest's command for this new West Tennessee expedition would total about 3,000 effectives. Forrest's strength seemed to ebb and flow like the tide.[5]

The two divisions of Buford and Chalmers did not march together, however. Forrest had received word that the enemy had concentrated on the east side of the Tennessee as if to cross, so Forrest had Buford strike out with the Kentucky Brigade to the northeast, to Lexington, Tennessee, bypassing Jackson. On station at Lexington, Buford would be in a "central position for observation" and directly below the Paris objective. When the National force did not venture across the Tennessee, however, Buford left Lexington, moving north himself to Huntington with Ed Crossland (commanding Lyon's Kentucky Brigade) on the October 24.[6]

Bell's Brigade was not with them. The march up from Corinth had convinced Bell that he was in no condition for active operations. His horses had not recovered from the rigors of the Middle Tennessee Raid; many were broken down and almost useless. For that matter, an alarming number of troopers were ill, including Tyree Bell himself. So, he appealed to Buford and Forrest to allow him and his West Tennesseans to have a couple of days at home to procure new mounts. Forrest, as had been his practice, agreed, delaying his movement to Paris two days, ordering Buford and Crossland to remain at Huntington, making themselves useful by sending details into the countryside to collar "absentees."[7]

Bell in the meantime marched west of Jackson past Mifflin to Lavinia, Tennessee, where he established his headquarters. Bell would remain in that vicinity until the October 23, when the brigade reassembled and marched east

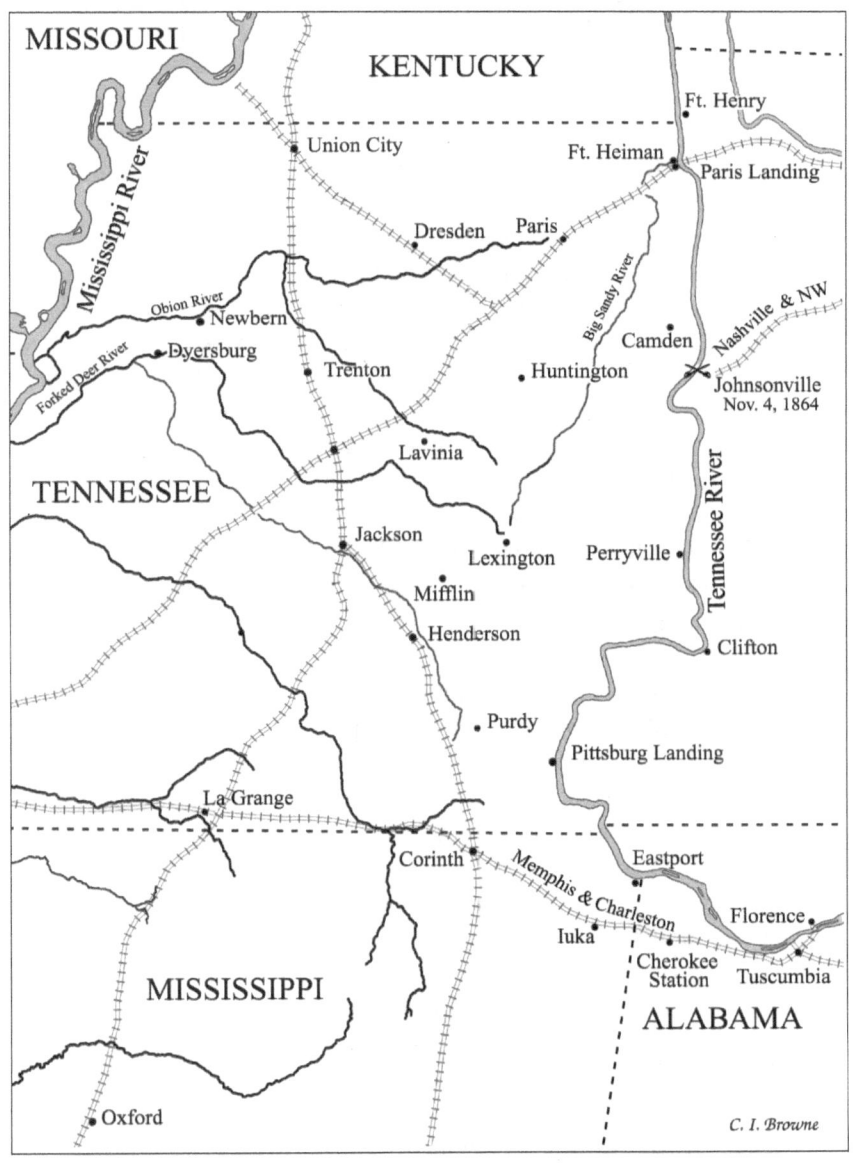

★ JOHNSONVILLE EXPEDITION, OCTOBER AND NOVEMBER 1864. COURTESY OF C. I. BROWNE.

to rejoin Buford in Huntington on October 24. Three days later, "by sunrise," Bell was riding north, advancing directly upon Paris, which he entered the morning of October 28. The good citizens thronged about him and his men, reminiscent of his arrival in Lexington, Kentucky, during the glory days of September 1862. The people of Paris "gave my command a banquet there that night," Bell remembered, "opened the Court House and danced nearly all night long." His old Paris friend, Gen. James Trimble Dunlap, quickly realized that Bell was not in good health and invited him to make his headquarters at his home where he could receive proper care.[8]

When Abe Buford came up to Paris the following day, it was with orders from Forrest to blockade the Tennessee River. The division commander split his force, riding north with the Kentucky Brigade close to the mouth of Big Sandy River. General Lyon was back, apparently relinquishing his departmental duties in Kentucky to help his old commander. With Lyon came a handful of experienced cannoneers, the pitiful remains of Cobb's Kentucky Battery, Army of Tennessee. These men had been mounted following the loss of Atlanta and returned home to serve under Lyon, their first battery commander. Buford hastened to occupy the abandoned Fort Heiman, sister of the ill-starred Fort Henry. Fort Heiman overlooked the Tennessee from the west bank, and into this fort would be placed two heavy guns—twenty-pounder Parrott rifles, sent especially for this mission from Mobile. The able battery commander, Edwin Walton, would supervise this section personally. Buford also brought along two ten-pounder rifles, and this section of the Hudson Battery would be directed by the experienced Sgt. Maj. Orlando M. Crozier and put into battery near the mouth of the Big Sandy, about one thousand yards above Paris Landing.[9] Morton's Battery of light three-inch field pieces was also split. Lt. Joe Mason's section, commanded by Sgt. Lemuel Zarring, would be firing at Paris Landing under the eyes of Morton and Bell while Saunders Sale's section, commanded by Lt. J. West Brown, would be positioned near the old Moody Landing, some eight hundred yards below Ft. Heiman.[10]

Bell and his brigade headed upstream in support of Zarring's section at Paris Landing and Brown's section at Moody Landing. Bell would be responsible for these artillery units manning the last firing positions against boats having passed Fort Heiman and attempting to reach Johnsonville; he and these two sections would also be the first line of defense against gunboats moving downstream to engage the guns at Fort Heiman or to assist cargo steamers or transports that had been attacked. Bell would be within reasonable supporting distance (five miles) of Buford, but both he and Buford looked to Chalmers at Paris as their general support or reserve. After all, the river attack was supposed to be an ambush, a total surprise.[11]

Bell began moving into position at Paris Landing on October 28 and complete his arrangements by nightfall. Newsom's and Wilson's smaller regiments were gone, busy picketing and scouting along the river all the way to Clifton. The main body, Barteau's and Russell's cavalry (except their sharpshooters), remained well back from the river, and details only came forward when needed to move guns or cut roads. They would play merely a support role in the river fights to come. Bell took elaborate care to hide Morton's caissons "back in the rear in a sink to cover them from sight of the river." He also masked his cannon close to the riverbank where they could be fired without the awkward and time-consuming practice of having to be rolled by hand into battery. Once the guns were in place, the supporting dismounted cavalry deployed, Buford and Bell had, in effect, "completed the blockade of the river." These raiders of Forrest "had moved north so swiftly," contends Johnsonville historian Donald Steenburn, "that the Federals did not dream that they were in the vicinity of the Tennessee River."[12]

Buford and Bell would not permit a round to be fired until all preparations were complete. They wisely allowed four shallow-draft steamers to pass the gauntlet of concealed firing positions headed downstream, virtually at point-blank range, without receiving a round. Hold your fire, Buford ordered. "These are empty boats going down after more supplies for Sherman's army. I want a loaded boat, a richer prize." So the gunners waited, displaying admirable forbearance throughout Friday, October 28.[13]

Their chance would come early the next day, Saturday, October 29, when the heavily laden steamer *Mazeppa* appeared, chugging up river with a barge in tow, heading for Johnsonville. Lieutenant Brown waited until she was past, then opened upon her stern as she approached Fort Heiman. Buford's twenty-pounders inside the fort had a perfect target. They unleashed three volleys that drove the astonished steamer to the opposite bank, where her crew jumped over the side. Buford went across river himself to supervise the *Mazeppa*'s capture and safe return to the west bank. He and his men were delighted to discover a rich cargo on board.[14]

The lighthearted Kentuckian sent a courier up to Paris Landing to let Bell know of his success, telling his old comrade that he had captured a treasure. Send some details down, he said, to help us unload the "army supplies, shoes, socks, and everything but whiskey." One demijohn of whiskey had been found, Buford told his friend, but he had plans for it. Tyree Bell did not require prompting. He went down to Fort Heiman himself, staff and work details in tow. We "got everything we needed or wanted," he recalled, "remained there a while and then back to my command." Hardly had they completed off-loading the cache of supplies, however, than three menacing gunboats appeared upstream and began to fire at long range. Buford felt it judicious to burn the *Mazeppa* as a precaution against her recapture. The precious cargo, nevertheless, had been saved, and Barteau's Tennesseans worked through the night hauling off their booty.[15]

The next day brought more steamers and more gunboats. The first, the steamer *Anna,* was allowed to pass Bell's sections, then received fire from the more powerful guns at Fort Heiman and quickly surrendered to Buford. As the Rebels watched her prepare to touch shore, the Union captain "hit full steam," and the steamboat raced downstream, zipping past the last section of guns. Not having been damaged badly, she hurried away to spread the alarm of concealed Confederate shore batteries to boats waiting in Paducah to begin their voyages upstream to Johnsonville.[16]

The Confederates were furious at this Yankee "perfidy." Soon thereafter the gunboat *Undine* appeared, heading downriver, escorting the transport *Venus.* The *Undine* was formidable, armed with eight twenty-four-pounders, one of the largest "tin-clads" on the Tennessee. Bell reserved his fire until both had passed downriver as ordered by Buford, then Bell had Sergeant Major Zarring run out his guns and blast the gunboat while Bell's sharpshooters by the dozen blinded the vessel by causing every opening on the port side to be fastened down. "In a very short time," Bell saw, Zarring's well-served guns "had her [*Undine*] crippled so badly that they could not control her. I ceased firing on her and ordered them to bring her ashore." The Yankees yelled back that they would bring her in as ordered, but the boat continued to drift downstream where it came under the long-range fire of Ed Walton's guns. At this point the *Undine* stopped and withdrew, taking cover behind the bend of the river, about midway between Bell and Buford, but out of range of both. There the Federals frantically attempted emergency repairs.[17]

The issue was settled not long after when Sgt. Maj. Crozier and the ten-pounders maneuvered on shore close enough to engage the gunboat at favorable range. Crozier, supported by the musket fire of Rucker's troops, newly arrived, drove the *Undine* to the opposite shore where her crew abandoned her. Troops under Col. David C. Kelley took possession of the *Undine* and Bell ordered Kelley to have "the boat brought to the shore." The *Venus,* lacking the means to resist, surrendered without a fight.[18]

General Chalmers gave a different version of what happened with the *Undine* and *Venus.* He came up to Paris Landing about this time, he said, and consulted with Bell. He ordered Bell "to move his artillery down the river to a point as nearly as possible opposite to the boats, and to drive them from their position." Bell cautiously reconnoitered and upon his return told Chalmers that he could not execute the order because of the nature of the intervening terrain. It was now that Colonel Rucker arrived on the scene and told Chalmers that he believed the ground should be reexamined, despite Bell's belief that it "was impracticable for artillery." While Rucker rode down to the bank, Chalmers and Bell were summoned back to the gun position at Paris Landing; a sternwheeler was approaching.[19]

Although the *Undine* and the *Venus* were in Confederate hands, this new steamer, the *J. W. Cheeseman,* evidently oblivious to the fate of her sister boats, thundered downstream. Bell reported that "a great many officers and their wives and friends" were aboard. Morton's guns opened and soon had the transport "so crippled that it was hauled to," Bell recalled. "My experience with the other boat had taught me a lesson and I ordered them to put a man in a small boat and give him the end of the cable and bring it ashore; and if they did not do so, in less than five minutes, I would sink it right where it was. Consequently they brought it to in a very short time."[20]

Bell took the officers and their wives off the boat, allowing them to take their personal property with them. He procured wagons and sent the little caravan back to the authorities at Paris. The *J. W. Cheeseman* "was loaded with a lot of sutler's stores, pickles, coffee, canned goods, etc.," recalled Rebel Pvt. James Dinkins, "No child ever anticipated more happiness, nor expected so many beautiful things would come to him on Christmas." When she was pulled to shore, the cavalrymen swarmed aboard and in short order the *J. W. Cheeseman* "was stripped of every thing worth moving. Barrels of pickles, hams, coffee, etc., lined the bank."[21]

Forrest arrived on the morning of October 31. He inspected the three captured boats and ordered the badly damaged *J. W. Cheeseman* burned. Having found the *Undine* and *Venus* serviceable, Forrest designated crews for them and placed his twenty-pounders aboard. He had the captured mechanics put the two vessels' engines and hulls in sailing order. The Confederates were thrilled at the prospect and up went the Confederate battle flag on their masts. When the two boats "rounded out into the stream, the troops drawn up in line made the air ring with cheer upon cheer." Their ambush having been compromised, Forrest now would advance upon Johnsonville itself with his cavalry and his "fleet."[22]

By noon, November 1, Bell's Brigade was moving upriver, parallel to the riverbank, laboring over roads turned to muck by the hard rains. Presently they halted, after having alternately ridden and tramped some fifteen miles, two of his regiments going into a large cornfield preparing to encamp. Their task on this trek had been to protect Forrest's two-boat navy from attack by Union gunboats downstream; Chalmers had performed the same mission up ahead along the brushy riverbank.

Unlike Chalmers's mounted shore contingent, the rear of the column, Bell noted, had "a gunboat sallying along parallel with us and throwing a shell at us every now and then," at one point, he continued, causing "a perfect stampede." Yankee thirty-two-pounder shells tore through the cypress tress and exploded in the brigade encampment, "producing confusion and naturally a first-class panic, not only among the horses, but among the men." Captain Morton was much amused seeing Bell's command, "always a great favorite with the artillery," thrown into chaos. Fear spared no one. "Gallant soldiers and otherwise intrepid officers," Morton observed, "could be seen running in almost every direction frequently running over one another."[23]

Bell and Major Allison at the time were absent, enjoying a good meal provided by a local in his log house well back from the river. Suddenly, their pleasant supper was interrupted by an excited member of Col. George H. Nixon's regiment, the Twenty-second Tennessee Cavalry, which contained many recruits. An embarrassed and irritated Bell made his apologies and thanked his host, then went outside and mounted his horse. Accompanied by the faithful Allison, he rode back through the thick darkness closer to the riverbank, toward the scene of action. When the disgusted Bell arrived, he was not in the mood for excuses and quickly "got things quieted." The remainder of the night would pass uneventfully as the Yankee gunboats quit shelling.[24]

The following evening, November 2, Bell's Brigade reached the shore opposite Johnsonville, and the next morning up came Buford's entire division, taking care to remain back "in the river bottom so far," Bell remembered, "that they did not discover us from Johnsonville."[25]

They would remain concealed in the soaked, swampy bogs for almost two days, moving their artillery up to favorable locations on the riverbank. With great labor they rolled, and in some instances carried, the cannon forward through "the bottomless 'bottom' across the river from Johnsonville." It proved, according to artillery commander Morton, "infinitely toilsome work."[26]

Some of the artillery went into battery immediately across the river from the town; others took position above and below to interdict anticipated attacks from nine Yankee gunboats. Fortunately Forrest's artillery had been augmented by the arrival of James C. Thrall's Battery and a section of Tom Rice's Battery, and when added to the other land batteries and the guns of the *Undine,* the Confederates could boast fourteen guns with which to oppose more than one hundred Federal guns.[27]

The artillery fight on November 4 resulted in the repulse of the Federal gunboat flotillas above and below the scene of the action. Forrest's land battery (Thrall's) above Johnsonville more than held its own, although the *Undine*, badly overmatched and manned by amateurs, became an easy target for the Union gunboats. To save her from capture, Forrest's sailors set her afire. Fortunately for the Confederates, the large Union fleet below, although blessed with overwhelming firepower, pulled away late in the morning, unwilling to venture up the narrow chute between Reynoldsburg Island and the western bank. To the Federal ship captains it looked like suicide to attempt it.[28]

So far everything had gone well. The artillery had been hauled to the riverbank and put into position without alerting the enemy across the river. Bell saw "ten or twelve transports and two or three wood gunboats anchored at the bank on the other side . . . The transports had passengers on them and when we got our batteries all ready, the General [Forrest] ordered the artillerymen to place their watches at the same time and at the same minute, open fire from the three batteries on the boats."[29]

At two o'clock the synchronized guns opened fire. Target acquisition had been predetermined—first, the gunboats and transports. The iron missiles from nowhere created pandemonium afloat and along the waterfront. Bell would never forget the scene: "Vessels afire and out of control drifted against others and spread the flames. We had all the boats in full blast burning, making the prettiest sight man ever saw on a river."[30]

For the unfortunates on the opposite bank, it was "surely a scary time," Bell recalled. "Men and ladies, all sizes and ages, were tumbling and rolling every way to get out of the way, but we kept up the fire continuously. They were firing back at us but doing us no harm at all." Actually the Federals helped the Rebel raiders, "setting fire to gunboats, transports and barges," wrote Forrest biographer Robert Selph Henry. "By dark the whole fleet had burned to the water's edge and sunk into the Tennessee."[31]

The Rebel gunners shifted their fire. Now they targeted the freight houses (one six-hundred-feet long), the two freight trains, and "about a half acre of the wharf that was covered solidly with army supplies" piled ten feet high. They sat there across the Tennessee, 394 yards away, at virtually point-blank range for field pieces. "Within two hours the whole place was ablaze, ashore and afloat, for a mile up and down the stream."[32]

The Confederates went wild with enthusiasm. Forrest, Buford, and Bell pushed a gun crew away from one of Morton's guns. Forrest, as gunner, sighted the piece, just as he had at Fort Pillow; Buford, as Number 1, rammed home the round; and Bell, as Number 4, prepared to pull the lanyard. Their spotter, Tom

Allison, yelled back target information from his position behind a tree on riverbank. When all was ready, Forrest shouted FIRE and Bell yanked the lanyard. What fun! For a moment they forgot the cares of war and fired away "with the enthusiasm of boy cannoneers on a Fourth of July."[33]

Darkness settled in and quieted the Confederate guns. It was time to go. Forrest had his men mount and they rode off to the south, "loaded with booty and floundering in the mud." Six miles they rode, to Camden, Tennessee, their way lit that November night by the lurid orange glare of Johnsonville's agony. Forrest would return to the riverbank for another look the next morning; then he too, convinced that nothing had been "left unconsumed," would turn south.[34]

The Johnsonville raid had been a spectacular success. The material damage inflicted upon the enemy was enormous: four gunboats destroyed, as well as fourteen steamers and seventeen barges. As these burnt to the waterline also perished all manner of quartermaster and commissary stores "estimated at from 75,000 to 120,000 tons." Also lost to the National cause were some 33 guns and 150 prisoners, as opposed to the Confederate loss of 20 men killed and 9 wounded, as well as the two big guns from Mobile captured along with the hulk of the *Venus*. The *Venus* herself was sunk on November 4 by Forrest's batteries at Johnsonville, but her two guns made a handsome new section for the Federal artillerists manning "Fort Johnson."[35]

As for Tyree Bell himself, Forrest commented simply that his brigade commander was "deserving of the highest commendation for [his] conduct on this as on all former occasions." Actually the Johnsonville affair was an artillery triumph, the cavalry remaining primarily in a support role. Even so, they too had cause to celebrate, these raiders of Forrest and Bell. They all had done very well.[36]

15

Hood's Invasion of Tennessee

Forrest knew he must hurry. In his pocket was a dispatch from Gen. Pierre G. T. Beauregard, commander of the Military Division of the West. No longer would Forrest and his cavalry be subject to the orders of Richard Taylor; rather Forrest and his command were to report to Gen. John Bell Hood "as soon as you have accomplished the objects of your present movement." Hood's Army of Tennessee, having abandoned its attempt to break Sherman's line of communications in North Georgia, had tortuously wound its way west and now stood poised to cross the Tennessee River at Florence. The invasion of Tennessee was imminent, waiting only, it was said, on Forrest's arrival.[1]

Invasion or not, it was impossible to hurry. "We were over a hundred miles from Florence, and the country was deluged with water," Bell recalled. "The roads were almost impassable, the worst roads on earth."[2] Hurry, indeed. Conditions only worsened, as if the rains conspired to wipe the glow from the faces of the Rebel raiders. They were so proud of their successes along the river. They were pleased with their new Yankee shoes and blankets and almost felt warm in the heavy blue uniforms, rain or no rain. And like Bell, some of them thought of the old Twelfth Tennessee ahead with Hood's army. Or what remained of it. Banish the past. It would be good to see old comrades again.

For now, though, they must endure the killing march to Florence. Virtually all the horses were spent, the artillery horses pitiful to behold. They double-teamed the heavy guns, then increased the twelve to sixteen, but the cold, the rain, and the ankle- and knee-deep muck defeated that plan, so riders were sent out to impress oxen from the locals along the line of march. Slow, so slow. Disheartened with the "untoward conditions," Captain Morton complained that daily progress had dropped to "two and a half miles." And, as if the mud and worn-out horses were not enough, the young artillerist recalled "blacksmithing forging facilities were so reduced that it was necessary to remove tires from farm wagons in order to make horse shoes and nails."[3]

For that matter, the unencumbered cavalry itself never made more than ten miles a day. The air continued heavy, cold, and damp, threatening rain, possible downpours. Everything seemed gray. To continue this dragging along the west bank of the Tennessee seemed to ensure a tramp of interminable duration. On the other hand, to cross the river and strike out southeast for Florence would reduce the journey by many miles and a significant number of days. So, when they reached Perryville, Tennessee, on November 6, Forrest attempted to shorten the route by crossing the river. Ed Rucker volunteered to try. The Tennessee was high, however, and rising by the hour. The audacious Rucker nevertheless managed to cross his four hundred troopers in "skiffs and flats," one of Duckworth's privates remembered, "swimming their horses behind." Some horses drowned, and the fast current and rampaging driftwood forced the Confederates to abort their perilous scheme. Rucker's Brigade would wind their way down the east bank of the river, but the remainder of Forrest's command would continue their tedious procession parallel to the west bank. Thus for another week Bell's Brigade marched around the great bend in the Tennessee, past Pittsburg Landing, Corinth, and Eastport, arriving in Iuka on November 14. When they reached Cherokee Station, their old base on the Memphis and Charleston, they encountered the logistical chaos that was the tail of Hood's army. From that point to Florence the road would become almost impassable from overuse; broken wagons, dead mules, and discarded army debris littered the sides of the road. Was General Hood advancing or retreating? The scene summoned visions of chasing after frightened Yankees following Brice's Crossroads.[4]

Then Bell and his men saw the proud Army of Tennessee, battered and tattered. "They looked sad and low-spirited," thought Pvt. Charles S. Coleman, a new recruit in Bell's Babies. "Some of the men were nearly barefoot and had few clothes, but the weather being warm they could stand it. Rations were scarce also, but they were ready to do or die in the attempt." Pvt. John Johnston saw them in even less flattering terms: "They were a very hardened, ill-clothed, dirty-looking set of fellows—but were laughing and jeering and cursing as if there were nothing serious in life—or death. . . . So Godless, and probably so soon to die."[5]

Bell's Brigade finally crossed the Tennessee River on Hood's pontoon bridge at Florence on November 18 and quickly united with the other elements of Forrest's Cavalry at Shoal Creek. Bell's boys felt good when they compared themselves to the ragged veterans of Gen. William H. "Red" Jackson's

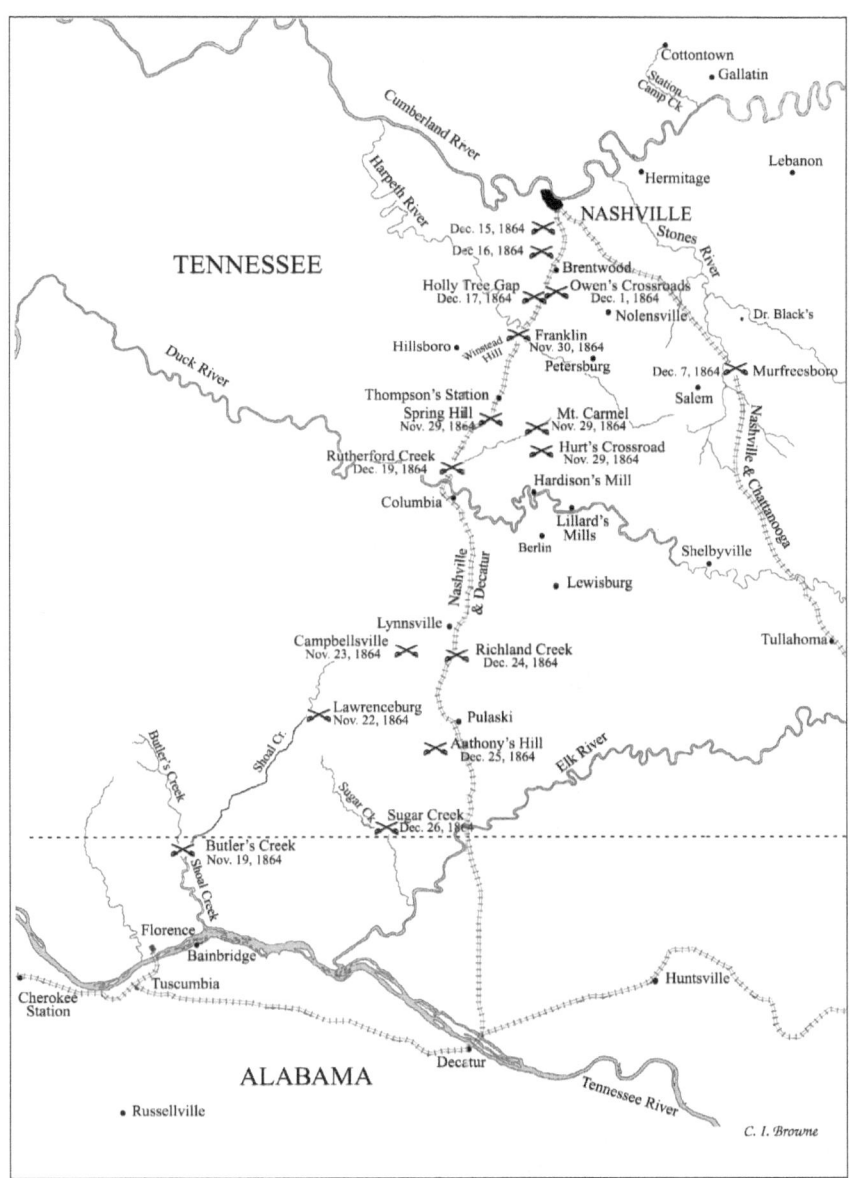

★ HOOD'S TENNESSEE CAMPAIGN, NOVEMBER AND DECEMBER 1864. COURTESY OF C. I. BROWNE.

cavalry, organic to Hood's Army of Tennessee. Their warm Yankee trousers and overcoats from Johnsonville caught the eye and envy of their new comrades. Jackson's Division consisted of Frank C. Armstrong's and Lawrence S. "Sul" Ross's brigades. They seemed fit and cocky, despite the rips and worn spots in their tunics and trousers. Red Jackson's troopers quickly dispelled any doubts about how they might meld, might get along, by welcoming Forrest's troopers with a cheer. Jackson himself, a veteran of the war in the west from days of Belmont, was said to be a pit bull in combat. Perhaps one could not expect him to be one of the boys like Buford, but Jackson was handsome and well-mannered, popular and competent, a cavalry leader with a professional background, the equal of Chalmers certainly. Also there was a new unit, mostly West Tennesseans, not quite a brigade in strength, being only two regiments. It was Brig. Gen. George C. Dibrell's old Tennessee Brigade now commanded by Col. Jacob B. Biffle. Forrest saw fit to assign Biffle and his men to Chalmers.[6]

Bell also had a new addition: Col. George H. Nixon's Regiment. Nixon, like Milton Russell, a former infantry regimental commander relegated to the status of supernumerary, had pulled together about 250 Middle Tennesseans into a regiment of cavalry, using key members of the sadly diminished 48th Tennessee Infantry as its nucleus. Nixon's Regiment (as it was known) had operated along the Tennessee River in North Alabama for a while, then joined Forrest in his Middle Tennessee and Johnsonville raids. Nixon, a Mexican War veteran, a lawyer by profession and a politician by nature, offered Bell experienced leadership, despite the "stampede" at Johnsonville. Bell needed Nixon and his men. Bell's Brigade had begun to dwindle following Johnsonville. Men had returned home for new horses to replace their jaded mounts; some had left for other reasons and would not be seen again. In all, Bell now had only 750 troopers in five sadly understrength regiments. Their sister unit, Ed Crossland's Kentucky Brigade, numbered even less—450.[7]

Forrest only had a few days to organize and rest his command for the heavy work ahead. On November 19, Jackson's and Buford's divisions moved from the Florence vicinity up the main Lawrenceburg Road (Andrew Jackson's old Military Road) close to Butler's Creek. In preparation for crossing the state line into Tennessee, Bell had troopers disperse to locate cattle and mills to grind meal for rations. They also were to keep an eye out for blacksmith facilities for shoeing horses. Once in Tennessee, the Buford-Jackson column was to advance to Lawrenceburg, then cut southeast toward Pulaski, held in strength by Federal Maj. Gen. John M. Schofield.[8]

There in the vicinity of Butler's Creek, south of Lawrenceburg, the Kentucky Brigade encountered Federal cavalry also out foraging. The enemy drove back Crossland's small band and managed to capture two of Buford's headquarters wagons. Frank Armstrong heard the firing and rushed his brigade to the scene, surprising and scattering the Federals, recapturing Buford's wagons. The Federals retreated east across Shoal Creek, pursued by Forrest's furious horsemen making "those hideous yells, such as only rebels can make." Ed Crossland, just recovered from his Harrisburg wound, was hit yet again, this time in the left heel.[9]

The role of Bell's Brigade in providing support for Hood's army would prove different than their previous assignments. In addition to reconnaissance, the brigade had to sweep away the enemy cavalry ahead of the army, to prevent Hood's infantry columns from being stopped or slowed. They also chased off details of Yankee cavalry seeking to gather intelligence about the movements of the Army of Tennessee, thus acting as a screen for the slow-moving parent body of infantry. Of course, such duty was tiring for men and mounts, and resulted in constant clashes with Federal cavalry as the army moved north. From the time they crossed the Tennessee line, according to Bell, "we commenced skirmishing with the enemy and kept it up until we got to Franklin, Tennessee. It was a kind of running fight with us, the Yankees running before us from place to place." The Federal cavalry at this point in the war had great respect for Forrest's troopers and tended to be quite cautious, too cautious to suit their new commander Bvt. Maj. Gen. James H. Wilson.[10]

Not that the bold Confederates acted foolhardy. An ambush might await them at any turn in the road, behind any dense tangle of undergrowth off to the side, or at any tree line on the edge of a field or clearing. In anticipation, Bell and his regimental commanders kept patrols well out to the flanks and dispatched far-ranging scouting parties constantly. Bell tried very hard to make his line of march unpredictable. Yet men would be shot by hidden assailants, despite the most meticulous precautions, and it was not uncommon to find dead men alongside the road, casualties of chance encounter and sniper fire. Fifteen-year-old Pvt. Charles Coleman, who had only recently donned the gray, would remember: "We drove them right along day after day, in small engagements and skirmishes with varying results. It was after one of these skirmishes that I first saw a dead Yankey on the road. He had been killed by some of our men and left there. Although I had heard a lot of firing and seen a great deal it was the sight of that dead Yank that made me realize what war meant."[11]

Forrest confronted a tough, determined opponent. The twenty-seven-year-old Wilson had come down from Nashville to take charge of the Federal cavalry personally. He commanded forty-eight hundred men, a jumble of units with a history of ineffectiveness. Wilson, like Joseph A. Mower and A. J. Smith, was a fighter; moreover, Wilson knew how to build a command and to breathe life and effectiveness into tired, pessimistic troopers. He had the absolute confidence of Ulysses S. Grant, general-in-chief of all Union Army operations, and he had the solid promise of many more troopers.

Whatever his reputation, Wilson was just another in the series of Yankee cavalry commanders. He must not be permitted to disrupt Hood's plans. The first objective for the invading Rebels was to cut off the retreat route of the Union troops concentrated at Pulaski under Schofield. To do this the Confederates had to interpose themselves between Pulaski and Nashville, and the first step must be to place cavalry astride Schofield's route of retreat. Therefore, after proceeding north from the Alabama-Tennessee line to the vicinity of Lawrenceburg, Bell's Brigade was to wheel right (or east) on the main Lawrenceburg Road as part of the Buford-Jackson strike force. They bivouacked in the snow the night of November 21, three miles outside of Lawrenceburg. "I never suffered so much before," recorded young Rebel Lieutenant R. J. Black, "for the length of time, with cold." No matter, the following morning it was "Boots and Saddles" as usual as they moved out to skirmish with enemy cavalry pickets. The Yankees contested any and every advance along the road leading to Pulaski, attempting to establish a line of battle whenever they had the chance.[12]

Buford and Jackson pushed on, Jackson driving down the main road, Buford's Division advancing rapidly on a parallel road to the north. When they encamped for the night, on November 23, the Confederates were about eight miles from Pulaski, but too late to cut off the Union retreat north from that point to Columbia.[13] The following morning Jackson and Buford, hard in pursuit of Schofield, turned north once again, this time toward Campbellsville, but Union cavalry awaited them in that little town. Buford, who arrived first, found himself outnumbered by Brig. Gen. Edward Hatch's cavalry division. Nevertheless he attacked Hatch with Bell's Brigade and Lt. Col. James K. Huey's tiny Kentucky Battalion. Both units fought with well, but it was the charge of John Newsom's Nineteenth Tennessee that met with dramatic success, "dispersing several regiments and capturing more than 100 prisoners." In fairness, it must be pointed out that the decisive element in this Confederate victory was the timely appearance of Red Jackson's Division. Jackson's men swung the tide of the cavalry battle and helped throw the Federals into hasty retreat. Indeed, Hatch's cavalrymen found themselves in a desperate fight just to evacuate Campbellsville before another Rebel cavalry attack cut off their escape route to Lynnsville and Schofield's infantry. Federal casualties ran high. In one company of twenty-five troopers, fourteen were killed. Newsom's regiment itself captured at least one hundred prisoners; Jackson's Division captured even more, in addition to four regimental flags and sixty-five head of cattle.[14]

On the evening of Thursday, November 25, Bell's Brigade, as a portion of the Buford-Jackson force, closed in on Columbia. Skirmishing was constant and the Yankee cavalry emboldened, having the fortifications of Columbia and solid infantry support at their backs. Great care had to taken to avoid or locate enemy snipers as well as practical precautions against surprise. Potential ambush sites must be cleared even if it resulted in the column moving in a stop-and-go fashion. At one point Pvt. D. B. Willard, of Barteau's Regiment, rode past a line of Union cavalry lurking in a hollow to his right. Willard pretended not to notice and quietly turned the head of his mount and doubled back with the intelligence. Immediately Bell pushed forward a heavy line of dismounted skirmishers with Willard as their guide. Once in position they attacked, routing the surprised Federals.[15]

Buford and Jackson moved up closer to Columbia. It fell to Bell to occupy the extreme Confederate right, his flank resting upon Duck River. Forrest now had the town invested and, having posted strong security, he awaited the coming of Hood and the infantry. To Bell's immediate front—about two hundred yards—were a line of rifle pits that held well-concealed sharpshooters. Forrest came up to inspect and saw the pits. He thought Barteau should move up closer. Barteau told the general about the sharpshooters. "Where?" Forrest countered. "Ride with me, General, and I will show you," responded Barteau. And so out rode Forrest and Barteau, accompanied by the ever-curious Buford. Almost immediately a volley rang out and one round killed Buford's mount. Forrest rode off, convinced.[16]

On November 27, Hood's infantry arrived before Columbia and relieved the cavalry. Bell's Brigade rode east for a day's rest to Berlin, Tennessee, south of Duck River on the Lewisburg-Franklin Pike. Hood and Forrest conferred that night, and Hood revealed his plan to cut Schofield's escape route to the north— the Columbia-Franklin-Nashville Pike. First, however, Forrest must cross the Duck and screen the passage of Hood's infantry across the river by pontoon bridge. Hood would then use back roads to move rapidly north to Spring Hill, seize that critical location and block Schofield's retreat toward Franklin and Nashville. They must exercise caution, however, for Schofield had already crossed to the north bank of the Duck and taken a strong defensive position. Rather than remain passive on the north bank, Schofield might strike out and catch Hood's infantry in the act of crossing.[17]

Forrest's first task was simply to get the cavalry over the river, fully aware that Wilson's Cavalry picketed if not controlled all the fords. Forrest directed

Buford to cross Duck River at Hardison's Mill near the Lewisburg-Franklin Pike, ten miles east of Columbia and six miles north of the division encampment at Berlin; Jackson was to cross one mile to the west toward Columbia; and Chalmers three miles farther west. Meanwhile, Forrest and his escort and Biffle's demi-brigade would cross five miles still farther west.

On November 28, as Buford and Bell advanced up the Lewisburg-Franklin Pike, they encountered a Union force that they managed to drive across the Duck by noon, but they found the ford at Hardison's Mill well guarded by a small fort on the far side; the river itself was high and swift, presenting more difficulties. Some of the Rebels traded shots with the Yankees on the other bank with long range rifles, while others built fires and visited local farms to kill hogs (it was hog-killing season). With their men thus engaged, but "not doing much good" militarily, Buford and Bell fretted about how they might get across the Duck. As Bell remembered: "Finally, Buford and myself fell on a plan by which we accomplished the crossing without any difficulty at all. The plan was this: we sent Newsom up the river until he got to a point where he could cross his regiment and come down the river until he got to the point where we were aiming to cross the river and at daylight to charge the Yankees and clear the way for us to cross. Which we did, and it worked admirably."[18]

Bell ordered Barteau and his men to cross the Duck. First Barteau built a raft with logs tied together with rope and halter straps, then called for twelve volunteers to cross on the raft. Once across they were to link up with Newsom's men and drive off the enemy, especially from a redoubt guarding the crossing. The Second Tennessee's amphibious adventure went awry, however, when the raft began to come apart halfway across Duck River. Quick-thinking Capt. Sam Barkley, Company A, tried to reach the men with a long pole, which failed. He searched up and down the bank frantically and luckily found a canoe that he managed to tie—one end to the raft and the other to the north bank, making a crude, unstable, floating bridge. The men scrambled ashore and immediately attacked the enemy stronghold. To aid them, Barteau had his regiment lead their horses to the bank, raise a mighty yell and swim the river. The Federals, attacked by three groups of Rebels—two by land and a third by water—abandoned the fort and fled with Barteau's water-capable Second Tennessee Cavalry in hot pursuit.[19]

Young General Wilson had made a mistake. As a result of faulty intelligence, he interpreted the Hardison's Mill crossing as a major cavalry advance up the Lewisburg-Franklin Pike toward Franklin itself. He had a fearful vision, it appears, of another Johnsonville raid, with Forrest bolting by him and attacking Franklin or even Nashville. Reports of "heavy force" came streaming in, convincing him that Rebel cavalry and infantry were advancing up the pike. Wilson determined to anticipate them and ordered his cavalry to pull back from the river crossings and concentrate at Hurt's Crossroads on the Lewisburg-Franklin Pike to block the direct route to Franklin. This decision allowed the remainder of Forrest's cavalry to cross Duck River and resulted in the Federals fleeing before Buford's and Bell's troopers, having to fight their way through Red Jackson's Division to escape. Wilson's mission as the "eyes and ears" of Schofield's force had been subordinated to blocking an imaginary strike. The Rebels, Schofield complained, had "forced a column of cavalry between General Wilson and me, and cut off all communication between us." Now, virtually unmolested, Hood could build his pontoon bridge at Davis' Ford, just east of Columbia, and by the morning of November 29, Patrick Cleburne's Division was across the Duck, leading the infantry on to Spring Hill.[20]

The balance of Bell's command also crossed Duck River that morning and rode north on the Lewisburg-Franklin Pike to Hurt's Crossroads, where they joined the rest of Forrest's Cavalry in the effort to drive Wilson's forces, concentrated at that point, up the pike. The Federals had cavalry strength roughly equal to Forrest's, but they proved unable to hold their ground. The running fight continued with Wilson's men, occasionally pausing to fight when they came upon a good position. The terrain, covered with cedar trees, seemed to be allied with the Federals—limiting mobility for horsemen. Certainly it made Forrest's repeated flanking maneuvers more difficult. Indeed, one of Chalmers's men was run through by a dead cedar limb during a mounted charge. Most of this "cavalry fighting" had to be done on foot. It was difficult for Bell to describe, much less remember, forty years later. So much of this dismounted cavalry action was chaotic and instinctive, contrasting plainly with the logical, linear movements of massed infantry, even the controlled rushes of skirmish lines.

This steady push north by Forrest continued to Mount Carmel, where a good road to Spring Hill crossed the Lewisburg-Franklin Pike. Here the Confederates confronted Wilson's forces in a strong defensive position overlooking the crossroads. Forrest threw a portion of Jackson's command against the prepared defenses, more as a demonstration than an attack; then his main force turned west toward Spring Hill. As the Confederates wheeled, the Federals made a surprise move themselves, abandoning Mount Carmel and retreating north up the pike, in effect disengaging from Jackson's advancing Confederates. Wilson still believed his proper course was to block Forrest's direct path toward Franklin. It had not occurred to him, apparently, that Forrest's objective was to neutralize the Federal cavalry and move west, throwing his force across Schofield's line of retreat.[21]

Bell and Buford raced with Forrest to Spring Hill. When Bell arrived, Forrest had already ordered an attack on the Federals defending the town by Armstrong's Brigade, Lt. Col. Raleigh R. White's Regiment (Biffle's Brigade), and a portion of the Kentucky Brigade led in person by Abe Buford. Armstrong and Buford succeeded in driving the Yankees back upon a strong position at the top of a hill. When the Confederates sought to continue their attack, however, they encountered murderous musketry and artillery fire. As Bell described it, "they had concentrated their forces and gave us a fight." Bell's Brigade was eager to join in as their commander formed them southeast of town. Forrest, however, had seen Schofield's wagon train hurrying into Spring Hill, and he asked Buford to attack the train with a regiment. Buford selected Wilson's Sixteenth Tennessee Cavalry, "armed with carbines and Navy sixes." Bell wanted some of the action himself, so, as often in the past, he turned brigade responsibility over to Milton Russell. He then found a fresh horse and rode off to join the fight.[22]

"When I got around to where the generals were," Bell recalled, "there was a column of infantry standing in full view between us and Spring Hill and Forrest told me he wanted Wilson to charge that column of infantry on horseback." Bell told his commander that he had anticipated such an order and intended to lead the regiment himself. Forrest replied he did not require that of him, but Bell insisted it made no difference; he "was going in with [Wilson]." Taking his place in the front rank, Bell remembered:

> We charged back and forward through this column of infantry, dispersing them and scattering them in every direction, wounding and killing a great many of them. In the charge, I had my horse mortally wounded but he did not fall with me. He remained on his feet until we finished the charge and got back to where we started from. I then discovered that my horse was badly wounded, from which he died that night. Colonel Wilson received a flesh wound about the face. With that exception, we sustained very few casualties, not one being killed.[23]

Forrest in his after-action report recalled "Colonel Wilson at the head of his splendid regiment made a gallant charge through an open field." As Wilson's charge ended, Forrest received orders from Hood to hold his position "at all hazards," as the head of the Rebel infantry column was only two miles away and rapidly advancing."[24]

Forrest immediately ordered up his command for another charge. Bell's Brigade arrived first. Like their commander, they were already dismounted, apparently eager for the fight. Cleburne's Division appeared soon after Bell received his orders to attack and the infantry moved forward, Bell's Brigade deploying and advancing on their right. Bell was short on ammunition, however, down to four rounds per man. The brigade had only been issued sixty rounds since they had struck out to cross Duck River, and three days of fighting had exhausted the supply. Forrest could furnish none because his ordnance wagons remained in Columbia. Once again Bell had run short, the same problem that had plagued him at Belmont. He was determined, nonetheless, not to let it jeopardize his mission. There was more to an assault than just blasting away with Navy sixes. Thus, with his brigade armed mostly with Rebel yells, Bell carried out the attack with what Forrest would later describe as "a promptness and energy and gallantry which I have never seen excelled."[25]

The Yankees had appeared determined, Bell thought:

> They had thrown up rail breastworks and were in heavy force at the top of the hill. I was ordered to charge this fort, which I did under one of the heaviest fires that I ever encountered during the whole march to Nashville.
>
> I charged through an open field and got up to the woods in which they were, crossed the fence and there I halted and took protection behind the trees. Being afraid they would charge me in this position and knowing I would be unable to repulse it, I ordered Major Allison to go back for reenforcement, which he proceeded to do and brought up Colonel Nixon's regiment under a very heavy fire.
>
> [John C. Brown's division and George W. Gordon's brigade of Cheatham's Corps] were immediately in our rear and they came to our assistance, but not until we had driven them back.[26]

Forrest took pride in Bell's success, noting in his report that "the enemy was driven from his rifle-pits, and fled toward Spring Hill." When the infantry came up they took over the position, and then Bell's Brigade withdrew. After issuing rations to his weary troopers, Bell gathered about him his most expert foragers and scroungers, sending them into the darkness of Spring Hill to find ammunition. Somehow, some way, the cartridge boxes must be replenished. While the hunt was on, Bell himself returned to the front.[27]

> I [Bell] walked up to Brown where he was standing in line of battle, and had a lively chat with him and Gordon, and told them the prospects for an infantry fight were pretty good, but as I had not been in an infantry fight in so long, that I would go in as a voluntary aid.

Then they got up a dispute between them, about who I should go with. Brown said I should go with him because he was ranking officer and Gordon said I should go with him, because he had my old command, the 12th Tennessee regiment. We sat and talked . . . , not having had the opportunity to talk for quite a while. Just then, orders were issued to Brown and Gordon to bivouac their [commands] and issue rations.[28]

Precious minutes passed. Brown had delayed his attack because he perceived the Federals had flanked him. As he talked with Bell, he awaited orders from his corps commander Frank Cheatham, who, after conferring with Hood, called off the attack until the next morning. Thus the Confederate thrust to cut the Columbia-Franklin Pike was aborted. Because Brown did not attack, Cleburne, waiting for the sound of Brown's guns as his signal, also failed to attack, and the way lay open for Schofield's army to pass by in the night marching straight for Franklin. According to Chalmers's staff officer, James Dinkins, Chalmers urged Brown to attack, but Brown replied emphatically that he had no orders to do so.[29]

Bell returned to the brigade bivouac where his men "had a great big log fire built up." He remained there readying the troops for the expected night operation until a courier rode up with orders to meet Bedford Forrest at Dr. George Peter's place. Bell did so, and Forrest directed him "to move next morning about three o'clock in the direction of Franklin." Forrest also told Bell "to send Major Allison [who had been raised in the area] down to Thompson's Station to Mr. [William W.] Buford's where he would find Generals Jackson and Armstrong and to give orders for General Jackson to take his command across the Franklin Pike to Carter's Creek Pike."[30]

Red Jackson, however, found his way blocked by Yankee infantry moving up the pike. He sent Allison back to Spring Hill to report to Forrest who asked the major to ride with him to Hood's headquarters. "It was then about three o'clock in the morning. Major Allison remained at Forrest's headquarters until the next morning and reported back to me."[31]

The next morning, Wednesday, November 30, 1864, Buford's Division mounted and struck out in a long column for Franklin. Bell's Brigade, accompanied by Forrest and his escort, led the march. After advancing about six miles up the pike they encountered Schofield's rear guard north of Thompson's Station. Red Jackson was there. He had been fighting all night in that vicinity, futilely attempting to block the pike to Franklin. Having failed, Jackson then pursued, nipping at the rear of Schofield's column. He was still engaged with the enemy cavalry when Bell came up. Bell immediately attacked. "We skirmished for some time," Bell wrote. "Finally they gave way and retreated back to Franklin." Buford with the Kentucky Brigade swung to the east, marching on Franklin by way of the Lewisburg Pike, while Bell, Jackson, and Forrest continued pressing down the Franklin-Columbia Pike. Bell's Brigade halted in the vicinity of Winstead Hill immediately south of Franklin. There the command waited for the arrival of the infantry. When Hood came up about 1 P.M., he deployed Alexander P. Stewart's Corps (who arrived about 2 P.M.) east of the Columbia-Franklin Pike along with Buford and Jackson. Chalmers took his division west of the pike and southwest of Franklin, closing the gap between the infantry and the Harpeth River.[32]

The Federals abandoned Winstead's Hill and withdrew into Franklin. Hood hastily called a council-of-war, which Forrest attended. About the same time a courier arrived at Bell's headquarters with a summons for Major Allison to report to General Hood "for the purpose of reconnoitering." Not long after, Tom Allison reported back to Bell. "He was the most disgusted man I ever saw," Bell recalled. "This fight was going to be exactly like the one at Harrisburg," Allison said. "We would be whipped in the same manner, having to go through an open plain, right up to the breastworks."[33] Forrest's Cavalry was to be fragmented, one division to the left of the infantry, two to the right. The command as such would not be employed in a flanking move as Forrest had suggested to Hood. Instead, Red Jackson's Division on the right would attempt such a stroke unsupported.[34]

True to Allison's words, Bell's Brigade would take position as dismounted infantry on the far right of the Army of Tennessee. They were to attack directly ahead against the waiting Federal cavalry south of the Harpeth. To his left front Bell could see Carnton, the home of John and Caroline Winder McGavock. He was just southeast of that handsome home, near Hughes' Ford on Harpeth River. From his position on the extreme right of Hood's massing infantry he could look to his immediate left and see W. W. Loring's Division drawn up in line of battle. How odd, Bell might have thought. Only yesterday he had sought to take part in an infantry assault. Perhaps he also thought of the Twelfth going in at Shiloh and Richmond. He could have laughed; these men of his today appeared almost ridiculous alongside their infantry comrades. But there they stood—Bell's Brigade—armed with their tiny regimental flags, their Navy sixes and shotguns, not to speak of their Yankee-blue trousers and jackets. Yet they extended Loring's right so that it connected with the Harpeth River, anchored it, in effect. To their rear stood their comrades of Buford's Division, supporting Hood's fragile right, with responsibility for the terrain from the Harpeth River around to the Lewisburg Pike.[35]

The Confederates stepped out at 4 P.M., and Bell's Brigade, dismounted and supported by Morton's artillery, quickly struck a heavy force of enemy cavalry, also dismounted. In effect, Bell and Buford were to shove Wilson's cavalry across Harpeth River, sealing the right flank of Hood's line. After about half an hour of heavy skirmishing, most of the Yankee cavalry began withdrawing across the Harpeth, but not those to Bell's immediate front. Supported by artillery fire from across the river, these Federals continued to fight with a fury. Bell turned to his friend Tom Allison and ordered him "to go back to General Forrest and tell him that it was an impossibility for me to advance and to send further orders." Forrest remarked to Allison, "Well, Bell can get in the hottest places in the quickest time of any man I ever saw." Bell found the Yankee fire to be "the hottest sort" and coming from "where it was least expected." The brigade withdrew and was replaced by infantry.[36]

Bell now received orders to remount and cross the Harpeth and to "proceed down the Lewisburg Pike toward Franklin." In effect the Confederate cavalry chieftain was replacing Jackson's Division with Buford's. Once on the north side of the river, at a point Bell designated as "Ewing's branch of the Lewisburg Pike," his troops again encountered a heavy enemy force, and the fighting grew even more fierce than on the south bank. Yankee field artillery joined in. It was well served, as usual, the fire of the fieldpieces being augmented by heavier caliber guns at Fort Granger. "Our whole line would have been swept away," declared one of Buford's troopers, "had we not been ordered to throw ourselves on the ground, not daring to raise our heads nor crawl forward even a few rods to give succor to the wounded and dying." The battle between Wilson's cavalry, suddenly grown tough and stubborn, and Forrest raged on the north side of the river until well after dark.[37]

Weary from a grueling day of fighting, Bell now received new orders: Reconnoiter on the north side of the Harpeth, he was told, and "go to the rear of the Federal army." Bell did so and remained north of the Harpeth far into the night. When Forrest learned of the infantry's disastrous frontal assault at Franklin, he disengaged from Wilson's front and brought most of his command back to the south side of the Harpeth. Bell, however, appears to have encamped on the north side.[38]

Having beaten back the assaults of Hood's Army of Tennessee with frightful loss, Schofield prudently decided to abandon Franklin in the night and continue his march to Nashville. While the Rebel infantry tended their dead and dying, Forrest set out in pursuit of Schofield at first light on December 1. Chalmers's Division pressed up the Hillsboro-Nashville Pike, Jackson pursued up the Franklin-Nashville Pike, while Buford moved a few miles to the east and took the Wilson Pike, which led north from Petersburg, Tennessee, to Brentwood. After a few miles Buford's troopers struck enemy cavalry. "It was the same kind of movement as before," Bell recorded. "We were skirmishing, small fighting with the enemy, from there to Nashville."[39]

The Federals tried to block Buford at Owen's Crossroads, denying him from making a flanking movement from the east against Schofield's main body marching north up the Franklin Pike. The Federals held their ground tenaciously. Forrest, who was at the scene of action, ordered Captain Morton to soften them up by sending some rounds into their midst. Simultaneously Buford was to assault. Bell's Brigade apparently carried out the main attack and did well, Nixon's Regiment especially, charging through the center of a Union brigade and putting them to flight. Clark Barteau and the Second Tennessee Cavalry met with similar success, driving the enemy in confusion from their front. Bell's Brigade captured several stands of colors at Owen's Crossroads and about one hundred prisoners. One of Barteau's privates, D. B. Willard, gathered up one man and five horses. As Willard "was taking his prisoner back to the guards another Confederate wanted to 'prowl him.' 'No,' said Willard, 'you cannot prowl this prisoner while he is in my possession.' After he had been turned over to the guards this prisoner showed how highly he appreciated the above remark by making Willard a present of seventy dollars in 'greenbacks,' saying at the same time, 'I had rather for you to have this money than any other living man.'"[40]

Forrest halted his cavalry six miles short of Nashville and had them bivouac. The next morning they approached nearer, Bell and his brigade riding on the Nolensville Pike to within view of the state Capitol. Acting upon orders from Forrest, Bell then established a chain of pickets to the east, across the Lebanon Pike, thus serving as the extreme right of the Army of Tennessee and ultimately as the high-water mark of Hood's desperate invasion. Reminiscent of Bragg at Chattanooga, Hood and his twenty-five thousand troops now besieged fortress Nashville defended by Thomas's army of sixty thousand, which would grow to seventy-one thousand within two weeks.[41]

Tyree Bell and his brigade had performed creditably during Hood's march from the Tennessee River to Nashville. It was a new and enlarging experience for Brigade Commander Bell. He handled orthodox cavalry responsibilities—picketing, intelligence gathering, screening—with seeming ease, although his opponents, it should be kept in mind, were often outnumbered and their organization and expectations under Wilson unfamiliar. Thus the enemy often appeared off-balance, if not incompetent. Bell's tactics at the Hardison Mill crossing merit praise and contributed to the demoralization of the Federal cavalry between Duck River and Spring Hill. At Spring Hill he fought with energy, eagerness, and determination. Indeed, considering Bell's age, his stamina throughout the invasion phase of Hood's Tennessee Campaign was unusual, if not remarkable.

Once again, it should be kept in mind, an assessment of Bell's performance is limited severely by the lack of after-action reports by him, his regimental commanders, or Abe Buford. Maybe it is fair to have expected more from Bell. Perhaps his dismounted cavalry at Franklin proved disappointing when compared with what the old Twelfth Tennessee might have done. It is true they did well enough protecting the right flank of the Army of Tennessee, but perhaps they could have pushed their attack more vigorously rather than throwing themselves on the ground and sending back to Forrest for help. But Tyree Bell was no fool. He could look to his left as well as straight ahead.

16

Hood's Retreat from Tennessee

Once John Bell Hood established his siege lines south of Nashville, he released Forrest's Cavalry to tear up the Nashville to Murfreesboro communications. Destroy the stockades and blockhouses protecting the Nashville & Chattanooga Railroad, he ordered, cut telegraph lines, burn bridges, twist rails, and gobble up isolated security units. Murfreesboro's garrison, almost eight thousand strong, must not be allowed to be a factor in the showdown between his army and that of Thomas. Bell's Brigade was an exception. The West Tennesseans were to remain on station, guarding the Army of Tennessee's right flank, picketing out to the Lebanon Pike. Somehow, despite this critical mission, Bell managed to persuade his friend Forrest to order him off to Gallatin, Tennessee, twenty miles to the northwest, on the opposite side of the Cumberland River.

First, as Bell prepared for crossing the Cumberland, he sent his pontoons to the spot he had chosen. As these wagons lumbered over the icy roads, Bell's headquarters, at least on the evening that he was to leave, miraculously was transformed from a command and control center into a cotillion. "My boys, the young ladies and young men were having a very nice time at Mrs. Smiley's," he noted. "They had a little dance, waiting for the time for me to go on over to Gallatin."[1]

Tyree himself was as excited as a nineteen-year-old private. He was going "to my old home" and would be able to visit relatives and old friends for the first time since the miserable retreat out of Kentucky in the fall of 1862. Colonel Bell had additional incentive. He would act as avenger for family and friends, intending to settle a score, reiver style, with "Old Payne." According to Bell, "the most nefarious scoundrel that ever was honored by a military title, who had been posted on these people at Gallatin nearly the whole of the war and in that length of time, had actually had a hundred men or more taken out and shot without any just cause whatever."[2]

"Old Payne" was Federal Brig. Gen. Eleazer Arthur Paine, an Ohioan almost exactly the same age as Bell. A West Point graduate and Seminole War veteran, Paine had proved incompetent in the field and had been relegated to rear-echelon duty in 1862, his principal assignment being the security of a short stretch of the Louisville & Nashville Railroad in Sumner County. Bell's quest for revenge reflects the attitude of Southern sympathizers in Gallatin and Paducah, and a number of smaller towns in Sumner County and Western Kentucky.[3]

An hour before most of the brigade was to ride off for Sumner County, however, a courier rode up to Mrs. Smiley's with a message for Bell. General Hood had canceled the Gallatin raid. It seemed that Maj. Gen. William B. Bate and his division, who served as Forrest's infantry as he confronted Murfreesboro, had been routed by Maj. Gen. Lovell H. Rousseau's Federals at Overall's Creek on December 4. Forrest was surprised and furious. He summoned Bell "as reenforcement." Forrest's Cavalry would teach this uppity Murfreesboro garrison a lesson. Bell obeyed promptly, of course, but was disappointed. "It was a very sore move," he wrote, "for I had anticipated the bright hopes of going over to my old home, where I was raised."[4]

It was just as well. Although Forrest appears to have been preparing, certainly considering, raids by Chalmers's and Buford's troops across the Cumberland during this time, Bell's proposed move to Gallatin had been anticipated by James H. Wilson, and Union cavalry were waiting for him. Moreover, the Union Navy's patrolling efforts on the Cumberland might well have jeopardized Bell's efforts to cross. Even if Bell had succeeded in reaching Gallatin, his desire to serve justice on Sumner County's tormentor Eleazer Paine would have been frustrated. Paine was gone, having been deactivated once again by higher authority.

So Bell and his brigade rode south toward Murfreesboro, leaving only Nixon's Regiment to picket the extended line from Murfreesboro Pike to the Cumberland River. When he reached the vicinity of Murfreesboro, Bell established his headquarters north of town, at Dr. Black's, a strategic point at the crossing of the East Fork of Stones River and at the intersection of Murfreesboro-Lebanon Road with the Nashville-La Vergne-Readyville Road. Forrest, however, had no intention of attacking the strong and elaborate Murfreesboro fortifications. These formidable defenses had been perfected over two years. Fortress Rosecrans itself enclosed about two hundred acres and contained about sixty guns. Forrest ordered Bell to bring his brigade and Morton's Battery to the east side of Murfreesboro, to Woodbury Pike. Forrest hoped, by means of demonstrations and false withdrawals west of town by Red Jackson's Division and Bate's infantry, to lure the Federal garrison out of their stronghold. If the ruse succeeded, and the enemy came out of their fortress, Forrest, Jackson, and Bate would deal with the sortie, while Bell would sneak in the back door to attack Murfreesboro.[5]

Having on hand some sixty-five hundred troops (his own command reinforced by Bate's Division and two small infantry brigades), Forrest advanced against Murfreesboro on a wide front, driving back the Federal pickets upon their main line. The Yankees took the bait. Curious and cocky, Rousseau sent out Maj. Gen. Robert H. Milroy with about thirty-three hundred troops (infantry, cavalry, and three artillery sections) as a reconnaissance in force. Forrest countered this attack down the Salem Pike with a planned withdrawal, a stand by his infantry, then a swift, surprising counterstroke on the flanks by his cavalry, a patent Forrest battle design. Initially the plan seemed to be working, but suddenly, inexplicably, the veteran Confederate infantry opposing Milroy panicked. They broke. Nothing could stop them, not the entreaties nor the threats of Forrest, nor the eloquence of Bate. They ran. In desperation, Forrest turned to Red Jackson's Division, ordering a counterattack against the enemy infantry by Armstrong's and Ross's brigades, hoping a cavalry charge might check the Federal onslaught. Cavalry could not be expected to stop infantry, however; stun them, perhaps; stop them, hardly. What did halt Milroy's foot soldiers and turn them about was the sound of firing from their rear, from inside Murfreesboro itself.[6]

While Milroy's column of combined arms had marched forth to do battle with Forrest, Buford and Bell conducted their demonstration on Murfreesboro itself, advancing down the Woodbury Pike with Bell's Brigade and one section of Morton's Battery. Bell, as he had for several days, rode alongside Clark Barteau. They moved forward into the suburbs and watched while Morton's gunners fired several at the courthouse. Emboldened, they ventured deeper into the town, gathering opposition with every step. It seemed like Memphis all over again. The fighting alerted Milroy's Yankees, however, and they hurried back to Murfreesboro. The diversion probably saved Bate's broken division from destruction.[7]

It was the Union artillery, however, not Milroy, that posed immediate danger to Bell. Rousseau had rallied his forces inside the town and brought up a battery to engage Morton. One of the enemy shells struck among Morton's battery horses and killed three. "I was preparing to retreat at the time," said Bell, "and I galloped up to where Morton was."

"Captain Morton," said Bell, "prepare your guns. I will send a detail here and will pull it off by hand and not let the Yankees have it."

Morton responded, "General, if you order me, I will do it, but if you do not, I will take the harness off the horses and park them on my gun and take the gun and harness off together."

"In the name of sense, Captain," Bell said, "if there is any chance for you to do such a thing, I will give you all the assistance I can."[8]

Bell directed Lt. Conquest C. Harris, his reliable ordnance officer, to choose twenty strong troopers, most of them from the Second Tennessee. Have them dismount and help Captain Morton, he directed. Morton had the trail lifted and the gun turned about. Off it went, pulled by hand down the road leading to Mulberry, Tennessee. Morton then "unbuckled the harness off the dead horses, packed them on his limbers." Pulled by Bell's cavalrymen, the guns rumbled off, all the while, Bell noted, "in the face of this large crowd [of Yankees] which had halted and were shooting at us." Only one of Bell's men was killed in this raid, fortunately, and Bell made sure his body was carried off as well. The Federals seemed content to see them go without pursuing. As one of Bell's men summarized nonchalantly, "We moved round and came in on the Woodbury pike and drove the Yanks into town and as time about is fair play they drove us out in a hurry." Bell marched back to the east, back down Woodbury Pike and there, behind the college, about a mile out, in what remained of a peach orchard, he brought the dead trooper on a caisson, "had a grave dug and buried him properly."[9]

Learning the attack on Murfreesboro had failed, Hood recalled Bate and ordered Forrest to continue the destruction of the railroad and to find forage for the animals. Buford, meanwhile, moved up to the Hermitage with the Kentucky Brigade and picketed along the Cumberland while Bell remained near Murfreesboro. Actually, this had become standard operating procedure; Buford's Division frequently functioned as two distinct units, Buford commanding the Kentuckians in person, Bell commanding the Tennesseans. Thus, Bell's mission following the "Second Battle of Murfreesboro," not unexpectedly, would differ from that of his division commander. Bell was to remain near Murfreesboro and, if Rousseau ventured forth, Bell was responsible. He also was to frustrate if not prevent the Union cavalry's foraging efforts and, far more important, he was to impede any advance by Rousseau threatening Hood's force at Nashville. According to Bell, it proved a relatively easy task. "Rousseau, once in a while, would send out a force from the fort, bantering me for a fight. I never failed to meet him and drive him back into the fort."[10]

Bell's memory conflicted with Rousseau's, certainly in regard to the ease of repelling forays by Union foragers. Bell had forgotten, apparently, that on December 10 and 11 he had reported to Forrest that he had too few men to stop these foraging parties, at least in the Murfreesboro–Liberty Pike area (immediately north of the Woodbury Pike). And Rousseau would report to Thomas on December 12: "The enemy's cavalry all around, but I think in small bodies. We forage without molestation."[11]

Once Bell spotted a small but venturesome Federal detail coming out to the east of his position near Dr. Black's. He told his Sumner County friend and adjutant, Capt. Reuben Clark, to take a company from the Second Tennessee and deal with them.

Regimental commander Clark Barteau intervened, however, and asked Bell if he might "take charge of the fight in person." Bell told Barteau that he "thought it was just a small squad of soldiers that had been left out and I wanted them driven back to their den, and I thought the detail [under Clark] was perfectly able to do it, but if he wanted to go, he might do so." And Barteau did so. For his trouble, Barteau received a musket ball in the leg, which splintered his shin bone, disabling him for the remainder of the war, and depriving Bell of perhaps his most able regimental commander.[12]

A "terrific snow storm" blew up during this time, and Rousseau, under cover of the storm, came forth, expecting to surprise Bell's unwary command. Bell fortunately had his brigade in hand and with the assistance of the miserable weather managed to convince the Federals to return to the comforts of Fortress Rosecrans. Bell then ordered his men back to their camp while he and his adjutant, Reuben Clark, sat their horses, observing. They heard a shot and spotted a Yankee sharpshooter off in the distance. He fired again, and Captain Clark told Bell he would ride over and check. It proved a mistake, as Bell relates:

> While over there, [Clark] was shot through the ankle. He came back and told me he had been shot, but he acted so cool about it, I thought it could not be so, and I told him I hoped it wasn't serious. He turned his boot around to me and the heel of his boot had been shot all to pieces and the blood was just streaming from his foot.
>
> He rode on down to my headquarters rapidly and Dr. [T. C.] McNeil of Paris, Tennessee, dressed his wound. Then I sent him down near Nashville on the Murfreesboro Pike to an old friend of mine, who was a Methodist preacher.[13]

This put Clark in danger, however, for a great battle loomed at Nashville. Bell sent Reuben's brother, Charlie (one of Newsom's men) to nurse him and also took the precaution of notifying his friend Frank Cheatham to alert him if he sensed imminent danger so that Clark might be removed to safety. Cheatham did send word on December 13 to get the adjutant away, so Bell sent his son Isaac up to O'Brien's to take Reuben south "to old man Jake Holland's, about eleven miles from Columbia."[14]

The Battle of Nashville, December 15–16, 1864, resulted in the most decisive major battle of the Civil War, as George H. Thomas routed Hood with ease and with very heavy loss. What remained of the Army of Tennessee fled down the Franklin Pike, threatened by Wilson's greatly strengthened cavalry force, which had executed to perfection an attack against the Rebel left flank and rear, overpowering Chalmers's force in the process. Forrest reacted by moving his cavalry to the Wilkinson Pike, six miles from Murfreesboro, and later on December 16 he ordered Buford to withdraw from his extended position east of Nashville. He wanted Buford to march south through the cold sleet and rain to the Franklin Pike to protect Hood's retreat.[15]

As for Tyree Bell, Forrest directed him to have the brigade ready "to move at a moment's notice," so Bell remained on high alert at Murfreesboro all during the morning of the December 15. Finally, a courier arrived from Hood's headquarters ordering Bell to move his brigade "to the rear of Hood's army as quick as possible." Bell and his men rode up the Nashville-Murfreesboro Pike until they neared the asylum.[16] "There we had to cross diagonally from the Nolensville Pike over to the Franklin Pike, Bell noted. With Maj. Tom Allison, "who knew the country well," as their guide, the brigade moved slowly through the rain and heavy darkness. "Major Allison took a man from every house," Bell recalled, "keeping him until we got to the first one beyond his house and, dropping him, we would get the man from the next house. We did this until we struck the Franklin Pike north of Hollow Tree Gap. We got there about two o'clock [A.M.]." As a precaution Bell sent Newsom and his Nineteenth Tennessee up Franklin Pike about a mile while the remainder of the command bivouacked.[17]

The next morning, however, Wilson's cavalry, in strong force, surprised and swept over Newsom's position, "capturing the colonel and about a half of his command," Bell lamented. "The other half came pouring down on the balance of the brigade." No defense could be organized, and when the Yankees crashed into the drowsy Second Tennessee, it became every man for himself. As Barteau's men attempted to mount and race through Hollow Tree Gap to escape, Bell hastily prepared an ambush at the far end of the gap, selecting a strong, concealed defensive position. For his force he employed a portion of Nixon's

Regiment, which had managed to retain its organization, the Rebel infantrymen on the hilltops, and a section of Morton's guns. This combined force opened fire on the Federals plunging through the gap, carrying with them a host of Confederate prisoners. The ambush startled the pursuers. Greeted with heavy Rebel musket and artillery fire, they fled, suffering about eighty casualties. Indeed, a large number of the most advanced Federal battalion surrendered. Bell's men grabbed their horses in numbers sufficient to mount a host of Confederate infantry, many of whom double-upped, enabling a number of stranded riflemen to make good their escape to the Harpeth River. All this was accomplished, incredulously, within sight of armed Federals who, according to Rebel Pvt. John Johnston, "withheld their fire on account of the presence of their comrades who were just captured."[18]

Bell himself described the Hollow Tree Gap ambush in these terms:

> After as many of the Yankee cavalry had crossed the gap and turned in to the road in pursuit of us, as I thought I could handle well, I told Morton to turn his battery aloose. He did so, and all [the Yankees] that had crossed the gap jumped off their horses and surrendered.
>
> I sent these prisoners up to General [S.D.] Lee by Capt. Joe Odom. The general sent them on south and Odom with them. Right there, I received information that General Lee was wounded and he left the field.[19]

This small cavalry rear-guard action marked the beginning of the systematic, effective employment of cavalry as a defensive screen for Hood's retreating army.[20] The Federal cavalry from this day forward would exercise far more caution in their pursuit, worrying about rushing into an ambush as they attempted to bring Hood's army to bay.

Bell now retreated along with the rear guard to the Harpeth River and crossed over the pontoon bridge. There on December 17 he received orders "to hold [protect] the rear of the army." Almost immediately, however, a scout reported Wilson's horsemen were "crossing the ford west of Franklin." Bell raced to the scene and put a portion of his command in position to check this threat. "I then galloped back to the pontoon bridge," he recalled, "just as the last of the troops were crossing and had it destroyed." This provided only a temporary respite, however. Maj. Gen. Carter L. Stevenson, now commanding the rear guard, spent that day—Saturday, December 17—harassed, virtually surrounded by Federals. Finally, Stevenson had his remaining infantry form a hollow square and attempt to back out of Franklin. Bell, meanwhile, had begun to retreat through the town himself, then across the old battlefield of November 30, and over Winstead Hill.[21] "We fought nearly constantly," Bell recalled, "the whole day and until some time in the dark, alternately fighting and falling back. The enemy pressed us hard. . . . One point particularly, late in the afternoon, they run in on us and got Buford cut off. The general [Buford] being on a better saddle horse than most of us, and being of such a powerful build, he knocked the federal down that attacked him with the butt of his pistol and leaped a ditch with his horse."[22]

Sporadic, sometimes desperate fighting continued all the way to Thompson's Station. When night fell, the infantry halted at that point while the cavalry continued on, encamping at Spring Hill. The following day, December 18, General Cheatham, now in command of the rear guard, established a line at Rutherford Creek, two miles below the village of Spring Hill in hope of securing safe passage of Hood's trains across the "greatly swollen" creek. This Rutherford Creek crossing was south of Spring Hill and almost three miles from the pontoon bridge Hood's engineers had constructed over Duck River.[23] When Bell reached Rutherford Creek, late on the afternoon of December 18, he received a message from Cheatham. Hood's wagon train was across, and now Cheatham and what remained of his corps (about fifteen hundred troops) had begun withdrawing across Rutherford Creek. If Bell could find another place to cross, Cheatham said, he might do so and his "command would be relieved after crossing." The brigade cared for their horses, looking out over the stubbled fields, enduring the slashing sleet while Bell's staff rode along the creekbank searching for a place to cross. Finally, one of Bell's staff located a feasible spot, and Bell quickly rode to the spot and took the brigade over. With Rutherford Creek at their backs, Bell remembered, we "were out of the fire of the enemy for the first time in three days and nights."[24]

Not only were they temporarily free of Wilson's pursuit, but Major Allison appeared out of nowhere with a huge basket of provisions which he and his servant, Wilson, had secured from his brother's home near Franklin. "We had not had time to eat anything," Bell recalled, "and if we had had time to eat, we could not have had anything to eat. We had cracklings, back-bone, spare ribs, etc., everything good at hog-killing time." If only a man could gain some hope from the leaden sky with its heavy clouds that seemed to hover over them. It was so cold.[25]

Soon word came to Bell that his brigade should move to the pontoon bridge and cross Duck River. The roads to the bridgehead, however, had turned into quagmires from the incessant rain and heavy use, presenting a formidable challenge. Nevertheless, the brigade managed to reach the bridge, and once across Bell was greeted by staff officers who reported "they had plenty of provisions and forage." After Bell's entire brigade had crossed the Duck and entered Columbia, Forrest came up to his exhausted brigade commander and asked him "to ride with him over to Hood's headquarters." The two did so and Bell listened as Forrest suggested that Hood "take the wagon train, crippled men and crippled horses and the artillery of the army and move on the next morning." Forrest told Hood that if an infantry division were left behind, he could guarantee to "hold the enemy in check" long enough for Hood to get a good head start south. Hood agreed and designated Maj. Gen. Edward C. Walthall's Division of infantry "to operate with Forrest's Cavalry in covering the retreat." Having made these dispositions, Hood started south with the army on December 20.[26]

Bell returned to his headquarters, took care to have his horse fed, then saddled up and rode out to Jake Holland's. There he found Reuben and Charlie Clark and Isaac, but he saw that Reuben was "not able to get up." He told his young adjutant to remain at Holland's and allow Wilson's men to capture him. Reuben, however, would have none of it. "He insisted that I should not leave him," Bell recalled, "that he would rather have his leg cut off than to be left there and be captured." Bell acquiesced. He had an ambulance set aside for Reuben and rigged properly. He saw that Reuben was put in the ambulance and sent him, Isaac, and Charlie south toward Pulaski.[27]

Bell himself remained two more days in and around Columbia as the Federals were stymied on the north bank of the Duck, not because of Confederate military action, necessarily, but because of their own logistical blunder. Wilson's pontoon train had been sent out the Murfreesboro Pike rather than down the Franklin Pike. All of this, of course, helped Hood "get a good start on his way south." By December 22, however, Wilson's pontoons had come up and the Yankee cavalry began crossing the Duck in heavy numbers, compelling the Confederate rear guard to abandon Columbia and retire in the direction of Pulaski. "From there on," Bell recalled, "it was almost a continual fight," with stands and attempted ambushes near Warfield's and at Lynnville.[28]

Forrest's dismounted cavalry would defend in depth, stationing an element of the command on a forward line while another portion of the command would select and fortify a defensive position to the rear of the first. When pressed, the first line would fall back upon the second for a determined stand in force. Reminiscent of Daniel Morgan's tactics employed at the Battle of Cowpens a century before, Forrest frequently utilized this technique when fighting defensively fighting with dismounted cavalry, much in the original concept of "dragoons." This technique, observed Col. Charles Olmstead, First Georgia Infantry, compelled the Yankees "to halt, reconnoitre and deploy and then feel our lines before advancing to the attack." All of which devoured time, "and time," noted Olmstead, "was what we were fighting for."[29]

Bell and Buford made a stand at Richland Creek, and it developed into a "a heavy fight." Jackson's Division joined in to bring the number of dismounted cavalry up to respectable strength. Then word came to Bell that Abe Buford had been wounded and was leaving the field. This left Bell in command of the division, but handicapped in that all of Buford's staff went with him. Bell had "no knowledge whatever" of the whereabouts of the Kentucky Brigade, commanded at this time by Lt. Col. Absalom R. Shacklett, Eighth Kentucky Infantry (mounted). The first order of business, then, was to get the Kentucky Brigade "in hand." Bell soon located them and immediately ordered them across Richland Creek. In fact, they were the last troops to cross before the bridge was set afire. The Confederates were too efficient, unfortunately. The burning of the bridge, Bell complained, "cut me off with a part of my escort."[30]

Just about this time a shell burst over Bell's head and the concussion threw him off his horse. "I fell on my feet," Bell remembered, "and was back on my horse in a second, just like a rubber ball." Shrapnel from the enemy shell, however, had struck his right eye and cheek, blinding him permanently in that eye.[31]

Bell and this fragment of his escort were not alone on the north bank of the creek, however. Chalmers was there, too, with a few from his command, and Lt. Col. William F. Taylor of the Seventh Tennessee Cavalry. The little group fled for their lives, trying to hide among the hills lining Richland Creek. Bell always remembered:

> The hills were steep and . . . there was a stream of Federal cavalry after us. One cavalryman had singled out General Chalmers and they, not having revolvers, were using their sabres entirely, and he had nearly reached Chalmers and was almost striking him with his sabre. Taylor, who was near him, drew his revolver and shot the Federal off his horse, thus relieving Chalmers.
>
> We run until we reached the top of the hill. There we halted, turned our force around facing our enemy and fired a volley in their faces, thus creating confusion in the Federal cavalry for several minutes. We turned and went down the hill, into the valley and up the other hill and did the same thing.[32]

Good fortune smiled upon them. In the distance they could see Walthall's infantry drawn up in line of battle in the creek bottom. Bell and his men struck a fence, threw off a few rails, jumped it, and raced across a wide cornfield to the creek bank. The Yankees, for some reason, allowed them to flee unmolested and just watched from the edge of the field. Bell found Richland Creek "swimming." Nevertheless, he and his Babies plunged in and swam their horses to the other bank. Awaiting them on the south side was Forrest, Walthall, and a welcome host of Confederates.[33]

Forrest and Walthall immediately saw Bell's bloody face and clothes. They tried to help him off his horse, but Bell stubbornly shook his head, "No." "My eye was paining me very much then," he remembered, then added the incredulous understatement, "but I knew I was not hurt and did not need any doctoring."[34]

"Well, get down and get in my ambulance," Forrest said impatiently. Bell again refused. "No, my ambulance is in good condition and I have a safe driver and if I go in an ambulance, I will go in my own." So, with that, Forrest told his mule-headed friend to turn over his brigade to one of his colonels and the two men rode off to Pulaski to have "a nice supper" at Tom Martin's.

When they arrived in Pulaski, however, Dr. J. P. McGee, who had been sent ahead to organize a hospital, met them. He took one look at Bell and wanted the bleeding brigadier placed in the hospital. Again Bell refused. "I told him that I was not hurt and the only thing I wanted was to have my face washed and stick up those cuts with court plaster and give me a clean shirt, that I wanted to go on and eat a good supper before the Yankees got to the town."[35]

Tyree Bell got his clean shirt and his handsome supper at Tom Martin's. Just as he and Forrest were finishing, however, in rode the Yankees. The two officers fled over the covered bridge across Richland Creek and, with the help of pickets, managed to set fire to it. The Yankee cavalry was too fast, however. They put out the fire, patched the bridge and came on in hot pursuit. Forrest and Bell took to the deep woods, however, and eluded them. Finally they reached camp, dismounted, and attempted to sleep, but it was very cold and Bell's face "was swollen up big" and hurting. Bell and Forrest wanted revenge on their tormentors; there on the south side of Richland Creek they set two ambushes, both of which were to prove highly successful. The first, at King's or Anthony's Hill, where the road from Pulaski to Bainbridge ran through a gap between two hills, resulted in total surprise and the Federals recoiled in confusion, leaving a fieldpiece in Confederate hands.[36]

This halted the pursuit of the Federal cavalry only momentarily, however, and the mounted portion of the Confederate rear guard rode off, this Christmas day, with the Yankees still on their heels. And so it continued all that day until they reached the banks of Sugar Creek, fourteen miles below Anthony's Hill. There they bivouacked, close to the north bank. Forrest and Bell decided to divide their party at this time, the stream being swollen and the road being narrow. They would cross at fords about a quarter mile apart.

The following day, December 26, carefully concealed along the south side of Sugar Creek, Bell's Brigade participated in the second ambush against Wilson's pursuing Federals. They had awakened to "one of the most dense fogs you ever saw," Bell recalled. "You could not distinguish anyone thirty yards in front of you." Assisted by Walthall's infantry, they set ambushes at both fords in heavy force and waited for the enemy to appear, With their ambush line close to the creek, and with Morton's Battery masked, they awaited the enemy's arrival. A large "mass" of Yankee came up to the opposite bank, but Bell and his comrades could not see them clearly because of the dense fog. They waited until the enemy had crossed and were almost upon them before they swept the Federal line with every weapon Forrest's and Walthall's men could bring to bear. We "drove them back into the creek," Bell recalled, "and captured prisoners and horses." The Federals broke off the pursuit and retreated.[37]

Bell immediately had his brigade remount, and they rode on toward Bainbridge, where the Confederates had constructed a pontoon bridge across the rapidly rising Tennessee River for Hood's army. Bell's Brigade bivouacked about ten miles away from the bridge, carefully stationing sufficient pickets to prevent another Hollow Tree Gap debacle. Word finally came for Bell and his men to cross the Tennessee, and they did so at night, December 27, being the last element of the army to cross. The flimsy pontoon bridge "was a mile and a half long," Bell remembered, "and we crossed in columns of twos, walked and led our horses." Once over the river they camped four or five miles south, thus ending the long, cold, disheartening retreat from Nashville.[38]

When Bell's Brigade crossed the Tennessee on the night of December 27 they could take pride in their role in Hood's invasion. For thirty-five days they had campaigned through the most severe weather Middle Tennessee had known in years, in the saddle almost constantly "most of the time both day and night," recalled one of Clark Barteau's privates, "with no intermission of cold, sleet, and snow." On the whole they had done very well, as had their commander. Although mauled initially at Hollow Tree Gap and forced to flee for their lives several times, they had fought valiantly and capably at Murfreesboro, Harpeth River, Richland Creek, Anthony's Hill, and Sugar Creek. Indeed, George H. Thomas, who knew the meaning of hard fighting, paid them and their comrades high praise: "The rearguard . . . was undaunted and firm, and did its work bravely to the last."[39]

Safe across the Tennessee, no longer fearing interference from the enemy, Bell's Brigade made its way west along the Memphis and Charleston Railroad toward Corinth. About two miles from Tuscumbia, Bell reached the house where Reuben Clark was being cared for. Charlie Clark was there, as was young Isaac. Reuben was dying. Bell always remembered the scene: "I got down and stayed with him as long as he was rational, as long as he could talk. I think nearly every single man of my brigade dismounted and went in and spoke to him and bid him goodbye and hardly a single one left with dry eyes. There were the fewest number of men in this world like Reuben D. Clark. He was the grandest noble man I ever knew."

Leaving Isaac and Charlie to bury his friend, Bell remounted and led what remained of his brigade toward Corinth.[40]

17

All Was Gloom

Upon his arrival at Corinth, Bell reported to Forrest's headquarters and learned the heartening news that Forrest intended to furlough for twenty days all troops who lived within a reasonable distance. These troopers from Mississippi, Alabama, and Tennessee were to return home to recruit as well as round up deserters and absentees; equally important, they were to search for serviceable horses. As extra incentive in their efforts to procure man and beast, Forrest promised them an additional twenty days' leave if they brought in a "deserter or a recruit well mounted." The poor Texans and men from Arkansas and Missouri, however, would remain behind in camp in North Mississippi, performing the lonely, dangerous drudgery of picket and outpost duty. The joyous Tennesseans going on leave were expected to keep their homeless trans-Mississippi comrades in mind as they set off to refit themselves—bring them back clothing, food, or some such luxury, Bell prompted.

Nearly everyone realized the horses had even a greater need than the men. Truly, the animals of Forrest's Cavalry were in miserable condition and "suffering badly for forage." On the long seventy-day march to Johnsonville, over to Nashville, and back to Corinth, virtually without rest, in wretched weather with insufficient forage, many horses had died and many had to be abandoned. Corinth and vicinity, although secure for the moment against the likes of James H. Wilson, hardly promised to improve their lot. The area had been stripped bare and the animals were on "one-third ration of corn per day," Forrest informed Taylor, "and if they remain much longer upon that allowance they will be worthless." It was a cruel irony; bring back the best horses only to watch them wither into nags from overwork and lack of food. After the fateful

219

★ Brig. Gen. James H. Wilson. Library of Congress.

December in Tennessee, Forrest, Bell, and their comrades hardly cared. One dared not think, one dared nt see beyond the end of his nose.[1]

As Bell had his command prepare rations for the march back home to West Tennessee, Col. William W. Faulkner approached him. The thirty-year-old Faulkner and Bell had been associated from time to time for over a year as senior officers in Buford's Division. A daring and charming Kentuckian, Faulkner had been fighting since the beginning of the war, had been captured at Island No. 10 and had escaped. He had seen action under Chalmers during the Vicksburg Campaign, but primarily served then and later as a partisan leader, bedeviling Federals throughout the Jackson Purchase. After Faulkner and his regiment, now known as the Twelfth Kentucky Cavalry, had come under Forrest's command, Faulkner seems to have performed bravely and competently, fighting as a dismounted cavalry commander. As a subordinate of Ed Crossland at Tupelo, he had received terrible wounds for his efforts. Faulkner had come to Corinth to rejoin the fight and to resume command of his Twelfth Kentucky.

There were problems, however. He was not universally admired by the members of his regiment, and the fiercely independent Faulkner could not be regarded as compatible with Tyree Bell. They had clashed at least once. While operating together earlier in 1864 in West Tennessee, Faulkner had disobeyed Bell. Bell went further, complaining that he "had no control over him whatever, he [Faulkner] went where he pleased and greatly to my detriment."[2]

Now Bell confronted a contrite Faulkner, however, and the latter pleaded with Bell, "saying that he knew he had done wrong before, but pledged me his word that he would obey every order issued to him if Forrest would let him have his command again." Forrest, however, wanted no part of Faulkner. Bell knew Forrest's feelings and refused to intercede on Faulkner's behalf. Besides, the sadly diminished band once known as Faulkner's Twelfth Kentucky Cavalry had already ridden off for Kentucky, evidently not bothering to wait for their old commander's return, not wanting, it seemed, to chance his reinstatement. No matter, Faulkner would not be denied. He pressed Bell, who finally relented and went with Faulkner to see Forrest. When they appeared at headquarters, Forrest lashed out at the Kentuckian. "He talked ugly to Faulkner," Bell reported, "telling him that he was no account." As anticipated, Forrest refused to reinstate Faulkner despite Bell's intercession, nor would he even allow Faulkner to accompany Bell's Brigade back to Tennessee.

Evidently Forrest rethought the matter after the two men left headquarters, and that night he summoned Bell. The two old comrades discussed Faulkner. "I suggested that it would be best to let him go with me," Bell recalled, "that he could get nearly all his command up again." Forrest trusted the judgment of his loyal lieutenant, and after further discussion reversed his decision. He called Faulkner back and told him: "If you will promise me when you get up into West Tennessee, that you will obey the orders that General [sic] Bell issues to you promptly and when he returns, come up and bring what command you can with you, I will let you go with them."[3]

Colonel Faulkner gave his word to Forrest and the next morning Bell's Brigade set out for Tennessee, Faulkner riding along as a member of the column. When they passed through Trenton, Bell "turned him aloose to go up into the edge of Kentucky, giving him so many days to report back to me. I must have given him two weeks at least."[4]

Bell was back home in Newbern by the night of January 6, greeted happily, it seemed, by "shoe-deep" snow. Isaac and his kinsman, Maj. Albert Harris, enjoyed themselves immensely the next day, sledding and going by friends' homes for visits and "treats." It seemed like Christmas. One lady in the neighborhood tried to "joke" Bell and Harris about their disastrous Middle Tennessee Campaign. They took it "finely," she reported, and promised "better luck next time." Miserable weather set in almost immediately, however, as though determined to keep everyone indoors—driving rain and sleet turning to hail and snow. It "fell incessantly" resulting in three inches of "soft and very sloppy" snow. On January 10 it turned off "clear and very cold." It was time to leave, Bell said, and at eleven that morning he and his men rode out of Newbern and began scouring the countryside for deserters and conscripts, and for horses. Bell would return home to Newbern at least once more before departing for good on January 19, having managed to remain at home through the first half of January 1865 and, according to his neighbor Harriet Haskins, busying himself "around there gathering up all the stragglers [he] could get."[5]

With Bell's departure, gloom set in with the civilians. Other soldiers, part of the wreckage of Hood's army, drifted into the village, some known, many unknown. Men were sad-faced, jumpy, desperate. Whom could one trust? The conversation of one of these gloomy survivors was "very desponding" to Mrs. Haskins, who wrote, "He speaks of defeat to our cause every where [and] hard times for us in here is expected, but I trust the good Lord will be with us through all."[6]

When Bell's Brigade reassembled in Trenton, Faulkner reported "to the day that he promised and he had nearly all his command with him in good condition." This pleased Bell. Moreover, most of the brigade seem to have procured fresh horses without much difficulty. Primarily they exchanged their worn-out mounts with patriotic friends and acquaintances, or with frightened, troubled farmer folk all too anxious to be rid of their narrow-eyed visitors. This "horse furlough," however, resulted in some fragmentation. In one instance, at least, some of his escort, his "Bell's Babies," found themselves unable to return to Corinth, cut off, in effect, and were ordered by other Confederate officials to stop chasing about the countryside and head south to Mobile. There they, like several thousand Army of Tennessee infantry and artillery, would become defenders of Spanish Fort and Blakely, returning to Bell's Brigade only after the fall of Mobile in April 1865.[7]

By January 25 Bell had returned to Mississippi. Almost immediately he encountered Col. Ed Crossland on his way to Kentucky to corral stragglers and deserters. Crossland wanted Faulkner and his regiment to accompany him and the Kentucky Brigade. Bell, however, having reconciled his differences with Faulkner, denied his friend Crossland, insisting he needed the Kentuckians. They would remain with his brigade. At this point Crossland pulled out an order from Forrest, directing Bell to turn over Colonel Faulkner to Crossland. The disappointed Bell complied, but noted, "I did so but very reluctantly."[8]

Soon after Crossland and Faulkner reached Dresden, Tennessee, a portion of the command, at least a company of Forrest's Cavalry, came upon some notorious, "outlawed" deserters, the McDougal brothers. Despite being assured they would not be arrested, these desperate Rebel "absentees" were ready to fight and risk death rather than be returned to the army. They started shooting, but they aimed not at Crossland's Kentuckians, only at Colonel Faulkner. Capt. H. A. Tyler, Bell later learned, "one of the men who was famous for gallantry, sat on his horse by the side of his command and allowed the fight to go on without moving his command one inch." Faulkner was killed as they stood by.[9]

It was certainly quieter and safer deep in Mississippi. For the week remaining in January, and for almost all of February, Bell and his brigade lingered in winter quarters at West Point. Forrest's decision concerning Faulkner had disappointed Bell, of course, but he displayed greater emotion—that of disgust—upon learning of the treatment the young colonel had received at the hands of his fellow Kentuckians. It seemed typical of the hard times in which they found themselves. The war had turned vicious.

Never one for despondency, Bell took up his duties with characteristic energy. He took pleasure in Forrest's greatly widened authority and responsibility. His old friend now commanded all the cavalry in Richard Taylor's Department of Alabama, Mississippi, and East Louisiana, an imposing military jurisdiction, notwithstanding the fact that the command consisted of "a paltry total of some 10,000 widely scattered troops." Moreover, as additional evidence of his abiding faith in Forrest, Taylor had granted his lieutenant control "of the District of Mississippi and East Louisiana, with authority to subdivide and organize at his discretion."[10]

Forrest, upon assumption of command, promptly shifted his headquarters first to Verona, then on March 1 to West Point, Mississippi, farther south on the Mobile and Ohio. He also reorganized his cavalry into three divisions, grouping all the Mississippians under Chalmers, the Kentuckians and Alabamians under Buford, and the Tennesseans under Red Jackson. He instructed Jackson to form two brigades, Bell to command one, "leaving the command of the other for future consideration." In addition to the two Tennessee brigades Jackson would also command Sul Ross's small Texas Brigade and Morton's Battery. As a reflection of the dwindling manpower, painful consolidation of proud regiments once again occurred: Newsom's and Russell's regiments were combined into one under Russell. The skeleton Second and Twenty-first Tennessee Cavalry were merged under Col. Andrew Wilson. Also consolidated were the Tenth and Eleventh Tennessee Cavalry, Col. Jacob B. Biffle commanding.[11]

During this quiet winter interlude, as the war wound down and the Confederacy teetered on the brink of extinction, official notice came of Forrest's promotion to lieutenant general and Bell to brigadier. Promoted with Tyree Bell was Col. Alexander W. Campbell of Jackson, Tennessee, who was named to

★ Brig. Gen. William H. Jackson. Tennessee State Library and Archives.

head Red Jackson's other Tennessee brigade. Campbell, a lawyer by profession, had led the Thirty-third Tennessee Infantry early in the war and been badly wounded. Staff duty under Polk and Pillow followed until Campbell's capture at Lexington, Tennessee, while attempting to round up conscripts. Although not exchanged until February 1865, Alexander Campbell returned to the West Tennessee–Mississippi theater and became Forrest's inspector general. He apparently impressed Forrest so much so that the latter gave him the unassigned Tennessee brigade.[12]

Abe Buford was gone. Nominally a division commander under Forrest, his brigades of Roddey, James H. Clanton, and Charles G. Armistead now constituted a paper command of Alabamians, scattered from Montevallo to Mobile.[13]

The swollen Tennessee River subsided finally from the winter rains, and March 1865 brought Yankee cavalry in heavy force to the south bank. They were commanded by Forrest's nemesis, the able, energetic Bvt. Maj. Gen. James H. Wilson. Wilson's objective was Selma, Alabama, the huge supply and munitions center, the logistical heart of the western Confederacy. Wilson came on rapidly. With him marched three divisions (some 12,500 troops), three batteries, and a train of 250 wagons guarded by 1,500 dismounted troopers. Wilson's men were armed with Spencer repeating carbines, giving them far greater firepower than any Confederate force they might encounter. Wilson intended to wreck Selma and knew that in the process he would have the chance to meet and destroy Forrest. To confront and repel this menace, Forrest sought to concentrate his widely scattered forces. He brought Chalmers's Division into Alabama while Red Jackson's division began its shift east, moving from West Point to Columbus, Mississippi. Upon his arrival at Columbus on March 28, Jackson received orders from Forrest to intercept a portion of Wilson's command, an isolated column perhaps. Jackson was to advance to Tuscaloosa, Alabama, to "whip and get rid of that column of the enemy as soon as possible." Forrest initially believed, it appears, that he was once again dealing with a Stephen Hurlbut or a Sooy Smith timidly poking into his fiefdom.[14]

Scarcely had they arrived in Tuscaloosa about noon, March 30, than Jackson's Division received orders to press on to Centerville to secure the bridge over the Cahaba. Forget the isolated column. Help was needed to protect Selma. Forrest hoped, once Jackson had crossed the Cahaba at Centerville, to throw his division to the rear of Wilson's column advancing south from Elyton (later known as Birmingham) through Montevallo. If this succeeded, Wilson would be caught between the undersized brigades of Roddey and Daniel W. Adams to his front (Chalmers with Armstrong's Brigade was hurrying to join them before Selma) and Jackson to his rear. Jackson and Bell, oddly, did not seem to be sufficiently concerned to press their march. Sending the column ahead, Jackson and Bell with a few staff officers remained behind in Tuscaloosa and had supper as guests of Col. John Blocker. Blocker was a cotton factor and sometime politician, a refugee from his plantation in Green County, Alabama, a passionate Rebel and a man of substance. He had raised and commanded a company for the Mexican War, then recruited and outfitted the Eleventh Alabama Infantry in 1861. He never commanded the latter, however, being declared over-age for field duty. His principal wartime accomplishment seems to have been establishing a reputation for entertaining Confederate guests lavishly, a fairly won distinction so far as Jackson and Bell were concerned. "I do assure you it was a treat," Bell wrote, "that we had not met up with in a great while, such a supper as we had that night at Blocker's." Like many Confederates, never troubled by over-mastering anxieties, Bell believed he might as well help himself to a proper dinner, and so he did. Having feasted and been entertained by the convivial Blocker, Jackson and Bell left their host about 11:00 that night and rode on through the darkness to where the division was encamped.[15]

All the while Bell and Red Jackson enjoyed their treat and rode blithely toward Centerville, James Wilson's subordinate, Brig. Gen. John T. Croxton, with a brigade of Federal cavalry, eighteen hundred strong, was marching from Elyton toward Tuscaloosa with the objective of capturing the town and destroying the bridge over the Black Warrior River. Once that had been accomplished Croxton was to proceed east to Selma and rejoin Wilson for the attack on that stronghold. Late in the afternoon of March 31, Croxton's column happened to strike perpendicularly the road over which Jackson's Division had just passed marching from Tuscaloosa to Centerville. Actually Jackson's cavalry had moved on east out of sight. Unknown to Croxton, trailing behind this long column of Rebel cavalry were Red Jackson's division train and John Morton's artillery. Thus Croxton had, in effect, cut the Rebel column in two. Uncertainty now struck. Croxton broke off his march to Tuscaloosa, aggressively deciding to follow and strike the rear of the Rebel cavalry column that had passed. He set out after Jackson and Bell and Campbell, then had a change of heart, stopped, and remembering Wilson's instructions, turned about. Marching west once again toward Tuscaloosa, he took another road, quite unintentionally, than that on which Jackson's trains and guns traveled, thus bypassing them. As he marched on toward Tuscaloosa, Croxton did take the precaution of protecting his rear, leaving behind a small rear guard.[16]

After Bell had bivouacked near Centerville on March 31, a few of his troopers informed him that "they were drawing forage from the same crib that the enemy were drawing from." Bell immediately rode to Jackson's headquarters and informed him. The two generals then devised a plan to strike at the nearby enemy, which happened to be the rear guard of Croxton's cavalry. They would attack the Federals in their camp before daylight. First, however, they had to locate precisely the bivouac, so Bell and a party of twenty carefully selected men rode about in the dark until they discovered the enemy's encampment. Without alerting the enemy, Bell and his fellow scouts now rode back to Jackson and reported what they had found. Jackson decided to attack with his entire division. Using good Forrest doctrine, Bell would swing wide to the northwest and strike the Elyton-Trion Road which intersected the Tuscaloosa Road at the village of Trion. Bell would then wheel south and move directly down that road upon the Yankee camp. Campbell and his brigade, in the meantime, would simply reverse their line of march and advance back down the Centerville-Tuscaloosa Road toward the tail of Croxton's force at Trion. Once in place, the two brigades would attack simultaneously.[17]

Bell moved out early, reached the Trion-Elyton Road, headed south cautiously, and arrived in the rear of the enemy cavalry column, all without being discovered. Then he and his men sat their horses and "waited to hear something from Campbell." But they heard nothing and, as dawn approached, Bell decided to attack alone. His troopers, "revolvers in hand," charged into the Federal camp, Andrew Wilson's regiment leading the attack, "stampeding them," Bell observed happily, "capturing some of their men and all of the cooking utensils and breakfast and provisions." One of Barteau's privates noted in his diary, "When Colonel Wilson's revolvers were playing upon the enemy in rapid succession, General Bell was heard to remark, 'That is the sweetest music I ever heard.'" Bell pursued Croxton's rear guard west toward Tuscaloosa, but tired of the chase and turned back, encamping midway between Tuscaloosa and Centerville. According to Bell, during the fight and pursuit, Campbell never showed up.[18]

That night scouts brought Bell more exciting intelligence. Another enemy cavalry force, Edward M. McCook's division, was advancing west toward them from Centerville—their objective! Bell wanted to repeat last night's success, so he remounted and led a scout of McCook's position. When he reported his findings to Red Jackson, the latter happily ordered him to attack McCook. Again, Campbell would be in support.[19]

Once more, it appears, Bell would attack on his own. Sunday morning, April 2, he planted Wilson's Sixteenth Tennessee Cavalry across the Tuscaloosa-Centerville Road at a point where the road crossed a ravine near Scottsville. He instructed Colonel Wilson to present McCook (who seemed to have deployed across the same road on a wide front) "a banter," a challenge or demonstration, then give way, hoping that McCook would follow in force, funneling his widely deployed force into a narrow, compact, road-bound column. This would lead McCook into an ambush, Bell's three other regiments being hidden in the woods on the side of the road. If all went as planned, Bell's bugle would be the signal for an assault by the entire brigade.

Wilson succeeded famously in drawing McCook across the ravine and down the road, the Yankees coming "gallantly to the attack." When McCook's leading elements reached the designated spot, Bell's bugle rang out. Wilson swung about and counterattacked. Milton Russell now turned "aloose" the balance of the brigade. They roared out upon McCook's men from two, perhaps three, sides, "stampeding McCook's whole division and giving them such a scare that they never halted to fire one time," Bell remembered proudly. McCook's cavalry turned about and scrambled back toward the Cahaba bridge, about twelve miles away. They and others of McCook's command quickly burned the bridge across the river before Bell could prevent it.[20]

Although the ambush seemed a success to Bell, McCook had the last laugh. Only a portion of his force had been engaged, and his mission was not to find and whip Rebel cavalry, but to provide cover for the remainder of his troopers back to the east, busy preparing the Cahaba bridge to be set afire. After being stung by Bell's ambush, McCook was able to retire down the Tuscaloosa-Centerville Road behind the Cahaba, leaving Jackson's big division stranded on the west bank, watching the conflagration, helpless to assist Bedford Forrest at Selma. McCook's spoiling attack had succeeded brilliantly.

Frustrated in his belated effort to cross to the east side of the Cahaba, Jackson had little choice but to set his entire division in motion for Marion, twenty miles northwest of Selma. All this time, it appears, Bell and Jackson had been operating in ignorance of Forrest's plight, his desperate running fight with the main portion of James Wilson's Federals north of Selma.

Forrest, outnumbered and outgunned and outgeneraled, had fallen back into the prepared defenses of Selma on April 2. There he attempted to defend the town and its three miles of fortifications with only Armstrong's Brigade of Chalmers's Division, a few troops from Crossland's Kentucky Brigade, Roddey's command, and local defense forces, in all about three thousand men. Wilson

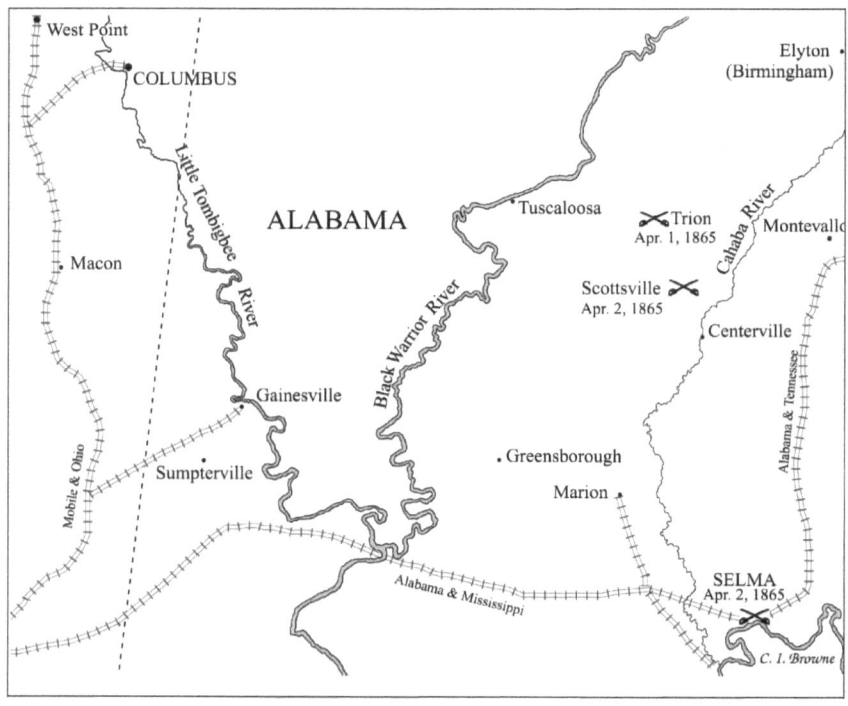

★ FIGHTING AGAINST WILSON IN ALABAMA, MARCH–MAY 1865. COURTESY OF C. I. BROWNE.

crashed into this thinly held line, overrunning it with relative ease. All was lost, and Forrest had to escape the best way he could.[21]

Jackson and Bell had failed Forrest. Concentrating on small tactical adventures of little consequence, they had allowed themselves to be occupied first by Croxton, then by McCook. Croxton, though beaten and forced to retreat, had diverted them from their objective: secure the Cahaba bridge and cross the river. Meanwhile, Edward McCook had moved swiftly, seized Centerville, and destroyed the bridge, thus isolating Jackson's critical command on the west bank of the Cahaba and rendering them useless for the defense of Selma.[22]

When Bell and Jackson reached Marion they were surprised to find survivors of the Selma battle, fragments of commands, dragging into the rendezvous point. Bad news piled upon bad news. Croxton had crossed to the west side of Black Warrior River and marched upon Tuscaloosa, capturing the town April 4. After a fight with Dan Adams's Brigade on April 6, Croxton would turn north and reestablish himself at Elyton. In Marion were the troops of Starke's Brigade, Chalmers's Division, and presently Forrest himself arrived from Selma with what remained of Armstrong's Brigade. "We met General Armstrong alone," Bell remembered. "He informed us of the fall of Selma," and of his desperate escape. "Armstrong was very much depressed indeed."[23]

Bell established his camp south of Marion and awaited developments. Forrest and James Wilson soon met under flag of truce at Cahaba on April 8 to discuss "the parole and exchange of the considerable number of prisoners which each side held." Afterwards Wilson returned to Selma and immediately rode off to the east, capturing Montgomery and winding his way virtually unopposed into Georgia, destroying Confederate facilities at will, seizing Columbus and Macon.[24]

Forrest and his troops did not follow Wilson, but remained inactive in the area between Marion and Gainesville, Alabama, close to the Mississippi border. Days turned into weeks. "We had a very fine time," Bell recalled. "It was a country where neither soldiers had been during the war and they were nice, charitable people, southern to the core and they gave us such treatment as we had not had since the early days of the war."[25]

According to Bell, he asked Forrest permission to take his brigade and go to Greensboro, Alabama, about fifteen miles west of Marion toward Gainesville. Red Jackson "decided to go with me," Bell recalled. "We went over and met with a warm reception and remained there for about two weeks." By this time serious negotiations for surrender were under way between Generals Richard Taylor and Edward R. S. Canby, whose forces had captured Mobile. During these last weeks in April, Forrest's forces, aware that the war was lost, gathered at or near Gainesville. Bell's Brigade continued to melt. Now it numbered less than one thousand effectives.[26]

Bell and his men spent their last days as Confederates at the little village of Sumpterville, some fourteen miles southwest of Gainesville. "All was gloom," remembered Col. David C. Kelley, "broken only by wild rumors." Debate raged among the men. Would they surrender? Would they continue the fight? Would they band together and ride off to Texas and Mexico? A group within Forrest's Cavalry urged the latter course. Prominent among them were two popular and influential leaders: Gov. Isham G. Harris and Gen. Hylan B. Lyon (recently returned from a disastrous attempt to organize and maintain a Department of Western Kentucky). Bell disagreed. He considered their ideas folly and attempted to speak against the plan, arguing for peace. "We paid no attention to him," remembered Sgt. J. G. Witherspoon, Nineteenth Tennessee Cavalry. The men were bitter and wild. Ultimately they turned to Forrest, who calmed them. They must accept the inevitable, he told them with disarming eloquence: "You have been good soldiers, you can be good citizens. Obey the laws, preserve your honor, and the government to which you have surrendered can afford to be and will be magnanimous." Forrest prevailed, and the command prepared for the shame of surrender.[27]

General Canby handled the situation wisely and kindly. "The details of surrender were all arranged without the appearance of a Federal officer in our camp," one young Rebel remembered. "The same being conducted in the most punctilious manner and without any effort to humiliate." Thus these Confederates of Forrest and Bell yielded and received their paroles at Gainesville, Alabama, May 10, 1865.[28]

In bidding good-bye to his men Tyree Bell echoed Forrest's advice. "Discharge as faithfully the duties of citizens as you have those of soldiers," he said, "and all may yet be well." He went further. "I am proud to be your commander; proud of the reputation you have won on so many bloody fields of battle, and proud of the firmness, consistency, and devotion you have displayed in the closing scene of this dark and fearful drama. . . . In your future prosperity and welfare I will ever feel a deep and abiding interest."[29]

18

Disappointment in Dyer County

It was over. Once he had received his parole, Tyree Bell did not linger in camp waiting until all his troops had received their own humbling piece of parchment authenticating them in the eyes of their former enemy. Instead, he let Major Allison handle that depressing task while he dispatched other staff members to the office of the Federal quartermaster in Gainesville. With the permission of Canby's paroling officer and the assistance of the Yankee quartermaster, the staff identified and retrieved Bell's headquarters wagon and his ambulance. They also requested and received two mule teams, which they promised would be turned back to the government once they arrived in Dyer County. Once they secured the teams, they proceeded to pack the wagon and ambulance with the general's personal effects and sufficient provisions and forage for the trip back to Newbern.

In the late spring of 1865, the four-hundred-mile trip from Gainesville, Alabama, to Newbern, Tennessee, had to be accomplished overland and in armed parties. The Mobile and Ohio Railroad, twenty miles from Gainesville, was wrecked and useful simply as a direction marker. Wagon roads north and west were available, but they were in poor repair and inefficiently located. The journey home to the land of the Forked Deer during those chaotic and dangerous days immediately after the surrender would prove long and tiring, but fortunately uneventful.

After reaching Newbern on May 20 and greeting friends and family with the news that "the boys will be along in a few days," General Bell, quite aware of his tender political status as a paroled Rebel senior officer, immediately had the wagon and ambulance unloaded. The next morning he and Isaac, with help from his servant Milus, hitched up the teams again and rode the twenty-five miles to Trenton, the nearest Union army post. There they turned over the ambulance, wagon, and teams to Federal authorities.

Now, with his military obligations at an end, Bell wheeled his horse about, faced west, and once more started toward Newbern. To stay.[1]

The transition from cavalry leader to civilian farmer was abrupt. Making a crop was of paramount importance, so he, Isaac, and Milus set to work in the cotton and corn fields. In response to President Andrew Johnson's May 29 Proclamation of Pardon and Amnesty, Bell made the eight-mile trip to the county seat at Dyersburg on Monday, July 17, and took the oath to "henceforth faithfully defend the Constitution of the United States and the Union of the States thereunder" and to "abide by and faithfully support all laws and proclamations which have been made during the existing rebellion with reference to the emancipation of slaves." The courthouse staff certified and supported his petition, concurring with Judge Isaac Sampson that Tyree H. Bell was worthy of clemency.[2]

By the end of September 1865, the financial concerns of civilian life had come to the forefront, and Bell found it necessary to pledge his 408 acres, his cultivated cotton and corn crops, five horses, a matched pair of mules, five head of young cattle, seven head of sheep, a four-horse wagon, a barouche, and two beds to satisfy an accumulation of $5,424.47 in debts incurred during the prewar years. His cousin, Allen Harris, the wealthiest man in Newbern, acted as trustee for the transaction, which required sale of the property if the debts were not repaid on or before October 15, 1867. It must have been painful to pledge land and livestock, but this was only the beginning. The decade following the war would be in sharp contrast to the 1850s, as property values, particularly farmland, continued to erode. There was virtually no cash as West Tennessee floundered in depression. For the most part, individual farmers like Bell relied on a primitive barter system to see them through.[3]

When the Harris brothers, Allen and Albert Gallatin, decided to go into the commission business in October 1865, Bell was glad to be made a partner, even though he could not contribute the same $2,500.00 that the Harrises and their other partners, John Fakes and George Miller, each supplied. Probably his reputation and numerous wartime and prewar contacts were thought to be equivalent, for it was agreed that he would be charged interest on the corporate debt as if he had bought an equal share. An office, known as Harris, Miller and Company, was opened at 11 Olive Street in the commercial district of St. Louis and another under the name of Bell, Harris and Company, Cotton and Tobacco Factors and General Merchandise, began operations at 114 Poydras Street in New Orleans as agents for their contracted farmers.[4]

These new business ventures, while moderately successful, did not raise money rapidly enough to satisfy Bell's debts. Consequently on February 21, 1866, Allen Harris, acting as his attorney in fact, sold two parcels of Bell's land. One tract of one hundred acres raised $5,000; the other ninety-six-acre parcel was sold for $1,400. Thus it appears Bell cleared, at least temporarily, his indebtedness. Quite possibly Bell was traveling on commission business at the time of the sale, as he does not seem to have been present, but by April 1866, he had returned to Dyer County and went to the courthouse to confirm the power of attorney under which the property had been sold.[5]

That same April Bell's old friend and chaplain, the Rev. Jack Mahon, and his former quartermaster, John Skeffington, were among the public-spirited citizens of Dyer County who took action regarding the desperate plight of former soldiers. In keeping with his pledge to his men in Gainesville, Bell became an enthusiastic participant in the new Dyer County Aid Society—dedicated to collecting contributions for "supplying those who need them with artificial limbs, helping the indigent, and relieving the families of the slain and the helpless." The Aid Society was organized with a central committee of five in Dyersburg and a subcommittee of four ladies and one gentleman in each civil district. At that first meeting, Saturday, April 14, 1866, at the Cumberland Presbyterian Church, plans were made for a benefit concert. General Bell moved that John Skeffington, Esq., of Dyersburg deliver an address on Saturday, April 28, about the objects and purposes of the society.[6]

With his real property reduced by half and the rising cost of labor making farming even more expensive, Bell devoted even greater attention and effort to the commission business. His primary role was traveling and soliciting accounts and transactions for the different houses. At the close of 1866, the St. Louis house was moved to Cincinnati. About the same time James Shane and Robert Herron, who had a commission business in Memphis, joined the firm with a one-sixth interest in the Cincinnati house and a one-half interest in the house at 280 Front Street in Memphis, which was known as Shane, Bell and Company. The New Orleans branch, Bell, Harris and Company, moved its offices a few blocks to 58 Carondelet Street, and Bell maintained a nearby part-time residence at 50 Carondelet.[7]

The end of 1866 also brought new changes in the family circle. Bell's eldest daughter, Susan, married Reuben Green Harrell on his twenty-first birthday. Among the many Dyer County families with distant kinship ties to Mary Walton Bell, the Harrells were also old friends, having lived just a short distance from Tyree and Mary Ann in Sumner County. They too had migrated to West Tennessee in the 1850s and settled east of Newbern in the Ninth Civil District.

Their two oldest sons, William and James, were among the first to enlist in the Newbern Blues, and William became captain of the company after Bell's promotion to lieutenant colonel, only to die in the fighting at Murfreesboro. Young Reuben joined Bell's Brigade even though he was underage and had remained with the general throughout the war.[8]

The year 1867 brought Tyree and Mary Ann Bell their first grandchild, Margaret "Maggy" Harrell, but business troubles mounted. The close of this year saw George Miller and John Fakes withdraw from the partnership. The New Orleans house closed, and the Memphis and Cincinnati offices conducted its business during 1868. Problems arose concerning a large shipment of tobacco consigned to the New Orleans office. Allen Harris decided to send the shipment to a firm in England, which soon became insolvent, and the tobacco was then shipped to Germany where it was eventually sold at very reduced prices. Many of the consignors felt the tobacco should have been sold at New Orleans prices and began a series of lawsuits that would last for many years. As the business was structured on an annual basis, Bell remained in the partnership through 1868, but decided at the end of the year to withdraw. He then took a similar position with William Glenn & Sons, Wholesale Grocers, in Cincinnati.[9]

The same year continued to be filled with family changes. Isaac, who had been working for the partnership, abandoned farming to seek employment in the mercantile business in Lexington, Tennessee. Soon Isaac met, courted, and married Miss Seraphina Elizabeth Smith. At the same time Sallie was courting her mother's cousin, Isaac Henry (Ike) Walton. In addition to being a family member, Ike also had served with General Bell at the end of the war. He first had enlisted in the Ninth Tennessee Cavalry and later served with John Hunt Morgan, fortunately avoiding capture in Morgan's Ohio raid. He then transferred to Forrest's Cavalry, Bell's brigade, where he was in service with his half-brother, Tyree Harris Walton, another early enlistee in the Newbern Blues who remained with Bell throughout the war. A tall, handsome, dark-haired man, Isaac was well known to both Tyree and Mary Ann Bell, and they knew he would take good care of their fun-loving second daughter. The young couple married on December 8, 1868.[10]

Life continued predictably for the next four years. Tyree Bell traveled on behalf of William Glenn & Sons; Mary Ann Walton Bell cared for their lively growing sons, John Richard, now twelve; Tyree Alexander "Burch," now fourteen; and Josiah Walton "Joe," now sixteen.[11] Burch and Joe, who had been toddlers during the war years, were now old enough and strong enough to help out on the farm.

★ TYREE H. BELL, ABOUT 1870. TENNESSEE STATE LIBRARY AND ARCHIVES.

The family was recovering financially. Instead of the labor-intensive tobacco crop that made up so much of their prewar produce, Tyree and the boys concentrated on growing corn and wheat. They also had enough land in cotton to produce five bales for sale in 1870. That year their farm products were valued at twenty-five hundred dollars, even though the number of livestock had been greatly reduced. Bell was solvent and could redirect his efforts.[12]

Early in 1872, General Bell resigned his position with William Glenn & Sons and threw his hat in the ring as a Democratic candidate for Congress. It is a testament to Bell's reputation and doggedness that he allowed himself to undertake such a campaign against well-known and experienced candidates, but hardly a tribute to his political acumen.

Robert P. Caldwell, former major of the Twelfth Tennessee and Bell's comrade of many battlefields, was running for reelection as a Democrat. Caldwell was an attorney practicing in Trenton. He had been a member of the Tennessee legislature for four years before the war and had served as attorney general of the Sixteenth Judicial Circuit of Tennessee in 1858. Gen. Alexander W. Campbell of Madison County, Bell's fellow brigade commander in 1865, was another popular candidate, but the eventual winner was the Republican David A. Nunn of Haywood County, a staunch Unionist. He, too, was an attorney and had served in the Tennessee legislature, 1865–67. In 1867 Nunn had been elected to Congress on the Republican ticket and was appointed by President Grant as minister to Ecuador in 1869 when he lost his seat to Caldwell. The Eighth Congressional District (Madison, Crockett, Haywood, Lauderdale, Dyer, Gibson, Weakley, Obion, and Lake Counties) was quite large, covering most of West Tennessee, and deeply divided politically in 1872.

Although Bell displayed strength in half the counties, he trailed the other candidates badly, even in Dyer. He polled about one hundred more votes than Nunn in Dyer, but came in second to Campbell; he lost to Caldwell in nearby Obion and Gibson, and in the large Madison County vote he garnered ninety to Caldwell's fifteen hundred and Nunn's thirteen hundred. Ultimately, Nunn benefited from the multiple Democratic entries and won handily. Bell seems to have succeeded only in taking votes from his fellow Democrats and contributing to Nunn's election. Undoubtedly, it proved a depressing experience.[13]

After nearly six years of business travel and appearances throughout West Tennessee during the election campaign, Bell was content to stay home and resume the life of a farmer and civic-minded citizen. Typical of his activities was service in 1874 as president of the board of directors of the annual Dyer County Fair.[14]

The long, complicated tobacco suits against Bell, Harris & Company finally ended, but unfortunately they generally resulted in damages being assessed against the firm. Although no longer a member of the partnership, Bell had become increasingly concerned about the financial dealings of the business. His worries were justified in January 1873 when his old friends, Ed Haskins and Guy Douglass, brought suit against him for notes which they insisted Allen Harris, his trustee, had not paid. In an effort to clarify his financial status, Bell entered into a suit with George Miller against their former partners, emphasizing that they had never received an accounting of the partnership activities. After Anderson & Richardson, attorneys for the Harrises, found numerous minute errors in the original bill of complaint, Bell and Miller filed a countercharge, which in effect accused the Harris brothers of delaying an accounting in order for the six-year statute of limitations to take effect, and of neglecting to collect on accounts payable in order to retain patrons for their own business. Bell and Miller also demanded a full accounting of the European tobacco fiasco. These suits and countersuits were in court through much of 1875 and certainly did nothing to enhance the strong sense of family loyalty that had previously existed among the extended Bell-Harris clan. The Bell family felt that Tyree's remaining assets had been wiped out because of mismanagement by at least one of his commission business partners.[15]

The early 1870s must have proven a disappointing period for Bell. Hard work had not produced the results he had anticipated—on the farm, in the political arena, and in the commission business. He had calculated on the advancing prosperity of Dyer County, the profits from the soil. That is why he had come west from Sumner. Instead he witnessed declining prices and foreclosures. He had watched his soldiers ride out of Alabama, sad that they had lost the struggle, but with their eyes full of hope. Now his boys had grown into needy veterans, and when they would visit him he must have suffered when he learned of their misfortunes. Men, his friends, felt helpless and angry.

National affairs also seemed in turmoil. The Panic of 1873 began in September, leading to a ten-day closing of the New York Stock Exchange, failure of the Northern Pacific Railroad and collapse of over five thousand businesses in the first year. Locally this had the long-term result of further reducing property values. The 115-acre Bell farm, worth $3,910.00 in 1874, had become devalued to $2,300 by 1875. Financial distress and fear proved fertile breeding ground for political and social unrest. Smoldering resentments from the war years flamed anew. August 1874 brought reports of an attack on nearby Trenton, Tennessee, by a large group of armed blacks with the intent of murdering certain whites and taking their farms. March 1875 saw the passage of the controversial and resented Civil Rights Act, which guaranteed equal rights for blacks in public places and erased some basic distinctions of color—blacks, for instance, could no longer be excluded from jury duty. To the eyes of many dismayed citizens of Dyer, however, it seemed that both economic conditions and race relations were at an all-time low. The weather had also contributed to the general malaise. Snow in Newbern reached fourteen inches in March. Hordes of army worms attacked the wheat and cotton crops, forcing the farmers to dig extensive ditches in an effort to halt their advance. By September 1875, chills and high fever had reached epidemic proportions.[16]

In this time of uneasiness, young Joe Bell, now twenty, is reported to have announced, "I'm going to get on my horse and ride to California!" He sounded like a prophet. There was magic to the word "California." It spelled opportunity, a place where one might begin again. Miss Mary's younger brother, John Walton, was among those Sumner County adventurers who had followed the lure of gold back in 1849, and surely he had told his young nephews stories of the fabled state even though he himself had not profited from the adventure. Then there were the California tales of the Russells and Nick Wyatt and Frank Cheatham and Black Bob McCulloch and dozens of others who had seen the "Promised Land." General Bell's old friend, the Rev. William Jackson Mahon, his son Rev. R. H. Mahon, and young Rev. A. W. Hunsaker were all transferring from the Memphis Conference of the Methodist Church to the Pacific Conference and could well have urged Bell to accompany them. Regardless of the specific catalyst, Dyer County had gone sour for Tyree Bell. It was time to go, and by autumn 1875, preparations were under way to move the entire Bell family to the far west.

19

South to West

On October 25, 1875, Tyree and Mary Ann sold their farm to their neighbor Herod A. Dean for $3,000.00. From the proceeds Allen Harris was to be paid $1,168.50 and two payments of $915.75 were to be made to Bell, all three notes falling due December 1, 1875. The Bells devoted November 1875 to packing household and personal belongings, making travel arrangements, disposing of other property, and preparing a large supply of food for the journey. Finally, on December 5, General Bell attempted to tie up his financial affairs in Tennessee by borrowing $1,200.00 from Thomas Cotton, giving him the two notes from Dean with the understanding that Cotton would keep the funds due him and send the balance to Bell in California.[1]

The general engaged one of Pullman's hotel cars for the journey, as well as a freight car for their family belongings and the horses to be taken along. The hotel car contained two drawing rooms, each with a sofa and two large easy chairs which made up at night into a double and single berth; a stateroom with two double berths; and six open sections of two double berths each, accommodations for twenty-two travelers. A fully equipped kitchen and the services of a cook, conductor, and two waiters were included, all for $85.00 per day, in addition to the regular fare. Certainly it seemed almost perfect accommodations for the large Bell party, which included General and Mrs. Bell and their four unmarried children, Cynthia, Burch, Joe and John; their daughter Susan, her husband Reuben Harrell, and their four little girls; and their daughter Sallie, her husband Isaac Walton, and their baby son Edgar. The Rev. Jack Mahon, his wife, their children, and three young bachelors—Bradley Doyle, the Rev. A. W. Hunsaker, and Ruben Harrell's cousin, Robert Harrell—completed the party. Plans were made for Isaac and his growing family to join them later, his responsibilities as

Henderson County Circuit Clerk preventing him from making the trip. How difficult it must have been for Cynthia to say good-bye, as she was newly engaged to young John P. Ledsinger, who promised to meet her out west. John was another of those distant kinfolk whose family had moved from Sumner County to West Tennessee, and he had served in General Bell's escort until the end of the war. The wedding would take place the following spring in California.[2]

The Bells' cross-continent railroad adventure took at least a week, perhaps longer, going by way of St. Louis, Council Bluffs, Salt Lake City, and Sacramento, then south down California's immense Central Valley. Delays abounded. The cars would sit interminably on sidetracks waiting to be hitched to the next westbound train, waiting for this, waiting for that. While sidetracked at the Council Bluffs, Iowa, depot, a large, menacing stranger entered the coach, but was informed he could not pass through this private car. He ignored this warning and continued through the car, whereupon General Bell grabbed him and forced him out the door. The women were terrified, knowing that they were in "Yankee" territory, and certain that Bell would be arrested for this action and possibly sent to jail. When the conductor arrived on the scene, however, he assured Bell and the ladies that the man was a big bully who had been causing much trouble. A guard was placed around their car until they were able to proceed the next morning. Incidents of this nature, played against the background of the feeling of turmoil they had left behind in Tennessee, added to the high state of excitement felt by the travelers.

The landscape contributed to the seesaw of emotions. Soon after leaving Council Bluffs they passed through the most barren country any of them had ever seen. Populated by prairie dogs and an occasional prairie chicken, this vast grassland seemed to stretch forever, until at last they reached the Rocky Mountains. Here the steep slopes and constant switchbacks of the roadbed added a new and troubling atmosphere of excitement. It was with a sense of relief that the party arrived at Sacramento, mingled with some sadness, for the Mahon family left the group at this point and traveled on to San Francisco, where Parson Jack took charge of the small Southern Methodist Church.[3]

The Bell party in their Pullman car continued south from Sacramento to Fresno County, chosen as their destination because young Reverend Hunsaker knew a fellow Southern Methodist minister there, the only person, it was said, any of them knew in the entire state of California. This fellow Tennessean, the Rev. Henry Avery, was ministering to a vast area and busy helping plan the first church of any denomination in the town of Fresno, where he preached the opening sermon on March 3, 1876. His small congregation, numbering about twelve, was soon augmented by the Bell family.

They arrived in Fresno at night, in a drizzling rain, and were met by the lantern-carrying hotel-keeper. This was another new experience, especially for the Bell women, who had done an occasional bit of traveling, but had always lodged with friends or family. The small, unpainted hotel building, with "walls of pine with some knotholes in them with one occasionally poked out," the dry goods boxes used for wash stands with tin pitchers and basins, were a great contrast to the marble-topped stands and china furnishings they had known in Tennessee, to say nothing of the dingy community roller-towel on the wall outside for those who had washed at the well.[4]

The hotel food was also indifferent, and Miss Mary was soon overheard to say, "Mr. Bell, can't you look around and find us a house we can move into and do our own cooking?" Nothing was to be had, accommodating the entire family, but Bell soon located a row of three small houses and rented them. Bell and his sons-in-law were busy meeting the local residents and soon became acquainted with Billy Cole, a sheep rancher from Missouri who owned a large ranch near Big Dry Creek and knew most of the valley residents. He put Bell in touch with William Glenn, another Tennessean who was settling his brother's estate. Glenn arranged for the Bells to rent a large brick house on a bluff east of King's River, where they moved the early part of 1876. Finding this property to his liking, Bell entered into an agreement to purchase it from the Glenn estate. Thus he, his sons, and sons-in-law were able to continue the farming that they knew so well. By March, General Bell was writing to his family back in Sumner County that "everything here looks like the middle of May, all kinds of garden vegetables are in their prime, the grass all over the plains is half-a-leg high, stock of all kinds sleek and fat without having been fed a single time throughout the winter, and with the finest prospects for a splendid wheat crop." The land not under cultivation was turning into a magic carpet of spring wildflowers, from which Miss Mary tried unsuccessfully to collect seeds to send back to Tennessee.[5]

Although Reuben Harrell, Isaac Walton, and Josiah and Tyree H. Bell all were registered voters, only T. H. Bell appears in the 1876 Fresno County tax records, paying $107.85 in real property taxes and $10.65 on personal property, which included $110 cash on hand, a $40 wagon, a $15 plow, five horses, five cows, seven calves, and $27 worth of poultry. The bold venture across the continent at last seemed to be successful.[6]

Life on the ranch, while filled with hard work, was also a time of homemade fun. Singing and dancing often filled the evening hours. Burch and Bob Harrell both played the violin while Ike Walton picked the banjo and could "sing the hit songs of the day with the best of them." Sallie always managed to learn the latest dance steps, and soon all ages were having a lively time.[7]

Summer's arrival brought more surprises. The lovely countryside changed to a dry, parched expanse, the beautiful wildflowers withered and died, and the temperatures reached unfamiliar heights. Soon Reuben Harrell's old war wound began acting up, an abscess causing him great pain. The family physician, Mississippian Robinson Cockrill of Centerville, Cal., despaired of Reuben's life and sent to Visalia for Dr. William Russell, brother of Bell's old compatriot, Milton Russell. Dr. Russell advised amputation. Both Dr. Cockrill and the family did not think Reuben would survive such an operation, so Russell was overruled. Reuben's days as a hardworking farmer were over, however, and the thigh wound would plague him the rest of his life.

The other family men were strong and healthy, however, so it was decided to farm an additional property across the river, closer to Centerville. Ike Walton and Joe Bell were sent over to manage this ranch. With Burch and John doing most of the work on the original ranch, General Bell became the messenger between the two operations. Once when traveling between ranches, Bell nearly met disaster. The melting of late spring snow caused sand to shift at the river ford. Although the general successfully crossed the ford, his two horses could not get a footing on the opposite bank, and the wagon he drove began slipping downstream. Walking out on the wagon tongue, the sixty-year-old Bell was able to unfasten the harness and lead the horses to safety, but the wagon floated away. It seemed like Hatchie River times all over again, he told his old friend, Milton Russell. Russell had come out to visit his two brothers who lived in Tulare County, south of Fresno, but spent a great deal of time with his old comrade of the Twelfth. Bell delighted in showing the colonel the ranch and introducing him to his grandchildren. He should have thanked Milton, and perhaps he did, for all those stirring campfire tales about the splendors of the far west.[8]

By 1878, the family had added three horses and three cows to their livestock, in addition to one hundred hogs and thirteen hundred goats. They also paid taxes on a forty-dollar sewing machine, furniture valued at forty dollars, and twenty dollars' worth of firearms. Despite this apparent success, the expensive notes due on the property forced Bell to give up the ranch. It reverted to the Glenn estate, and the general had little choice but to move the family to a property near the Cole family. The federal government made some new valley land available for homesteads about this time, and the Bells thought they saw an opportunity. The men filed on several adjacent quarter sections—due west of the river bluff property.

What a difference three miles could make. The valley land was virtually flat, and frequent sandstorms added to the discomfort of summer's hundred-degree heat. The men hurried to build dwelling houses while the women and children remained in the cooler foothills. About the same time, the frequent letters to Tennessee began bringing relatives to Fresno County. First to arrive from Old Sumner were Conquest Cross Harris, General Bell's cousin and former chief of ordnance, with his younger brother, Milus King Harris, just out of law school. Conquest also homesteaded a quarter section on the plains, and M. K. began his practice in Fresno City. Next to come was Mary's younger brother, Dr. Isaac Alexander Walton, with his four grown sons, Josiah, Charles, John, and Isaac, his three daughters and three younger sons. There were now three men named Isaac Walton all living in the same general area, forcing each of them to use his middle initial in business dealings and leading to a wide variety of nicknames.[9]

As the family became well established in the county, General Bell renewed his interest in Democratic Party politics. When the 1879 county Central Committee Convention was held at Magnolia Hall in Fresno, he was chosen temporary chairman. Later during the proceedings he was elected delegate to the Sixth Senatorial District Convention and with M. K. Harris was elected to the county Central Committee for the following term. The general was not the only publicly active family member at this time, however. The many homesteaders on the plains needed to form a school district of their own, which was organized as the Bethel District on May 15, 1879, with Reuben Harrell as one of the trustees. This school, located at Central and Bethel Avenues, was built on a corner of Burch's homestead land, and did double duty as a community church.

Although the family nominally belonged to the Southern Methodist congregation in Fresno, the distance made it impossible for them to attend services regularly, so they were delighted to offer hospitality to the Methodist ministers whose turn it was to preach at Bethel. The Bethel community soon had need for another church-related institution—a cemetery. It was not too long after moving to the plains that young John Ledsinger, Cynthia's husband, died of tuberculosis on September 15, 1881, followed almost immediately by Miss Mary, beloved wife, mother, and grandmother, who died on September 20 at age sixty-one. Theirs were the first burials in what would become a family plot in Bethel Cemetery, also on Burch's land, and today part of the Sanger Cemetery District. As the family drew even closer in this time of sadness, they also became more involved in church activities. Both General Bell and his son-in-law Ike acted as trustees for the Wildflower Circuit of the Methodist Episcopal Church South when Oscar McConnel gave land for a church building, and Bell also acted for the Kingsburg Circuit when Andrew Farley donated land.[10]

The year 1883 brought further family changes. Isaac Bell finally concluded his business in Tennessee and brought his family to Fresno County, where he homesteaded a quarter-section farm south and west of the Bethel area. When the summer heat became unbearable, most of the family took to the mountains. John Bell would fit out his lumber wagon for passengers, and drive a six- or eight-horse team on the two-day trip. Burch Bell had fifteen hundred to two thousand head of sheep pastured in the mountains in the summer, and the older boys, James and Will Bell, and Edgar Walton, were his eager summer ranch-hands. Burch and Reuben Harrell decided to try the general merchandise business in Fresno. They soon found that their knowledge of buying and selling goods was not sufficient to ensure success, and by 1886 they had closed their store. Both however, decided they liked town life and remained in Fresno.[11]

The hotly contested 1884 presidential election found Tyree Bell again in the midst of politics, serving as inspector in the Bethel precinct, with Conquest C. Harris as judge, for the Democratic primary election. Bell's fondness for brass bands and his familiarity with marching drills were put to good use by the Democratic Club. The uniformed "brigade" made frequent appearances in Fresno and throughout the county, adding much to the election color and excitement.

Conquest Harris had also joined the active Blue and Gray Veterans organization and urged his old commander to participate. At the December 6, 1884, camp meeting, seventy-year-old Tyree H. Bell, "a distinguished brigade commander under General Forrest" became a willing recruit.[12]

General Bell had made his home with Burch since Mary's death and found Fresno to his liking. Nevertheless, he continued to divide his time among his children and to oversee the properties that they retained in the Bethel district. Early 1885 was filled with preparations for a "Grand Promenade Concert and Social" given by the Blue and Gray Vets at Fresno's Grady Opera House. General Bell was local assistant for the Mendocino District, which included Bethel. The Fresno City Band played a "Grand Potpourri of Southern Melodies," and after the program and a campfire supper of hot coffee, beans, and hardtack, the hall was cleared for dancing. Springtime found Bell as inspector and Ike Walton as judge for the county election held at the Bethel schoolhouse, and during the summer, Bell and his son Isaac were paid by the county for further election service.[13]

December 1885 brought the news that General Bell had been appointed receiver of the U.S. land office in Visalia. This position as a bonded officer required him to receive all monies owed for public land and to provide the secretary of the treasury with an accounting of the same. For this service, he would be paid 1 percent of all money he collected. He would work closely with the land office registrar, who received a copy of the available plats from the surveyor general and kept records of their purchase. Exciting as this news was, it necessitated more change, primarily a move to Tulare County to be near the land office. Bell quickly decided that Isaac, with his experience as Henderson County court clerk, would be a great help as clerk in the land office. Consequently, Isaac—or "I. T." as he was known—disposed of his Fresno County farm and moved to Visalia, where he and Lizzie provided temporary quarters for General Bell in their rented Court Street home.[14]

Visalia had been established in 1852, twenty years before Fresno, and incorporated in 1874. It was the county seat of Tulare County, which covers 4,935 square miles, more territory than the state of Connecticut.[15] The vast area stretched from the fertile San Joachin Valley to the summit of the Sierra Nevadas. Located thirty miles southeast of Bethel, Visalia was not unfamiliar. Colonel Milton Russell and his brother, Dr. William Russell, lived there, not to speak of the Rev. Jack Mahon, who had been presiding elder of the Visalia District, long one of the centers of Southern Methodism. The Bell's Court Street home was only a short distance from the "Old South" Church at the corner of Court and School Streets, which soon became the center of family social activities. Fundraising "dime socials" sponsored in private homes by the Southern Methodist Ladies Aid Society also helped introduce new residents to the townsfolk. It was not long before General Bell, in his habitual black suit, beard, and coat-tails flying, was racing his horse down Court Street in friendly competition with other gentlemen. It brought to mind tales of Abe Buford and his unbeatable stallions.[16]

"Doing a land office business" had real meaning during this period. In the fourth quarter of 1887, for example, over 130,200 acres were processed with fees totaling $50,389.08, causing the local newspaper to comment on the great activity at the office. In addition to farmers' homesteads, much timber land in the mountains was included in these transactions. With Isaac on hand as clerk, assisted by J. T. Hyde, the experienced register, Bell did not find it necessary to be in the land office daily. Over seventy years old, he remained strong and erect, radiating exuberance and vitality. Always physically active, he loved to saddle his horse or hitch up his buggy to ride across the countryside and call on family and friends.

Since Mary's death, the family had begun to scatter, so the general made frequent visits to Bethel, Fresno, and San Francisco, where Burch was courting one of the former Bethel schoolteachers. On such a trip in July 1886 he had an interesting encounter on the train. The conductor knew him well and encouraged him to enter a coach occupied by some Northern gentlemen. Bell demurred but the conductor insisted, telling him that there was no one else in the coach and he would not disturb them. Besides, one of the travelers was General Sherman, en route to a Grand Army of the Republic reunion in San Francisco. Bell decided to take advantage of the opportunity. Walking into the car, Bell made straight for

Sherman's seat and after introducing himself said, "General Sherman, I am glad to meet you, sir." With this Sherman nudged his staff officer saying, "You are mistaken, this is General Sherman." Bell replied, "If no one had told me, General, I would have recognized you, so there's no use in playing with me." The end result was a pleasant conversation about old times which occupied the remainder of the three-hundred-mile journey.[17]

In 1887, Bell and his son bought adjacent properties on Goshen Avenue in the new "Stephenson Addition" to Visalia. Isaac began building his two-story house in late spring, and Maud Harrell came down as her grandfather's housekeeper. That summer General Bell purchased a lot and started to build his new home. Although the Harrell girls took care of their grandfather's day-to-day household needs, Isaac's wife, Lizzie, did most of his entertaining. It was most likely at these dinners parties at home that General Bell, drawing on his experience with the Fresno Blue and Grey Veterans, persuaded those gentlemen responsible for the annual Decoration Day ceremonies to include both Union and Confederate soldiers in the remembrances. Thus he is credited with bringing the Civil War to an end in Tulare County.[18]

Dr. Fielding A. Combs, a fellow Southern Methodist and active Democrat, and like Bell, a widower, soon became a good friend. These two old Southern gentlemen went off fishing together whenever possible, and Combs introduced the Bells to the beautiful Mineral King area where he had previously lived. Soon this became a favorite summer retreat, despite the five-day trip required. In addition to his land office duties, General Bell filled his time with visits to Fresno, politics, and church activities. Closer to home, the members of the Methodist Episcopal Church, South, decided to make improvements to their building, and Isaac was on the fund-raising committee. This led to another series of dime socials which featured good food, musical-literary programs, and lively parlor games, such as keeping a feather aloft, at which "Gen. Bell and Dr. Combs both proved themselves to be great blowers." The gregarious Bell was never a lonely man.[19]

The year 1888 was again an election year, and Bell became actively involved. Burch decided to seek the office of Fresno County recorder, and Grover Cleveland was running for re-election. The Visalia campaign opened with a torchlight procession on Court Street led by General Bell, and on this splendid occasion Bell's Drum Corps, outfitted in C & T (Cleveland & vice presidential candidate Allen G. Thurman) uniforms, made their first appearance. During the rest of the campaign season, Bell and his Drum Corps would make numerous appearances all over the valley in support of the Democratic ticket. Burch was elected county recorder, but President Cleveland went down to defeat. After the election, Maggie Harrell remarked, "Just imagine, the people prefer that man Harrison to Cleveland." Bell replied, "No, no, Maggie, Harrison is a very fine man," despite the fact that his election cost Bell his land office position.[20]

Bell's term as receiver ended October 1, 1889. Immediately he filed "a contest" on a quarter-section of land homesteaded by Volney Baker, a piece of land reputed to contain choice timber. Bell failed to displace Baker, but his land office experience had taught him and his sons much about federal land law and real estate. Isaac soon opened a real estate office and Bell decided to again make Fresno his home.[21] The stream of relatives from Tennessee had continued, bringing Isaac Walton's younger brother, Bell's nephew Kleber Miller Bell, and assorted Harrises. Other than helping them get acquainted, there was plenty to occupy Bell: summers spent in the mountains, church activities, politics, and Confederate Veterans' affairs. Sadly these veterans' activities also included attending old comrades' funerals, such as the one held May 5, 1893, when Bell's old friend Milton Russell died in Traver and was buried in Visalia.[22]

Tyree Bell was content to assume the role of patriarch, letting his sons, sons-in-law, and grandsons carry on the day-to-day family business activities. He now made his home with the Harrells. His daughter Sue had diligently cared for him ever since Miss Mary's death, sending her daughters to keep his Visalia house in order and making his shirts and waistcoats to conceal "an enlargement on his breast caused by a fragment of a shell" that had struck him at Shiloh. Reuben would yield his dinner table seat as head of the house to him, and Bell particularly enjoyed carving the meat with all due ceremony.[23]

Fresno Democrats had the same patriarchal regard for him and honored him as one of the gentlemen selected to receive Mayor Edward B. Pond, Democratic candidate for governor, on his October 8, 1890, visit to Fresno. A huge crowd, led by the local brass band, greeted the candidate at the train station, then formed into a parade to the Hughes Hotel for a reception. In the evening another torchlight parade of over eight hundred wound its way through the center of Fresno, where bonfires "brilliantly illuminated several of the street corners along the line of march." Upon arrival at the Riggs Theater, the band played several lively tunes and then the Democratic Committee vice presidents, including General Bell, were introduced and escorted to seats on the stage.[24]

Ultimately the Fresno Blue and Gray Veterans organization disintegrated, being supplanted by an active Grand Army of the Republic post and the newly formed United Confederate Veterans. By 1895 the Sterling Price UCV Camp was holding annual reunions of veterans in gray, and in 1900 Commanding General John B. Gordon appointed Bell to lead the California Brigade in the Pacific Division. This indicates the importance of his services on behalf of the

★ *Top:* Bell Home on Goshen Avenue in Visalia, California. Collection of Connie Moretti. *Above:* Bell-Cole Family Reunion, 1899–1901. Courtesy of Col. George Kastner, Fresno, California.

organization and the esteem in which he was held by the veterans, given that several former Confederate general officers were living in California. It may seem unusual to have appointed an eighty-four-year-old to a position of responsibility, but Bell, the general with the dead eye, maintained a cheerful, interested outlook on life. His footsteps, many thought, were as vigorous at eighty as those of a younger man. A glimpse of him in 1897 comes from the *Visalia Times Delta:*

> General Tyree H. Bell, a young man who lives in Fresno, is in Visalia on a business trip. General Bell was born in 1815, but there is nothing in his walk or talk to indicate he has passed the half century mark of life. He drove from Fresno yesterday, a distance of 47 miles. After supper with the family of his son, I. T. Bell, the latter remarked that he was going to church, he supposed his father was too tired to go. The general thought that a walk around town would rest him up and straighten out his legs after the long ride, so he refused to go to bed with the children and spent the evening listening to one of Rev. Ross' most convincing sermons.
> There are few men who carry their age like General Bell.[25]

At about this time, the Harrells moved from their San Pablo Avenue home to a new residence at the corner of O and Merced Streets. This location was much to Bell's liking, just three blocks northeast of St. Paul's Methodist Church, two blocks up the street from Burch and M. K. Harris, who lived next to each other on O Street, and six blocks west of his fellow Confederate, Dr. T. R. Meux. After supper and a short nap, the general would call for his hat and cane and suggest a visit to these and other friends and relatives.[26]

In 1897, the survivors of Forrest's Cavalry, meeting in Nashville, formed an organization and adopted a constitution. Tyree Bell now found himself a UCV major general, commanding the Second Division of Forrest's Veterans Cavalry composed of "Bell's old Tennessee brigade and all other Veterans not otherwise assigned." Plans were made to meet at Brice's Crossroads on June 10–11, 1900. Bell requested that Tom Allison replace him, but the idea of attending a reunion began to take hold.

In February 1901, those raising funds for the Forrest equestrian monument resolved to lay the cornerstone during the coming May reunion in Memphis. This was the final spur needed to bring Bell back to Tennessee. By the start of April he had received a warm letter from Col. Charles W. Anderson (Forrest's former aide-de-camp) asking him to name his staff officers. This Bell did, striking a balance between those on the west coast who could assist him regularly, and those in Tennessee who might be expected to attend the Memphis reunion. Hamilton Parks, Jr., one of Milton Russell's troopers and an old friend from Dyer County, was now a successful Nashville attorney. Parks made a special request of Bell to attend this reunion and then come to Nashville and visit him. Such an invitation, combined with plans to honor Forrest's men at the reunion, made Bell determined to go. The family did not think that he, at the age of eighty-five, should attempt the trip alone, and because none of them could go with him, they urged him not to attend. When he told them, "If I knew I would lose my right arm, I would go," it was clear how much the trip meant. Plans were soon under way.[27]

On May 12, 1901, the Fresno United Confederate Veterans held their annual meeting and elected General Bell as their official delegate to the Memphis meeting. Several of the crowd paid warm personal tributes to Bell, who, temporarily putting aside his abhorrence of speaking, responded with feeling.[28]

The next day he was off, catching the evening Southern Pacific train, "bound for his old home in Gallatin, Sumner County, Tennessee." A crowd of friends and Confederate veterans were at the depot to say farewell. Many of them believed it might be a year before they saw their friend again.

How different this cross-country journey would prove. Railroad transportation had changed greatly—faster, safer, more comfortable. What had been a vast, empty prairie a quarter-century before was now speckled with farms and towns. Bell arrived in Nashville sometime before May 21, as noted in the *Nashville American,* and became the house guest of W. T. Hardison.

> The presence of Gen. Bell in Tennessee . . . will be glad news to many Confederate veterans to whom his name is familiar as one of the most gallant and popular brigade commanders of Forrest's cavalry corps. . . . He has come across the continent to meet his old comrades at the Memphis Reunion, at which it is believed there will be the largest gathering of the survivors of the great cavalry leader's troopers since their surrender. . . . Gen. Bell is wonderfully well preserved and in excellent spirits.[29]

Plans for the Memphis gathering had been under way for months. By this time the committee was preparing for thirty thousand veterans and over one hundred thousand visitors. Special agents were detailed to meet each incoming train seventy-five miles outside the city, confirm hotel reservations, and distribute vouchers. A tent camp was prepared for those veterans not housed in hotels or with townspeople, and ten thousand cots and pillows were solicited for their use. An elaborate series of arches and a court of honor was designed for Main Street between North and South Court, with a reviewing stand on the west side of Court Square. This was far more elaborate than any reunion "hitherto attempted." In addition to the parade of veterans, a special flower parade, featuring decorated tally-ho's, coaches, and pony carts led by the Robert E. Lee

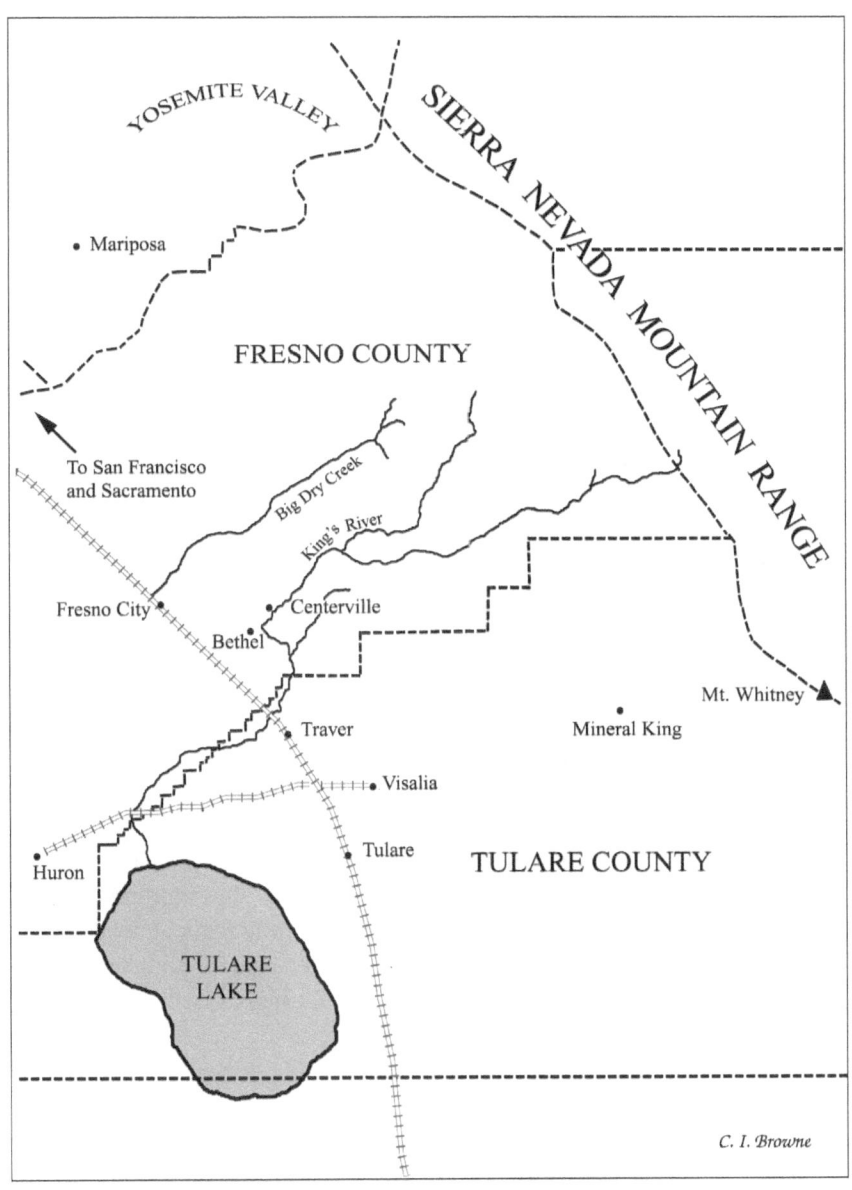

★ CENTRAL CALIFORNIA, 1876–1902. COURTESY OF C. I. BROWNE.

pony was added to the program. The chairman of the horse and carriage committee prepared to rent three to five hundred horses and wished "the people would wake up to the fact that we need every good horse that we can lay hands on." A post office known as Reunion Station was scheduled to open in the specially constructed Confederate Hall on the Memphis bluff. Among the many amusements planned for the veterans was a baseball game between the professional Little Rock and Memphis teams. Two carnivals were scheduled to be in town, and numerous musical performances were planned. Each UCV reunion since the first in 1890 had attracted a larger crowd, and the special appeal of Memphis with its many reminders of Bedford Forrest guaranteed that this eleventh gathering would be the largest ever.[30]

Between his arrival in Nashville about May 20 and his departure for Memphis with the delegates a week later, General Bell was warmly welcomed and grandly entertained. He dined with Tom Allison soon after his arrival and soon made Major Allison's place his Nashville headquarters. Sumner County beckoned, however. Although both his brother and sister had died, their spouses and most of their children still lived nearby, not to speak of numerous cousins and in-laws spread throughout the county. Bell spent the weekend before the Memphis reunion in the Gallatin area. This was perfect timing, as Saturday was Confederate Memorial Day, with ceremonies at the Methodist Church. After the opening prayer, Bell was introduced as "one of the greatest Generals of the South, Gen. Tyree Bell of Forrest's Cavalry." As he was introduced, all the old soldiers arose and saluted him. After saying a few words about his early years in Sumner County and giving encouragement and reassurance to his old comrades, he was overwhelmed with emotion and ended his remarks by saying, "I feel so happy that I cannot say what I want to say." The trip had proven all he had hoped for, and the reunion festivities were still ahead.[31]

Memphis proved delightful. Bell mingled with his old comrades and participated in every event. Oratory consumed Tuesday when threatening weather caused the postponement of the gala floral parade and the fireworks display. Wednesday began with a special memorial service in honor of Forrest at the Cumberland Presbyterian Church, where he had worshiped. From the opening notes of "America" played by the orchestra to the closing of the "Star Spangled Banner" and the "Bonnie Blue Flag," this was an impressive occasion. UCV Gen. D. C. Kelley gave the main eulogy; the Rev. G. T. Stainback, who had been Forrest's pastor, also spoke. Bell's former Chaplain, R. H. Mahon, gave the benediction. Throughout the services, General Bell had an honored seat on the left of the pulpit, and Forrest's son and grandchildren filled the front pew. In the afternoon, a reception in honor of Gen. John B. Gordon, given at the home of

Mr. and Mrs. J. T. Latham, included General Bell among the honored guests. The floral parade also filled a part of the afternoon, with prizes awarded that evening at the United Sons of Confederate Veterans ball. The Sons' ball featured the "Southern Cross Drill," a series of marching formations originally devised by Johnson's Island prisoners to pass the time, now performed by a company of thirty-two uniformed veterans partnered by thirty-two young ladies in white dresses and Confederate colors. The drill was "a very popular social amusement with the young ladies and the old veterans."[32]

Thursday, Forrest Day at the reunion, began at 10:30 A.M. with the grand parade of fifteen thousand veterans, Forrest's men occupying the place of honor at the end of the parade. Leading the first unit were one hundred musicians combined from three reunion bands. Next came General Gordon, commander of the UCV, with Generals Joe Wheeler and Fitzhugh Lee, all on horseback. Each unit was preceded by a carriage with the sponsors and maids of honor chosen for the occasion. After each division, from Virginia to Tennessee, had passed in review, finally it was Bell's turn.[33]

"Forrest's cavalry corps made one of the best shows in the parade," noted a reporter for the Memphis *Commercial Appeal:*

> The corps was divided into two divisions, the first division commanded by Maj. Gen. Tyree H. Bell of California and the second division commanded by Maj. Gen. E. W. Rucker of Birmingham, Ala. General Bell came all the way from California for the first time in many years to join his old comrades and pay tribute once more to the memory of his former leader. . . . The cavalry feature of this corps was carried out in the fullest detail. The sponsors and their maids of honor, instead of riding in carriages and looking beautiful in flounces and laces, rode horseback and looked charming in neat fitting suits of gray, with yellow trimmings. The young ladies handled their steeds like true horsewomen and never troubled their veteran escorts about the management of their mounts. . . . After the sponsors and their escorts came the surviving members of the escort company of Gen. Forrest. They were not many but they got the glad hand. Then came the Bluff City Grays and the members of Gen. Forrest's old regiment, and then followed the two divisions of Forrest's cavalry corps. All were mounted and the thousand horsemen in gray made an imposing sight.[34]

Tyree Bell certainly graced this huge mounted company. One of the eldest surviving generals, he had spent much of his life on horseback, and to one newspaperman "looked like some splendidly proportioned statue when mounted."[35]

At two o'clock the same afternoon came the long-awaited event at Forrest Park. Generals Kelley, Rucker, and Bell arrived as a party with their sponsors and maids of honor, and were assigned to places of prominence. General Gordon called the crowd to order and introduced General Kelley, who gave a detailed and inspiring address on Forrest's life and career. Following his speech, several ladies recited poems including "The Wizard of the Saddle."[36]

The glorious three-day event had come to an end. Memphis, a city of about 75,000, had seen her population doubled by the 165,000 visitors, and had acquitted herself well. The general opinion was that there had never been such a successful reunion. Dozens of poignant incidents of recognition were reported, and as one Nashville veteran said: "I saw Gen. Bell shake hands with men and recognize men whom he had not seen before in thirty-five years. He not only recognized these men but asked of the whereabouts of some of the absent ones whom he had always associated with those present. He exhibited the most remarkable memory, I think, I have ever seen. He told the men that he had come 3,000 miles to see them, and he had, too, for he had come from California, through Texas and down by New Orleans."[37]

The survivors of Bell's former regiments had given him an enthusiastic ovation; they recalled that he had been the kindest officer to his men and never demanded more of them than he would do himself. "There was not a man in his Brigade," a reporter noted, "that did not love him for his fine character both in camp and field." General Bell said he had enjoyed the reunion so much that he felt more than repaid for his long journey across the continent.[38]

Following his return to Nashville after the reunion, Bell made his "headquarters" with Hamilton Parks and launched a series of meetings with his surviving comrades with the aim of producing an accurate history of their operations during the "late unpleasantness." During these months he was the guest of numerous friends and comrades who were "vieing with each other in making him the object of all possible graces of hospitality." In addition to staying with Hamilton Parks, he was a guest of Gen. William H. "Red" Jackson at Belle Meade for a week; spent several weeks off and on with his nephew, Bennet D. Bell, in Gallatin; and visited Dyer County in the late autumn. As Bell himself said, "I am really living about." M. K. Harris, Bell's cousin from Fresno, visited Sumner County relatives during this period and especially enjoyed a dinner given for him and Bell by Judge and Mrs. B. D. Bell. Although he didn't say so, no doubt M. K. had an additional commission from the Fresno family to check on the general. Certainly Harris sent home a good report, for Bell was having a wonderful time and seemed fit. As the old man told a reporter: "Well, you know, I have been away from Middle Tennessee for a long, long while, in fact, since 1875, and though many changes have taken place since that period, I want to tell you that there are many old land marks throughout this section which are familiar to me. Up until the time I was fifty years old I was about as well acquainted in Nashville as I was in Sumner County."[39]

At the Memphis reunion, the veterans had voted to hold their twelfth reunion in Dallas, and by early April 1902, preparations were well under way. General Bell would be doing double duty at Dallas, serving in General Kelley's place as head of Forrest's Cavalry Corps and also commanding the UCV Pacific Division. Several special appointments of Texas residents to staff positions were made, including Bell's grand-niece, Lily Vertrees Bell, as a maid of honor for the corps.[40]

Once again the reunion visitors more than doubled the size of the host city but, lacking the special emphasis on Forrest, the Confederate invasion of Dallas was smaller than that of Memphis. The program of the three-day gathering was much the same as in years before.[41] In the huge parade of aging veterans, nine bands were interspersed with the units of marching men, and this year Forrest's men followed the Tennessee Division. "Gen. Tyree H. Bell, commanding the Forrest cavalry corps, rode in a carriage with Miss Donelson, sponsor, and Miss Bell, chief maid of honor," a newspaper reporter noted. "Behind them were the men who had followed that intrepid cavalry leader, Forrest. The battle flag of the Sixteenth Confederate Cavalry was carried by S. C. Buck of Stephensville, Tex., who was attired in his old war uniform." Buck had been the original color-bearer of the regiment, and as he marched by the side of Bell, he was "the proudest soldier in that great procession, and well he might be, carrying the old flag that he loved so dearly."[42]

After the Dallas reunion, General Bell returned to Tennessee, to his nephew's home in Gallatin, rather than journey on to California. His health, which had been less than robust at the Dallas reunion, became a matter of increasing concern to family and friends. Bell continued to meet with his former staff members regarding the history of Forrest's Corps, but by the beginning of July, his health had deteriorated. Indeed, he was described as in an enfeebled condition, probably having suffered a slight stroke. During the second week of August Bell appeared to have had a second stroke, and as soon as he could walk about unassisted, he announced he wanted to go back home to California. It would be a long trip by rail, via New Orleans, and the family was anxious. It had been his stubborn determination, however, that had brought him to Tennessee in the first place, and carried him through the emotional stress of the reunions. Now he was equally determined to return home. On Wednesday, August 20, 1902, he left Gallatin by train.

In New Orleans the next morning Bell found that he hardly had the strength to get off the train. He attempted to walk to the Southern Pacific depot, but failed and became confused. A kindly porter, Brou Maths, took charge at this point and found the feeble old man a wheelchair. Assisted by a wagon driver, August Blanchard, Maths wheeled Bell to the office of the station agent who telephoned Dr. Daniel S. Brosnan to come to the depot. The young doctor hurried to the station and found Bell unconscious. He immediately ordered an ambulance and had the general taken to the New Orleans Sanitarium on Carondelet Street.

Although Dr. Brosnan had General Bell placed in one of the best rooms at the sanatorium, with two nurses assigned to care for him, it was a while before his identity became known. Finally, by searching his pockets, which contained a few letters and his credentials to the Dallas reunion, and his telescope valise which contained other personal papers, the hospital staff identified him and began trying to locate his family. On Monday, August 25, Bell rallied and tried to speak, but had difficulty being understood. He had a money order that needed signing, and made it known that he needed his glasses, but they could not be found. Two days later Sue Harrell received a telegram informing her that her father was seriously ill at New Orleans. Dr. Brosnan's examination had revealed that General Bell's condition was critical. A blood clot on the brain caused a partial paralysis, aggravating an already serious heart condition, and the excessive late summer heat combined with his stout physique had led to his collapse.[43]

Dr. Brosnan restricted Bell's visitors to four close connections, although many more would have visited the stricken general had it been permitted. George Moorman, Adjutant General of the UCV, immediately set out for New Orleans from Mandeville, Louisiana. He went directly to the sanatorium and although not allowed to see the general, continued to visit the infirmary daily. Capt. James Dinkins, a former Memphis resident who had served with Bell, also concerned himself with the general's welfare, as did an unidentified woman who sent flowers daily.

The first impulse of the Bell family was to hurry to New Orleans; however, it was felt that he would not last until they could arrive, so they depended upon frequent telegrams to keep them apprised of his condition. By Friday, Bell lapsed into unconsciousness, and he died at 10:41 P.M., Saturday, August 30, just one week short of his eighty-seventh birthday. Confederate comrades procured a new gray uniform and prepared the body for shipment to California.[44]

Tyree Bell was not allowed to pass unnoticed to his grave. Beginning with an account of "Gen. Tyree H. Bell Fatally Injured" in the August 28, 1902, edition of the Memphis *Commercial Appeal* and fanned by the New Orleans *Daily Picayune* on August 30, newspapers across the country reported increasingly dramatic tales of his collapse. From relatively tame accounts of "mystery in the case" arising from his unconscious state, these grew to reports that the "Confederate General was assaulted in New Orleans." The *New York Sun* reported that he died as a result of injuries after suffering a blow on the head, and this report quickly spread from coast to coast, distressing Bell's friends. Soon the *San Francisco Chronicle* asserted "Bell's Death Due to a Blow," and the *Fresno Morning Republican* stated that he had met thugs in New Orleans and was found unconscious after having made stout resistance. A special from the New Orleans *Times-Democrat* to Fresno gave the information that

> General Bell was picked up on a bench in the Southern Pacific railroad depot, in this city, in an unconscious condition. He was without a coat, and his shirt was torn almost into strips. At his side lay a broken walking stick. Robbery is supposed to have been the motive for the crime. Money and railroad tickets that he is known to have had when he reached this city from a visit to friends at Gallatin, Tenn., had disappeared when he was found. While there is little doubt that he was robbed, and most foully, and that he made desperate resistance, the affair is wrapped in the deepest mystery.[45]

These journalistic exaggerations eventually led to a thorough police investigation, but before that occurred, General Bell's body arrived in Fresno and his funeral was arranged for 10 A.M. on his birthday, Saturday, September 6. The Methodist Church was crowded with hundreds who came to pay their last respects. Many beautiful floral offerings adorned his casket, and six former Confederates served as his pallbearers. Clergymen J. A. Batchelor and J. J. N. Kenney, who conducted the service, both spoke highly of the departed, not only as a soldier, but also as a human being. Then the long funeral procession made its way over the fifteen dusty miles from downtown Fresno out to little Bethel Cemetery, where Tyree Bell was laid to rest beside his beloved Miss Mary.[46]

By September 8, Judge J. H. Clack, former Nashville chief of police, had arrived in New Orleans to carry out an inquiry into the circumstances of Bell's death, while others were reporting, "The police have done practically nothing towards running down the person or persons who assaulted General Bell as all evidence points to a tragic death." Clack had come at the request of Hamilton

Parks, John W. Morton, and Charles W. Anderson, "prominent Tennesseans and friends of General Bell." Quietly Clack began his investigation. Four members of the New Orleans Police Department reported the precise details of Bell's arrival, and Dr. Brosnan testified that not only did Bell have money in his possession, but that his body bore no marks of violence and he was "positive that there was no foul play." Nevertheless it was widely reported that Clack and his party would continue on to California and there exhume the general's body. Fortunately calmer views prevailed. Judge Clack reported he "was able to establish clearly that General Bell's death was due solely to a sudden stroke of apoplexy," and the body was allowed to remain undisturbed.[47]

In its death notice of Tyree Harris Bell, the New Orleans *Daily Picayune* referred to this Tennessee farmer turned instant soldier as "Forrest's right arm." Nothing could have pleased him more.[48]

Of course, newspapers are prone to indulge in overstatement at the time of an old man's death. There seems to be merit, nevertheless, in the *Picayune*'s assertion. Forrest did depend upon Bell; this is demonstrated over and over again throughout the latter half of 1863 and all through the war days of 1864–65. Bell was Forrest's principal recruiter; Bell was his disciplinarian; Bell was his confidant. Not only were the two men comfortable in each other's company, but often they appear to have thought alike. Bell understood about rapid division and reconcentration in the presence of a hesitant or slow-moving enemy. Bell, like Forrest, sought the opportunity to shift from the strategic defensive to tactical offensive. Hit-and-run tactics suited him, the bloodline of the reiver, so to speak. He was a natural combat leader—demonstrating repeatedly his love of the assault, particularly the surprise attack and the counterattack; witness Hollow Tree Gap, Brice's Crossroads, the bridge over the Wolf River at LaFayette, the sudden moves against Athens and Columbia. Bell could balance Abe Buford's Falstaff and James Chalmers's prickliness and Red Jackson's sometime lack of focus. Bell seems to have been supremely confident; no dragon of doubt shared his blanket. Men trusted him. They would fight for him, follow him. He was a natural leader and he knew the art of cooperation. He could fight alongside a Black Bob McCulloch, a Hylan Lyon, or an Edmund Rucker.

It would not be exaggeration, perhaps, to regard this Dyer County farmer as the glue for Forrest's Cavalry during the last half of the war. Bell knew instinctively how to get the best from a William W. Faulkner and an Andrew N. Wilson and a George H. Nixon. He could soften up a Braxton Bragg and breathe confidence into a Milton Russell. He could push a herd of cattle and a long train of wagons through dangerous country and he could drive a herd of sullen Rebel malingerers and retreads away from home and transform them, through politic but firm discipline and constant drill, into effective dragoons.

Bell showed adaptability and flexibility throughout the Civil War, moving from infantry to cavalry, from small unit commander to brigade leader, and sometimes division commander. He could operate independently. Although the tactics and demands for Forrest's and Bell's type of cavalry changed during the Tennessee Campaign, both showed they could excel in that traditional close support role. Bell could raid, he could scout, he could patrol, he could fight mounted or dismounted—cavalry versus cavalry, cavalry versus infantry. He learned the most effective use of sharpshooters, of artillery; indeed, he won the admiration of artilleryman John Morton and his gunners. They liked to fight beside Bell's Tennesseans; they could depend upon Bell's Brigade. Bell could judge terrain, the advantages that could be obtained from it militarily. He continued to grow as a soldier, thereby winning the praise of his subordinates, not to speak of the support and positive statements of Frank Cheatham, of Pres Smith, of Edmund Kirby Smith, of Gideon Pillow, of Leonidas Polk, of Red Jackson, and of Abe Buford.

This Dyer County farmer-soldier loved good whiskey and he loved a good laugh. He could be kind and conciliatory; he could be stern, uncompromising, and threatening. He was a warrior—brave, even audacious. He shined in adversity. He could stand physical abuse and exposure. He could fight while wounded. He could lead footsore men into the wilderness and come out with them mounted. He could fight well with indifferent horseflesh and antique weapons. He was energetic, resourceful, and responsible. He did his duty.

Tyree Harris Bell was the lieutenant for whom Bedford Forrest would risk his life. Forrest's "right arm" might not be hyperbole after all.

Notes

Abbreviations

General

AAG	Assistant Adjutant General
CSR	Compiled Service Record
G.O.	General Order
RG	Record Group
S.O.	Special Order
THB	Tyree H. Bell

Repositories

DU	Duke University Library, Durham, N.C.
LOC	Library of Congress, Washington, D.C.
NA	National Archives, Washington, D.C.
SHC	Southern Historical Collection, University of North Carolina, Chapel Hill
SIU	Southern Illinois University, Morris Library, Carbondale
TSLA	Tennessee State Library and Archives, Nashville

Books, Periodicals, and Documents

ANB	*American National Biography*
B&L	*Battles and Leaders of the Civil War*
CV	*Confederate Veteran*
DAB	*Dictionary of American Biography*
NOR	*Official Records of the Union and Confederate Navies in the War of the Rebellion*
OR	*The War of the Rebellion: A Compilation of the Official Records of the Union and Confederate Armies.* Unless otherwise indicated, all volumes cited throughout the notes are from Series I.
SHSP	*Southern Historical Society Papers*
THQ	*Tennessee Historical Quarterly*
WTHSP	*West Tennessee Historical Society Papers*

1. Excitement Reigned Supreme

1. Tyree Harris Bell Autobiography, *Confederate Veteran* Papers, William R. Perkins Library, Duke Univ.
2. Ibid.
3. Tyree Rodes Harris (1765–1841) had emigrated to Kentucky as a young man, bringing two slaves with him. He freed these slaves before his death and gave them a home on his farm. They remained on the place until their deaths. Milus K. Harris [Dove Branham Harris], *The Harris Family and Others* (1928; reprint, Redondo Beach, Cal.: C. W. Moretti, 1987), 8, 16, 22; *Biographical Directory of the Kentucky General Assembly* (Frankfort: Kentucky Historical Society, 1964), 143, 148.
4. *Gallatin Union,* Dec. 21, 1838; THB Autobiography; Jeanette T. Acklen, comp., *Tennessee Records: Tombstone Inscriptions and Manuscripts* (1933; reprint, Baltimore: Genealogical Publishing, 1994), 103.
5. Walter T. Durham, *The Great Leap Westward: A History of Sumner County, Tennessee, From Its Beginnings to 1805* (Gallatin, Tenn.: Sumner County Public Library Board, 1969), 168 (quotations). Isaac Walton, raised an Episcopalian, became a zealous convert to Methodism. Because the primitive log church could not seat the crowds who came to hear the preaching, a large shed was constructed for camp meetings and "cabins were built for those who camped on the grounds," all this on land that Isaac had given. Lily Cartwright Bell, *History of the Dickinson Road* (Nashville: Robert Cartwright Chapter, DAR, 1936), 38–39 (quotation). Lily Cartwright was the wife of Judge Bennett Douglass Bell, THB's nephew.

6. Josiah Walton obituary, Nashville *Christian Advocate,* Mar. 18, 1858; Durham, *The Great Leap Westward,* 66, 69, 72, 75, 133–34, 168; Harriette S. Arnow, *Flowering of the Cumberland* (New York: Macmillan Co., 1963), 378–81; John Carr, *Early Times in Middle Tennessee* (Nashville: E. Stevenson & F. A. Owen, 1857), 46; Bell, *History of the Dickinson Road,* 38 (quotation); Weston A. Goodspeed, ed., *History of Tennessee* (Nashville: Goodspeed Publishing Co., 1887), 924.
7. J. T. McAllister, *Virginia Militia in the Revolutionary War* (Hot Springs, Va., McAllister Publ. Co., 1913), 175; Henry C. Peden, Jr., *Revolutionary Patriots of Montgomery County, Maryland, 1776–1783* (Westminster, Md.: Family Line Publications, 1996), 24, 28; George N. MacKenzie, ed., *Colonial Families of the United States of America,* 7 vols. (Baltimore: Seaforth Press, 1996), 2:56–71; Margaret B. Farnham to Craig Mathews, Apr. 27, 1952, Craig Mathews Collection, TSLA; George M. Fraser, *The Steel Bonnets: The Story of the Anglo-Scottish Border Reivers* (New York: Alfred A. Knopf, 1972), chap. 1 *passim.*
8. Margaret Bell Harrell Farnham, *South to West* (1947; reprint, Redondo Beach, Cal.: C. W. Moretti, 1987), 20–21.
9. Harris, *Harris Family,* 42.
10. Ibid., 41; Farnham, *South to West,* 15.
11. Harris, *Harris Family,* 15, 20, 28–29, 42; Walter T. Durham, *Old Sumner* (Gallatin, Tenn.: Sumner County Public Library Board, 1972), 4–5; Joyce M. Murray, *Sumner County, Tennessee, Deed Abstracts 1806–1817* (Wolfe City, Tex.: Henington Publ. Co., 1989), 81, 130; Edythe R. Whitley, *Marriages of Sumner County, Tennessee 1787–1838* (Baltimore: Genealogical Publishing Co., 1981), 47, 75; 1820 census, Sumner County, Tennessee, 139, shows two young men, one age 16–18 and one age 18–25, living in the Absalom Bell household. It seems likely that one of these is John Wesley, age twenty-five. All three males were engaged in manufacturing.
12. Thomas Beall's will had been probated earlier, but the real property was partitioned when the family could not agree on the division after the death of Susannah H. Beall.
13. 1860 Census, Sumner County, Tenn., 104; 1812 tax list, Garrard County, Ky., 4; Absalom B. Bell CSR, 2nd Regiment (Jennings) Ky. Vols., War of 1812; Garrard County, Ky., Marriage Register, 1797–1853, 97 (Absalom was possibly Susannah's second choice, given that an earlier marriage bond, signed by her uncle John Heard, was filed by Asa Hubbard in 1809); Jay Guy Cisco, *Historic Sumner County, Tennessee with Genealogies of the Bledsoe, Cage and Douglass Families* (1909; reprint, Nashville: Charles Elder, 1971), 211–12, 225; Ezra J. Warner, *Generals in Gray: Lives of the Confederate Commanders* (Baton Rouge: Louisiana State Univ. Press, 1964), 59; THB Autobiography; 1816, 1817 tax lists, Garrard County, Ky., 6, 20; Deed Book E, Garrard County, Ky., 254–55;

Will Book F, Mason County, Ky., 360–61 (will of Thomas Allen Beall); Deed Book 51, 421, Mason Co., Ky. (Beall estate partition deed); 1820 Census, Sumner County, Tenn.; 1830 Census, Sumner County, Tenn., 154; Deed Book 16, 320, Sumner County, Tenn.; 1840 Census, Sumner County, Tenn., 396; Deed Book 19, 88–89, 322–23, Sumner County, Tenn.; 1850 Census, Sumner County, Tenn., 248; 1870 Census, Sumner County, Tenn., 710 (It is unknown why Absalom is listed in this census as Adaline); Era W. Stinson and Elizabeth Sue Spurlock, *Sumner County, Tennessee, Marriages 1839–1875* (Bowling Green, Ky.: n.p., 1985), 9, 38. It is possible Absalom Bell had no namesakes because there was no potential material benefit for a child bearing his name. Most grandchildren, nephews, etc., enjoyed a close connection to the relative for whom they were named, often being left special bequests in their wills.

14. Harris, *Harris Family*, 22; THB Autobiography; Case 1243, Garrard Co., Ky. Circuit Court Records, Kentucky Department of Archives and Libraries.
15. Stinson and Spurlock, *Sumner County, Tennessee, Marriages*, 9; THB Autobiography; Farnham, *South to West*, 15, 23.
16. Harris, *Harris Family*, 49. This Scots-Irish custom of the infair at the groom's home the day after the wedding was replaced in the twentieth century by the groom's family hosting the rehearsal dinner.
17. THB Autobiography; Farnham, *South to West*, 34–35; 1850, 1860 Censuses, Sumner County, Tenn.
18. Sumner County, Tenn. Deed Books 21, 258; 22, 50.
19. Jane G. Buchanan, *Thomas Thompson and Ann Finney of Colonial Pennsylvania and North Carolina* (Oak Ridge, Tenn.: n.p., 1987), 202, 223–27; Farnham, *South to West*, 9.
20. Connie W. Moretti, "Newbern, Tennessee, on the Eve of the War Between the States"; THB Autobiography.
21. THB Autobiography.
22. Ibid.; 1860 census, slave schedule, and agricultural schedule, Dyer Co., Tenn.; Connie W. Moretti, "Newbern, Tennessee, on the Eve of the Civil War."

2. Belmont

1. Earl Willoughby, "Tyree Bell Moves to Dyer County."
2. THB Autobiography.
3. Ibid. Occasionally Walton wrote or copied letters for Jackson in the First Seminole War as AAG for the Tennessee Volunteer Mounted Gunmen, but this organization had quarreled with Jackson earlier in the Creek War that preceded the Battle of New Orleans. Indeed, these Tennesseans believed their term of enlistment was up and they went home. Jackson called it desertion. Apparently Walton made his peace with Jackson, however, for he was listed

as the future president's private secretary in 1818. Farnham, *South and West*, 8–9; Goodspeed, *History of Tennessee*, 924.

4. THB Autobiography; Farnham, *South to West*, 8–9.
5. Earl Willoughby, "12th, 22nd & 47th Regiments"; Apr. 24, 1861, entry, Hiram R. Andrew McCorkle Diary, TSLA.
6. Albert L. Hulme and James A. Hulme, *A History of Dyer County* (Dyersburg: n.p., 1982), 356; THB Autobiography.
7. Bell's cousin and Newbern postmaster Albert G. Harris was elected first lieutenant.
8. Pillow styled himself "The Major General Commanding The Army of Tennessee" in his correspondence. The major general was unceremoniously demoted by Jefferson Davis, however, when Tennessee's troops entered the Confederate Army. Henceforward, this major general of the U.S. Army in Mexico in 1847, and of the state of Tennessee in 1861, would be Brigadier General Pillow. No longer could he officially promise appointments to colonel in the name of the Provisional Army. S.O. 307, June 21, 1861, Correspondence of G. J. Pillow, RG 109, NA; Nathaniel C. Hughes, Jr., and Roy P. Stonesifer, *The Life and Wars of Gideon J. Pillow* (Chapel Hill: Univ. of North Carolina Press, 1993), 158–63, 172–73; THB Autobiography (quotation).
9. THB Autobiography. Unmentioned by THB and quietly complicating this tidy arrangement was Harris's widespread militia organization. Indeed, just as the Tennessee troops were turned over to the Confederacy, THB was listed as colonel, 137th Regiment, 18th Brigade, commanded by Congressman John C. D. Atkins. THB's subordinate officers as shown on July 7, 1861, would form the nucleus of his recruiting efforts and of his cavalry brigade two years later: Lt. Col. M. J. Burton, 1st Maj. R. G. Sinclair, 2nd Maj. Elijah P. Kirk, and company-grade officers R. N. Butterworth, William A. Dawson, S. S. Hall, Robert L. Doke, Tyree C. Harris, Ed T. Haskins, G. K. McGee, Daniel E. Parker, J. W. Rudder, William H. Todd, J. W. Wood, and T. B. Wyse. Commission Books, 1840–1861, Tennessee State Militia, TSLA; Robert M. McBride and Daniel M. Robison, eds., *Biographical Directory of the Tennessee General Assembly.* 5 vols. (Nashville: Tennessee Historical Commission, 1975), 1:20–21. See also Thomas L. Connelly, *Army of the Heartland: The Army of Tennessee, 1861–1862* (Baton Rouge: Louisiana State Univ. Press, 1967), 32, 37–38.
10. Hulme, *History of Dyer County,* 356; THB CSR; John B. Lindsley, ed., *The Military Annals of Tennessee* (Nashville: J. M. Lindsley & Co., 1886), 307.
11. Dyer County men continued to wait, however. Almost four complete companies of them would join the Forty-seventh Tennessee Infantry in December 1861. Tennessee Civil War Centennial Commission, *Tennesseans in the Civil War: A Military History of Confederate and Union Units with Available Rosters of Personnel,* 2 vols. (Nashville: Civil War Centennial Commission, 1964–65), 1:277.

12. McBride and Robison, eds., *Biographical Directory of the Tennessee General Assembly,* 1:110–11; U.S. House of Representatives, *Biographical Directory of the American Congress, 1774–1949,* 81st Cong. 2nd Sess., 1950. H. Doc. 607, 936; William S. Speer, *Sketches of Prominent Tennesseans* (Nashville: A. B. Tavel, 1888), 194–96; R. P. Caldwell, *Sketches of the Bench and Bar of Tennessee* (Knoxville, Tenn.: Ogden Bros. & Co., 1898), 369–70.
13. Earl Willoughby, "Noble, True and Brave: The 12th Tennessee Volunteers"; *Tennesseans in the Civil War,* 1:198–99; Harris, *Harris Family,* 8–11; 12th Tenn. Inf. CSRs; *CV* 21: 213. THB's Kentuckians came from Fulton, Graves, and Hickman Counties. Lindsley, *Military Annals of Tennessee,* 307.
14. 12th Tenn. Inf. CSRs; Willoughby, "Noble, True and Brave."
15. *Tennesseans in the Civil War,* 1:199; Willoughby, "Noble, True and Brave;" Brent A. Cox, "From a Finer Cast: The History of the 12th Tennessee Regiment" (quotations).
16. THB Autobiography.
17. Born December 15, 1825, Russell was the son of James and Mary Cowan Russell of Lincoln County, Tenn. George Washington Cullum, *Biographical Register of the U.S. Military Academy at West Point, N.Y., from Its Establishment, March 16, 1802, to the Army Re-organization of 1866–67* (New York: D. Van Nostrand, 1868), 218; Brent A. Cox, "The Secrets of Heroism."
18. Visalia, Cal., *Weekly Delta,* Jan. 17, 1886; Dec. 21, 1893; Columbus, Ky., *Daily Confederate News,* Nov. 12, 1861; U.S. Military Academy Cadet Application Papers, 1805–1866, RG 94, NA; *CV* 6: 529; Lindsley, *Military Annals of Tennessee,* 307; Robert M. Russell Papers in possession of Brent A. Cox, Milan, Tenn.; Memphis *Commercial Appeal,* June 2, 1949; Visalia, Cal., *Daily Times,* May 5, 1895.
19. Clement A. Evans, ed., *Confederate Military History,* extended ed., 19 vols. (1899; reprint, Wilmington, N.C.: Thomas Broadfoot Publ., 1987–1989), 10:8–9; Hughes and Stonesifer, *Pillow,* 169.
20. *Tennesseans in the Civil War,* 1:201, 221.
21. THB to Charles C. Jones, Nov. 14, 1875, Charles C. Jones Papers, DU; THB Autobiography; *Tennesseans in the Civil War,* 1:198–99, 201, 221; Willoughby, "Noble, True and Brave"; Goodspeed, *History of Tennessee,* 913–14; Mamie Yeary, comp., *Reminiscences of the Boys in Gray, 1861–1865* (Dallas: Smith & Lamar, 1912), 50. THB's Confederate appointment as lieutenant colonel is dated August 7, 1861, although his name appears on a register of Commissioned Officers, Provisional Army, Confederate States, as lieutenant colonel, June 3, 1861, "Comd'g 12th Regiment." THB CSR.
22. July 29, 1861, entry, Fielder Diary, TSLA; Christopher Losson, *Tennessee's Forgotten Warriors: Frank Cheatham and His Confederate Division* (Knoxville: Univ. of Tennessee Press, 1990), 28–31; Hughes and Stonesifer, *Pillow,* 162, 170.

23. July 29, 1861, entry, Fielder Diary; Lindsley, *Military Annals of Tennessee*, 307 (quotation).
24. THB to Quartermaster General, Jan. 12, 1862, THB CSR. This would be a recurring problem with THB. See also his letter explaining irregularities in the fourth quarter, 1861, and first quarter, 1862, THB to Quartermaster General, Jan. 21, 1863, Letters Received, QM Dept., RG 109, NA.
25. Hughes and Stonesifer, *Pillow*, 193–94; Connelly, *Army of the Heartland*, 50–53; THB Autobiography (quotation).
26. Sept. 2, 5, 1861, entries, Fielder Diary.
27. River people called them the "Chalk Bluffs" because of their bright coffee color. French explorers Fr. Jacques Marquette and Louis Jolliet had named them the Iron Banks. Bell's men usually referred to the heights less elegantly as "the hill." Nathaniel Cheairs Hughes, Jr., *The Battle of Belmont: Grant Strikes South* (Chapel Hill: Univ. of North Carolina Press, 1991), 36.
28. Sept. 8, 14, 1861, entries, Fielder Diary (quotations).
29. William W. House to Miss Mollie, Sept. 18, 1861, quoted in Willoughby, "Noble, Brave and True."
30. Fall 1861 entries, Fielder Diary; Hughes, *Belmont*, 30, 36–37; Hughes and Stonesifer, *Pillow*, 196.
31. Willoughby, "Noble, Brave and True" (first quotation); Joseph Jones to Frances D. Polk, Mar. 26, 1870, Polk Papers, Univ. of the South Library (second quotation).
32. Hughes and Stonesifer, *Pillow*, 196–97; Nov. 7, 1861, entry, Fielder Diary (first, second quotations); THB to R. M. Russell, Nov. 9, 1861, Civil War Documents, SIU; Columbus (Ky.) *Daily Confederate News*, Nov. 12, 1861; THB Autobiography.
33. THB Autobiography (quotations); Hughes, *Belmont*, 68–69, 74. Capt. Marsh Polk commented sharply about Pillow's actions in a letter to his wife:

> Dearest Eva . . . I would just as lieve fight under Pillow as any man but the more I see of him the greater contempt I have for him. This is ours and might injure me if revealed, but Eva he showed ignorance in the arrangement of the Belmont Battle that would have disgraced a six months old cadet; his personal bravery is undoubted for he was as cool as a cucumber and fought well but his general ship was abominable. I have never mentioned it to a soul and you must not let anyone see it but your Pa, and he under promise of silence, at least until I am out of service. General Pillow changed Beltzhoover's plan of battle and planted his guns and infantry within easy range of a woods, his own men out in the field and the enemy under cover of the trees, among which with their blue coats our men could hardly see them. It was the fire from the

woods mentioned that broke Tappan's and Wright's and Freeman's undisciplined troops and lost Beltzhoover's Battery, called the Watson Battery. The evening of the fight when I was landing my battery Col. Beltzhoover came up to me and said Captain let [me] go with you. I said Colonel take my battery, I will serve as chief of action under you. I could not help saying it, the tears were running down the old fellow's cheeks, his horse had been shot under him, his coat pierced through and his sword scabbard shattered by bullets. Col. Watson (the gentleman who paid $35,000 for the battery) stood by, his eyes fairly glowing, and after I stopped he wrung my hand and said, 'Polk, I'll go with you, by God.' I offered him my spare horse but he would not have it. He fired the two last guns of the battery himself. . . .

> Marshall Tate Polk to Eva Bills Polk, Nov. 11, 1861, Virginia Prichard Polk Papers, Inverness, Miss.

34. Hughes, *Belmont,* 75.
35. Ibid., 52–53, 205.
36. Nov. 7, 1861, entry, Fielder Diary (first quotation); THB to RMR, Nov. 9, 1861, SIU (second, third quotations). *OR* 3:332–33.
37. Nov. 7, 1861, entry, James N. Rosser Diary, Civil War Collection, TSLA (first quotation). THB Autobiography (second quotation). THB would lose at least two horses at Belmont, being reimbursed seven hundred dollars by the War Department "for five horses killed & disabled by the enemy." J. L. Lea to Quartermaster General, n.d., Letters Received, AG & QMG, RG 109, NA (third quotation).
38. Hughes, *Belmont,* 94–95; Nov. 7, 1861, entry, Fielder Diary (first quotation); THB to RMR, Nov. 9, 1861, SIU (second–fifth quotations).
39. Nov. 7, 1861, entry, Fielder Diary.
40. *OR* 3:333; THB to R. M. Russell, Nov. 9, 1861, SIU; Hughes and Stonesifer, *Pillow,* 200–201; Farnham, *South to West,* 21; Willoughby, "'Noble, True and Brave.'"
41. Hughes and Stonesifer, *Pillow,* 202.
42. THB to RMR, Nov. 9, 1861, SIU (first quotation); Nov. 7, 1861, entry, Fielder Diary (second quotation); Hughes, *Belmont,* 143–44; THB Autobiography (third, fourth quotations).
43. THB Autobiography (quotations); Lindsley, *Military Annals of Tennessee,* 307; Dec. 16, 1861, entry, Fielder Diary.
44. Hughes, *Belmont,* 87–88, 119, 155, 181, 202–5.
45. THB Autobiography; W. S. Bell CSR; *OR* 8:128, 778, 781, 786.
46. Hughes, *Belmont,* 181, 216, 269 n. 23.
47. Nov. 8–9, 1861, entries, Fielder Diary; Hughes, *Belmont,* 179.

48. *OR* 3:333; THB to RMR, Nov. 9, 1861, SIU (quotation).
49. Hughes, *Belmont,* 185; Nov. 26–27, 1861, entries, Fielder Diary; Hughes and Stonesifer, *Pillow,* 204–5; *OR* 3:313–30.
50. Hughes and Stonesifer, *Pillow,* 200; *OR* 3:339–40 (quotation), 369.
51. THB Autobiography (quotation).

3. Shiloh

1. Losson, *Tennessee's Forgotten Warriors,* 40; Joseph H. Parks, *General Leonidas Polk CSA: The Fighting Bishop,* 189 (quotation), 194–97.
2. Hughes and Stonesifer, *Pillow,* 205–6 (quotation); Dec. 18, 1861, entry, Fielder Diary. Columbus was the northern terminus of the Mobile and Ohio; the track led directly south to Union City, continuing on to Trenton, Humboldt, and Jackson.
3. Dec. 18, 1861, entry, Fielder Diary (quotation).
4. R. M. Russell to G. Williamson, Feb. 2, 1862, R. M. Russell CSR (quotation). See also Nathaniel C. Hughes, Jr., *The Civil War Memoir of Philip Daingerfield Stephenson, D.D.* (1995; reprint, Baton Rouge: Louisiana State Univ. Press, 1998), 40–48.
5. Alfred J. Vaughan, *Personal Record of the Thirteenth Regiment Tennessee Infantry* (Memphis, Tenn.: S.C. Toof & Co., 1897), 15 (quotation).
6. It is not known where young Bell died, nor of what cause. It is assumed he died in camp at Columbus, rather than on sick leave at Newbern, because his CSR gives date of death with no explanation. J. W. Bell CSR; Lindsley, *Military Annals of Tennessee,* 310; Connie W. Moretti, "Descendants of Tyree Rodes Harris," http://members.aol.com/cwmoretti/family/page 2.htm.
7. Dec. 30, 1861, entry, Fielder Diary; Hughes and Stonesifer, *Pillow,* 208.
8. *OR* 3:313–24; 4:539; Connelly, *Army of the Heartland,* 104–5; Parks, *Polk,* 200, 203; Hughes and Stonesifer, *Pillow,* 207; Dec. 30–31, 1861, entries, Fielder Diary (quotations).
9. Lindsley, *Military Annals of Tennessee,* 307 (first–third quotations); Jan. 1–3, 1862, entries, Fielder Diary (fourth quotation); *OR* 7:803, 813, 816, 826. James Lusk Alcorn would remain popular with many Mississippians despite his Civil War misadventures. A Whig-turned-Republican, he would represent them as senator and governor throughout the Reconstruction period. Bruce S. Allardice, *More Generals in Gray* (Baton Rouge: Louisiana State Univ. Press, 1995), 17–18.
10. Hughes and Stonesifer, *Pillow,* 209–10.
11. Jan. and Feb. 1862 entries, Fielder Diary; Nov. 1861 entries, H. R. A. McCorkle Diary; Willoughby, "Noble, True and Brave."
12. Feb. 16, 17, 20, 1862, entries, Fielder Diary (quotation).
13. Jan. 19, 1862, entry, Fielder Diary (quotation).

14. Parks, *Polk,* 213–14; Connelly, *Army of the Heartland,* 132; Feb. 16–28, 1862, entries, Fielder Diary (quotations); Losson, *Tennessee's Forgotten Warriors,* 41.
15. Mar. 1–4, 1862, entries, Fielder Diary (quotation).
16. THB Autobiography; Cox, "From a Finer Cast: the History of the 12th Tennessee Regiment"; Mar. 5–12, 1862, entries, Fielder Diary.
17. Warner, *Generals in Gray,* 51–52; Mar. 13–15, 1862, entries, Fielder Diary.
18. Lindsley, *Military Annals of Tennessee,* 307; Mar. 17–22, 1862, entries, Fielder Diary (quotation).
19. Mar. 22–Apr. 1, 1862, entries, Fielder Diary.
20. S.O. No. 469, First Corps, Army of the Mississippi. *OR* 1:382–83; *Tennessee in the Civil War,* 1:199. On April 7, 1862, Dyer County's Forty-seventh Tennessee would arrive and also be assigned to Polk.
21. Parks, *Polk,* 227–28; Daniel, *Shiloh: The Battle that Changed the Civil War* (New York: Simon & Schuster, 1997), 121–23; Apr. 1–4, 1862, entries, Fielder Diary; Connelly, *Army of the Heartland,* 155.
22. THB Autobiography; *OR* 10(1):414; Apr. 5, 1862, entry, Fielder Diary.
23. Wiley Sword, *Shiloh: Bloody April* (Dayton, Ohio: Morningside Press, 1983), 186; Daniel, *Shiloh,* 167–68 (second, third quotations); THB Autobiography (first, fourth quotations); *OR* 10(1):416; Willoughby, "Dyer County and the Civil War"; Connelly, *Army of the Heartland,* 160–61.
24. Sword, *Shiloh: Bloody April,* 192; Apr. 6, 1862, entry, Lemuel A. Scarborough Diary, Emory Univ.; Daniel, *Shiloh,* 157 (third quotation), 168, 170; *OR* 10(1):408, 422–23 (first quotation) 262, 423; *CV* 6 (Nov. 1898): 529 (second quotation).
25. *OR* 10(1):423 (quotation).
26. *OR* 10(1):423; Daniel, *Shiloh,* 179–80 (quotation); Diane Neal and Thomas W. Kremm, *The Lion of the South: General Thomas C. Hindman* (Macon, Ga.: Mercer Univ. Press, 1993), 108.
27. *OR* 10(1):423 (quotation); THB Autobiography; Apr. 6, 1862, entry, Fielder Diary; Willoughby, "Dyer County in the Civil War."
28. THB Autobiography; *OR* 10(1):417–18, 423; Lindsley, *Military Annals of Tennessee,* 486; Joseph H. Parks, *General Leonidas Polk* (Baton Rouge: Louisiana State Univ. Press, 1962), 234; Willoughby, "Dyer County in the Civil War."
29. THB remembered being carried to an "extreme eastern" captured camp. THB Autobiography.
30. THB Autobiography; *OR* 10(1):418, 423; Willoughby, "Dyer County in the Civil War"; Sam D. Elliott, *Soldier of Tennessee: General Alexander P. Stewart and the Civil War in the West* (Baton Rouge: Louisiana State Univ. Press, 1999), 44.
31. Apr. 6, 1862, entry, William Mays journal, quoted in Willoughby, "Dyer County in the Civil War" (first quotation); Apr. 6, 22, 1862, entries, Fielder

Diary (second, third quotations); Apr. 6, 1862, entry, Thomas Firth Diary, Confederate Collection, TSLA (fourth quotation). These Yankee rifles "of every description" had to be surrendered to the Ordnance Department late in June, thus preventing a logistical nightmare for the regiment.

32. THB Autobiography; Apr. 7, 1862, entry, William Mays journal, quoted in Willoughby, "Dyer County in the Civil War"; Daniel, *Shiloh,* 284; *OR* 10(1): 404, 416, 423 (quotations); Apr. 7, 1862, entry, Fielder Diary; Lindsley, *Military Annals of Tennessee,* 308; Connelly, *Army of the Heartland,* 175.
33. William Mays journal, quoted in Willoughby, "Dyer County in the Civil War" (first quotation); THB Autobiography (second quotation).
34. THB Autobiography (quotation). The Rev. W. J. "Jack" Mahon, a Methodist pastor, was chaplain of the Twenty-second Tennessee at the time, but a close friend of THB.
35. THB Autobiography; Lindsley, *Military Annals of Tennessee,* 308; Apr. 7, 1862, entry, William Mays Journal, quoted in Willoughby, "Dyer County in the Civil War"; *OR* 10(1):395.
36. Lindsley, *Military Annals of Tennessee,* 486. See Nathaniel C. Hughes, Jr., *The Pride of the Confederate Artillery: The Washington Artillery in the Army of Tennessee* (Baton Rouge: Louisiana State Univ. Press, 1997), 27–29.
37. *OR* 10(1):419.
38. George C. Porter, "The Twelfth," quoted in Brent Cox, "Secrets of Heroism."
39. *Tennesseans in the Civil War,* 1:199.
40. May 8, 1862, entry, Fielder Diary; *Tennesseans in the Civil War,* 1:199; *OR* 17(2):603.
41. Excess officers "who are not included among rank and file, and stand in the third rank on parade, when the troops are drawn up in double ranks."
42. R. M. Russell CSR; Application of Annie J. Russell Wade, UDC Applications, vol. 6, box 3, TSLA; Brent Cox, "Secrets of Heroism," "Colonel Robert M. Russell."
43. THB Autobiography. Harris was a wealthy farmer-doctor of Newbern and THB's cousin, son of Brightberry Harris and Sally Walton. Westbrook was also a neighbor at Newbern and would become surgeon of Russell's Twentieth Tennessee Cavalry as the war wore on. McBride and Robinson, *Biographical Directory,* 1:384–85; Earl Willoughby, "Confederate Surgeons from Dyer Co."
44. THB Autobiography (quotation); May 28, 1862, entry, Fielder Diary. THB's traveling companions were Maj. W. P. Fowlks, Capt. W. L. Fowlks, Mr. Harrel, and Mr. Fuller. Perhaps as a precaution, Bell sold ninety-six acres of land to William Morris the week he returned to the army. Dyer Co., Tenn. Deed Book N, 53.
45. S.O. #69, Hdq. 1st Corps, Army of the West, June 17, 1862, RG 109 (quotation); THB to AG, May 25, 1863, Letters Received by the War Department, RG 109, NA; *OR* 17(2):603.

46. Warner, *Generals in Gray,* 283–84; Hughes, *Belmont,* 43, 139–40, 165–68; Hughes and Stonesifer, *Pillow,* 52, 189, 204; *OR* 10(1):442–43; 30(2):79; *Tennesseans in the Civil War,* 1:199–200, 310.
47. Lindsley, *Military Annals of Tennessee,* 308–9.
48. Losson, *Tennessee's Forgotten Warriors,* 57 (first quotation); B. F. Cheatham to Secretary of War, Feb. 2, 1863, Letters Received by the Confederate Secretary of War (M437) RG 109, NA.
49. THB Autobiography.
50. Nathaniel C. Hughes, Jr., *General William J. Hardee: Old Reliable* (Baton Rouge: Louisiana State Univ. Press, 1965), 119; Grady McWhiney, *Braxton Bragg and Confederate Defeat,* vol. 1: *Field Command* (New York: Columbia Univ. Press, 1969), 262–63.
51. Bell, Autobiography; June 25–28, July 6, 19, 1862, entries, Fielder Diary; *OR* 10(1):783.
52. McWhiney, *Braxton Bragg,* 267–68; Connelly, *Army of the Heartland,* 195–202.
53. Hughes, *Hardee,* 120; *OR* 16(2):759; THB Autobiography; Losson, *Tennessee's Forgotten Warriors,* 60.
54. July 25, 1862, entry, Fielder Diary; THB Autobiography.

4. Banners to the Breeze

1. July 26–31, 1862, entries, Fielder Diary (quotations); THB Autobiography.
2. July 31–Aug. 5, 1862, entries, Fielder Diary; THB Autobiography (quotations).
3. Losson, *Tennessee's Forgotten Warriors,* 301 n. 39; Roy Morris, Jr., "Battle in the Bluegrass." *Civil War Times Illustrated* 27:15; Joseph H. Parks, *General Edmund Kirby Smith, C.S.A.* (Baton Rouge: Louisiana State Univ. Press, 1954), 201; *OR* 16(2):744–45, 748–49; 16(1):1089; Connelly, *Army of the Heartland,* 207.
4. See Kirby Smith's letters to Bragg of Aug. 9, 1862, and to Jefferson Davis two days later. *OR* 16(2):748, 752–53. Joe Wheeler explained it well: "General Smith had at first contemplated cutting off the supplies of the garrison at Cumberland Gap, but learning that they were well provisioned, and seeing the difficulty of supplying his own troops in the poor and barren region of southeastern Kentucky, he determined to push rapidly on to the rich blue-grass region in the central part of the state." Joseph Wheeler, "Bragg's Invasion of Kentucky," in *Battles and Leaders of the Civil War,* ed. Robert Underwood Johnson and Clarence Clough Buel, 3:4.
5. Howell and Elizabeth Purdue, *Pat Cleburne, Confederate General* (Hillsboro, Tex.: Hill Junior College Press, 1973), 134; Parks, *Kirby Smith,* 202. Bankhead's Battery, commanded by Capt. William L. Scott, was detached from its parent unit and remained with Cheatham's Division throughout the

Kentucky Campaign. It was Kirby Smith's responsibility to provide the field artillery for Pres Smith's detached brigade. Edmondson's company of sharpshooters, sometimes listed separately in the brigade's table of organization, maneuvered and fought independently of their parent unit—the 154th Senior Infantry. Aug. 7–8, 1862, entries, Fielder Diary; *OR* 16(2):744–45; Purdue and Purdue, *Pat Cleburne,* 134. Also see Captain Scott's account, Lindsley, *Military Annals of Tennessee,* 792.

6. THB Autobiography.
7. Aug. 9–10, 1862, entries, Fielder Diary.
8. Parks, *Kirby Smith,* 204 (quotation); Ted R. Worley, ed., *The War Memoirs of Captain John W. Lavender, C.S.A.* (Pine Bluff, Ark.: W. M. Hackett and D. R. Perdue, 1956), 20; *OR* 16(2):753–554. Bell refers to Rogers' Gap as Big Tree Gap in his Autobiography.
9. THB Autobiography (quotations); *OR* 16(2):753–54; Aug. 13–14, 1862, entries, Fielder Diary. Kirby Smith was wise. Rogers' Gap was "a nearly impassable notch on the crest of the Cumberland Mountains which rose a thousand feet above the surrounding hills, with nothing but a horse trail through it." D. Warren Lambert, *When the Ripe Pears Fell: The Battle of Richmond, Kentucky* (Richmond, Ky.: Madison County Historical Society, 1995), 7–8.
10. THB Autobiography (quotations). According to Lt. Col. James A. Williamson, Second Arkansas Mounted Rifles, Pres Smith's brigade was the first across the Cumberland Mountains. Wesley T. Leeper, *Rebels Valiant: Second Arkansas Mounted Rifles (Dismounted)* (Little Rock, Ark.: Pioneer Press, 1964), 103.
11. Aug. 21, 1862, entry, Fielder Diary; THB Autobiography.
12. THB Autobiography.
13. Aug. 25–26, 1862, entries, Fielder Diary (quotations); Peter F. Hammond, "General Kirby Smith's Campaign in Kentucky in 1862," *SHSP* 10 (1882): 247; 9 (1881): 247–48; J. G. Law, "Diary of the Rev. J. G. Law," *SHSP* 12 (1882): 391, 394; Frank T. Ryan, "The Kentucky Campaign and the Battle of Richmond, *CV* 26 (Apr. 1918): 158; Edwin L. Drake, ed. *Annals of the Army of Tennessee* (Nashville: A. D. Haynes, 1878), 199; Connelly, *Army of the Heartland,* 214.
14. Ryan, "The Kentucky Campaign," *CV* 26 (Apr. 1918): 158.
15. Irving A. Buck, *Cleburne and His Command,* ed. T. R. Hay (1908; reprint, Dayton, Ohio: Morningside Bookshop, 1992), 104; Parks, *Kirby Smith,* 210–22; Aug. 27–28, 1862, entries, Fielder Diary (first, second quotations); Ryan, "Kentucky Campaign," *CV* 26: 158–59 (third, fourth quotations).
16. Lambert, *Richmond,* 43; Drake, *Annals of the Army of Tennessee,* 199 (first quotation); Robert H. Dacus, *Reminiscences of Company "H," First Arkansas Mounted Rifles* (Dardanelle, Ark.: Post Dispatch Print, 1897) n.p.; *OR* 16(1):944; Hammond, "General Kirby Smith's Campaign in Kentucky in 1862," *SHSP* 9:249; Morris, "Battle in the Blue Grass," 27:21 (second quotation).

17. THB, Autobiography; Edwin H. Rennolds, *A History of the Henry County Commands* (1904; reprint, Kennesaw, Ga.: Continental Book Co., 1961), 12.
18. Hammond, "General Kirby Smith's Campaign in Kentucky in 1862," *SHSP* 9:250 (quotation); Aug. 30, 1862, entry, Fielder Diary; Buck, *Cleburne,* 105; Purdue, *Pat Cleburne,* 105; Wheeler, "Bragg's Invasion of Kentucky," *B&L* 3:4; Drake, *Annals of the Army of Tennessee,* 202–3; James Lee McDonough, *War in Kentucky, from Shiloh to Perryville* (Knoxville: Univ. of Tennessee Press, 1994), 133.
19. Buck, *Cleburne,* 105–6; Hammond, "General Kirby Smith's Campaign in Kentucky in 1862," *SHSP* 9:250; Purdue, *Pat Cleburne,* 106.
20. Morris, "Battle in the Bluegrass," 22 (first quotation); THB Autobiography (second, third, fourth, fifth quotations); *OR* 16(1):947.
21. THB Autobiography (quotations).
22. *OR* 16(1):932, 934, 946; Buck, *Cleburne,* 105–6; Hammond, "General Kirby Smith's Campaign in Kentucky in 1862" *SHSP* 9:250; THB Autobiography; Craig L. Symonds, *Stonewall of the West: Patrick Cleburne & the Civil War* (Lawrence: Univ. Press of Kansas, 1997), 90–91.
23. Vaughan had been elected colonel of the regiment Dec. 4, 1861. James D. West, "The Thirteenth Tennessee Regiment—Confederate States of America," *Tennessee Historical Magazine* 7 (Oct. 1921): 180–93.
24. *OR* 16(1):934; Ryan, "Kentucky Campaign," *CV* 26: 159.
25. *OR* 16(1):947 (first quotation); Lavender, *War Memoirs,* 23–24 (second quotation).
26. Hammond, "General Kirby Smith's Campaign in Kentucky in 1862," *SHSP* 9:253; Morris, "Battle in the Bluegrass," 23.
27. Ryan, "Kentucky Campaign," *CV* 26: 160; *OR* 16(1):940–41, 947, 950–51; Connelly, *Army of the Heartland,* 215–16. It is unclear, however, that M. R. Hill, who had been at Knoxville, was at Richmond or even made the march into Kentucky. The regiment could have been commanded by Capt. William M. Watkins who would lead it at the Battle of Murfreesboro four months later.
28. *OR* 16(1):941, 951 (first, third quotations); Vaughan, *Personal Record,* 21 (second quotation); THB Autobiography (fourth quotation); Evans, *Confederate Military History,* 10:46 (fifth quotation).
29. THB Autobiography (first quotation); *OR* 16(1):932, 941, 948 (second quotation); "The Fighting Forty Eighth Tennessee Regiment," *CV* 2 (Feb. 1884): 248; Lambert, *Battle of Richmond,* 139–40.
30. THB appears to be mistaken when he credits Nelson's escape to young Henry Clay to whose plantation he had fled. Nelson had escaped to the home of Cassius M. Clay, Kentucky Unionist and general officer. It seems C. M. Clay was not at home. He had run afoul of the peremptory Nelson on August 25, and been relieved of his command. His services not desired, Clay appears to have returned to Frankfort, where he was to address the legislature on August 27.

Thus THB might be referring to C. M. Clay's son rather than Henry Clay's. THB Autobiography; Charles C. Gilbert, "Bragg's Invasion of Kentucky," *Southern Bivouac* 4 (Sept. 1885): 220; Lambert, *Battle of Richmond*, 19–21.

31. Vaughan, *Personal Record*, 21 (first quotation); THB Autobiography; Morris, "Battle in the Bluegrass," 23; Lindsley, *Military Annals of Tennessee*, 309; *OR* 16(1):935; Ryan, "Kentucky Campaign," *CV* 26: 160; Symonds, *Stonewall of the West*, 92.
32. Vaughan, *Personal Record*, 21. D. Warren Lambert, historian of the Battle of Richmond, echoes these sentiments. "The absence of any reports at regimental or battery level in Kirby Smith's army . . . is a major frustration for the researcher." Lambert, *Battle of Richmond*, 246.
33. Aug. 30, 1862, entry, Fielder Diary; *OR* 16(1):948.

5. My Old Kentucky Home

1. Aug. 31, 1862, entry, Fielder Diary; Vaughan, *Personal Record*, 9–10.
2. THB Autobiography; Sept. 1, 1862, entry, Fielder Diary.
3. THB Autobiography (first, second, fifth quotations); Sept. 1, 1862, entry, Fielder Diary (third, fourth quotations).
4. THB Autobiography (second quotation); Sept. 2, 1862, entry, Fielder Diary (first quotation).
5. THB Autobiography.
6. *OR* 16(1):932; Sept. 2, 1862, entry, Fielder Diary (quotations).
7. Leeper, *Rebels Valiant*, 110; Vaughan, *Personal Record*, 23; Basil W. Duke, "Morgan's Cavalry During the Bragg Invasion," *B&L* 3:26; THB Autobiography (second quotation); "The Fighting Forty Eighth Tennessee Regiment," *Southern Bivouac*, 2 (Feb. 1884): 248 (third quotation).
8. In his Autobiography, THB mistakenly recalled the enemy retreated across the Ohio. Instead, most of the Federals continued their retreat west through Lexington toward Louisville.
9. Parks, *Kirby Smith*, 221; THB Autobiography (quotations); Sept. 5–8, 1862, entries, Fielder Diary.
10. Sept. 9, 1862, entry, Fielder Diary; Basil W. Duke, *History of Morgan's Cavalry* (1867; reprint, Indianapolis: Indiana Univ. Press, 1960), 237 (quotation).
11. Lowell H. Harrison, "Abraham Buford," *ANB* 3:878; Warner, *Generals in Gray*, 39.
12. THB Autobiography (quotation); *OR* 16(2):807; Sept. 10–16, 1862, entries, Fielder Diary.
13. *OR* 16(2):812; THB Autobiography (quotations); Sept. 16–17, 1862, entries, Fielder Diary. Among their visitors was Mrs. John C. Breckinridge, but apparently she did not, or was not allowed to, join the infantry column.
14. Sept. 19–22, 1862, entries, Fielder Diary.

15. Parks, *Kirby Smith*, 225–26; *OR* 16(2):850, 855, 861; Connelly, *Army of the Heartland*, 244; Symonds, *Stonewall of the West*, 93; Sept. 23–Oct. 3, 1862, entries, Fielder Diary.
16. Oct. 1–7, 1862, entries, Fielder Diary (first, second, third quotations); Parks, *Kirby Smith*, 225–26; Symonds, *Stonewall of the West*, 93; Purdue, *Pat Cleburne*, 144–45.
17. Oct. 7–8, 15, 1862, entries, Fielder Diary.
18. *OR* 16(1):1096; Lindsley, *Military Annals of Tennessee*, 309; Losson, *Tennessee's Forgotten Warriors*, 301 n. 39; Kenneth A. Hafendorfer, *Perryville: Battle for Kentucky* (Louisville, Ky.: K H Press, 1991), 360, 367, 374; Vaughan, *Personal Record*, 23.
19. Symonds, *Stonewall of the West*, 97; Losson, *Tennessee's Forgotten Warriors*, 74–75; Parks, *Kirby Smith*, 237–39.
20. THB probably knew Frank L. Wolford (1817–1895). Wolford had raised the First Kentucky Cavalry, USA, in Garrard and nearby counties. Essentially he was a partisan leader who by 1864 commanded a division but was deemed incompetent by Maj. Gen. John M. Schofield. Wolford, a popular conservative Democrat, openly criticized Lincoln's policy of using black troops and for his outspoken opposition he was placed under arrest and forced to resign. Henry Deeks, "Civil War Images," *Civil War News* (May 2001): 49.
21. THB Autobiography; Oct. 12–13, 1862, entries, Fielder Diary; McBride and Robison, eds., *Biographical Directory of the Tennessee General Assembly*, 1:206–207. Craig was probably Capt. S. Craig, a former officer in the Forty-eighth Tennessee, at that time an aide on Donelson's staff.
22. THB Autobiography.
23. Oct. 15–26, 1862, entries (first, second, third, fifth quotations), Fielder Diary; THB Autobiography; Vaughan, *Personal Record*, 23 (fourth quotation); McDonough, *War in Kentucky*, 310–12.

6. Shelbyville

1. *OR* 16(2):982; THB Autobiography; Oct. 30–Nov. 10, 1862, entries, Fielder Diary.
2. Lindsley, *Military Annals of Tennessee*, 309; Nov. 10–21, 1862, entries, Fielder Diary; *OR* 16(2):982–83; THB Autobiography.
3. *OR* 30(1):12, 16, 34–35; Nov. 21–Dec. 8, 1862, entries, Fielder Diary; THB Autobiography; *CV* 6 (Nov. 1898): 529.
4. THB Autobiography (last quotation); Dec. 9, 1862, entry, Fielder Diary (first–third quotations).
5. *OR* 23(2):734; Dec. 17–24, 1862, entries, Fielder Diary (quotations). Two weeks later Fielder would report that henceforward the "old 12th" was to be known as the First Battalion or Right Wing; the Forty-seventh, the Second

Battalion or Left Wing. Fielder, happily, was reinstated as captain of combined companies A and E. Jan. 12, 1863, entry, Fielder Diary.
6. Dec. 21, 24, 1862; Jan. 7, 1863, entries, Fielder Diary; Lindsley, *Military Annals of Tennessee*, 309; THB Autobiography (quotations); *Tennesseans in the Civil War*, 1:198, 200, 278; Brian S. Wills, *Battle from the Start: A Life of Nathan Bedford Forrest* (New York: Harper Collins, 1992), 88–89; Losson, *Tennessee's Forgotten Warriors*, 78.
7. *OR* 17(1):561–62; 593; Brent A. Cox, "The Battle of Trenton, December 20, 1862."
8. Jan. 7, 1863, entries, Fielder Diary; Lindsley, *Military Annals of Tennessee*, 309; THB Autobiography (quotations); *Tennesseans in the Civil War*, 1:198, 200, 278; Wills, *Battle from the Start*, 88–89; *OR* 20(1):744–45; Cozzens, *No Better Place to Die: The Battle of Stones River* (Urbana: Univ. of Illinois Press, 1990), 114–55.
9. THB Autobiography; *Tennesseans in the Civil War*, 1:278.
10. Officers of the 12/47th Tenn. Vol. Inf. to Secretary of War, Feb. 2, 1863; B. F. Cheatham to Secretary of War, Feb. 2, 1863, Letters Received by the Confederate Secretary of War (M437) RG 109, NA.
11. Longtime adjutant of the Forty-seventh Tennessee, Richardson became Bell's AAAG (acting assistant adjutant general) and would serve Bell faithfully throughout the war. T. E. Richardson CSR, M331, RG 109, NA.
12. THB Autobiography.
13. Ibid.
14. Ibid. For another instance of THB's strict enforcement, see his letter to Maj. Gen. Patton Anderson, Feb. 24, 1863, THB CSR.
15. Feb. 23–26; Mar. 29–31, 1863, entries, Fielder Diary (first, second quotations); Brigade and Division inspection reports, Mar. 1863, Inspection Reports and Related Records Received by the Inspection Branch, RG 109, NA (third–fifth quotations).
16. Mar. 25; Apr. 1–3, 15–16, 1863, entries, Fielder Diary (first, second quotations); THB Autobiography (remaining quotations).
17. THB Autobiography (quotations).
18. Hughes and Stonesifer, *Pillow*, 261–67; *OR* 23(2):827; *OR* 39(2):648 (first quotation); John A. Wyeth, *Life of General Nathan Bedford Forrest* (1899; reprint, Dayton, Ohio: Morningside Bookshop, 1975), 279 (second quotation).
19. The cavalry headquartered at Spring Hill consisted of two divisions commanded by brigadier generals, Frank C. Armstrong and "Red" Jackson, both former officers in the prewar U.S. Army, the "Old Army." Robert S. Henry, *First with the Most—Forrest* (Indianapolis: Bobbs-Merrill Co., 1944), 122, 160–61; Jan. 30; May 21, 1863, entries, Fielder Diary; Wills, *Battle from the Start*, 121.
20. According to Captain Fielder, Bell, true to his promise to Bragg to be easily available "if needed," appears to have visited Shelbyville on May 5, probably

in the company of Pillow, then returned almost immediately to Columbia. Bell maintained "I staid the thirty days out." May 5, 25, 1863, entries, Fielder Diary; Bell Autobiography (quotations).
21. Apr. 30–May 14; May 25, 1863, entries, Fielder Diary.
22. May 21, 1863, entry, Fielder Diary; Earl Willoughby, "Colonel Dawson & the Shadow War"; *Tennesseans in the Civil War,* 1:88.
23. Thomas H. Baker to James A. Seddon, May 10, 1863, Letters Received, Confederate Secretary of War (M437), RG 109, NA.
24. May 25, 1863, entry, Fielder Diary; Earl Willoughby, "Chasing Guerrillas: The West Tennessee Campaign" (quotation); Willoughby, "Home-made Yankees"; Willoughby, "A Hot-bed of Traitors"; June 23, 1862–Feb. 9, 1863, entries, McCorkle Diary.
25. Benjamin F. Cooling, *Fort Donelson's Legacy: War and Society in Kentucky and Tennessee, 1862–1863* (Knoxville: Univ. of Tennessee Press, 1997), 250 (first quotation). According to historian Robert M. McBride, "Correspondence of [Hurst's] superior officers lends credence to such charges and indicates that money so collected was not turned over to Federal authorities." McBride, *Biographical Directory of the Tennessee General Assembly,* 2:444 (quotations). Cavalryman John Johnston spoke for many of his fellow West Tennesseans in characterizing Hurst's regiment as "a notorious gang organized in the backwoods of McNairy and other Counties, along the Tennessee River mainly, and noted for their propensity to plunder and murder." John Johnston Reminiscences.
26. Cooling, *Fort Donelson's Legacy,* 250. See also Gary Blankinship, "Colonel Fielding Hurst and the Hurst Nation," *WTHSP* 34 (1980): 71–87; Willoughby, "Home-made Yankees"; Willoughby, "Chasing Guerrillas."
27. Branch, "Robert Vinkler Richardson," *Dictionary of North Carolina Biography,* 5:217–18.
28. Stephen V. Ash, *When the Yankees Came: Conflict and Chaos in the Occupied South, 1861–1865* (Chapel Hill: Univ. of North Carolina Press, 1995), 106.
29. When the actual election was held in August 1863, both Atkins and Caruthers won. Atkins returned to serve in Richmond. Caruthers, however, because of a technicality in Tennessee election law, would never serve as governor. This was not known to Bell and Fielder at the time of the convention, however. Because of the provision in the Tennessee constitution that he be qualified before holding office and given that qualification consisted of an official vote count by the speaker of the senate in the presence of the General Assembly and the formal swearing-in ceremony (a virtual impossibility in the summer of 1863), Caruthers was never qualified and Isham G. Harris would remain governor, "in the absence of a successor." Kenneth C. Martis, *The Historical Atlas of the Congresses of the Confederate States of America, 1861–1865* (New York: Simon & Schuster, 1994), 68; June 11, 16–18, 1863, entries, Fielder Diary;

G. W. Watters, "Isham Green Harris, Civil War Governor and Senator from Tennessee, 1818–1897" (Ph.D. dissertation, Florida State Univ., 1977), 120.
30. June 21, July 14, 1863, entries, Fielder Diary; THB Autobiography (quotation).

7. Slipping Back to West Tennessee

1. Cooling, *Fort Donelson's Legacy,* 265–66 (quotation), 280.
2. Roy Morris, Jr., "Fort Pillow: Massacre or Madness," *America's Civil War* 29 (Nov. 2000): 26. In lieu of a study of partisan activity in West Tennessee and the Jackson Purchase region of Kentucky, understanding may be gained from B. F. Cooling's work on Middle and East Tennessee—*Fort Donelson's Legacy.* Also see Cooling's chapter in Daniel E. Sutherland, ed., *Guerillas, Unionists, and Violence on the Confederate Home Front* (Fayetteville: Univ. of Arkansas Press, 1999).
3. Hughes and Stonesifer, *Pillow,* 267 (quotations).
4. Special Orders #255, July 19, 1863, Volunteer and Conscript Bureau, THB CSR; *OR* 23(1):844; 23(2):532–33; 39(2):762.
5. Special Orders #255, July 19, 1863, Volunteer and Conscript Bureau, THB CSR; *OR* 39 (2):647.
6. Special Orders #50, Oct. 20, 1863, Volunteer and Conscript Bureau, THB CSR.
7. 1850, 1860 Henry Co., Tenn. Censuses; *Tennesseans in the Civil War,* 1:109; H. C. Greer file, in possession of Bruce S. Allardice.
8. Evans, *Confederate Military History,* 10:75; *Tennesseans in the Civil War,* 1:110–11; J. F. Newsom file, in possession of Bruce S. Allardice.
9. *Tennesseans in the Civil War,* 1:99, 112, 292; A. N. Wilson file, in possession of Bruce S. Allardice.
10. *Tennesseans in the Civil War,* 1:110.
11. L. M. Nutt to N. B. Forrest, Nov. 8, 1866, Nutt Papers, SHC.
12. *OR* 30(2):655 (quotation). First Lieutenant Thomas E. Richardson, onetime adjutant of the Forty-seventh Tennessee, who was assisting Bell, was captured while recruiting, Aug. 8, 1863. T. E. Richardson, CSR, G&S File (M331), RG 109.
13. *OR* 30(2):650, 652–55 (quotation); 30(3):750, 789, 890.
14. *OR* 32(1):613.
15. Bragg continued to support Bell in West Tennessee well into October 1863. Endorsements by B. Bragg, Oct. 1, 1863 on S.O. #255, Volunteer & Conscription Bureau, July 19, 1863, and THB to B. F. Cheatham, [Sept.?] 1863, THB CSR; *Tennesseeans in the Civil War,* 1:80–81; Cooling, *Fort Donelson's Legacy,* 280.
16. L. M. Nutt to N. B. Forrest, Nov. 8, 1866, Nutt Papers.
17. Ibid. (quotations). Russell's whereabouts and activities, throughout his life, are frustrating to reconstruct, but especially from June 1862 to November 1863.

Compounding the problem are the presence of Col. A. A. Russell, Fourth Alabama, who fought under Chalmers and Forrest, and Capt. Milton Russell, Fifty-first Indiana, one of Col. Abel Streight's key subordinates.

18. THB Autobiography; Oct. 13–17, 1863, entries, Fielder Diary; "Judge W. W. McDowell," *CV* 13 (Oct. 1905): 468; Charles S. Coleman statement, *CV* 35 (Dec. 1927): 467; James H. Mathes, *The Old Guard in Gray: Researches in the Annals of the Confederate Historical Association. Sketches of Memphis Veterans, etc.* (Memphis, Tenn.: S. C. Toof, 1897), 22; *Tennesseans in the Civil War,* 1:111. Some of Bell's troops encamped at Moulton, Ala., just to the east of Russellville. James J. White questionnaire, *Tennessee Civil War Veterans Questionnaires,* comp. Gustavus W. Dyer and John Trotwood Moore; ed. Collen M. Elliott and Louise A. Moxley, 5 vols. (Easley, S.C.: Southern Historical Press, 1985), 5:2173.

19. J. Davis to N. B. Forrest, Oct. 29, 1863, N. B. Forrest CSR (M331), RG 109, NA; James L. Lea CSR; to AG, endorsement of B. Bragg, Oct. 10, 1863, on THB to W. W. Mackall, Oct. 1863, THB MSR; THB Autobiography (quotations); Thomas Jordan and J. P. Pryor, *The Campaigns of Lieut.-Gen. N. B. Forrest, and of Forrest's Cavalry* (New Orleans: Blelock & Co., 1868), 358; Oct. 13–17, 1863, entries, Fielder Diary; Hudson Strode, *Jefferson Davis, 1801–1861,* 3 vols. (New York: Harcourt, Brace and Co., 1955–1964), 2:482–83; Steven E. Woodworth, *Jefferson Davis and His Generals* (Lawrence: Univ. Press of Kansas, 1990), 243–44; Wyeth, *Forrest,* 274–75 (last quotation).

20. J. J. White questionnaire, *Tennessee Civil War Veterans Questionnaires,* 5:2173; *OR* 39(2):647.

21. THB Autobiography.

22. Ibid. (first, second quotations); *OR* 3(3):336; 39(2):647 (third quotation).

23. THB Autobiography; *OR* 31(3):336, 343; 39(2):647–48; Wyeth, *Forrest,* 275 (quotation); Elisha T. Hollis, "Diary of Captain Elisha Tompkin Hollis," ed. William W. Chester, *WTHSP* 39 (1985): 84–85; THB CSR.

24. William Alderson, ed., "Forrest's March Out of West Tennessee: Recollections of a Private (John Johnston)," *WTHSP* 12 (1958): 139 (quotation); THB Autobiography; Dec. 6, 1863, entry, McCorkle Diary. "It can be assumed that the camp mentioned was situated in or near Newbern. Col. Bell's Plantation was located on Haskins Lane on the outskirts of the village near Church Grove and presumably this is where the camp was located. This site has sometimes been confused with the camps at Trenton and Eaton." Earl Willoughby, "Church Grove & Camp Bell during the Civil War."

25. Robert S. Henry, *Forrest* (Indianapolis: Bobbs-Merrill Co., 1944), 200–201; Dept. of the West, S.O. 245, Nov. 14, 1864, RG 109, NA (quotation); *OR* 31(3):645, 694, 789; Jordan and Pryor, *Campaigns of General Forrest,* 357–59; *Nashville American,* June 3, 1901; Wills, *Battle from the Start,* 143–49.

26. *OR* 31(3):646 (quotations), 694, 704–5, 730–32, 745, 751; S. D. Lee, "The War in Mississippi after the Fall of Vicksburg, July 4, 1863," *Publications of the Mississippi Historical Society,* 10:48–49.
27. Henry, *Forrest,* 204 (quotation); *OR* 31(3):668, 678–79, 684; Jordan and Pryor, *Campaigns of General Forrest,* 362–63; R. R. Hancock, *Hancock's Diary: Or, a History of the Second Tennessee Confederate Cavalry, with Sketches of First and Seventh Battalions; also Portraits and Biographical Sketches* (1887; reprint, Dayton, Ohio: Morningside Bookshop, 1981), 289–90; Lindsley, *Military Annals of Tennessee,* 640.
28. John Johnston Reminiscences; *OR* 31(3):763–65, 772; 31(1):576–77; Jordan and Pryor, *Campaigns of General Forrest,* 363–65; John W. Morton, *The Artillery of Nathan Bedford Forrest's Cavalry* (1909; reprint, Paris, Tenn.: Guild Press, 1988), 135 (quotation).
29. Jordan and Pryor, *Campaigns of General Forrest,* 365; Henry, *Forrest,* 204–5; Herman M. Hattaway, *General Stephen D. Lee* (Jackson: Univ. Press of Mississippi, 1976), 105.
30. Jordan and Pryor, *Campaigns of General Forrest,* 365; Wills, *Battle from the Start,* 152; *OR* 31(3):449 (quotation).
31. THB Autobiography; *OR* 31(1):853–54 (first quotation); Wills, *Battle from the Start,* 153 (second quotation).
32. THB Autobiography (quotation); Henry, *Forrest,* 207; *OR* 31(1):607 (second quotation); Wyeth, *Forrest,* 281.
33. Capt. John Skifington was assistant quartermaster for Francis M. Stewart's recently organized Fifteenth Tennessee Cavalry, the nucleus of which was Dawson's Tennessee Partisan Rangers Battalion. Joseph H. Crute, Jr., *Units of the Confederate States Army* (Midlothian, Va.: Derwent Books, 1987), 289; *Tennesseans in the Civil War,* 2:368.
34. *OR* 31(1):613; Henry, *Forrest,* 208 (first quotation); THB Autobiography (second quotation); Wyeth, *Forrest,* 284.
35. Jordan and Pryor, *Campaigns of General Forrest,* 367.
36. THB Autobiography (quotation); Jordan and Pryor, *Campaigns of General Forrest,* 370.
37. Jordan and Pryor, *Campaigns of General Forrest,* 370; THB Autobiography (quotations); Henry, *Forrest,* 209.
38. THB Autobiography (quotation).
39. *OR* 31(3):493, 620–21; THB Autobiography; Jordan and Pryor, *Campaigns of General Forrest,* 375–76; Wyeth, *Forrest,* 287–88; Wills, *Battle from the Start,* 155; Lytle, *Bedford Forrest and His Critter Company,* 255; Johnston, "Forrest's March Out of West Tennessee," *WTHSP* 12 (1958): 146.
40. THB Autobiography (quotation); Henry, *Forrest,* 211–13; *Cincinnati Commercial,* Jan. 12, 1864, quoted in Jordan and Pryor, *Campaigns of General Forrest,* 379–80; Morton, *Artillery of Forrest's Cavalry,* 139.

41. THB Autobiography (quotation); Henry, *Forrest,* 211–13; Jordan and Pryor, *Campaigns of General Forrest,* 379–80; Morton, *Artillery of Forrest's Cavalry,* 139; Jan. 23, 1864, entry, Hollis Diary. A drawing by the Union spy C. C. Bell (sometime member of Chalmers's staff) exists of the encampment at Como. See William B. Feis, "Charles S. Bell, Union Scout," *North and South* 4 (June 2001): 32.

8. Bell's Brigade

1. James Harvey Mathes, *General Forrest* (New York: D. Appleton & Co., 1902), 170; Jordan and Pryor, *Campaigns of General Forrest,* 381 (quotation); *OR* 32(2):546–47, 617.
2. R. M. Russell to L. Polk, Dec. 30, 1863, R. M. Russell CSR; *OR* 31(3):868, 876.
3. *OR* 31(3):817; *OR* 32(1):342.
4. Jordan and Pryor, *Campaigns of General Forrest,* 382 (quotation); Lee, "The War in Mississippi after the Fall of Vicksburg, July 4, 1863," *PMHS* 10 (1909): 52; *OR* 32(2):614; Mathes, *Forrest,* 171. Although appointed brigadier December 3, 1863, Richardson's "nomination was returned by the Senate at the request of President Davis," Feb. 9, 1864. Warner, *Generals in Gray,* 256.
5. *OR* 32(2):614; 32(3):593–94; *Tennesseans in the Civil War,* 1:93–95, 97–100, 102–4; Lindsley, *Military Annals of Tennessee,* 611–25, 737–41. Lt. Col. Henry C. Greer's Partisan Ranger Regiment, which was listed as Bell's fifth regiment in G.O. #3, January 25, 1864, would be folded into the Twentieth Tennessee Cavalry within six weeks, Greer becoming lieutenant colonel of the consolidated regiment. See Randel M. Price, "20th Tennessee Cavalry, CSA." *http://www.familytreemaker.com/cgi-bin/iff; Tennesseans in the Civil War,* 1:109.
6. R. D. Clark CSR, G&S; *CV* 6 (1898): 500; THB Autobiography.
7. T. F. P. Allison CSR, G&S; McBride, *Biographical Directory of the Tennessee General Assembly,* 2:17; Evans, *Confederate Military History,* 10:353–54; *CV* 4 (July 1896): 237; 21 (Sept. 1913): 451.
8. R. M. Russell to A. G., May 1864, R. H. Mahon CSR, G&S.
9. THB Autobiography. John L. Bell, AAG, who was not a relative, actually did not join the staff until May 8, 1864. There would be still other staff members of course: Capt. William K. Bennett would replace Jo Lea; Capt. D. M. Womack would replace Albert Harris as brigade commissary; 1st. Lt. Pleasant A. Smith would join in February 1865 as AAG; and Capt. Thomas Rudd Wingo, late in the war, as brigade surgeon. Among the couriers serving the staff and Bell were Absalom DeBerry Hurt and nineteen-year-old Reuben Green Harrell (1845–1920), Bell's future son-in-law. The latter, probably in 1865, would

move up to become an AAG. Lt. James T. Dunlap, formerly Tenth Tennessee Infantry, was assigned to THB by Forrest, December 22, 1863, and would become provost marshal of Bell's Brigade, February 2, 1864. Eventually he would leave the staff and become one of Russell's Twentieth Tennessee troopers. See documents presented to War Department, Letters Received by the Confederate Adjutant and Inspector General (M474), RG 109, NA.

10. Jan. 24–31, 1864, entries, Hollis Diary, *WTHSP* 39 (1985): 90–91; Jordan and Pryor, *Campaigns of General Forrest*, 382 (first quotation); J. J. White questionnaire, *Tennessee Civil War Veterans Questionnaires*, 5:2173 (second quotation).
11. Evans, *Confederate Military History*, 12:344–45.
12. *OR* 32(2):650; Feb. 1–5, 1864, entries, Hollis Diary, *WTHSP* 39 (1985): 91 (quotations).
13. *OR* 32(1):346–47 (quotations).
14. Jordan and Pryor, *Campaigns of General Forrest*, 384–85 (quotation); Feb. 12, 1864, entry, Hollis Diary; *Hancock's Diary*, 309–10. See Henry, *First with the Most*, 214–15.
15. THB Autobiography (first quotation); Jordan and Pryor, *Campaigns of General Forrest*, 384–85 (second quotation).
16. Feb. 12, 1864, entry, Hollis Diary; *Hancock's Diary*, 309–10 (first quotation); THB Autobiography (third–fifth quotations); Dinkins, "Forrest's Wonderful Achievements," *CV* 35 (Jan. 1927): 12 (second quotation); John M. Hubbard, *Notes of a Private* (St. Louis: Nixon-Jones Printing Co., 1911), 130–31.
17. N. B. Forrest to S. Cooper, Feb. 5, 1864; J. W. C. Atkins to S. Cooper, Feb. 9, 15, 1864, THB CSR; *OR* 32(1):342; 32(3):608–9.
18. Feb. 13–18, 1864, entries, Hollis Diary; THB Autobiography; *OR* 32(1):348–49; Wills, *Battle from the Start*, 158–59; Jordan and Pryor, *Campaigns of General Forrest*, 384–87; Lee, "The War in Mississippi," 53–54; Mathes, *Forrest*, 178, 184.
19. THB Autobiography.
20. David Knapp, Jr., *The Confederate Horsemen* (New York: Vantage Press, 1996), 248–50. See: Mathes, *Old Guard in Gray*, 33–35; *Hancock's Diary*, 578–79; Evans, *Confederate Military History*, 10:368–69; Jonathan M. Atkins, "Race, Freedom, and the Confederate Cause," *Journal of East Tennessee History* 70 (1998): 34–61; Rennolds, *Henry County Commands*, 259.
21. *OR* 32(1):351 (quotation); Jordan and Pryor, *Campaigns of General Forrest*, 390–401; *Hancock's Diary*, 320–24; Mathes, *Old Guard in Gray*, 34–35; Wills, *Battle from the Start*, 162–67; John M. Hubbard, *Notes of a Private* (St. Louis: Nixon-Jones Printing Co., 1911), 93–94; Morton, *The Artillery of Nathan Bedford Forrest's Cavalry*, 152–53; Rennolds, *Henry County Commands*, 259–60; Price, "20th Tennessee Cavalry."

9. A Dash into Kentucky

1. *OR* 32(2):801; Mathes, *Forrest,* 187; Muster rolls, Twentieth Tennessee Cavalry, RG 109 (M268), NA; *Hancock's Diary,* 331 (quotations).
2. Henry, *Forrest,* 235; Morton, *Artillery of Forrest's Cavalry,* 160 (quotation).
3. Mercer Otey, "Story of Our Great War," *CV* 9 (1901): 110.
4. In effect, Jeff Forrest's brigade was "divided up among the other brigades." Even his Alabama regiment soon would be transferred to Newsom's Nineteenth Tennessee Cavalry. *Hancock's Diary,* 332 (quotation). For information about Thompson himself, see Evans, *Confederate Military History,* 11:551.
5. A. Buford CSR (M331); Lowell H. Harrison, "Abraham Buford," *ANB* 3:878–79; Chalmers, "Forrest and His Campaigns" *SHSP* 7: 470; *OR* 32(3):594, 660; Henry, *First with the Most,* 235–36; *Hancock's Diary,* 332; Wills, *Battle from the Start,* 169; THB Autobiography; Henry George, *History of the 3d, 7th, 8th and 12th Kentucky C.S.A.* (1911; reprint, Lyndon, Ky.: Walthen Historic Press, 1970), 149.
6. This land between the Tennessee and Mississippi Rivers, West Tennessee and Southwest Kentucky, once occupied by the Chickasaws, had been ceded to the United States by that group of tribes in 1818 under the Treaty of Tecumseh, negotiated by Andrew Jackson and Isaac Shelby. The area would be known to American citizens as the "Jackson Purchase."
7. Jordan and Pryor, *Campaigns of General Forrest,* 406–7, 413; Wills, *Battle from the Start,* 171 (quotation).
8. THB Autobiography; Henry, *First with the Most,* 237; *Hancock's Diary,* 340 (quotation); *OR* 32(1):611.
9. Otey, "Story of Our Great War," *CV* 9 (1901): 110.
10. Ibid. In 1879 Buford sold Enquirer to Gen. Red Jackson who, with his father-in-law William G. Harding, operated Belle Meade, a horse farm of national reputation. Buford and Jackson would remain fast friends and competitors into the twentieth century. Ridley Wills, II, *The History of Belle Meade: Mansion, Plantation, and Stud* (Nashville: Vanderbilt Univ. Press, 1991), 179, 285.
11. *OR* 32(3):664–65 (first quotation), 117–19 (second–fourth quotations); Wills, *Battle from the Start,* 172; Henry, *First with the Most,* 238.
12. Muster rolls, Twentieth Tennessee Cavalry (M268), RG 109, NA (quotation).
13. Jordan and Pryor, *Campaigns of General Forrest,* 409–11, 413 n; THB Autobiography; Wyeth, *Forrest,* 330; J. V. Greif, "Forrest's Raid on Paducah," *CV* 5 (May 1897): 212–13; George, *3d, 7th, 8th and 12th Kentucky,* 76; Mar. 24–25, 1864, entries, Hollis Diary; Mar. 22–27, 1864, entries, Hanson Hard Diary, LC; *Hancock's Diary,* 341; Mathes, *Forrest,* 202; Evans, *Confederate Military History,* 11:332–34.
14. Jordan and Pryor, *Campaigns of General Forrest,* 410; *OR* 32(1):547.
15. *OR* 32(1):548.

16. Wills, *Battle from the Start,* 177; THB Autobiography (quotation). Bell and many of his contemporaries, particularly Confederate soldiers, used the term "Dutch" to refer to German immigrants.
17. Jordan and Pryor, *Campaigns of General Forrest,* 413–15; *Hancock's Diary,* 345 (quotation).
18. N.B. Forrest to Jefferson Davis, April [n.d.], 1864, quoted in *Papers of Jefferson Davis,* 10:436-37.
19. *OR* 32(3):736, 609; Jordan and Pryor, *Campaigns of General Forrest,* 415; THB; Apr. 4–6, 1864, entries, Hollis Diary; THB Autobiography; Apr. 2–3, 1864, entries, Fielder Diary; Morton, *Artillery of Forrest's Cavalry,* 167.
20. Jordan and Pryor, *Campaigns of General Forrest,* 416.
21. Ibid.

10. Fort Pillow

1. *OR* 32(1):585, 623.
2. For the history of Fort Pillow from its construction to the time of its destruction by Forrest, see Robert C. Mainfort, Jr., "A Folk Art Map of Fort Pillow," *WTHSP* (Dec. 1986): 72–81; and Lonnie D. Maness, "Fort Pillow under Confederate and Union Control," *WTHSP* 38 (1984): 84–98; Wills, *Battle from the Start,* 178; Edward F. Williams, III, *Confederate Victories at Fort Pillow* (Memphis, Tenn.: Nathan Bedford Forrest Trail Committee, 1973), 31.
3. Patricia E. Coats and Robert C. Mainfort, Jr. "Soldiering at Fort Pillow, 1862–1864: An Excerpt from the Civil War Memoirs of Addison Sleeth," *WTHSP* 36 (1982): 77, 87–88, 90; B. Franklin Cooling, longtime student of this transition into violent irregular conflict in Tennessee, offers a perceptive essay: "A People's War: Partisan Conflict in Tennessee and Kentucky," in Daniel E. Sutherland, ed., *Guerrillas, Unionists, and Violence on the Confederate Home Front* (Fayetteville: Univ. of Arkansas Press, 1999).
4. Henry, *First with the Most,* 249; John Cimprich and Robert C. Mainfort, Jr., "Fort Pillow Revisited: New Evidence about an Old Controversy," *Civil War History* 28 (Winter 1982): 302.
5. *OR* 32(1):609 (quotations).
6. For biographical sketches of the Bradfords, see Charles L. Lufkin, "'Not Heard from Since April 12, 1864': The Thirteenth Tennessee Cavalry, U.S.A." *THQ* 45 (Spring 1986): 138n; Earl Willoughby, "Under the Black Flag"; Henry, *First with the Most,* 249. It is interesting how some historians tend to treat Bradford (age thirty-seven) as "young." See William R. Brooksher, "Betwixt Wind and Water," *Civil War Times Illustrated* 32 (Nov. 1993): 68.
7. *OR* 32(2):311; Robert C. Mainfort, Jr., *Archaeological Investigations at Fort Pillow State Historic Area: 1976–1978* (Nashville: Tennessee Department of Conservation, 1980), 3; Jordan and Pryor, *Campaigns of General Forrest,* 432

(quotation). Confusion arises about the proper designation of Bradford's command. Frequently referred to as the Thirteenth Tennessee Cavalry, U.S.A. in the *OR*, it had no connection with that East Tennessee regiment and for the sake of simplicity is referred to here as Bradford's Battalion. The four companies had been raised at Union City just after Christmas 1863. *Tennesseans in the Civil War,* 1:353. See also William F. and Theodore (Theodorick F.) Bradford CSRs in muster rolls of the Bradford Battalion and of Fourteenth Tennessee Cavalry, U.S.A. (M395), RG 94, NA.

8. Paul Horton, "'Submitting to the Shadow of Slavery': The Secession Crisis and Civil War in Alabama's Lawrence County," *Civil War History* 44 (June 1998): 130. About 40 percent of the Fort Anderson garrison were members of the First Kentucky Heavy Artillery (Colored). Ronald K. Huch, "Fort Pillow Massacre: The Aftermath of Paducah," *Illinois State Historical Society Journal* 66 (Spring 1973): 62–70.

9. *Tennesseans in the Civil War,* 1:353, 396; John Cimprich and Robert C. Mainfort, Jr., "The Fort Pillow Massacre: A Statistical Note," *Journal of American History* 76 (Dec. 1989): 836–37; John L. Jordan, "Was There a Massacre at Fort Pillow?" *THQ* 6 (1947): 102, 104; John Cimprich and Robert C. Mainfort, Jr., "Dr. Fitch's Report on the Fort Pillow Massacre," *THQ* 44 (Spring 1985): 29; Jordan and Pryor, *Campaigns of General Forrest,* 422–24.

10. *OR* 32(1):620; Henry, *First with the Most,* 246; Wyeth, *Forrest,* 338–39.

11. *OR* 32(1):620; THB Autobiography; Lois D. Bejach, "The Journal of a Civil War 'Commando,' DeWitt Clinton Fort," *WTHSP* 2 (1948): 19.

12. THB Autobiography (quotations).

13. Ibid.; Apr. 9–10, 1864, entries, Hollis Diary; *Hancock's Diary,* 351; A. V. Clark to sisters Henrietta Ray and Judith Porter, Apr. 14, 1864, A. V. Clark Letters (quotations); Apr. 10–11, 1864, entries, W. R. Dyer Diary.

14. Bejach, "Journal of a Civil War 'Commando,'" 19 (quotation); Apr. 11–12, 1864, entries, W. R. Dyer Diary; Apr. 11, 1864, entry, Hollis Diary; Charles W. Anderson, "The True Story of Fort Pillow," *CV* 4 (1896): 322; Jordan and Pryor, *Campaigns of General Forrest,* 424; *Hancock's Diary,* 352. Walton commanded what remained of Capt. Alfred Hudson's Mississippi battery which had been captured at Vicksburg. Hudson had been killed at Shiloh, but the name lingered, as would its original name: The Pettus Flying Artillery. Within Forrest's command, however, "the battery was always called Walton's Battery." James Dinkins, *1861 to 1865 Personal Recollections and Experiences in the Confederate Army. By an Old Johnnie* (Cincinnati: Robert Clarke Co., 1897), 208 (quotation).

15. *House of Representatives Executive Document No. 65. Reports of the Committee on the Conduct of the War: Fort Pillow Massacre.* 38th Cong., 1st sess. (Washington: U.S. Government Printing Office, 1864), 3; *Hancock's Diary,* 353.

16. The fort held six fieldpieces but only five, apparently, were used against the approaching Rebels.

17. Mathes, *Forrest,* 217; THB Autobiography (first quotation); Wyeth, *Forrest,* 339, 390, 428; *NOR* 26: 225; James Dinkins, "The Capture of Fort Pillow," *CV* 33 (Dec. 1925): 460; Henry, *First with the Most,* 250 (second quotation); Bejach, "Journal of a Civil War 'Commando,'" 19; *OR* 32(1):621 (third quotation), 614; Lufkin, "Thirteenth Cavalry," 143; Albert E. Castel, "The Fort Pillow Massacre: A Fresh Examination of the Evidence," *Civil War History* 4 (1958): 39; log of *New Era* quoted in Cimprich and Mainfort, "Fort Pillow Revisited," 28:294; John A. Wyeth, "The Storming of Fort Pillow," *Harper's New Monthly Magazine* 99 (Sept. 1899): 596.
18. THB Autobiography; A. V. Clark to sisters Henrietta Ray and Judith Porter, Apr. 14, 1864, Clark Letters; Jordan and Pryor, *Campaigns of General Forrest,* 428 (quotation).
19. Wyeth, *Forrest,* 340.
20. Jordan and Pryor, *Campaigns of General Forrest,* 428–29; Dinkins, "Capture of Fort Pillow," 460; Jack Hurst, *Nathan Bedford Forrest, a Biography* (New York: Alfred A. Knopf, 1993), 167.
21. THB Autobiography (quotations); J. J. White Questionnaire, *Tennessee Civil War Veterans Questionnaires,* 5:2173–74; Lonnie D. Maness, "The Fort Pillow Massacre: Fact or Fiction," *THQ* 45 (1986): 300, 304; Jordan and Pryor, *Campaigns of General Forrest,* 429; Henry, *First with the Most,* 251.
22. THB Autobiography; *OR* 32(1):596, 559 (first quotation); Henry, *First with the Most,* 250–51; Wyeth, *Forrest,* 343 (second, third quotations); A.V. Clark to sisters, Apr. 14, 1864, Clark Letters; *Hancock's Diary,* 356. One of the wounded was Bell's surgeon, Dr. John R. Westbrook of Newbern.
23. It has been generally accepted that Forrest arrived at 10 A.M. on the 12th. Bell, however, states emphatically that he arrived "considerably later." THB Autobiography.
24. THB Autobiography (quotation); OR 32(1):614. For an analysis of the strengths and weaknesses of Fort Pillow see Jordan, "Was There a Massacre?" 6:103, 131.
25. THB Autobiography (quotations). Both Bell and R. R. Hancock set Forrest's arrival at 1–1:30 P.M. *Hancock's Diary,* 592.
26. THB Autobiography (first, third quotations); *OR* 32(1):560 (second quotation), 594, 609, 621; Jordan and Pryor, *Campaigns of General Forrest,* 431–32; Wills, *Battle from the Start,* 182–83.
27. Wyeth, *Forrest,* 336; Castel, "Fort Pillow Massacre," 39; Cimprich and Mainfort, "Dr. Fitch's Report," 29; Anderson, "True Story," *CV* 4: 322.
28. *OR* 32(1):615; Henry, *First with the Most,* 254; THB Autobiography; Eddy W. Davison and Dan Foxx, "Our Journey to the Most Controversial Battlefield in America," *CV* (Sons of Confederate Veterans Series, 1980–) 6 (2001): 22; Wyeth, *Forrest,* 386n. Barteau's Second Tennessee was positioned so that when they charged, the left of the regiment would strike the northwest corner

of the fort with the right wing of the regiment extending west "down the bluff toward the river."
29. Apr. 12, 1864, entry, Hollis diary. For Forrest's communications with Bradford see *OR* 32(1):594, 596–97.
30. *Hancock's Diary,* 366 (first quotation); Anderson, "The True Story," 324 (second–fourth quotations); Dinkins, *Personal Recollections,* 154.
31. *Hancock's Diary,* 366 (quotation).
32. *OR* 32(1):561 (quotation), 564.
33. Wyeth, *Forrest,* 383.
34. Bell's memory does not quite agree with that of J. C. McAdoo, who maintains that he was allowed to fill his canteen from such a barrel by the "guard who had been placed to watch it by General Bell." Wyeth, *Forrest,* 389.
35. Jordan and Pryor *(Forrest)* maintained that many of the defenders were intoxicated—"few were not, to some degree, under the influence of liquor. . . . A number of barrels of whiskey and beer were found disposed at convenient points in the works. . . ." Dr. Wyeth took care to point out that "about an hour before the assault" some of McCullough's men "gained access to a supply of whiskey" in one of the Union quartermaster buildings. One of McCullough's Texans, Clinton Fort, emphatically agreed. Jordan and Pryor, *Campaigns of General Forrest,* 440–41n.; Wyeth, *Forrest,* 350, 367, 382–83; Wyeth, "Storming of Fort Pillow," 603; Bejach, "Journal of a 'Civil War Commando,'" 18–19; May 13, 1864, (Atlanta) *Memphis Appeal* (the *Appeal* was being published in Atlanta at this time); Maness, "Fort Pillow under Confederate & Union Control," *WTHSP* 38: 95n.
36. THB Autobiography (quotation). Forrest biographers Robert Selph Henry and John A. Wyeth credit one of Barteau's men, Pvt. John Doak Carr, with having cut down the fort's banner, and Forrest's provost-marshal, John Goodwin, wrote Polk a week after the battle that "General Forrest wishes particular mention made of the large flag captured by Colonel Bell's brigade at Fort Pillow." Henry, *First with the Most,* 256; Wyeth, *Forrest,* 356, 385n; *OR* 32(1):619 (quotation), 621.
37. *OR* 32(1):621 (first quotation); THB Autobiography (second, third quotations).
38. Cimprich and Mainfort, "Dr. Fitch's Report," 31 (first quotation); *OR* 32(1):615 (second quotation), 612 (third quotation); THB Autobiography (fourth quotation). The number of Federal casualties is crucial in determining the truth about Fort Pillow, but that number as well as the actual number of defenders has been in dispute since 1864. Following exhaustive research, coupled with complex yet judicious calculation and analysis, John Cimprich and Robert C. Mainfort, Jr., have provided an authoritative study: "The Fort Pillow Massacre: A Statistical Note," *Journal of American History* 76 (Dec. 1989): 830–37. See also the earlier study by John L. Jordan, "Was There a Massacre at Fort Pillow?" 111–16; Albert E. Castel, *Articles of War* (Mechanicsburg, Pa.: Stackpole Books, 2001), 88–89; Maness, "Fort Pillow Massacre," 306.

39. George Bodnia, ed., "Fort Pillow 'Massacre' Observations of a Minnesotan," *Minnesota History* 43 (Spring 1973): 188 (quotation).
40. THB Autobiography (all quotations); Anderson, "The True Story," 324; Wyeth maintains that Forrest fired upon the *New Era* rather the *Olive Branch*. Wyeth, *Forrest,* 356.
41. THB Autobiography (second, third quotations); Cimprich and Mainfort, "Dr. Fitch's Report," 31, 36 (first quotation); Jordan and Pryor, *Campaigns of General Forrest,* 440–41 (fourth quotation).
42. Cimprich, "Dr. Fitch's Report," 36–37 (quotations); Bodnia, "Fort Pillow Massacre," 188.
43. THB Autobiography.
44. May 13, 1864, (Atlanta) *Memphis Appeal*.
45. S. H. Caldwell to wife, Apr. 15, 1864; *Tennessee Civil War Veterans Questionnaires,* 4:61. Rennolds, *Henry County Commands,* 297. Caldwell's estimate of the strength of the garrison is too high, as is his estimate of the number of Union soldiers killed.
46. A. V. Clark to sisters Henrietta Ray and Judith Porter, Apr. 14, 1864, Clark Letters.
47. Apr. 12, 1864, entry, W. R. Dyer Diary.
48. (Atlanta) *Memphis Appeal,* May 2, 1864; THB Autobiography; Wyeth, *Forrest,* 357, 384; *OR* 32(1):616; Apr. 12, 1864, entry, W. R. Dyer diary; *Hancock's Diary,* 361, 364; Cimprich and Mainfort, "Dr. Fitch's Report," 38.
49. Apr. 13, 1864, entry, Hollis Diary; Apr. 13, 1864, entry, W. R. Dyer Diary.
50. THB Autobiography; *NOR* 26:225 (first quotation); *OR* 32(1):571 (second quotation); 32 (3):777; Anderson, "The True Story," 324.
51. Apr. 14–20, 1864, entries, Hollis Diary; Jordan and Pryor, *Campaigns of General Forrest,* 455–56; THB Autobiography; *OR* 32(3):777, 798.
52. Wyeth, *Forrest,* 361n (quotations); *House Document No. 65,* 6, 101–3.
53. Wyeth, *Forrest,* 361n; Henry, *First with the Most,* 269.
54. May 13, 1864, (Atlanta) *Memphis Appeal*.
55. THB Autobiography; Cimprich and Mainfort, "The Fort Pillow Massacre: A Statistical Note," 835–37; *OR* 32(1):610 (first quotation); 623 (second quotation).
56. THB quoted "under oath" in Wyeth, *Forrest,* 384–90.

11. Brice's Crossroads

1. Apr. 14–20, 1864, entries, Hollis Diary; Jordan and Pryor, *Campaigns of General Forrest,* 455–56; THB Autobiography; *OR* 32(3):777, 797–98; *Hancock's Diary,* 369n.
2. THB Autobiography (third–fifth quotations); Edwin C. Bearss, *Forrest at Brice's Cross Roads and in North Mississippi in 1864* (Dayton, Ohio: Morningside

Bookshop, 1979), 11; *OR* 32(3):769 (first quotation), 777 (second quotation), 798, 800; Apr. 23, 1864, entry, Hollis Diary.
3. THB Autobiography; Jordan and Pryor, *Campaigns of General Forrest,* 456–57, 460n; Henry, *First with the Most,* 274–75. Forrest with his staff and escort was following the ponderous column but turned off to engage and blunt the advance of a large Federal force of cavalry and infantry near Somerville.
4. Ken R. Knopp, "Summary of Hodge's Inspection Report for Forrest's Cavalry." This report with its supporting documents may be found in RG 109 (M935), NA.
5. *OR* 39(2):601.
6. Henry, *First with the Most,* 279; *OR* 39(2):642.
7. F. M. O'Daniel to J. A. Seddon, Aug. 25, 1864; J. S. Dawson to J. A. Seddon, Feb. 1, 1864, Letters Received, Secretary of War, RG 109, NA; Inspection Report, Vaughan's Brigade, Aug. 19, 1864, Inspection Reports and Related Records Received by the Inspection Branch, RG 109, NA.
8. F. M. O'Daniel to J. A. Seddon, Aug. 25, 1864; J. S. Dawson to J. A. Seddon, Feb. 1, 1864, Letters Received, Secretary of War, RG 109, NA. One of the officers examining Forrest's muster rolls and busy reclaiming absentees was Capt. Alfred Fielder. May 10–29, 1864, entries, Fielder Diary.
9. May 24, 1864, entry, Hollis diary.
10. Wills, *Battle from the Start,* 201–2; Stuart W. Sanders, "Confederate Raider's Kentucky Rampage," *America's Civil War* 12 (July 1999): 30–32.
11. THB Autobiography; Henry, *First with the Most,* 282; *OR* 39(1):222 (quotation).
12. Bearss, *Forrest at Brice's Cross Roads,* 60; Hancock, *Hancock's Diary,* 377; Wills, *Battle from the Start,* 203; Morton, *Artillery of Forrest's Cavalry,* 171; Lindsley, *Military Annals of Tennessee,* 640; Mark Grimsley, "A Civilian at Brice's Cross Roads," *Civil War Times Illustrated* 32 (Jan. 1994): 39 (quotation); Rennolds, *Henry County Commands,* 237.
13. Henry, *First with the Most,* 282 (first, second quotations); *OR* 32(3):411 (third quotation).
14. THB Autobiography; *OR* 39(1):222; Jordan and Pryor, *Campaigns of General Forrest,* 464; *Hancock's Diary,* 378; Wyeth, *Forrest,* 399; Henry, *First with the Most,* 284; Wills, *Battle from the Start,* 203–4.
15. June 7–8, 1864, entries, Hollis Diary; *Hancock's Diary,* 379–80; Bearss, *Forrest at Brice's Crossroads,* 61, 379.
16. THB Autobiography; *OR* 39(1):222; Jordan and Pryor, *Campaigns of General Forrest,* 464; Henry, *First with the Most,* 284.
17. *OR* 39(2):85,638; *Hancock's Diary,* 380.
18. *Hancock's Diary,* 381.
19. Bearss, *Forrest at Brice's Cross Roads,* 62–63; *Hancock's Diary,* 65.
20. *OR* 39(1):119 (quotation); Jordan and Pryor, *Campaigns of General Forrest,* 467; Bearss, *Forrest at Brice's Cross Roads,* 64; *Hancock's Diary,* 281–82.

21. THB Autobiography (quotations); *OR* 39(1):222.
22. Bearss, *Forrest at Brice's Cross Roads,* 64; *Hancock's Diary,* 282 (first quotation).
23. Wyeth, *Forrest,* 409 (quotation).
24. *OR* 39(1):223; John A. Wyeth, "Major-General Forrest at Brice's Cross-Roads," *Harper's New Monthly Magazine* 98 (Dec. 1898): 534 (quotations); Wills, *Battle from the Start,* 208.
25. *Nashville American,* June 3, 1901 (first quotation); THB Autobiography (second quotation); Morton, *Artillery of Forrest's Cavalry,* 175.
26. *Hancock's Diary,* 282–84; THB Autobiography; Jordan and Pryor, *Campaigns of General Forrest,* 467, 470; Bearss, *Forrest at Brice's Crossroads,* 71, 77.
27. Prussian Field Marshal Gebbard Leberecht Friedrich von Blücher fought well in several major battles against Napoleon, but he gained immortality at Waterloo where his timely arrival turned possible defeat into victory for the Duke of Wellington and the Allied army.
28. Henry, *First with the Most,* 290–93; Jordan and Pryor, *Campaigns of General Forrest,* 467 (first quotation); subsequent quotations from George, *History of the 3d, 7th, 8th and 12th Kentucky C.S.A.,* 92, quoted in Bearss, *Forrest at Brice's Crossroads,* 80 n46. The Terry statement is similar to that attributed to Rucker in Wyeth, *Forrest,* 400; *OR* 39(1):223; Hord, "Brice's X Roads from a Private's View," *CV* 12 (Aug. 1905): 529; *Hancock's Diary,* 391–92.

   Bell's Autobiography specifically states that at this point, not on the road leading to Carrollville hours earlier, "Forrest directed me to send one of [the regiments of] my brigade to the rear of the army, therefore I ordered Colonel Barteau with the 2nd Tennessee to move around the enemy, so as not to be discovered and reach the rear of their wagon train as quick as possible." Although this would seem to make good sense tactically and be quite in keeping with Forrest's methods, it contradicts Forrest's own report and a mound of subsequent accounts of the battle, virtually all of which, however, are based on Forrest's report. Clark Barteau's diary itself, as quoted in Wyeth's biography of Forrest, is vague as to place and time. "My instructions," wrote Barteau, "were to take my regiment, numbering then 250 men, across the country by out-of-the-way routes, to slip in upon the Federal flank and rear, and to attack them in co-operation with Forrest's force in front. . . . I succeeded in reaching the Federal rear just as the fighting seemed heaviest in front." Jonas Jutton's "Incidents of the Battle of Brice's Cross Roads," which appeared in the *Nashville American* in 1906, would seem to support Bell's explanation, however. Jutton's account has scout Tom Henderson, acting on Forrest's specific instructions after the battle commenced, discovering a crossing of Tishomingo Creek and leading young Capt. Francis M. McRae and Maj. Oliver B. Farris, commanding elements of the Second Tennessee, across the creek, to strike Sturgis's army in the rear.

   It leads one to question why Forrest would detach a portion of a regiment, only 250 men, at Carrollville, so far from the battlefield and have them move some five miles cross-country over uncertain if not unknown trails against an enemy column of cavalry and infantry whose location Forrest had not yet fixed. It seems to make more sense to have Forrest order Bell to detach a regiment or a portion thereof after they had arrived at the battlefield, to follow Henderson down Tishomingo Creek, cross, then seek the enemy's flank and rear.

By 11 A.M. Forrest had Sturgis's position fixed. He knew Yankee infantry was very close, coming up the Ripley road at the double-quick, and he knew how to cross the difficult (deep with steep banks) Tishomingo Creek, and at his side he had a reliable guide who had just tested the crossing. Granted, the Second Tennessee would also have to use the "woods and by-ways" for its flanking movement, just as it would have during a sweep from Old Carrollville, but only over a short distance and not out of hearing of the battle itself, and not beyond recall. It need not be some deep flanking movement at that point.

Whichever explanation is correct, Forrest came up with a timely, imaginative, and highly effective tactical expedient that succeeded famously.

29. THB Autobiography; *OR* 39(1):223; Parker Hills, "A Study in Warfighting: Nathan Bedford Forrest and the Battle of Brice's Crossroads," *Papers of the Blue and Gray Education Society* 2 (Fall 1995): 33; Wyeth, *Forrest,* 413; George, *History of the 3d, 7th, 8th and 12th Kentucky C.S.A.,* 89; Bearss, *Forrest at Brice's Cross Roads,* 78.
30. Jordan and Pryor, *Campaigns of General Forrest,* 472; THB Autobiography (quotation).
31. *OR* 39(1):223 (quotation); THB Autobiography; Rennolds, *Henry County Commands,* 262; Wyeth, "Forrest at Brice's Cross-Roads," 98:530.
32. Bell is listed in official documents as John L., John S., and John E. He was from McLemoresville (Carroll County) and had begun his service as a lieutenant in Company C, Twenty-second Tennessee Infantry. His relationship to THB, if any, has not been determined. He had become THB's AIG May 5, 1864. J. L. Bell CSR.
33. THB Autobiography (quotations); Wyeth, *Forrest,* 394, 413; June 10, 1864, entry, W.R. Dyer Diary.
34. THB Autobiography (quotations); I. T. Bell CSR; *CV* 22 (1914): 420; Young, *Seventh Tennessee Cavalry,* 91. It appears Isaac was unauthorized. Gen. S. D. Lee had disapproved Isaac as an ADC for Brigade Commander Col. Tyree Bell in May 1864, contending that an ADC "is only allowed to a general officer." I. T. Bell CSR.
35. THB Autobiography (quotations). Of Caldwell's four sons, only one, Surgeon Samuel H., would survive the war. Rennolds, *Henry County Commands,* 297.
36. *Hancock's Diary,* 386–87; Jordan and Pryor, *Campaigns of General Forrest,* 472; *OR* 39(1):223; THB Autobiography.
37. THB Autobiography (quotation).

38. Wyeth, *Forrest*, 416; THB Autobiography (quotations).
39. Jordan and Pryor, *Campaigns of General Forrest*, 472–73, 473n; *Hancock's Diary*, 386; George, *History of the 3d, 7th, 8th, and 12 Kentucky, C.S.A.*, 89. THB Autobiography (quotations).
40. *Hancock's Diary*, 388; THB Autobiography (quotation).
41. Wyeth, *Forrest*, 416; Otey, "Story of Our Great War," *CV* 9 (1901): 153 (quotations).
42. *Hancock's Diary*, 391–92. Several companies of the Second Cavalry had been detailed during the approach march and before Barteau made his flanking maneuver.
43. Jordan and Pryor, *Campaigns of General Forrest*, 476; Hord, "Brice's X Roads from a Private's View" *CV* 12 (Aug. 1905): 529–30; *Hancock's Diary*, 391–92; Henry, *First with the Most*, 291–93; Wills, *Battle from the Start*, 211.
44. Morton, *Artillery of Forrest's Cavalry*, 176–77; Hubbard, *Notes of a Private*, 115–16 (quotation); Wyeth, *Forrest*, 419.
45. Wills, *Battle from the Start*, 213; Jordan and Pryor, *Campaigns of General Forrest*, 474–75 (quotations); *Hancock's Diary*, 388–89; Wyeth, *Forrest*, 418; Hubbard, *Notes of a Private*, 111; Yeary, *Reminiscences of the Boys in Gray*, 767; Bearss, *Forrest at Brice's Cross Roads*, 103; N. B Forrest to C. C. Washburn, June 23, 1864, NBF CSR.
46. Jordan and Pryor, *Campaigns of General Forrest*, 476.
47. Ibid., 477 (quotation); *OR* 39(1):223; Young, *Seventh Cavalry*, 95; Dan C. Jones to Mrs. Rebecca P. Leech, June 13, 1864, in J. L. Douthat, ed., *Shelby County, Tennessee W.P.A. Records* (Signal Mountain, Tenn.: Mountain Press, 1993), 86; Morton, *Artillery of Forrest's Cavalry*, 180.
48. *OR* 39(2):224; Jordan and Pryor, *Campaigns of General Forrest*, 477; Henry, *First with the Most*, 297; THB Autobiography (second, third quotations); Bearss, *Forrest at Brice's Crossroads*, 119, 127 (first quotation).
49. Jordan and Pryor, *Campaigns of General Forrest*, 479; THB Autobiography (quotation).
50. THB Autobiography (quotation); Jordan and Pryor, *Campaigns of General Forrest*, 480; Bearss, *Forrest at Brice's Crossroads*, 131.
51. Hord, "Pursuit of Gen. Sturgis," 18 (first quotation); Wyeth, *Forrest*, 423; THB Autobiography (third, fourth quotations); *OR* 39(2):224; A. V. Clark to sister, Henrietta Ray, Clark Letters (second quotation); William S. Speer, *Sketches of Prominent Tennesseans* (Nashville: Albert B. Tavel, 1888), 38; *CV* 13 (Oct. 1905): 465. The "uncle" was Lawrence Walker, Mary Ann's uncle, and the younger brother of her mother, Sarah Walker Walton. He returned to Tennessee after the war.
52. June 12–21, 1864, entries, Hollis Diary.
53. *Nashville American*, June 3, 1901 (quotation); Wyeth, *Forrest*, 413; Henry *First with the Most*, 299.

54. Hylan Lyon would receive an overdue promotion to brigadier general within a week following Brice's Crossroads. Warner, *Generals in Gray,* 197.
55. *OR* 39(2):229.
56. Ibid., 230–31.

12. Harrisburg

1. Jordan and Pryor, *Campaigns of General Forrest,* 492n; Bearss, *Forrest at Brice's Cross Roads,* 145–51.
2. Michael B. Ballard, "The Battle of Tupelo," *Papers of the Blue and Gray Education Society* 3 (1996): 9; Wills, *Battle from the Start,* 217–19.
3. *OR* 39(1):121 (quotation); Lee, "The War in Mississippi," 58–59.
4. *Hancock's Diary,* 409–10; *OR* 39(1):321–25; Hattaway, *General Stephen D. Lee,* 116–19; Henry, *First with the Most,* 311–13; Bearss, *Forrest at Brice's Cross Roads,* 162.
5. Allardice, *More Generals in Gray,* 146–47.
6. OR 39(1):320; (2):674–77; Henry, First with the Most, 313; Bearss, *Forrest at Brice's Cross Roads,* 163. Smith had left LaGrange July 5. His cavalry meanwhile had started south from Saulsbury on a parallel road, successfully screening Smith's column for a day.
7. July 8–12, 1864, entries, Hollis Diary; *OR* 39(1):320 (quotation), 329, 346; *Hancock's Diary,* 411; Jordan and Pryor, *Campaigns of General Forrest,* 499.
8. *OR* 39(1):321 (quotation).
9. Ibid., 346 (quotation); *Hancock's Diary,* 415.
10. Ballard, "Battle of Tupelo," 15–16 (quotation); *OR* 39(1):250–51, 346; Henry, *First with the Most,* 314–15.
11. Lee, "The War in Mississippi," 60; July 13, 1864, entry, Hollis Diary; *OR* 39(1):321–22, 346–47 (quotation); Henry, *First with the Most,* 314; Bearss, *Forrest at Brice's Cross Roads,* 185.
12. Forrest had gathered up men who, for various reasons, were without serviceable mounts. He gave them the unwelcome news that they would be trained as a special infantry unit and hoped that their numbers would reach brigade strength. By adding all manner of wandering functionaries—guards, purchasing agents, factory and farm employees—he did manage to pull together sufficient manpower (about a thousand men) to justify assigning Hylan B. Lyon to command and entitling it an "infantry division." The heart of this curious brigade-strength organization would be Lt. Col. Daniel Beltzhoover's orphan battalion of heavy artillerists. *OR* 39(1):335; Wills, *Battle from the Start,* 220; Henry, *First with the Most,* 312.
13. *Biographical Directory of Congress,* 1037; George, *History of the 3d, 7th, 8th, and 12 Kentucky, C.S.A.,* 146.

14. *Hancock's Diary,* 417–18; *OR* 39(1):321, 336 (first quotation), 347 (second–fourth quotations); Jordan and Pryor, *Campaigns of General Forrest,* 504; Ballard, "Battle of Tupelo," 21–26; Lindsley, *Military Annals of Tennessee,* 618–19.
15. *Hancock's Diary,* 421(quotation); Bearss, *Forrest at Brice's Cross Roads,* 185; Hubbard, *Notes of a Private,* 124; Wyeth, *Forrest,* 440; Henry, *First with the Most,* 315–16; Morton, *Artillery of Forrest's Cavalry,* 204–5; *OR* 39(1):322.
16. See Henry, *First with the Most,* 317–18; Bearss, *Forrest at Brice's Cross Roads,* 198–99.
17. Hattaway, *General Stephen D. Lee,* 120–21; Henry, *First with the Most,* 318–19; Morton, *Artillery of Forrest's Cavalry,* 208; Jordan and Pryor, *Campaigns of General Forrest,* 334; *OR* 39(1):330 (quotation).
18. *OR* 39(1):322, 330.
19. Ibid., 330; Henry, *First with the Most,* 320; Memphis *Commercial Appeal,* Mar. 16, 1902.
20. Bearss, *Forrest at Brice's Cross Roads,* 202; *OR* 39(1):331.
21. Ed Crossland would excuse the lack of order, contending that "it was impossible to restrain the ardor" of the Kentuckians. *OR* 39(1):336.
22. *OR* 39(1):347, 349 (quotation); Stephen D. Lee, "Battle of Harrisburg, or Tupelo," *Publications of the Mississippi Historical Society* 6 (1902): 44; Ballard, "Battle of Tupelo," 35.
23. THB to J. W. Morton, Feb. 20, 1902, reproduced in Memphis *Commercial Appeal,* Mar. 16, 1902(first quotation); *OR* 39(1):331 (sixth quotation), 347 (third quotation), 322 (fifth quotation); *Hancock's Diary,* 424(fourth quotation); Morton, *Artillery of Forrest's Cavalry,* 209; Wills, *Battle from the Start,* 227–28 (seventh quotation); Jordan and Pryor, *Campaigns of General Forrest,* 510; Ballard, "Battle of Tupelo," 43 (second quotation); July 14, 1864, entry, W. R. Dyer Diary; Lee, "Battle of Harrisburg," 48; Wyeth, *Forrest,* 451–52.
24. Dinkins, *Personal Recollections,* 169.
25. Memphis *Commercial Appeal,* Mar. 16, 1902 (quotations).
26. *OR* 39(1):331; Memphis *Commercial Appeal,* Mar. 16, 1902.
27. Jordan and Pryor, *Campaigns of General Forrest,* 513–14; *OR* 39(1):331 (quotation), 347–48; Ballard, "Battle of Tupelo," 49.
28. *OR* 39(1):331, 323 (first quotation), 348, 337, 343 (third quotation); Wyeth, *Forrest,* 454 (second quotation); George, *History of the 3d, 7th, 8th, and 12 Kentucky, C.S.A.,* 103; Hurst, *Forrest,* 408; Bearss, *Forrest at Brice's Cross Roads,* 224–26; Henry, *First with the Most,* 325; Lee, "Battle of Harrisburg," 49. Lt. Col. A. R. Shacklett, Eighth Kentucky Mounted Infantry, replaced Crossland in command of the Kentucky Brigade. *OR* 39(1):337.
29. *OR* 39(1):337; Hubbard, *Notes of a Private,* 130 (quotations); Rennolds, *Henry County Commands,* 263.

30. Patricia L. Faust, ed., *Historical Times Illustrated Encyclopedia of the Civil War* (New York: Harper & Row, 1986), 765.
31. Henry, *First with the Most*, 326.
32. *OR* 39(1):324, 333; Wills, *Battle from the Start*, 228–29; Jordan and Pryor, *Campaigns of General Forrest*, 506; *CV* 32 (June 1924): 243; Hattaway, *Stephen D. Lee*, 123. THB saw fit to mention in his letter to Morton forty years later that his horse was shot twice at Harrisburg. Memphis *Commercial Appeal*, Mar. 16, 1902.
33. *OR* 39(1):332 (first quotation); Lindsley, *Military Annals of Tennessee*, 619 (second quotation); Chalmers, "Forrest and His Campaigns," 477 (third quotation); Bearss, *Forrest at Brice's Cross Roads*, 215 (fourth quotation).
34. Memphis *Commercial Appeal*, Mar. 16, 1902.

13. Cheer Up

1. *Hancock's Diary*, 439; Hubbard, *Notes of a Private*, 135; Bearss, *Forrest at Brice's Cross Roads*, 247–48.
2. *OR* 39(2):748 (quotation).
3. Ibid., 744, 748 (first quotation), 756 (second quotation); 39(1):871. Lyon's place would be taken temporarily by Ed Crossland and at one point by William W. Faulkner, colonel of the Twelfth Kentucky Cavalry.
4. Jordan and Pryor, *Campaigns of General Forrest*, 527; Dinkins, *Personal Recollections*, 171 (quotation); Morton, *Artillery of Forrest's Cavalry*, 217; Henry, *First with the Most*, 332; *Hancock's Diary*, 442.
5. *OR* 39(2):775; Wills, *Battle from the Start*, 238; Jordan and Pryor, *Campaigns of General Forrest*, 532; Henry, *First with the Most*, 332–33.
6. *OR* 39(2):783 (first, second quotations), 787 (third quotation).
7. *Hancock's Diary*, 444–46; Hubbard, *Notes of a Private*, 139; Morton, *Artillery of Forrest's Cavalry*, 217–19 (first quotation); Chalmers, "Forrest and His Campaigns," 478; Bearss, *Forrest at Brice's Cross Roads and in North Mississippi in 1864*, 282; *OR* 39(2):788; Wyeth, *Forrest*, 469; Aug. 20, 1864, entry, H. R. A. McCorkle Diary (second quotation). For the resourcefulness employed in the bridging of both creeks see Jordan and Pryor, *Campaigns of General Forrest*, 535–36.
8. Henry, *First with the Most*, 336–37; *Hancock's Diary*, 447–48.
9. Bearss, *Forrest at Brice's Cross Roads*, 290.
10. Henry, *First with the Most*, 339 (quotation), 340–41; Jordan and Pryor, *Campaigns of General Forrest*, 543. *Hancock's Diary*, 452; Hubbard, *Notes of a Private*, 145; Lindsley, *Military Annals of Tennessee*, 619; Dinkins, *Personal Recollections*, 187–88. Complicating accounts of the Memphis raid is the presence of Col. William B. Bell, the commander of the Eighth Iowa Infantry.

11. *OR* 39(1):468–84; 39(2):787; Jordan and Pryor, *Campaigns of General Forrest*, 546–47; *Hancock's Diary*, 459–60 (quotation). Once Smith learned that he had been duped by Forrest, he pushed through Chalmers's weak screen into Oxford and proceeded to burn all public buildings and some private homes. An accompanying newspaper correspondent noted that Oxford had become "smoldering ruins." Henry, *First with the Most*, 339–41.
12. Wills, *Battle from the Start*, 244–46; Henry, *First with the Most*, 343 (quotation).
13. Wyeth, *Forrest*, 468.
14. *OR* 39(2):796–97 (first quotation), 812 (second quotation), 813, 815, 819 (third quotation); Henry, *First with the Most*, 347.
15. *OR* 52(2):731(quotation).
16. Richard Taylor, *Destruction and Reconstruction: Personal Experiences of the Late War* (New York: D. Appleton and Co., 1879), 198–99 (first quotation); *OR* 52(2):731–32 (second quotation).
17. *Hancock's Diary*, 462; Dinkins, *Personal Recollections*, 198; Henry, *First with the Most*, 351.
18. Sept. 16–18, 1864, entries, Hollis Diary; *OR* 39(2):839–40; 39(1):542; Jordan and Pryor, *Campaigns of General Forrest*, 558; Henry, *First with the Most*, 351; *Hancock's Diary*, 462–63; Lindsley, *Military Annals of Tennessee*, 619.
19. Jordan and Pryor, *Campaigns of General Forrest*, 561n; *OR* 39(2):845, 849, 859; George, *History of the 3d, 7th, 8th, and 12 Kentucky, C.S.A.*, 119; Henry, *First with the Most*, 350–52.
20. Lindsley, *Military Annals of Tennessee*, 619 (first quotation); Henry, *First with the Most*, 352; *OR* 39(1):542; *Hancock's Diary*, 464 (second, third quotations); William T. Alderson, "The Civil War Reminiscences of John Johnston, 1861–1865. *THQ* 14: 44.
21. *OR* 39(1):542.
22. *Hancock's Diary*, 465; *OR* 39(1):542–43; John Johnston Reminiscences; Wyeth, *Forrest*, 488–89.
23. When the Confederate War Department folded the Forty-eighth Tennessee Infantry into the Thirty-fifth, the officers of the Forty-eighth became supernumeraries and set out to recruit themselves a regiment. They succeeded and began operating in the Tennessee River Valley. These mounted troops were known as Nixon's Regiment, Twentieth Tennessee Cavalry, or Twenty-second Tennessee Cavalry. *Tennesseans in the Civil War*, 1:104.
24. Lindsley, *Military Annals of Tennessee*, 738–39.
25. *OR* 39(1):543–44; Sept. 24, 1864, entry, Hollis Diary; Wills, *Battle from the Start*, 252; *Hancock's Diary*, 466–67; Lindsley, *Military Annals of Tennessee*, 620; Henry, *First with the Most*, 354–55; Price, "20th Tennessee Cavalry."
26. Lindsley, *Military Annals of Tennessee*, 739; Alderson, "Reminiscences of John Johnston," *THQ* 14: 51; *Tennesseans in the Civil War*, 1:91. The Fifteenth

was yet another West Tennessee regiment, heavy with men from Dyer County. Its original commander, Col. Francis M. Stewart, had fallen out with Forrest, however, over the appointment of Rucker to succeed Neely.
27. Henry, *First with the Most,* 354–56; *OR* 39(2):870, 874, 876; 39(1):544–45; Lindsley, *Military Annals of Tennessee,* 620; Jordan and Pryor, *Campaigns of General Forrest,* 564–65.
28. Jordan and Pryor, *Campaigns of General Forrest,* 571–73; *OR* 39(2):878; 39(1):545–46.
29. Henry, *First with the Most,* 356–59; 39(1):546; Jordan and Pryor, *Campaigns of General Forrest,* 574; *Hancock's Diary,* 478–79.
30. *OR* 39(1):546; Hubbard, *Notes of a Private,* 167–68 (quotation).
31. Henry, *First with the Most,* 359.
32. Jordan and Pryor, *Campaigns of General Forrest,* 576 (quotations).
33. Oct. 1, 1864, entry, H.R.A. McCorkle Diary; *OR* 39(1):547 (quotations); Young, *Seventh Tennessee Cavalry,* 108; Henry, *First with the Most,* 360–61.
34. Henry, *First with the Most,* 361 (quotation); Jordan and Pryor, *Campaigns of General Forrest,* 578–80; *OR* 39(1):547.
35. For the story of Morgan's North Alabama adventures, see Nathaniel C. Hughes, Jr. and Gordon Whitney, *Jefferson Davis in Blue: The Life of Sherman's Relentless Warrior* (Baton Rouge: Louisiana State Univ. Press, 2002), 290.
36. *OR* 39(1):547, 548; Jordan and Pryor, *Campaigns of General Forrest,* 580–81; *Hancock's Diary,* 488–90; Henry, *First with the Most,* 361–64. Forrest devoted a paragraph of his official report to this remarkable and heroic rearguard stand. See also Young, *Seventh Tennessee Cavalry,* 112n.
37. Lindsley, *Military Annals of Tennessee,* 621; Jordan and Pryor, *Campaigns of General Forrest,* 582.
38. *OR* 39(2):878; 39(1):548–49 (quotation).

14. Johnsonville

1. *OR* 39(3):810, 812.
2. Ibid., 815–16 (quotations).
3. Donald H. Steenburn, *Silent Echoes of Johnsonville: Rebel Cavalry & Yankee Gunboats* (Rogersville, Ala.: Elk River Press, 1994), 5–6.
4. At this time, while Rucker recuperated from his wounds received at Harrisburg, his brigade was commanded by Lt. Col. David C. Kelley, major of Forrest's original battalion in 1861. Mathes, *Forrest,* 297; *Tennesseans in the Civil War,* 1:55.
5. Oct. 16–24, 1864, entries, Hollis Diary; *Hancock's Diary,* 493; *OR* 39(3):837; Wyeth, *Forrest,* 520; *OR* 39(3):833.
6. Jordan and Pryor, *Campaigns of General Forrest,* 587–88 (quotation).
7. *OR* 39(3):833; Jordan and Pryor, *Campaigns of General Forrest,* 590.

8. Oct. 15–28, 1864, entries, McCorkle Diary; *Hancock's Diary,* 493–94; Wyeth, *Forrest,* 519; THB Autobiography (quotations). Dunlap was a veteran Tennessee legislator and an attorney in Paris. He had been prominent in the Tennessee militia, but during the war seems to have been content with his civilian role as state comptroller. See McBride and Robison, *Biographical Directory,* 1:217.
9. Walton would be commanding Lt. Willis O. Hunter's section of his battery; Crozier would handle Lt. Milton H. Trantham's section. Evans, *Confederate Military History,* 11:500; John W. Morton, "Raid of Forrest's Cavalry on the Tennessee River in 1864" *SHSP* 10 (1881): 261–62. For Lyon's whereabouts during Fall 1864, see Stuart W. Sanders, "Confederate Raider's Kentucky Rampage," *America's Civil War* 12 (July 1999): 33.
10. *Hancock's Diary,* 494; Steenburn, *Silent Echoes,* 25; Morton, "Raid of Forrest's Cavalry," 10:261.
11. *OR* 39(1):870.
12. THB Autobiography (first quotation); Wills, *Battle from the Start,* 263 (second quotation); Steenburn, *Silent Echoes,* 23 (third quotation).
13. *Hancock's Diary,* 495 (quotation); Wills, *Battle from the Start,* 265.
14. Wills, *Battle from the Start,* 264–65; Jordan and Pryor, *Campaigns of General Forrest,* 592; Steenburn, *Silent Echoes,* 28.
15. THB Autobiography (quotations); Jordan and Pryor, *Campaigns of General Forrest,* 593; *Hancock's Diary,* 497; Wyeth, *Forrest,* 521; Dinkins *Personal Recollections,* 201.
16. Wills, *Battle from the Start,* 264 (quotation); Jordan and Pryor, *Campaigns of General Forrest,* 593; Morton, *Artillery of Forrest's Cavalry,* 247–48.
17. Henry, *First with the Most,* 373–74 (first quotation); *Hancock's Diary,* 498; THB Autobiography (second quotation); Steenburn, *Silent Echoes,* 42–44; Jordan and Pryor, *Campaigns of General Forrest,* 594–97. Conspicuous among the sharpshooters were the Alabama Cadets fresh from the campus at Tuscaloosa. D. W. Sanders, "Hood's Tennessee Campaign," *Southern Bivouac* 3 (1885–86): 248.
18. *OR* 39(1):872–73; Henry, *First with the Most,* 373–74; *Hancock's Diary,* 498; THB Autobiography (quotation); Steenburn, *Silent Echoes,* 42–44; Wills, *Battle from the Start,* 265; Dinkins, *Personal Recollections,* 202; John A. Eisterhold, "Fort Heiman: Forgotten Fortress." *WTHSP* 28 (1974): 52–53.
19. *OR* 39(1):872 (quotations). The relationship of Chalmers and Bell cannot be documented. Their accounts often contradict, and each general appears to have minimized the other's role. According to Chalmers, Rucker attacked the *Undine* and *Venus* with Crozier's ten-pounders, the Fifteenth Tennessee Cavalry, and the Twenty-sixth Tennessee Cavalry Battalion. The latter unit, commanded by Col. D. C. Kelley, captured the *Venus,* then crossed the river and seized the *Undine.* Chalmers soon after ordered Bell to move his brigade downstream and rejoin Buford at Fort Heiman. In his after-action report Chalmers emphatically denied

that Bell, his cavalrymen, or the guns under his command engaged the *Undine*. Bell in his Autobiography argues strongly to the contrary, stating "About the time we [he and Morton] got these things all wound up, Chalmers came in sight, Rucker's Brigade being a part of his division." Forrest's after-action report evades the issue, complimenting Kelley, as Chalmers and Bell had, but assigning the responsibility for damaging the *Undine* to "my batteries." This war of words would continue thirty-five years, Morton and Capt. Anderson being drawn into the parchment quarrel with Chalmers and Rucker. *OR* 39(1):870, 873; Steenburg, *Silent Echoes,* 70–72; THB Autobiography.
20. THB Autobiography.
21. Ibid.; Dinkins, *Personal Recollections,* 204 (quotations); Steenburn, *Silent Echoes,* 71.
22. Dinkins, *Personal Recollections,* 205; Wyeth, *Forrest,* 523; Jordan and Pryor, *Campaigns of General Forrest,* 596–97 (quotation); Hurst, *Forrest,* 225. Former Dyer County sheriff, Lt. Col. Bill Dawson, Fifteenth Tennessee Cavalry, veteran of many West Tennessee encounters and Milton Russell's right-hand man, would command Forrest's little fleet.
23. THB Autobiography (first, second quotations); John W. Morton, "Battle of Johnsonville," *SHSP* 10 (1881): 472 (third, fourth quotations).
24. THB Autobiography; S. R. Latta to J. W. Morton, Feb. 27, 1896, quoted in *Dyer County Herald,* Mar. 14, 1896; John W. Morton, "Battle of Johnsonville," *SHSP* 10 (1881): 472 (quotation); Jordan and Pryor, *Campaigns of General Forrest,* 598–99; Henry, *First with the Most,* 374; *Hancock's Diary,* 504. In fairness to Nixon it should be pointed out that his command had conducted an independent raid upon the Nashville & Northwestern Railroad previous to joining Forrest on the west bank of the Tennessee. Lindsley, *Military Annals of Tennessee,* 739.
25. THB Autobiography (quotation).
26. Henry, *First with the Most,* 375 (first quotation); Morton, *Artillery of Forrest's Cavalry,* 254 (second quotation); Jordan and Pryor, *Campaigns of General Forrest,* 601.
27. Two of Forrest's cannon, his potent twenty-pounders, had been lost on November 2 when the *Venus* had fallen victim to two strong and well-served Union gunboats. Henry, *First with the Most,* 375–76; *OR* 39(1):870; Steenburn, *Silent Echoes,* 48.
28. Edward F. Williams, III. "The Johnsonville Raid and Nathan Bedford Forrest State Park," *THQ* 28: 239; Wills, *Battle from the Start,* 269; Steenburn, *Silent Echoes,* 54–58; Henry, *First with the Most,* 376–77; *OR* 39(1):871.
29. THB Autobiography (quotation).
30. Henry, *First with the Most,* 377; THB Autobiography (quotation); Jordan and Pryor, *Campaigns of General Forrest,* 602–3.
31. THB Autobiography (first quotation); Dinkins, *Personal Recollections,* 206–7; Henry, *First with the Most,* 377 (second quotation).

32. Steenburn, *Silent Echoes*, 10–13; THB Autobiography (first quotation); Henry, *First with the Most*, 377–78 (second quotation).
33. Manuscript notes, unsigned, Morton Scrapbook, quoted in Henry, *First with the Most*, 378 (quotation); Morton, "Battle of Johnsonville." *SHSP* 10:482–83; Wills, *Battle from the Start*, 271; J. W. Morton to S. R. Latta, Feb. 27, 1896, quoted in 1902 *Nashville American* clipping, Morton Scrapbooks, TSLA.
34. Nov. 5, 1864, entry, Hollis Diary; Henry, *First with the Most*, 378 (first quotation); *Hancock's Diary*, 508; Steenburn, *Silent Echoes*, 65; Jordan and Pryor, *Campaigns of General Forrest*, 605 (second quotation).
35. *OR* 39(1):870–71; Henry, *First with the Most*, 375, 378–79 (quotation); Steenburn, *Silent Echoes*, 65, 83–84.
36. *OR* 39(1):871.

15. Hood's Invasion of Tennessee

1. *OR* 39(3):845, 853 (quotation); Wiley Sword, *Embrace an Angry Wind: The Confederacy's Last Hurrah: Spring Hill, Franklin, and Nashville* (New York: Harper Collins, 1992), 67; Henry, *First with the Most*, 379.
2. THB Autobiography (quotations).
3. Jordan and Pryor, *Campaigns of General Forrest*, 606; Morton, *Artillery of Forrest's Cavalry*, 367–68 (quotations).
4. Young, *Seventh Tennessee Cavalry*, 116 (quotation); *OR* 45(1):735, 751–52; 39(2):290; Jordan and Pryor, *Campaigns of General Forrest*, 607–8; *Hancock's Diary*, 509; Steenburn, *Silent Echoes of Johnsonville*, 82; Dinkins, *Personal Recollections*, 221–23.
5. Charles S. Coleman Memoirs (first quotation); John Johnston Reminiscences (second quotation).
6. Jordan and Pryor, *Campaigns of General Forrest*, 611; Dinkins, *Personal Recollections*, 222; *OR* 45(1):1211, 752; Morton, *Artillery of Forrest's Cavalry*, 269.
7. *Tennesseeans in the Civil War*, 1:93–94, 97–100, 104–5, 280; McBride, *Biographical Directory of the Tennessee General Assembly*, 1:555; *OR* 39(2):806; Nov. 7, 1864, entry, Hollis Diary; THB to N. B. Forrest, Dec. 11, 1864, Nutt Papers, SHC; Henry, *First with the Most*, 384; Jordan and Pryor, *Campaigns of General Forrest*, 611 n. For an account of one of Bell's officers who returned home at this time and never returned, see Hollis Diary, Nov. 7, 1864–Feb. 2, 1865 entries; Price, "20th Tennessee Cavalry, CSA," 5.
8. THB Autobiography; N. B. Forrest to W. H. Jackson, Nov. 19, 1864, Nutt Papers; *OR* 45(1):752.
9. Jordan and Pryor, *Campaigns of Forrest's Cavalry*, 613; Wyeth, *Forrest*, 535; *OR* 45(1):585 (quotation), 945, 961; Casualty List of Forrest's Command, Nov. 1864, TSLA.
10. THB Autobiography (quotation).

11. Coleman Memoirs.
12. Young, *Seventh Tennessee Cavalry,* 117 (quotation); *OR* 45(1):657, 752, 586; *Hancock's Diary,* 511–12.
13. *OR* 45(1):143–44, 575–76, 945, 586; N. B. Forrest to W. H. Jackson, Nov. 23, 1864, Nutt Papers; *Hancock's Diary,* 512. On November 20 Chalmers's headquarters wagons had been captured and Forrest's dispatches regarding the planned movement fell into enemy hands. Consequently Schofield immediately took precautions—beginning the evacuation of Pulaski and sending cavalry to contest the Confederate cavalry's advance from Lawrenceburg. It seems that Hood's plan to cut off Schofield's retreat was doomed to failure before his forces had left Florence.
14. *Hancock's Diary,* 512–13; *OR* 45(1):752, 768, 586–87, 576; Jordan and Pryor, *Campaigns of General Forrest,* 617–18.
15. *Hancock's Diary,* 513.
16. Ibid., 513–14 (quotations).
17. Ibid., 513–14; *OR* 45(1):752; Thomas R. Hay, *Hood's Tennessee Campaign* (1929; reprint, Dayton, Ohio: Morningside Bookshop, 1976), 82; Sword, *Embrace an Angry Wind,* 96–97.
18. THB Autobiography. Pvt. R. R. Hancock, Second Tennessee Cavalry, contradicts Bell's version, asserting that it was Barteau who was sent upriver to make a crossing with a handful of men on a raft. Barteau succeeded in getting close to the Yankee fort and raising such a ruckus that it allowed the main body of cavalry to cross the river and chase the enemy from the fort. *Hancock's Diary,* 514–16.
19. *Hancock's Diary,* 515–16; *OR* 45(1):1123–24.
20. Henry, *First with the Most,* 389; *OR* 45(1):341 (quotation), 550, 588, 769, 742, 1122–23, 1110–11.
21. *OR* 45(1):752; Jordan and Pryor, *Campaigns of General Forrest,* 621; Dinkins, *Personal Recollections,* 228–29; John Johnston Reminiscences; John E. Fisher, *They Rode with Forrest and Wheeler: A Chronicle of Five Tennessee Brothers' Service in the Confederate Western Cavalry* (Jefferson, N.C.: McFarland & Co., 1995), 152.
22. THB Autobiography (quotations). When Wilson heard the firing from Schofield's direction, he sent a message in which he questioned what all the firing was about.
23. Ibid.
24. *OR* 45(1):753 (quotations). Several sources have claimed that Chalmers led the charge of Wilson's regiment at the request of Forrest. This assumption appears to be based on the account of Dinkins, *Personal Recollections,* 230–31, that J. P. Young claimed Chalmers affirmed in his comprehensive article on Spring Hill (*CV* 16 [1908]: 31). Chalmers was on the scene when the Fourteenth Tennessee Cavalry (White's) of his division took part in the first charge

on the Spring Hill fortifications as described in Forrest's after-action report (*OR* 45 [1]: 54). Chalmers would have been likely to have led this charge that involved a hastily assembled mix of units. This charge, probably also mounted, appears to have been confused with Wilson's mounted charge. When describing the second charge, Forrest specifically states that he asked Buford to send him a regiment, and Buford sent Wilson's Sixteenth.

The sharp repulse and heavy casualties attributed to Wilson's charge by numerous sources also seems to better match Forrest's description of the Armstrong-White charge as well as Pvt. John Johnston's recollection of his participation in the attack of White's Fourteenth Tennessee (Johnston Reminiscences). For that matter, there well may have been yet another charge before Forrest arrived on the field—that of Rucker's Brigade, Chalmers's Division, as described by Dinkins and Johnston.

Bell's Autobiography provides little help. The order of events seems jumbled and, as usual, disappointingly terse. Forrest's report has been used as the ultimate authority.

25. Wills, *Battle from the Start*, 282; Henry, *First with the Most*, 390–91; James L. McDonough and Thomas L. Connelly, *Five Tragic Hours: The Battle of Franklin* (Knoxville: Univ. of Tennessee Press, 1983), 46; *OR* 45(1):753 (quotation); Jordan and Pryor, *Campaigns of General Forrest*, 623, 623n; Hay, *Hood's Tennessee Campaign*, 87; Symonds, *Stonewall of the West*, 251–53.
26. THB Autobiography.
27. *OR* 45(1):753 (quotation); Jordan and Pryor, *Campaigns of General Forrest*, 623; Dinkins, *Personal Recollections*, 231.
28. THB Autobiography.
29. Sword, *Embrace an Angry Wind*, 133–37; Dinkins, *Personal Recollections*, 232.
30. THB Autobiography.
31. Ibid.
32. Ibid. (quotation); *OR* 45(1):240, 753–54; Henry, *First with the Most*, 396–98; Jordan and Pryor, *Campaigns of General Forrest*, 625; Wyeth, *Forrest*, 482.
33. THB Autobiography (quotations); Hay, *Hood's Tennessee Campaign*, 120. THB had unlimited confidence in Allison. Years later he would describe his friend as "one of the bravest and truest soldiers I ever knew. Even though while a Quartermaster he always took a chance in the hottest of the fights." *Nashville American*, June 3, 1901.
34. THB Autobiography; Jordan and Pryor, *Campaigns of General Forrest*, 626.
35. THB Autobiography; *OR* 45(1):754.
36. THB Autobiography.
37. Morton, *Artillery of Forrest's Cavalry*, 273; THB Autobiography (first, second quotation); Sword, *Embrace an Angry Wind*, 218 (third quotation); *OR* 45(1):331, 338; Wyeth, *Forrest*, 545; Horn, *Army of Tennessee*, 401–2.
38. THB Autobiography (quotation).

39. Jordan and Pryor, *Campaigns of General Forrest,* 629; THB Autobiography (quotation).
40. *OR* 45(1):754, 1184, 560; Lindsley, *Military Annals of Tennessee,* 740; Morton, *Artillery of Forrest's Cavalry,* 277; *Hancock's Diary,* 522, 522n (quotation). Confusion exists about the location of this fight. Some sources state "Wilson's Cross." This crossroads did not exist until after the war when Concord Road was extended beyond Wilson's Pike. Federal reports mention "Wilson's Mill," but that would have been too far south to provide security for the road leading to Franklin Pike. Owen's Crossroads location described in Forrest's report would have been a section of Wilson Pike between Crockett Road and a southern split of Concord that existed at that time. In support of this location are family-owned relics from a cavalry skirmish that occurred in the front lot of the Knox-Crockett House. See George R. Knox, *The Crockett House* (Williamson County Historical Society Publication #22, Spring 1971). Also supporting this location is a conversation of Jim Browne with Richard Carlton Fulcher, who described finding minie balls in a firing line pattern near the location of the southern split of Concord Road.
41. Lindsley, *Military Annals of Tennessee,* 621; Jordan and Pryor, *Campaigns of General Forrest,* 629–30; *OR* 45(1):754; Fisher, *They Rode with Forrest and Wheeler,* 162.

16. Hood's Retreat from Tennessee

1. *OR* 45(1):754 (first quotation); THB Autobiography (second quotation); Sword, *Embrace an Angry Wind,* 293; Jordan and Pryor, *Campaigns of General Forrest,* 630. One may infer from Bell's memoir that the river crossing he intended using for the Gallatin raid was near the mouth of Stones River, probably on the Nashville-Lebanon Pike. Mrs. Smiley was probably Mrs. Alexander E. Smiley, forty-five, with her sixty-eight-year-old husband and daughters Alene, seventeen, and Sallie, sixteen.
2. THB Autobiography (quotations).
3. At the time Bell plotted revenge, however, Paine was "awaiting orders," but was not in Sumner County. Warner, *Generals in Blue,* 355–56. See Hughes, *Belmont,* 46, 56, 195, for Paine's inability to handle troops and bringing upon himself the anger of C. F. Smith and U. S. Grant. For Paine's repression of Gallatin and Hartsville, as well as his propensity for summary executions, see also Feb. 1864 entries, Alice Williamson Diary, DU; Walter T. Durham, *Rebellion Revisited, a History of Sumner County from 1861 to 1870* (Gallatin, Tenn.: Sumner County Museum Assoc., 1982), 189, 192, 222.
4. Wills, *Battle from the Start,* 286–87 (first quotation); THB Autobiography (second quotation). For an account of Bate's disastrous defeats, see Hughes, *The Civil War Memoir of Philip Daingerfield Stephenson,* 296–303.

5. *OR* 45(1):755; THB Autobiography; Henry, *First with the Most,* 403.
6. Hurst, *Forrest,* 238–40; Wills, *Battle from the Start,* 287–88; *OR* 45(1):755, 613, 746–47; Jordan and Pryor, *Campaigns of General Forrest,* 632–33; Wyeth, *Forrest,* 550–52; Fisher, *They Rode with Forrest and Wheeler,* 164; Losson, *Tennessee's Forgotten Warriors,* 234. Milroy had fought unsuccessfully against "Stonewall" Jackson in the Shenandoah Valley in 1862; then his command of six thousand men was demolished at Winchester by Richard Ewell in June 1863. Exonerated by a court of inquiry, Milroy had been sent to George H. Thomas for reassignment in late 1864. Warner, *Generals in Blue,* 326.
7. THB Autobiography; Henry, *First with the Most,* 405; *OR* 45(1):613, 618, 756; Morton, *Artillery of Nathan Bedford Forrest's Cavalry,* 281–82; *Hancock's Diary,* 525; Jordan and Pryor, *Campaigns of General Forrest,* 633; Hay, *Hood's Tennessee Campaign,* 141.
8. THB Autobiography.
9. Ibid. (first–third quotations); Jordan and Pryor, *Campaigns of General Forrest,* 634; *Hancock's Diary,* 527; Morton, *Artillery of Forrest's Cavalry,* 281–82; Dec. 7, 1864, entry, H. R. A. McCorkle Diary (fourth quotation).
10. THB Autobiography (quotations).
11. N. B. Forrest to W. H. Jackson, Dec. 10, 1864; THB to N. B. Forrest, Dec. 10–12, 1864, Nutt Papers; *OR* 45(1):615.
12. HB Autobiography (quotations); Dec. 6, 1864, entry, H. R. A. McCorkle Diary; Lindsley, *Military Annals of Tennessee,* 622; *Hancock's Diary,* 525–26.
13. THB Autobiography (quotation); H. R. A. McCorkle Diary, Dec. 9, 1864, entry; Charles S. Coleman Memoirs. THB identified the Methodist pastor as Mr. Larry O'Brien.
14. THB Autobiography (quotation).
15. Jordan and Pryor, *Campaigns of General Forrest,* 635.
16. Wilson and the Sixteenth Tennessee Cavalry had been detached December 16 with instructions to "go into the southeastern portion of Wilson County in search of a Federal Tennessee Regiment, commanded by Colonel Blackburn." As he sought Blackburn, Wilson received a dispatch recalling him, and he rejoined Bell December 18 between Rutherford Creek and Duck River. *Hancock's Diary,* 531. Lt. Col. Joseph H. Blackburn, Fourth Tennessee Mounted Infantry (USA), would gain a reputation the following spring by capturing the notorious Rebel, Champ Ferguson.
17. THB Autobiography (quotations). It would appear Bell arrived there late in the night of December 16 and deployed Newsom near the Isola Bella house, south of where Granny White Pike intersected the Franklin Pike in Brentwood.
18. THB Autobiography (first quotation); Lindsley, *Military Annals of Tennessee,* 740; Alderson, "The Civil War Reminiscences of John Johnston," *THQ* 14: 151; *Hancock's Diary,* 532–34 (second quotation).

19. THB Autobiography. Joseph T. E. Odom formerly commanded a company in the Seventh Tennessee Cavalry Battalion, then had become Clark Barteau's adjutant. At Hollow Tree Gap he was assisting Barteau's successor, Lt. Col. George H. Morton, the Scotsman who had displayed great leadership as an enlisted man, then as company commander. See *Hancock's Diary,* 581–83.
20. Virtually all of the guns of the Army of Tennessee had been captured, and the artillerymen who had escaped plodded alongside the infantry.
21. THB Autobiography (quotations); Sword, *Embrace an Angry Wind,* 398–400.
22. THB Autobiography (quotations). Robert S. Henry, making use of other sources, gives a more dramatic account. "Buford found himself engaged with three Union horsemen. One he shot, the second he clubbed with his empty pistol, the third he grabbed by the hair and dragged from his saddle." Henry, *First with the Most,* 411.
23. Forrest, meanwhile, was still making his way cross-country from Murfreesboro to Lillard's Mills on Duck River with prisoners, wagons, and a herd of cattle, arriving at Columbia on December 18.
24. THB Autobiography (quotations); *OR* 45(1):756; Wills, *Battle from the Start,* 289; Jordan and Pryor, *Campaigns of General Forrest,* 636, 644–45; *Hancock's Diary,* 538–40; Losson, *Tennessee's Forgotten Warriors,* 240; Connelly, *Autumn of Glory,* 512.
25. THB Autobiography.
26. Ibid. (quotations); Henry, *First with the Most,* 412; *OR* 45(1):757.; Jordan and Pryor, *Campaigns of General Forrest,* 645–46; Morton, *Artillery of Forrest's Cavalry,* 290–91. In addition to the cavalry and Walthall's troops, Forrest's command consisted of five diminished infantry brigades, about nineteen hundred men, many of whom were shoeless.
27. THB Autobiography (quotations).
28. Ibid.; *OR* 45(1):757.
29. Charles H. Olmstead, "Rear Guard Service in Tennessee," Olmstead Papers, Georgia Historical Society, quoted in Wills, *Battle from the Start,* 291.
30. THB Autobiography (quotations); Henry, *First with the Most,* 414; *OR* 45(1):757; Wyeth, *Forrest,* 564.
31. THB Autobiography (quotation).
32. Ibid.
33. Ibid.
34. Ibid. (quotations).
35. Ibid. (quotations).
36. THB Autobiography; Jordan and Pryor, *Campaigns of General Forrest,* 649–51; Chalmers, "Forrest and His Campaigns," 483; Henry, *First with the Most,* 414–15; *OR* 45(1):758; Morton, *Artillery of Forrest's Cavalry,* 296; Sword, *Embrace an Angry Wind,* 417–18; Mathes, *Forrest,* 327–28.

37. THB Autobiography (quotations); Henry, *First with the Most*, 414–15; *OR* 45(1):58; Morton, *Artillery of Forrest's Cavalry*, 298–99; Mathes, *Forrest*, 329–30; Wyeth, *Forrest*, 572; Fisher, *They Rode with Forrest and Wheeler*, 178; Sword, *Embrace an Angry Wind*, 419.
38. Charles S. Coleman Memoirs; THB Autobiography (quotation); Sword, *Embrace an Angry Wind*, 421; *OR* 45(1):758.
39. Lindsley, *Military Annals of Tennessee*, 622 (first quotation); *OR* 45(1):42 (second quotation).
40. "Since the war his relatives have had his remains moved home to Sumner County where his mother lived. His mother had four sons. All went into the war and three were killed, only one coming back to her and that was Charlie Clark, the one who stayed with Reuben." THB Autobiography.

17. All Was Gloom

1. Henry, *First with the Most*, 418 (first quotation); *OR* 45(2):748, 751–52 (second quotation), 756 (third quotation); Lindsley, *Military Annals of Tennessee*, 781; Wyeth, *Forrest*, 577. Joining Bell's men for the journey back to Dyer County would be Capt. Alfred Fielder, who had been badly wounded at the Battle of Atlanta, convalesced in North Carolina, and granted a thirty-day leave. Jan. 4, 1865, entry, Fielder Diary.
2. THB Autobiography (quotation); Bruce S. Allardice to N. C. Hughes, Oct. 18, 2000; Cooling, *Legacy*, 72. Enthusiasts of the period often confuse Faulkner with the novelist William Faulkner's great-grandfather, William Clark Falkner (the novelist added the *u* to the family name). Falkner (1825–1889) was born near the Tennessee-Virginia and migrated to North Mississippi about 1840, settling near Ripley. A prominent, popular man, he became brigadier general of Mississippi militia just before the war, but when things became serious, the general assumed the modest rank of captain, commanding the Magnolia Rifles, a unit he raised himself. No matter, Falkner would continue to be called "general" and would be the model for Faulkner's Colonel Sartoris. For more information about the Captain/General Falkner, see Joseph Blotner, *Faulkner, a Biography* (New York: Random House, 1974).
3. THB Autobiography.
4. Ibid.
5. Jan. 6–28, 1865, entries, Harriett Jane Haskins Diary, in possession of Earl Willoughby, Dyersburg, Tenn.; THB Autobiography.
6. Jan. 6–28, 1865, entries, Haskins Diary.
7. THB Autobiography (first quotation); Coleman Memoirs (second, third quotations).
8. THB Autobiography (quotations).

9. Ibid. (quotations); Jan. 6–28, 1865, entries, Haskins Diary; George, *History of the 3d, 7th, 8th and 12th Kentucky C.S.A.,* 139; Lindsley, *Military Annals of Tennessee,* 781; Henry, *First with the Most,* 486; John Johnston Reminiscences; B. S. Allardice to N. C. Hughes, Oct. 18, 2000. Bell further described the incident: "Dr. Thomas Edwards, who had been in the army in the forepart of the war, but had been discharged on account of his health failing him, that being his home at present. In the heat of the fight, he ran out into the street between them, did everything he could to stop the fighting and to prevent them killing Faulkner, but they killed him right there and he fell off his horse dead. That is the last I knew of the Faulkner Regiment."
10. *OR* 49(1):938; T. Michael Parrish, *Richard Taylor: Soldier Prince of Dixie* (Chapel Hill: Univ. of North Carolina Press, 1992), 406; Hurst, *Forrest,* 245 (first quotation); Wills, *Battle from the Start,* 299; Henry, *First with the Most,* 420 (second quotation).
11. *OR* 49(1):972, 992; 49(2):1280; Chalmers, "Forrest and His Campaigns" 7:485; Lindsley, *Military Annals of Tennessee,* 622; Wyeth, *Forrest,* 581.
12. Jordan and Pryor, *Campaigns of General Forrest,* 656–57; *OR* 49(2):991; Henry, *First with the Most,* 425; THB Autobiography; Warner, *Generals in Gray,* 42. Campbell and THB received their promotions to brigadier general the same day, but Secretary of War John C. Breckinridge proposed, and the Confederate Senate agreed, that THB's date of rank should be Feb. 28, 1865, Campbell's March 1. The presence of Campbell and the promotion of Peter B. Starke of Armstrong's command to brigadier meant that Black Bob McCullough, who had served Forrest so well, would no longer exercise brigade command. Confederate States of America Senate, *Journal of the Congress of the Confederate States of America* 7 vols. (Washington, D.C.: U.S. Government Printing Office, 1904–1905), 7:632.
13. Jordan and Pryor, *Campaigns of General Forrest,* 658.
14. Henry, *First with the Most,* 427; THB Autobiography; *OR* 49(2):1160; Young, *Seventh Tennessee Cavalry,* 135.
15. Wills, *Battle from the Start,* 306; *OR* 49(2):1181; THB Autobiography; Thomas McA. Owen, *History of Alabama and Dictionary of Alabama Biography,* 4 vols. (Chicago: F. J. Clark Publishing Co., 1921), 3:165 (quotation).
16. Hubbard, *Notes of a Private,* 186–87; Wyeth, *Forrest,* 590–91.
17. THB Autobiography.
18. Lindsley, *Military Annals of Tennessee,* 623 (second quotation); THB Autobiography (first, third, fourth quotations); *OR* 49(1):357; 419–21; Young, *Seventh Tennessee Cavalry,* 136; Edward G. Longacre, *Grant's Cavalryman: The Life and Wars of General James H. Wilson* (Mechanicsburg, Pa.: Stackpole Books, 1972), 204; James P. Jones, *Yankee Blitzkrieg: Wilson's Raid Through Alabama and Georgia* (Athens: Univ. of Georgia Press, 1976), 60–62; Rex

Miller, *Croxton's Raid* (Ft. Collins, Colo.: Old Army Press, 1979), 28–36; Hancock's Diary 550n (fifth quotation); Wyeth, *Forrest,* 589–92.
19. THB Autobiography; *OR* 49(1):350–51, 417.
20. THB Autobiography (quotations); *OR* 49(1):360–61; John Johnston Reminiscences; Jones, *Yankee Blitzkrieg,* 67–69; Morton, *Artillery of Forrest's Cavalry,* 310–311; *Hancock's Diary,* 556–57.
21. Henry, *First with the Most,* 431–32; Mathes, *Forrest,* 346–48. For Forrest's futile defense of Selma see: Jones, *Yankee Blitzkrieg,* 84–91; Wills, *Battle from the Start,* 308–11; Parish, *Richard Taylor,* 434–35.
22. Jordan and Pryor, *Campaigns of General Forrest,* 672. Chalmers disagrees with this assessment. He believed that Forrest, not Jackson, gave the order for the division to turn on Croxton. Chalmers, "Forrest and His Campaigns" 7:485.
23. Henry, *First with the Most,* 432–33; THB Autobiography (quotations); Lindsley, *Military Annals of Tennessee,* 623.
24. Henry, *First with the Most,* 434 (quotation).
25. THB Autobiography (quotations).
26. Ibid. (first quotation); *OR* 49(2):1280.
27. THB Autobiography; Henry, *First with the Most,* 436–38 (second, third quotations); Sanders, "Confederate Raider's Kentucky Rampage," 12:36; J. G. Witherspoon, "General Forrest's Military Strategy," *CV* 23 (July 1915): 317; John Johnston Reminiscences.
28. Hubbard, *Notes of a Private,* 194 (quotation); THB Autobiography; Lindsley, *Military Annals of Tennessee,* 623.
29. "Brig. Gen. T. H. Bell's Farewell," *CV* 5 (July 1897): 363.

18. Disappointment in Dyer County

1. THB Autobiography; May 1865 entries, Haskins Diary; Mathes, *Old Guard in Gray,* 165; THB to Charles C. Jones, Nov. 14, 1875, Jones Papers, DU.
2. THB Pardon application, May 11, 1865, and Amnesty Oath, July 17, 1865, Pardon Petitions and Related Papers Submitted in Response to President Andrew Johnson's Amnesty Proclamation of May 29, 1865 (M1003), RG 109, NA.
3. Dyer Co., Tenn. Deed Book N, 235.
4. Dyer Co., Tenn., Chancery Court Records, Book C, 437–42; Charles Gardner, comp., *Gardner's New Orleans Directory for 1866* (New Orleans: Charles Gardner, 1866), 79; *Edwards' Annual Directory for the City of St. Louis for 1866* (St. Louis: Edwards, Greenough & Deved, 1866), 79, 222, 430.
5. Dyer County Tenn., Deed Book N, 324–25, 347.
6. Dyersburg, Tenn. *State Gazette,* Apr. 21, 1866.
7. Dyer County, Tenn., Chancery Court Record Book C, 437–42; *Williams Cincinnati Directory, 1867* (Cincinnati: Williams & Co., 1867), 235; T. M. Halpin,

comp., *Halpin's City Directory of Memphis, 1867–68* (Memphis: Bulletin Publ. Co., 1868), 46, 222. For the rising cost of labor see 1860, 1870 Dyer Co., Tenn. censuses, Schedules 6 and 7.

8. Byron and Barbara Sistler, *Dyer County, Tennessee, Marriages, 1860–1879* (Nashville: Byron Sistler & Associates, 1989), 21; Paul E. Vandor, *History of Fresno, California, with Biographical Sketches* (Los Angeles: Historic Record Co., 1919), 663–64; 1850 Sumner Co., Tenn. census, 381, 345; Muster roll of Company A, Twelfth Tennessee Infantry, Oct. 31, 1861; R. Harrell CSR; Farnham, *South to West,* 24; Mrs. Harrell and Mary Ann Bell's uncle John's third wife were first cousins, as found in the genealogical research of Connie W. Moretti.

9. 1870 Dyer Co., Tenn. census, 104; UDC Application of Margaret Harrell Farnham; Dyer Co., Tenn., Chancery Court Book C, 654–56; Nashville *Daily News,* Sept. 1, 1902; *Williams Cincinnati Directory, 1872,* 116, 132.

10. *Memorial and Biographical History of the Counties of Fresno, Tulare, and Kern, California* (Chicago: Lewis Publishing, 1891), 637–38; *Sacramento Bee,* Sept. 28, 1929; Muster Roll, Company B, Ninth Tennessee Cavalry; *Great Register of Voters, Fresno County, California, 1892,* Mendocino Dist., #129; *Dyer County Marriages,* 21. Isaac Henry Walton was the son of John B. and Minerva Willis Carr Walton. John B., the youngest son of Isaac and Catherine Perry Walton, born 1808, was twenty years younger than Josiah Walton, Mary Ann's father, and just twelve years older than Mary Ann. Tyree Harris "Tack" Walton was born during John B.'s second marriage to Lorana Spears, and was seven years older than Isaac Henry.

11. Grandchildren arrived pell-mell: little John Walton in November 1869, Willie Maud Harrell in February 1870, James Warren Bell in August 1870, Bell Walton and Myrtle Eloise Harrell in 1872.

12. 1870 Dyer Co., Tenn. census, 102, 104, and Agricultural Schedule, 58; 1870 Obion Co., Tenn. census, 221; Harris, *Harris Family,* 16–17.

13. *Biographical Directory of the United States Congress, 1774–1949* (Washington: Government Printing Office, 1950), 936, 1624; Tally Sheets, Certificates of Election, Statewide General Election, Nov. 5, 1872, Record Group 87, TSLA; Kenneth C. Martis, *Historical Atlas of United States Congressional Districts, 1789–1983* (New York: Free Press, 1982), 268; *Memphis Avalanche,* Nov. 4–9, 1872; Memphis *Daily Appeal,* Nov. 4–9, 1872; Nashville *Union and American,* Nov. 4–11, 1872.

14. Dyersburg, Tenn., *State Gazette,* Aug. 29, 1874.

15. Dyer Co. Chancery Court Records Book C 437–42; Book D 85–89, 213, 654–57; *Fresno Morning Republican,* Sept. 2, 1901. For an example of the suits for damages against Bell, Harris and Co., see Dyer Co. Court Minutes, Feb. 12–14, 1872.

16. Arthur M. Schlesinger, Jr., ed., *Almanac of American History* (New York: Barnes & Noble, 1993), 324–28 (second quotation); Dyer Co. Property Tax List, 1874, Dist. 6, 1; 1875, Dist. 6, 1; Dyersburg, Tenn., *State Gazette,* Aug. 29, 1874 (first quotation); Hulme, *History of Dyer County,* 360.

19. South to West

1. Farnham, *South to West,* 7; Walter T. Durham, *Volunteer Forty-Niners: Tennesseans and the California Gold Rush* (Nashville: Vanderbilt Univ. Press, 1997), 107, 231; Dyer Co. Deed Book R, 291–92; Dyer Co. Chancery Court, Book D, 656.
2. Farnham, *South to West,* 10; Charles Nordhoff, *California for Health, Pleasure and Residence: A Book for Travellers and Settlers* (1873; reprint, Berkeley, Cal.: Ten Speed Press, 1973), 28–29; 1880 Merced Co., Cal. census, 362c; 1880 San Joachin Co., Cal. census, 208d; *Memorial and Biographical History of the Counties of Fresno, Tulare, and Kern, California,* 637–38; J. P. Ledsinger CSR. Ledsinger's mother was one of the Sumner Co. Brown family, related to Tyree Bell; John and Cynthia were third cousins.
3. Nordhoff, *California for Travellers and Settlers,* 34–35; Farnham, *South to West,* 10–12; J. C. Simmons, *History of Southern Methodism on the Pacific Coast* (Nashville: Southern Methodist Publishing House, 1886), 401.
4. Farnham, *South to West,* 12 (quotation); *History of Fresno County, California with Illustrations* (San Francisco: Wallace W. Elliott & Co., 1882), 125.
5. Fresno Co., Cal. Deed Book B, 412–14; Gallatin, Tenn., *Gallatin Examiner,* Mar. 31, 1876 (quotation); Farnham, *South to West,* 12–14.
6. Fresno Co. Great Register of Voters 1876, Nos. 192, 193, 1525, 1592; Fresno Co. Assessment Book, 1876–77.
7. Farnham, *South to West,* 13 (quotation).
8. Ibid., 13–16.
9. Fresno Co. tax lists, 1878, 1879; Fresno Co. land management records, 1878; "Conquest Cross Harris," *Military Images* 21 (Nov.–Dec., 1999): 34–36; *Fresno Morning Republican,* Dec. 6, 1934. Paul E. Vandor, *History of Fresno, California, with Biographical Sketches* (Los Angeles: Historic Record Co., 1919), 1194. Walton family lore indicates the Isaac Waltons were variously known as Ike, Dr. Ike, and Young Ike or Black Ike (Isaac Henry) based somewhat on hair color.
10. Fresno, Cal., *Fresno Weekly Expositor,* June 25, 1879, Sept. 20, 1881; Fresno Co. deed books, 1879–81.
11. Farnham, *South to West,* 16–17, 20; U.S. Land Management Records, Fresno Co., Cal., 1880–92; *Memorial and Biographical History of the Counties of Fresno, Tulare, and Kern, California,* 637–38; Vandor, *History of Fresno County,* 663–64.

12. *Fresno Weekly Expositor,* June 18, July 31, Aug. 27, Sept. 19, Dec. 10, (quotation), 1884.
13. Ibid., Jan. 21, Feb. 18, Apr. 15, July 15, 1885.
14. Visalia, Cal., *Weekly Delta,* Dec. 10, 1885; David Henry, U.S. Land Office, to C. W. Moretti, Apr. 17, 2001; *Memorial and Biographical History of the Counties of Fresno, Tulare, and Kern, California,* 637–38; Visalia, Cal., *Times-Delta,* Sept. 20, 1952.
15. When the Bells arrived, adjacent King's County was still a part of Tulare.
16. "Tulare County History," http://www.cagenweb.com/cpl/tulare; *Story of Tulare County and Visalia* (Los Angeles: Title Insurance and Trust Co., 1955), 9–11; Visalia, *Weekly Delta,* Jan. 7, 1886; *Southern Methodism on the Pacific Coast,* 402; Leon L. Loofbourow, *Cross in the Sunset: The Development of Methodism in the California-Nevada Annual Conference of the Methodist Church and Its Predecessors* (Berkeley: Historical Society of the California-Nevada Annual Conference of the Methodist Church, 1966), 162; Farnham, *South to West,* 23–24; *Visalia Times Delta,* Jan. 7, 1886; Visalia Scrapbook, California History Room, Tulare County Library, Visalia, Cal.
17. Visalia *Weekly Delta,* Oct. 30, 1886, Oct. 27, 1887, Jan. 12, June 21, Dec. 20, 1888; *Nashville Daily News,* Sept. 29, 1901 (quotation). Sherman's diaries at Notre Dame University indicate his plans for this trip but do not list daily events.
18. Tulare Co. Deed Book, 1887, 182–83, 409; Visalia, Cal. Tax Assessor's Map Book 93, 17; Visalia *Weekly Delta,* May 19, Aug. 25, 1887; Farnham, *South to West,* 20; 1880 Tulare Co., Cal. census, 18d; Annie R. Mitchell, *Historical Landmarks in Tulare County* (Fresno, Cal.: Valley Publishers, 1983), 17.
19. Visalia *Weekly Delta,* May 26, 1887; Mar. 7, Oct. 31, Nov. 7 (quotation) 1889; Fresno *Weekly Expositor,* Jan. 11, 1888; Allen Johnson and Dumas Malone, eds., *Dictionary of American Biography,* 21 vols. (New York: Charles Scribner's Sons, 1928–37), 3:103–105; Visalia *Times-Delta,* Sept. 20, 1952.
20. *Memorial and Biographical History of the Counties of Fresno, Tulare, and Kern, California,* 637–38; Visalia *Times Delta,* Sept. 20, 1952; Farnham, *South to West,* 21.
21. Visalia, Cal., *Weekly Delta,* Oct. 3, 1889; Fresno Co., Cal., *Great Register of Voters,* 1892, No. 646; Fresno, Cal.: *Daily Evening Expositor,* July 9, 1890.
22. Traver, Cal., *Traver Advocate,* May 11, 1893. The Harrises' move to California included several of A. G. Harris's children from Dyer County as well as others from Sumner County.
23. Farnham, *South to West,* 21 (first quotation).
24. Fresno, Cal., *Fresno Weekly Expositor,* Oct. 3, 8, 9, 1890 (quotation). Edward B. Pond was born Sept. 7, 1833, in New York and came to California in 1854. He served as mayor of San Francisco, 1887–1890.

25. Visalia *Times Delta,* Oct. 31, 1952.
26. *Fresno Evening Expositor,* June 16, 1890; *Fresno Weekly Expositor,* May 1, 1895; *CV* 8 (1900): 148, 238, 349; Farnham, *South to West,* 22. Records of the UCV are few. Those in California were donated to the World War II paper drives, since all the veterans had died; therefore any history of the camps and division in that area must be pieced together from notices in *CV* and local newspapers. Since the Fresno commander, H. St. George Hopkins, was the former commander of the Blue and Gray Veterans, it is probable that the Stonewall Jackson Camp was formed when that organization folded. The 1880 California census records show that Brig. Gen. George B. Cosby lived in the Sacramento area with Brig. Gen. Henry Brevard Davidson in the Bay area.
27. *CV* 6 (Apr. 1898): 157; 8 (1900): 301, 237 (first quotation); 9 (1901): 99; second quotation attributed to Mary Bell Browne by grandson Jim Browne; Farnham, *South to West,* 22 (second quotation). THB appointed Tennesseans Hamilton Parks, T. F. P. Allison, Guy Douglass, Pleas Smith, Gid Lauderdale, Dr. Sam Caldwell, William Gay, Henderson Dawson, Egbert E. Tansil, George F. Hager, and James H. Bate, and Californians I. T. Bell, Dr. Thomas R. Meux, W. P. Maupin, E. D. Edwards, C. C. Clay, W. H. Martin and C. C. Harris to his staff. THB to C. W. Anderson, Apr. 13, 1901, Morton Scrapbook (vol. 3), TSLA.
28. *Fresno Morning Republican,* May 12, 1901.
29. Ibid., May 14, 1901 (first quotation); *Nashville American,* May 22, 1901 (second quotation).
30. Memphis *Commercial Appeal,* Apr. 6, 9, 12, 14 (first quotation), 21 (second quotation) 1901; *Nashville American,* Apr. 6, Apr. 21, 1901; May 28, 1901.
31. *Nashville American,* May 21, 25, 26 (quotations), 1901.
32. Ibid., May 25, 29, 1901; Farnham, *South to West,* 10; Memphis *Commercial Appeal,* May 27, 29 (quotation), 30 1901; *CV* (1901): 150, 244; *Nashville Banner,* May 29, 1901.
33. *Nashville American,* Apr. 21, 1901; Memphis *Commercial Appeal,* May 31, 1901.
34. Memphis *Commercial Appeal,* May 31, 1901.
35. Farnham, *South to West,* 16.
36. Memphis *Commercial Appeal,* May 31, 1901.
37. Ibid.
38. Ibid., June 1, 1901; *Nashville American,* June 3, 1901 (quotation); Farnham, *South to West,* 23.
39. *Nashville Daily News,* Sept. 28, 1901 (first and second quotations); *Nashville American,* Sept. 1, 1902 (third and fourth quotations); Arahwana H. Ridens, *Dyer County and Newbern, Tennessee: Being a History of 39 of the Earliest Families of this County* (Easley, S.C.: Southern Historical Press, 1979), 53; Harris, *Harris Family,* 16.

40. *Nashville American,* May 30, 1901, Apr. 16, 1902; *CV* 10 (1902): 150, 179–80; Dallas, Tex., *Morning News,* Apr. 23, 1902. Lily Vertrees Bell was the daughter of Martha H. and Tyree L. Bell, the son of THB's brother Thomas.
41. *CV* 10 (1902): 195–96; Dallas, Tex., *Morning News,* Apr. 20, 23, 1902.
42. Dallas, Tex., *Morning News,* Apr. 24, 25 (first, second quotations), 1902; *CV* 10 (1902): 221 (third quotation).
43. *Fresno Republican,* Sept. 2, 11, 1902; New Orleans *Daily Picayune,* Aug. 31, 1902; *Fresno Weekly Democrat,* Aug. 27, 1902; Jack D. Welsh, *Medical Histories of the Confederate Generals* (Kent, Ohio: Kent State Univ. Press, 1995), 20.
44. New Orleans *Daily Picayune,* Aug. 31, 1902; Visalia *Tulare County Times,* Sept. 11, 1902; Memphis *Commercial Appeal,* Sept. 6, 1902; *Fresno Morning Republican,* Sept. 2, 1902; Visalia *Daily Delta,* Sept. 2, 7, 1902; Orleans Parish Death Certificate, 128 (1902), 201.
45. Memphis *Commercial Appeal,* Aug. 28, 1902 (first quotation); New Orleans *Daily Picayune,* Aug. 31, 1902; *San Francisco Chronicle,* Sept. 1, 1902 (second quotation); *Fresno Morning Republican,* Sept. 3, 1902 (third quotation).
46. *Visalia Times Delta,* Sept. 5, 7, 1902; unidentified Nashville newspaper account, Sept. 1, 1902; *Fresno Morning Republican,* Sept. 7, 1902; C. I. Miller to Craig Mathews, Dec. 3, 1951, Craig Mathews Collection, TSLA.
47. *San Francisco Chronicle,* Sept. 10, 1902 (second quotation); Oct. 1, 1902 (first quotation); Visalia, *Tulare County Times,* Sept. 11, 1902 (third quotation).
48. New Orleans *Daily Picayune,* Aug. 31, 1902.

Bibliography

Primary Sources

Manuscripts

Coleman, Charles S., Memoirs, in possession of Gordon L. Johnson, Wonewoc, Wisc.

Collection of Brent A. Cox, Milan, Tenn.
    J. A. Crutchfield Letters
    Robert M. Russell Papers

Haskins, Harriet Jane, Diary, in possession of Earl Willoughby Dyersburg, Tenn.

Library of Congress, Washington, D.C.
    Hanson Hard Memoir

Louisiana State Univ. Library, Baton Rouge, La.
    Samuel W. Ferguson Papers

Memphis-Shelby County Public Library, Memphis, Tenn.
    Nathan Bedford Forrest Collection
    Goodman Collection
    Gideon J. Pillow Papers

National Archives and Record Service, Washington, D.C.
    RG 94 Records of the Adjutant General's Office
    U.S. Military Academy Cadet Application Papers, 1805–1866
    RG 109 War Department Collection of Confederate Records
        Compiled Service Records of Confederate Generals and Staff

Officers, and Non Regimental Enlisted Men (M331)
> Letters Received by the Confederate Secretary of War (M437)
>
> Letters Received by the Confederate Quartermaster General (M469)
>
> Letters Received by the Confederate Adjutant and Inspector General (M474)
>
> Letters Sent by the Confederate Secretary of War (M522)
>
> Letters and Telegrams Sent by the Confederate Adjutant and Inspector General (M627)

Inspection Reports and Related Records Received by the Inspection Branch (M935)

George Moorman Papers

Pardon Petitions and Related Papers Submitted in Response to President Andrew Johnson's Amnesty Proclamation of May 29, 1865 (M1003)

Gideon J. Pillow Papers

Records of the Army of Tennessee

Orders and Circulars of Lt. Gen. Nathan B. Forrest's Cavalry, 1863–65

Nathan B. Forrest Papers

Polk, Virginia Prichard, Papers, Inverness, Miss.

Southern Illinois Univ., Morris Library, Carbondale, Ill.
> Tyree H. Bell Report of the Battle of Belmont

Tennessee State Library and Archives, Nashville, Tenn.
> Newton Cannon Papers
>
> Robert H. Cartmell Papers
>
> Civil War Collection (Confederate)
>> Achilles V. Clark Letters
>> Thomas J. Firth Memoirs
>> John Johnston Reminiscences
>> Samuel Latta Letters
>> W. R. Dyer Diary
>
> Military Units Collection
>> James N. Rosser Diary
>
> Joseph D. Clark Papers
>
> Monroe Cockrell Papers
>
> Election Returns, Statewide General Election, Nov. 5, 1872 (RG 87)
>
> Craig Mathews Collection
>> Sketch of Tyree H. Bell

Hiram R. Andrew McCorkle Diary
William H. McRaven Papers
>Sketch of Tyree H. Bell
Tennessee Authors and Writings on Tennessee
>Jay G. Cisco, "Tyree H. Bell"
Tennessee Historical Society Collection
>Alfred T. Fielder Diary

Univ. of Arkansas Libraries, Fayetteville, Ark.
>William S. Ray Reminiscences

Univ. of Memphis Library
>Mississippi Valley Collection
>>Civil War Collection
>West Tennessee Historical Society Collection
>>Hammer-Stacy Papers
>>Merriwether Family Papers

Univ. of North Carolina, Southern Historical Collection Chapel Hill, N.C.
>Garnett Andrews Papers
>Leroy M. Nutt Papers

Univ. of Tennessee Library, Knoxville, Tenn.
>McClung Collection

William R. Perkins Library, Duke Univ., Durham, N.C.
>Monroe Cockrell Papers
>Charles Colcock Jones Papers
>*Confederate Veteran* Papers
>>Tyree Harris Bell Autobiography
>Nathan B. Forrest Papers

Virginia Polytechnic Institute, Blacksburg, Va.
>Robert Selph Henry Papers

State of Tennessee Court Cases

Southern Express v. Glenn, 1886

Collected Works, Memoirs, Letters, Diaries, Reminiscences, and Unit Histories

Agnew, Samuel A. "Battle of Tishomingo Creek." *Confederate Veteran* 8 (1900): 401–3.

Alderson, William T. "The Civil War Reminiscences of John Johnston, 1861–1865." *Tennessee Historical Quarterly* 14:43–81, 142–75.

Anderson, Charles W. "The True Story of Fort Pillow." *Confederate Veteran* 4 (1896): 387.

Barteau, Clark R. *A Brief Review* (Hartsville, Tenn.: n.p., 1861).

Bejach, Lois D. "The Journal of a Civil War 'Commando,' DeWitt Clinton Fort." *West Tennessee Historical Society Papers* 2 (1948): 5–32.

Brewer, Theodore F., "Storming of Fort Pillow." *Confederate Veteran* 33 (December 1925): 459, 478.

Buck, Irving A. *Cleburne and His Command.* Edited by T. R. Hay. 1908. Reprint, Dayton, Ohio: Morningside Bookshop, 1992.

Carter, Theodore G. "Reply to 'Experiences at Harrisburg'" *Confederate Veteran* 14 (1906): 309–11.

Chalmers, James R. "Forrest and His Campaigns." *Southern Historical Society Papers* 7 (1879): 449–86.

Cimprich, John, and Robert C. Mainfort, Jr. "Dr. Fitch's Report on the Fort Pillow Massacre." *Tennessee Historical Quarterly* 44 (Spring 1985): 27–39.

Clark, Achilles V. "A Letter of Account. Edited by Dan E. Pomeroy. *Civil War Times Illustrated* 24 (June 1985): 24–25.

Coats, Patricia E., and Robert C. Mainfort, Jr. "Soldiering at Fort Pillow, 1862–1864: An Excerpt from the Civil War Memoirs of Addison Sleeth." *West Tennessee Historical Society Papers* 36 (1982): 72–90.

Cook, V. Y. "Forrest's Efforts to Save Selma." *Confederate Veteran* 26 (1918): 151–52.

Cowen, E. G. "Battle of Johnsonville." *Confederate Veteran* 22 (1914): 174–75.

Crist, Lynda, et al., eds. *The Papers of Jefferson Davis.* 11 vols. Baton Rouge: Louisiana State University Press, 1983–2003.

Dacus, Robert H. *Reminiscences of Company "H," First Arkansas Mounted Rifles.* Dardanelle, Ark.: *Post Dispatch Print,* 1897.

Dinkins, James. "The Capture of Fort Pillow." *Confederate Veteran* 33 (Dec. 1925): 460–62.

———. *1861 to 1865 Personal Recollections and Experiences in the Confederate Army. By an Old Johnnie.* Cincinnati: Robert Clarke Co., 1897.

———. "Forrest's Wonderful Achievements." *Confederate Veteran* 35 (Jan. 1927): 10–13.

Duke, Basil W. *A History of Morgan's Cavalry.* Edited by Cecil F. Holland. Bloomington: Indiana Univ. Press, 1960.

———. "Morgan's Cavalry During the Bragg Invasion," *Battles and Leaders* 3:26–28.

"The Fighting Forty Eighth Tennessee Regiment," *Southern Bivouac* 2 (Feb. 1884): 246–51.

Fitch, Charles. "Capture of Fort Pillow—Vindication of General Chalmers by a Federal Officer." *Southern Historical Society Papers* 7 (1879): 439–41.

Gilbert, Charles C. "Bragg's Invasion of Kentucky," *Southern Bivouac* 4 (Sept. 1885): 217–22.

Greif, J. V. "Forrest's Raid on Paducah" *Confederate Veteran* (Sons of Confederate Veterans Series, 1980–) 5 (1977): 212–13.

Hammond, Peter F. "General Kirby Smith's Campaign in Kentucky in 1862." *Southern Historical Society Papers* 9 (1881): 225–33, 246–54, 289–97, 455–62; 10 (1882): 270–76.

Hancock, R. R. *Hancock's Diary: or, a History of the Second Tennessee Confederate Cavalry, with Sketches of First and Seventh Battalions; also Portraits and Biographical Sketches.* Reprint, Dayton, Ohio: Morningside Bookshop, 1981.

Henry, Robert S. *As They Saw Forrest: Some Recollections and Comments of Contemporaries.* Jackson, Tenn.: McCowat-Mercer Press, 1956.

Hollis, Elisha T. "Diary of Captain Elisha Tompkin Hollis." Edited by William W. Chester. *West Tennessee Historical Society Papers* 39 (1985): 82–118.

Hood, John Bell. *Advance and Retreat: Personal Experiences in the United States and Confederate States Armies.* New Orleans: Hood Orphan Memorial Fund, 1880. Reprint, Bloomington: Indiana Univ. Press, 1959.

Hord, Henry E. "Brice's X Roads From a Private's View." *Confederate Veteran* 12 (Nov. 1904): 529–30.

———. "Personal Experiences at Harrisburg." *Confederate Veteran* 13 (Aug. 1905): 361–63.

———. "Pursuit of Gen. Sturgis." *Confederate Veteran* 13 (Jan. 1905): 17–18.

Hubbard, John M. *Notes of a Private.* St. Louis: Nixon-Jones Printing Co., 1911.

Johnson, Robert T., and Clarence C. Buel, eds. *Battles and Leaders of the Civil War.* 4 vols. New York: Thomas Yoseloff, Inc., 1956.

Johnston, John. "Forrest's March Out of West Tennessee, December, 1863." Edited by William Alderson. *West Tennessee Historical Society Papers* 12 (1958): 138–48.

Johnston, Joseph E. *Narrative of Military Operations, Directed, During the Late War Between the States.* New York: D. Appleton & Co., 1874.

Jordan, Thomas, and J. P. Pryor. *The Campaigns of Lieut.-Gen. N. B. Forrest, and of Forrest's Cavalry.* New Orleans: Blelock & Co., 1868.

Law, J. G. "Diary of the Rev. J. G. Law." *Southern Historical Society Papers* 11 (1883): 175–81, 297–303; 12 (1884): 390–95, 460–65, 538–43.

Lee, Stephen D. "Battle of Brice's Cross Roads or Tishomingo Creek, June 2nd to 12th, 1864." *Publications of the Mississippi Historical Society* 6 (1902): 27–38.

———. "Battle of Harrisburg, or Tupelo." *Publications of the Mississippi Historical Society* 6 (1902): 38–52.

———. "The War in Mississippi After the Fall of Vicksburg, July 4, 1863." *Publications of the Mississippi Historical Society* 10 (1909): 47–62.

Leeper, Wesley T. *Rebels Valiant: Second Arkansas Mounted Rifles (Dismounted)* Little Rock, Ark.: Pioneer Press, 1964.

Morton, John W. *The Artillery of Nathan Bedford Forrest's Cavalry.* 1909. Reprint, Paris, Tenn.: Guild Press, 1988.

———. "Battle of Johnsonville." *Southern Historical Society Papers* 10 (1881): 471–88.

———. "Raid of Forrest's Cavalry on the Tennessee River in 1864." *Southern Historical Society Papers* 10 (1881): 261–68.

Otey, Mercer. "Story of Our Great War." *Confederate Veteran* 9 (1901): 107–10, 153–54.

Pinckney, T. F. "At the Fall of Selma, Ala." *Confederate Veteran* 40 (1932): 53.

Puryear, G. J. "No Man's Battle." *Confederate Veteran* 22 (Nov. 1914): 510.

Rennolds, Edwin H. *A History of the Henry County Commands.* 1904. Reprint. Kennesaw, Ga.: Continental Book Co., 1961.

Robinson, Charles. "Fort Pillow 'Massacre' Observations of a Minnesotan." Edited by George Bodnia. *Minnesota History* 43 (Spring 1973): 186–90.

Ryan, Frank T. "The Kentucky Campaign and the Battle of Richmond. *Confederate Veteran* 26 (Apr. 1918): 158–60.

Sanders, D. W. "Hood's Tennessee Campaign." *Southern Bivouac* III (1885–86): 97–104, 145–53, 193–203, 241–52, 289–94, 350–66.

Tennessee Civil War Veterans Questionnaires. Compiled by Gustavus W. Dyer and John Trotwood Moore. Collen M. Elliott and Louise A. Moxley, eds. 5 vols. Easley, S.C.: Southern Historical Press, 1985.

Taylor, Richard. *Destruction and Reconstruction: Personal Experiences of the Late War.* New York: D. Appleton and Co., 1879.

Tyler, H. A. "Forrest Covers Hood's Retreat." *Confederate Veteran* 12 (1904): 436.

Vaughan, Alfred J. *Personal Record of the Thirteenth Regiment Tennessee Infantry.* Memphis, Tenn.: S.C. Toof & Co., 1897.

Wheeler, Joseph. "Bragg's Invasion of Kentucky. *Battles and Leaders* 3: 1–25.

Wilson, James H. *Under the Old Flag: Recollections of Military Operations in the War for the Union, the Spanish War, the Boxer Rebellion, etc.* New York: D. Appleton & Co., 1912.

Witherspoon, J. G. "General Forrest's Military Strategy," *Confederate Veteran* 23 (July 1915): 317–18.

Witherspoon, William. *Reminiscences of a Scout, Spy and Soldier of Forrest's Cavalry.* Jackson, Tenn.: McCowat-Mercer Printing Co., 1910.

Worley, Ted R., ed. *The War Memoirs of Captain John W. Lavender, C.S.A.* Pine Bluff, Ark.: W. M. Hackett and D. R. Perdue, 1956.

John A. Wyeth. "Major-General Forrest at Brice's Cross-Roads." *Harper's New Monthly Magazine* 98 (Dec. 1898): 530–45.

———. "The Storming of Fort Pillow." *Harper's New Monthly Magazine* 99 (Sept. 1899): 595–607.

Yeary, Mamie, comp. *Reminiscences of the Boys in Gray, 1861–1865.* Dallas, Tex.: Smith & Lamar, 1912.

Young, John P. *The Seventh Tennessee Cavalry (Confederate): A History.* Nashville: M. E. Church, South, 1890.

Newspapers

Atlanta, Ga. *Memphis Appeal,* 1864.

Dallas, Tex. *Dallas Morning News,* 1902

Dyersburg, Tenn. *Dyer County Herald,* 1896.

Dyersburg, Tenn. *State Gazette,* 1866.

Fresno, Cal. *Fresno Morning Republican,* 1901, 1934.

Fresno, Cal. *Fresno Weekly Expositor,* 1879, 1881, 1884.

Gallatin, Tenn. *Gallatin Examiner,* 1876.

Memphis, Tenn. *Daily Appeal,* 1861.

Memphis, Tenn. *Commercial Appeal,* 1902.

Mobile Advertiser and Register, 1864.

Nashville American, 1901, 1906.

Nashville Daily News, 1901–1902.

Nashville Tennessean, 1941.

New Orleans, La. *Daily Picayune,* 1878, 1902.

Sacramento, Cal. *Sacramento Bee,* 1929.

San Francisco Chronicle, 1902.

Traver, Cal. *Traver Advocate,* 1893.

Visalia, Cal. *Tulare County Times,* 1902.

Visalia, Cal. *Daily Times,* 1893.

Visalia, Cal. *Times-Delta,* 1952.

Visalia, Cal. *Weekly Delta,* 1885–1889.

Government Documents

Confederate States of America. *Journal of the Congress of the Confederate States of America, 1861–1865.* 7 vols. Washington, D.C.: U.S. Government Printing Office, 1904–5.

Dyer County, Tennessee. Chancery Court Record Book C, D.

———. Deed Books B, N, R.

Fresno Co., California. *Great Register of Voters, Fresno County, California, 1892.*

———. Deed Books 1879–81.

Garrard County, Kentucky. Deed Book E.

———. 1816, 1817 Tax Lists.

Mason County, Kentucky. Deed Book 51.

———. Will Book F.

Orleans Parish, Louisiana. Death Records, Vol. 128.

Sumner County, Tennessee. Chancery Court Records.

———. Circuit Court Minute Book.

———. Deed Book A, 16, 19, 21.

U.S. Bureau of Land Management. Land and Mineral Reservation Patents Granted, Fresno Co., Cal., 1880–92.

———. Census of Davidson County, Tennessee, 1860.

———. Census of Dyer County, Tennessee, 1850–70 (Slave, Agricultural and Manufacturing schedules).

———. Census of Fresno County, California, 1880.

———. Census of Merced County, California, 1880.

———. Census of San Joachin County, California, 1880.

———. Census of Sumner County, Tennessee, 1820–70 (Slave, Agricultural and Manufacturing schedules).

U.S. Congress. House Executive Document No. 65. *Reports of the Committee on the Conduct of the War: Fort Pillow Massacre.* 38th Cong., 1st sess. Washington: U.S. Government Printing Office, 1864.

———. Senate Committee Reports, 38th Cong. 1st sess., No. 63.

U.S. Navy Department. *Official Records of the Union and Confederate Navies In the War of the Rebellion.* 30 vols. Washington, D.C.: U.S. Government Printing Office, 1894–1927.

U.S. War Department. *The War of the Rebellion: A Compilation of the Official Records of the Union and Confederate Armies.* 70 vols. in 127 and index. Washington, D.C.: U.S. Government Printing Office, 1880–1901.

Secondary Sources

Books

Alexander, Mai. *Dyer County.* Dyersburg, Tenn.: Wallace Printing Co., 1974.

Ash, Stephen V. *Middle Tennessee Society Transformed, 1860–1870: War and Peace in the Upper South.* Baton Rouge: Louisiana State Univ. Press, 1988.

———. *When the Yankees Came: Conflict & Chaos in the Occupied South, 1861–1865.* Chapel Hill: Univ. of North Carolina Press, 1995.

Bearss, Edwin C. *Forrest at Brice's Cross Roads and in North Mississippi in 1864.* Dayton, Ohio: Morningside Bookshop, 1979.

Caldwell, Joshua William. *Sketches of the Bench and Bar of Tennessee.* Knoxville, Tenn., 1898.

Castel, Albert E. *Articles of War.* Mechanicsburg, Pa.: Stackpole Books, 2001.

Connelly, Thomas Lawrence. *Army of the Heartland: The Army of Tennessee, 1861–1862.* Baton Rouge: Louisiana State Univ. Press, 1967.

———. *Autumn of Glory.* Baton Rouge: Louisiana State Univ. Press, 1971.

Cooling, Benjamin F. *Fort Donelson's Legacy: War and Society in Kentucky and Tennessee, 1862–1863.* Knoxville: Univ. of Tennessee Press, 1997.

Cornish, Dudley T. *The Sable Arm: Negro Troops in the Union Army, 1861–1865.* New York: Longman's Green & Co., 1956.

Culp, Frederick M., and Mrs. Robert E. Ross. *Gibson County, Past and Present.* Trenton, Tenn.: Gibson County Historical Soc., 1961.

Daniel, Larry J. *Shiloh: The Battle That Changed the Civil War.* New York: Simon & Schuster, 1997.

Davis, James D. *History of Memphis.* Memphis, Tenn.: Hite, Crumpton and Kelly, 1873.

Drake, Edwin L., ed. *Annals of the Army of Tennessee.* Nashville: A. D. Haynes, 1878.

Durham, Walter T. *Old Sumner.* Gallatin, Tenn.: Sumner County Public Library Board, 1972.

———. *Rebellion Revisited, a History of Sumner County from 1861 to 1870.* Gallatin, Tenn.: Sumner County Museum Assoc., 1982.

———. *Volunteer Forty-Niners: Tennesseans and the California Gold Rush.* Nashville: Vanderbilt Univ. Press, 1997.

Dyer, John P. *"Fightin' Joe" Wheeler.* Baton Rouge: Louisiana State Univ. Press, 1941.

Edwards' Annual Directory for the City of St. Louis for 1866. St. Louis: Edwards, Greenough & Deved, 1866.

Elliott, Sam D. *Soldier of Tennessee: General Alexander P. Stewart and the Civil War in the West.* Baton Rouge: Louisiana State Univ. Press, 1999.

Evans, Clement A., ed. *Confederate Military History.* Extended edition. 19 vols. 1899. Reprint, Wilmington, N.C.: Thomas Broadfoot Publ., 1987–1989.

Farnham, Margaret Bell Harrell. *South to West.* 1947. Reprint. Redondo Beach, Cal.: C. W. Moretti, 1987.

Fisher, John E. *They Rode with Forrest and Wheeler: A Chronicle of Five Tennessee Brother's Service in the Confederate Western Cavalry.* Jefferson, N.C.: McFarland & Co., 1995.

Fuchs, Richard L. *An Unerring Fire: The Massacre at Fort Pillow.* Rutherford, N.J.: Fairleigh Dickinson Univ. Press, 1994.

Gardner, Charles, comp. *Gardner's New Orleans Directory for 1866.* New Orleans: Charles Gardner, 1866.

Gillum, James L. *Prominent Tennesseans, 1796–1938.* Lewisburg, Tenn.: Who's Who Publishing Co., 1940.

George, Henry. *History of the 3d, 7th, 8th and 12th Kentucky C.S.A.* 1911. Lyndon, Ky.: Walthen Historic Press, 1970.

Glatthaar, Joseph T. *Forged in Battle: the Civil War Alliance of Black Soldiers and White Officers.* New York: Free Press, 1990.

Halpin, T. M., comp. *Halpin's City Directory of Memphis, 1867–68.* Memphis, Tenn.: Bulletin Publ. Co., 1868.

Harris, Milus K. [Dove Branham Harris]. *The Harris Family and Others.* 1928. Reprint. Redondo Beach, Cal.: C. W. Moretti, 1987.

Hattaway, Herman M. *General Stephen D. Lee.* Jackson: Univ. Press of Mississippi, 1976.

Hay, Thomas Robson. *Hood's Tennessee Campaign.* 1929. Reprint Dayton, Ohio: Morningside Bookshop, 1976.

Henry, Robert S. *"First with the Most" Forrest.* Indianapolis: Bobbs-Merrill Co., 1944.

History of Fresno County, California with Illustrations. San Francisco: Wallace W. Elliott & Co., 1882.

History of Tennessee . . . together with an Historical and a Biographical Sketch of Gibson, Obion, Dyer, Weakley and Lake Counties. Nashville: Goodspeed Publ. Co., 1887.

Horn, Stanley F. *The Army of Tennessee.* Norman: Univ. of Oklahoma Press, 1941.

Hughes, Nathaniel Cheairs, Jr. *The Battle of Belmont: Grant Strikes South.* Chapel Hill: Univ. of North Carolina Press, 1991.

Hughes, Nathaniel Cheairs, Jr., and Roy P. Stonesifer. *The Life and Wars of Gideon J. Pillow.* Chapel Hill: Univ. of North Carolina Press, 1993.

Hulme, Albert L., and James A. Hulme. *A History of Dyer County.* Dyersburg: n.p., 1982.

Hurst, Jack. *Nathan Bedford Forrest, a Biography.* New York: Alfred A. Knopf, 1993.

Jones, James P. *Yankee Blitzkrieg: Wilson's Raid through Alabama and Georgia.* Athens: Univ. of Georgia Press, 1976.

Klebenow, Anne. *200 Years through 200 Stories.* Knoxville: Univ. of Tennessee Press, 1996.

Knapp, David, Jr. *The Confederate Horsemen.* New York: Vantage Press, 1996.

Lambert, D. Warren. *When the Ripe Pears Fell: The Battle of Richmond, Kentucky.* Richmond, Ky.: Madison County Historical Society, 1995.

Lindsley, John B., ed. *The Military Annals of Tennessee.* Nashville: J. M. Lindsley & Co., 1886.

Longacre, Edward G. *Grant's Cavalryman: The Life and Wars of General James H. Wilson.* Mechanicsburg, Pa.: Stackpole Books, 1972.

Loofbourow, Leon L. *Cross in the Sunset: The Development of Methodism in the California-Nevada Annual Conference of the Methodist Church and Its Predecessors.* Berkeley: Historical Society of the California-Nevada Annual Conference of the Methodist Church, 1966.

Losson, Christopher. *Tennessee's Forgotten Warriors: Frank Cheatham and His Confederate Division.* Knoxville: Univ. of Tennessee Press, 1990.

Lytle, Andrew N. *Bedford Forrest and His Critter Company.* New York: G. P. Putnam's Sons, 1931.

McBride, Robert M., and Daniel M. Robison, eds. *Biographical Directory of the*

Tennessee General Assembly. 5 vols. Nashville: Tennessee State Library and Archives, 1975–.

McDonough, James Lee. *War in Kentucky, from Shiloh to Perryville.* Knoxville: Univ. of Tennessee Press, 1994.

McWhiney, Grady. *Braxton Bragg and Confederate Defeat.* Vol. 1: *Field Command.* New York: Columbia Univ. Press, 1969.

Mainfort, Robert C., Jr. *Archaeological Investigations at Fort Pillow State Historic Area: 1976–1978.* Nashville: Tennessee Department of Conservation, 1980.

Maness, Lonnie E. *An Untutored Genius: The Military Career of General Nathan Bedford Forrest.* Oxford, Miss.: Guild Bindery Press, 1990.

Martis, Kenneth C. *The Historical Atlas of the Congresses of the Confederate States of America, 1861–1865.* New York: Simon & Schuster, 1994.

———. *Historical Atlas of United States Congressional Districts, 1789–1983.* New York: Free Press, 1982.

Mathes, James Harvey. *General Forrest.* New York: D. Appleton & Co., 1902.

———. *The Old Guard in Gray: Researches in the Annals of the Confederate Historical Association. Sketches of Memphis Veterans, etc.* Memphis, Tenn.: S. C. Toof, 1897.

Memorial and Biographical History of the Counties of Fresno, Tulare, and Kern, California. Chicago: Lewis Publishing, 1891.

Memphis Bar Association. *Bench and Bar of Memphis: Memorial.* Memphis: n.p., n.d.

Menefee, Eugene L., and Fred A. Dodge. *History of Tulare and Kings Counties California.* Los Angles: n.p., 1913.

Miller, Rex. *Croxton's Raid.* Ft. Collins, Colo.: Old Army Press, 1979.

Mitchell, Annie R. *Historical Landmarks in Tulare County.* Fresno, Cal.: Valley Publishers, 1983.

Nordhoff, Charles. *California for Health, Pleasure and Residence: A Book for Travellers and Settlers.* 1873. Reprint. Berkeley, Cal.: Ten Speed Press, 1973.

Owen, Thomas McA. *History of Alabama and Dictionary of Alabama Biography.* 4 vols. Chicago: F. J. Clark Publishing Co., 1921.

Parks, Joseph H. *General Edmund Kirby Smith, C.S.A.* Baton Rouge: Louisiana State Univ. Press, 1954.

———. *General Leonidas Polk CSA: The Fighting Bishop.* Baton Rouge: Louisiana State Univ. Press, 1962.

Parrish, T. Michael. *Richard Taylor: Soldier Prince of Dixie.* Chapel Hill: Univ. of North Carolina Press, 1992.

Purdue, Howell, and Elizabeth Purdue. *Pat Cleburne, Confederate General.* Hillsboro, Tex.: Hill Junior College Press, 1973.

Ridens, Arahwana H. *Dyer County and Newbern, Tennessee: Being a History of 39 of the Earliest Families of this County.* Easley, S.C.: Southern Historical Press, 1979.

Ridley, Bromfield L. *Battles and Sketches of the Army of Tennessee.* Mexico, Mo.: Missouri Printing and Publishing Co., 1906.

Rowland, Dunbar. *Military History of Mississippi, 1803–1898.* Spartanburg, S.C.: Reprint Co., 1978.

Sheppard, Eric W. *Bedford Forrest: The Confederacy's Greatest Cavalryman.* New York: Dial Press, 1930.

Sistler, Byron and Barbara. *Dyer County, Tennessee, Marriages, 1860–1879.* Nashville: Byron Sistler & Associates, 1989.

Snider, Margaret C., and Joan H. Yorganson. *Sumner County Cemeteries.* Owensboro, Ky.: McDowell Publ. Co., 1981.

Speer, William S. *Sketches of Prominent Tennesseans.* Nashville: A. B. Tavel, 1888.

Steenburn, Donald H. *The Man Called Gurley.* Meridianville, Ala.: Elk River Press, 1999.

———. *Silent Echoes of Johnsonville: Rebel Cavalry & Yankee Gunboats.* Rogersville, Ala.: Elk River Press, 1994.

Stinson, Era W., and Elizabeth S. Spurlock. *Sumner County, Tennessee Marriages, 1839–1875.* Bowling Green, Ky.: n.p., 1985.

Sutherland, Daniel E., ed. *Guerrillas, Unionists, and Violence on the Confederate Home Front.* Fayetteville: Univ. of Arkansas Press, 1999.

Sword, Wiley. *Embrace an Angry Wind: The Confederacy's Last Hurrah: Spring Hill, Franklin, and Nashville.* New York: Harper Collins, 1992.

———. *Shiloh: Bloody April.* Dayton, Ohio: Morningside Press, 1983.

Symonds, Craig L. *Joseph E. Johnston, a Civil War Biography.* New York: W. W. Norton and Co., 1992.

———. *Stonewall of the West: Patrick Cleburne & the Civil War.* Lawrence: Univ. Press of Kansas, 1997.

Tennessee Civil War Centennial Commission.. *Tennesseans in the Civil War: A Military History of Confederate and Union Units with Available Rosters of Personnel.* Nashville: Civil War Centennial Commission, 1964–65.

The Story of Tulare County and Visalia. Los Angeles: Title Insurance and Trust Co., 1955.

United Daughters of the Confederacy, Tennessee Division. *Confederate Patriot Index, 1894–1924.* 3 vols. Nashville: UDC, Tennessee Div., 1976.

Vandor, Paul E. *History of Fresno, California, with Biographical Sketches.* Los Angeles: Historic Record Co., 1919.

Williams Cincinnati Directory, 1867. Cincinnati: Williams & Co., 1867.

Williams, Edward F., III. *Confederate Victories at Fort Pillow.* Memphis, Tenn.: Nathan Bedford Forrest Trail Committee, 1973.

Wills, Brian S. *A Battle from the Start: A Life of Nathan Bedford Forrest.* New York: Harper Collins, 1992.

Wills, Ridley II. *The History of Belle Meade: Mansion, Plantation and Stud.* Nashville: Vanderbilt Univ. Press, 1991.

Winters, Donald L. *Tennessee Farming, Tennessee Farmers: Antebellum Agriculture in the Upper South.* Knoxville: Univ. of Tennessee Press, 1994.

Wyeth, John A. *Life of General Nathan Bedford Forrest.* 1899. Reprint. Dayton, Ohio: Morningside Bookshop, 1975.

Articles and Parts of Books

Atkins, Jonathan M. "Race, Freedom, and the Confederate Cause," *Journal of East Tennessee History* 70 (1998): 34–61.

Ballard, Michael B. "The Battle of Tupelo." *Papers of the Blue and Gray Education Society* No. 3 (1996).

Basler, Roy P. "And for His Widow and His Orphan." *Quarterly Journal of the Library of Congress* 27 (Oct. 1970): 291–94.

Branch, Paul, Jr. "Robert Vinkler Richardson," William Powell, ed. *Dictionary of North Carolina Biography* 6 vols. Chapel Hill: Univ. of North Carolina Press, 1979–1996. 5:217–18.

Brooksher, William R. "Betwixt Wind and Water." *Civil War Times Illustrated* 32 (Nov. 1993): 64–83.

Carlisle, Rodney P. "Nathan Bedford Forrest." *American National Biography* 8:262–64.

Castel, Albert. "The Fort Pillow Massacre: A Fresh Examination of the Evidence." *Civil War History* 4 (1958): 37–50.

———. "Fort Pillow: Victory or Massacre." *American History Illustrated* 4 (Apr. 1974): 4–11, 46–48.

Cimprich, John, and Robert C. Mainfort, Jr. "Fort Pillow Revisited: New Evidence about an Old Controversy." *Civil War History* 28 (Winter 1982): 293–306.

———. "The Fort Pillow Massacre: A Statistical Note." *Journal of American History* 76 (Dec. 1989): 830–37.

Cunningham, S. A. "Tyree H. Bell." *Confederate Veteran* 6 (1898): 529.

Davison, Eddy W., and Dan Foxx. "Our Journey to the Most Controversial Battlefield in America." *Confederate Veteran* (Sons of Confederate Veterans Series, 1980–) 6 (2001): 12–33.

Eisterhold, John A. "Fort Heiman: Forgotten Fortress." *West Tennessee Historical Society Papers* 28 (1974): 43–54.

Grimsley, Mark. "A Civilian at Brice's Cross Roads." *Civil War Times Illustrated* 32 (Jan. 1994): 39–41, 73.

———. "Leader of the Klan: The Life of Nathan Bedford Forrest." *Civil War Times Illustrated* 32 (Jan. 1994): 34–41, 63–71.

———. "Race in the Civil War." *North & South* 4 (Mar. 2001): 36–46, 52–55.

Harris, William C. "James Ronald Chalmers." *American National Biography* 4:627–28.

Harrison, Lowell H. "Abraham Buford." *American National Biography* 3:878–79.

Hills, Parker. "A Study in Warfighting: Nathan Bedford Forrest and the Battle of Brice's Crossroads." *Papers of the Blue and Gray Education Society* 2 (Fall 1995): 1–64.

Horton, Paul. "'Submitting to the Shadow of Slavery': The Secession Crisis and Civil War in Alabama's Lawrence County." *Civil War History* 44 (June 1998): 111–36.

Huch, Ronald K. "Fort Pillow Massacre: The Aftermath of Paducah." *Illinois State Historical Society Journal* 66 (Spring 1973): 65–70.

Jones, James P. "Brig. General James Camp Tappan, C.S.A." *Phillips County Historical Quarterly* 3 (1965).

Jordan, John L. "Was There a Massacre at Fort Pillow?" *Tennessee Historical Quarterly* 6 (1947): 99–133.

Leftwich, William G., Jr. "The Battle of Brice's Cross Roads. *West Tennessee Historical Society Papers* 20 (1966): 5–19.

Luckett, William W. "Bedford Forrest at the Battle of Brice's Cross Roads." Memphis *Commercial Appeal*. June 4, 1939.

Lufkin, Charles L. "'Not Heard From Since April 12, 1864': The Thirteenth Tennessee Cavalry, U.S.A." *Tennessee Historical Quarterly* 45 (1986): 133–51.

Mainfort, Robert C., Jr. "A Folk Art Map of Fort Pillow." *West Tennessee Historical Society Papers* 40 (Dec. 1986): 72–81.

Maness, Lonnie D. "The Fort Pillow Massacre: Fact or Fiction." *Tennessee Historical Quarterly* 45 (1986): 287–315.

———. "Fort Pillow under Confederate and Union Control." *West Tennessee Historical Society Papers* 38 (1984): 84–98.

———. "A Ruse That Worked: The Capture of Union City, 1864." *West Tennessee Historical Society Papers* 30 (1976): 91–103.

Moore, Kenneth B. "Fort Pillow, Forrest, and the United States Colored Troops in 1864." *Tennessee Historical Quarterly* 54 (Summer 1995): 112–23.

Moran, Nathan K. "'No Alternative Left': State and County Government in Northwest Tennessee During the Union Invasion, January–June, 1862." *West Tennessee Historical Society Papers* 46 (1992): 13–33.

Moretti, Connie Walton. "Brigadier General Tyree Harris Bell, Postwar Californian." *United Daughters of the Confederacy Magazine* 63 (Sept. 2000): 14–16.

Morris, Roy, Jr. "Battle in the Bluegrass." *Civil War Times Illustrated* 27 (1988): 15–16, 20–23.

———. "Fort Pillow: Massacre or Madness." *America's Civil War* 29 (Nov. 2000): 26–32.

Sanders, Stuart W. "Confederate Raider's Kentucky Rampage." *America's Civil War* 12 (July 1999): 30–36.

Stanchak, John E. "A Legacy of Controversy: Fort Pillow Still Stands." *Civil War Times Illustrated* 32 (Sept. 1993): 18, 25, 75–76, 78.

Tap, Bruce. "These Devils Are Not Fit to Live on God's Earth: War Crimes and the Committee on the Conduct of the War." *Civil War History* 42 (June 1996): 116–32.

Weller, Jac. "Nathan Bedford Forrest: An Analysis of Untutored Military Genius." *Tennessee Historical Quarterly* 18 (1959): 213–51.

West, James D. "The Thirteenth Tennessee Regiment—Confederate States of America." *Tennessee Historical Magazine* 7 (Oct. 1921): 180–93.

Williams, Edward F., III. "The Johnsonville Raid and Nathan Bedford Forrest State Park." *Tennessee Historical Quarterly* 28 (1969): 72–80.

Wyeth, John A. "Major-General Forrest at Brice's Cross-Roads." *Harper's New Monthly Magazine* 98 (Dec. 1898): 530–45.

———. "The Storming of Fort Pillow." *Harper's New Monthly Magazine* 99 (Sept. 1899): 595–607.

Unpublished Studies

Cox, Brent A. "The Battle of Trenton, December 20, 1862."

———. "Colonel Robert M. Russell."

———. "From a Finer Cast: The History of the 12th Tennessee Regiment."

———. "Gibson County in the Civil War."

———. "John Russell Dance."

———. "The Secrets of Heroism."

Moretti, Connie W. "Newbern, Tennessee, on the Eve of the War Between the States."

Willoughby, Earl. "Chasing Guerrillas: The West Tennessee Campaign."

———. "Church Grove & Camp Bell during the Civil War."

———. "Colonel Dawson and the Shadow War."

———. "Confederate Surgeons from Dyer County."

———. "Dyer County and the Civil War."

———. "Home-made Yankees."

———. "A Hot-bed of Traitors."

———. "'Noble, True and Brave': The 12th Tennessee Volunteers."

———. "12th, 22nd & 47th Regiments."

———. "Tyree Bell Moves to Dyer County."

———. "Under the Black Flag."

Internet Sources

Moretti, Connie W. "Descendants of Tyree Rodes Harris." *http://members.aol.com/cwmoretti/family.htm*

Price, Randel M. "20th Tennessee Cavalry, CSA, Descriptive Notes on Battles." *http://www.familytreemaker.com/cgi-bin/iff*

"Tulare County History." *http://www.cagenweb.com/cpl/tulare*

Index

Abbeville, Miss., encounter at, 105, 146, 153
Abernathy, John T., 76
Adams, Daniel W., 225, 228
Adams, William, 6–7
Adams, William Wirt, 168
Agnew, Samuel A., 136
Alabama and Florida Railroad, 49
Alabama River, 49
Alabama troops: 11th Infantry, 225
Alcorn, James L., 31–32, 269n.9
Allison, Thomas F. P., 95, 100–101, 121, 187–88, 199–201, 210, 212, 231, 249–50, 303n.33
Anderson and Richardson, 236
Anderson, Charles W., 102–4, 121, 123, 127, 130, 140, 142, 148, 172, 249, 258
Anderson, James Patton, 277n.14
Anthony's [King's] Hill, battle of, 215–16
Appler, Jesse J., 38
Arkansas troops: 2nd Mounted Rifles, 273n.10; 4th Infantry, 59; 13th Infantry, 19
Armistead, Charles G., 224
Armstrong, Frank Crawford, ix, 192–93, 200, 225, 229, 277n.19
Armstrong's Brigade, 229
Army of Kentucky, 64, 69
Army of Tennessee, 73, 75–76, 78–80, 82–83, 86, 89–90, 92, 107, 132–33, 135, 165, 189, 192–93, 201, 210
Army of the Cumberland, 89, 174
Army of the Mississippi, 36, 41, 44, 47–48, 69
Army of Northern Virginia, 132

Army of the West, 44
Asboth, Alexander S., 85
Asbury, Francis, 3,
Ash, Stephen V., 83
Athens, Ala., 171–73
Atkins, John DeWitt Clinton, 79, 83, 104, 115, 265n.9
Atlanta, Ga., 49, 90, 152, 177, 179
Austin, Tex., 15
Avery, Henry, 240

Bainbridge, Tenn., 215
Baker, Volney, 247
Baldwyn, Miss., 137–40
Ballentine, John G., 89
Barboursville, Ky., 52, 54–55
Barkley, Sam, 196
Barteau, Clark R., 100, 105, 120–21, 123–24, 130–31, 137–38, 145, 149, 154–55, 161–62, 167, 170, 172, 176, 183–84, 195–96, 203, 209–10, 216, 227, 291n.28
Batchelor, J. A., 257
Bate, William Brimage, 206–7
Beall, Ninian, 3–4
Beall, Thomas Allen Beall (grandfather), 3, 6, 12n.12
Bearss, Edwin Cole, 162
Beauregard, Pierre G. T., 33, 35–36, 41, 189
Beddo, Absalom, 3–4,
Beechgrove, Tenn., 74
Bell-Cole Family Reunion, 248
Bell, Harris & Company, 232–33, 236

333

Bell, Absalom B.(father), 5–6, 263nn.11, 13
Bell, Bennett Douglass, 254, 262n.5
Bell, C. C. (Charles S.), 282n.41
Bell, Cynthia Ann (daughter), 7, 239–40
Bell, Isaac Thomas "I. T.," (son), 7, 9, 14, 90, 101, 105, 143, 147–48, 210, 217, 231–32, 234, 239, 243–45, 247–48, 292n.34
Bell, James William (son), 7, 9, 14, 30, 629n.6
Bell, James, 244
Bell, John L., 143, 292n.32
Bell, John Richard, 234, 239, 242, 244
Bell, John Wesley, 263n.11
Bell, Josiah Walton "Joe" (son), 7, 234, 237, 239, 241
Bell, Kleber Miller, 247
Bell, Lily Cartwright (Mrs. B. D.), 262n 5
Bell, Lily Vertrees, 255
Bell, Mary Ann Walton (Mrs. Tyree H.), 3, 5–9, 11, 30, 44, 78–80, 233, 239, 241, 243
Bell, Russell (son), 7–8
Bell, Sarah Catherine "Sallie" (daughter), 7, 234
Bell, Seraphina Elizabeth Smith "Lizzie" (Mrs. Isaac T.), 234, 245–46
Bell, Susan (daughter), 7
Bell, Susannah Harris (mother), 2, 5, 263nn.12, 13
Bell, Thomas (uncle), 6,
Bell, Tyree Alexander "Burch" (son), 7, 234, 239, 241–42, 244–46, 249
Bell, Will, 244
Bell, William B., 296n.10
Bell, William S., 25
Bell's Brigade, 94, 100, 102–3, 105, 108, 113, 118, 120, 127, 136–38, 140, 147–48, 154–57, 159–61, 165–66, 170, 173, 175, 180, 185–86, 190, 194–95, 198–203, 205, 216, 221–22, 229, 234, 259
Bell's Drum Corps, 246
Bell's Escort ("Bell's Babies"), 89, 143, 190, 215, 222
Belle Meade, 254, 284n.10
Belmont, battle of, 19–25, 26, 46, 138
Beltzhoover, Daniel, 267n.33, 294n.12
Benicia Barracks, Calif., 15
Bennett, William K, 282n.9
Berlin, Tenn., 196

Bethel, Tenn., 35
Bethel, Calif., 243–45
Bethel Cemetery, 243, 257
Bethel (Calif.) School District, 243
Bettis, Mr., 71
Biffle, Jacob B., 192, 196, 223
Biffle's Brigade, 198
Big Creek Gap, 52
Big Dry Creek, 241
Big Hill, Ky., 54–55, 70
Big Pond, Ky., 67
Big Sandy River, 179, 182
Bird's Point Brigade, 25
Bird's Point, Mo., 26
Black, Dr. (house), 206–9
Black, R. J., 194
Black Warrior River, 226
Blackland, Miss., 138, 146
Blakely, 222
Blanchard, August, 256
Bledsoe's Creek, 5–6,
Blocker, John, 225
Bluff City Grays, 253
Bolivar, Tenn., 95
Booneville, Miss., 137–40
Booth, Lionel F., 116–17, 119, 123
Bouton, Edward, 157
Bowling Green, Ky., 32
Bradford, Theodorick, 116, 120, 128
Bradford, William F., 82, 115–17, 121, 123, 127–29, 285nn.6, 7
Bradford's Battalion, 116–17
Bragg, Braxton, 33–34, 36–37, 39–40, 44, 46–47, 51, 68–70, 73, 76, 79–80, 83, 88–90, 92, 132, 258, 277n.20, 279n.15
Branham, John, 5,
Breckinridge, John C., 36–37
Breckinridge, Mary Cyrene (Mrs. J. C.), 66, 275n.13
Brentwood, Tenn., 203
Brice, Mr. and Mrs. William (house), 143–45, 148
Brice's Crossroads, 136, 139
Brice's Crossroads, battle of, xi, 139–49
Brooks, J. J., 51
Brosnan, Daniel S., 256, 258
Brown, Francis, 5
Brown, John C., 199–200
Brown, Joseph E., 151, 169
Brown, Tully, 159

Brown, West, 182–83
Brownsville, Tenn., 115, 127, 131
Bryantsville, Ky., 54, 69
Buck, S. C., 255
Buford, Abraham "Abe" ix, 66–67, 107, 110, 112–13, 131–32, 137–42, 149, 155–58, 160–61, 168, 173, 175–76, 180, 182–84, 187–88, 192–96, 198, 201, 208, 210, 212, 214, 223–24, 258–59, 284n.10, 306n.22
Buford's Division, 132, 137, 153–55, 157, 160, 166, 170, 194, 200, 220
Buford, William W., 200
Buell, Don Carlos, 32, 36, 47, 51, 68
Burch, John C., 13
Burroughs, John, 6,
Burton, M. J., 265n.9
Busby, Elijah, 6,
Butler's Creek, 192
Butterworth, R. N., 265n.9
Byrnes, Robert, 32

Cahaba River, 225, 227–29
Cairo, Ill., 20
Cairo, Tenn., 5,
Caldwell, Robert Porter, 13–14, 24, 36, 39–41, 43, 101, 126, 143, 235–36
Caldwell, Samuel H., 24, 126, 128, 289n.45
Calhoun, Dr., 160
California, 238–49
Camden, Tenn., 88, 109, 188
Camp Bell (Newbern), 91
Camp Bell (Trenton), 88, 91, 95
Camp Beauregard, 31, 34
Camp Brown, Tenn., 15, 17, 34
Camp Dick Robinson, 69–70
Camp Johnston, Mo., 22
Campbell, Alexander W., 223–24, 226, 235, 308n.12
Campbellsville, Tenn., 191, 194
Canby, Edward R. S., 229–31
Caney Fork, Tenn., 3
Carlisle Barracks, Pa., 108
Carnton, 201
Carr, John Doak, 288n.36
Carroll County, Tenn., 13, 131
Caruthers, Robert L., 83
Centerville, Ala., 225–26, 228–29
Centerville, Calif., 242
"Chalk Bluffs," Ky., 31, 267n.27

Chalmers, James R., ix, 87, 93–94, 98, 100, 118, 120, 124–30, 153, 156, 162, 167–68, 170, 179–80, 182, 184–86, 192 196, 200–201, 206, 210, 214, 219, 223, 225, 258, 282n.41, 299n.19, 302n.24
Chalmers's Division, 108, 117, 134, 157, 160–61, 166, 169–70, 180, 225, 228
Chaplin River, 69
Charleston, Mo., battle of, 25
Chattanooga, Tenn., 25, 47, 49–50, 89, 94
Cheatham, Benjamin F. "Frank," 16, 24–25, 36, 40, 43, 45–46, 48–50, 68, 75–76, 81, 90, 199–200, 209–10, 212, 237–38, 259
Cheatham's Division, 32, 73, 272 n.5
Cheatham's Corps, 199
J. W. Cheeseman (steamer), 185
Cherokee Station, Ala., 137, 139, 170, 172–74, 176–77, 179, 190
Cherryville, Tenn., 118, 131
Chickamauga, battle of, 89–90
Chickasaw Indians, 284n.6
Chiwapa Creek, 154
Church Grove, Tenn., 9, 280n.24
Churchill, Thomas J., 59–60
Churchill's Division, 52, 57
Cimprich, John, 288n.38
Cincinnati, Ohio, 5, 67, 233–34
Cincinnati Commercial, 98
Clack, J. H., 257
Clanton, James H., 224
Clark, Achilles V., 118, 126, 128, 148
Clark, Gen. Charles, 35, 38, 42–43, 46
Clark's Division, 37
Clark, Charlie, 209, 217
Clark, Reuben Douglas, 96–97, 100, 209–10, 217, 307n.40
Clarksville, Tenn., 18–19, 26, 29,
Clay, Cassius M., 274n.30
Clay, Henry, 274n.30
Clay, Henry, Jr., 274n.30
Cleburne, Patrick R., 51, 57–58, 68, 200
Cleburne's Brigade, 37, 55
Cleburne's Division, 52–53, 55, 68, 198
Cleveland, Grover, 246–47
Clinch River, 52, 73
Clifton, Tenn., 75, 89, 183
Clinton, Tenn., 52
Coal Creek, Tenn., 16, 120, 122
Cockrill, Robinson, 242
Coffeeville, Miss., 105

Colbert's Shoals, 171–72
Coldwater River, 98, 167
Cole, Billy, 241–42
Coleman, Charles S., 190, 193
Collierville, Tenn., 97–98
Columbia, Tenn., 44, 75, 79–80, 175, 177, 194–96, 199, 210, 213, 277n.20
Columbus, Ga., 229
Columbus, Ky., 16–19, 25–26, 29–33, 85, 88, 94, 115–16, 119, 269nn.2, 6
Columbus, Miss., 107, 153
Combs, Fielding A., 246
Committee on the Conduct of the War, 129–30
Como, Miss., 95, 98–99, 101, 109, 282n.41
Confederate Troops: 8th Cav., 168
Confederate Veteran, x
Cooling, Benjamin F., 82, 279n.2, 285n.3
Coonewah Creek, 155
Coonewah Crossroads, engagement at, 146, 155–56, 162
Coosa River, 90
Corinth, Miss., 35–37, 41–42, 44, 85, 88–89, 91, 93, 95, 108, 117, 132, 136–38, 153, 170, 179–80, 190, 217, 219–20, 222
Cotton, Thomas, 239
Cottontown, Tenn., 7–9
Council Bluffs, Ia., 240
Courtland, Ala., 117
Covington, Ky., 54, 67
Covington, Tenn., 5, 128
Crab Orchard, Ky., 70–72
Craig, Tal, 71, 276n.21
Creek War, 264n.3
Crittenden, Ky., 67
Cromwell, Oliver, 3,
Crossland, Edward, 111–13, 155–57, 160–61, 168, 180, 192–93, 220, 222, 296n.3
Croxton, John T., 225–27
Crozier, Orlando M., 182, 184
Cruft, Charles, 57
Cumberland Gap, 51–52, 70, 72
Cumberland Law School, 100
Cumberland Mountain, 52
Cumberland River, 5, 18, 205–6
Cynthiana, Ky., 54, 66–67
Cypress Creek, engagement at, 176

Dallas, Tex., 255
Dalton, Ga., 135

Daniel, Larry, 37
Davis, Jefferson, 16, 29, 47, 64, 67, 89–90, 92, 102, 112, 151, 169, 265n.8, 282n.4
Davis, Mrs. Jefferson, 112
Davis's Mill, 147
Dawson, William A., 80–82, 265n.9, 300n.22
Dean, Herod A., 239
Decatur, Ala., 171–72, 175
Decoration Day, 246
Democratic Party, 243, 247
Department of Alabama, Mississippi, and East Louisiana, 99, 153, 165, 223
Department of East Tennessee, 51
Department of Mississippi and Eastern Louisiana, 81, 223
Department of the West, 86
Department of Western Kentucky, 230
Desha, Mary Breckinridge, 66
Dibrell, George C., 192
Dick Keys (steamer), 49
Dick's River, 69–70
Dickinson, Benjamin F., 76
Dinkins, James, 185, 200, 256
District of the Gulf, 165
District of West Tennessee, 167
Dodds, George W. D., 110
Doke, Robert L., 265n.9
Donelson, Daniel S., 70–72, 100
Donelson, Miss, 255
Dougherty, Henry, 24–26
Dougherty, Mrs. Henry 26
Douglas Chapel, 2
Douglass Family, 6
Douglass, Guy, 78, 236
Douglass, Martha Harris (Mrs. Guy), 78
Douglass, Sarah Ann Bell, 6
Doyle, Bradley, 239
Dresden, Tenn., 111, 181, 222
Duck River, 78, 175, 195–97, 199, 204, 212
Duckworth, William L., 93, 108, 110, 128, 190
Duke, Basil, 66
Dunlap, James T., 182, 282n.9, 299n.8
Durham, Walter, 3,
Dyer County, Tenn., 1, 8–9, 13, 29, 44, 63, 78, 80–83, 86, 116, 131, 231–38, 249, 254, 265n.11
Dyer County Aid Society, 233
Dyer County Fair, 236

Dyer, William R., 126, 128
Dyersburg, Tenn., 11, 77, 82, 116, 232–33

East Pasagoula, Miss., 15
Eastport, Miss., 179, 181, 190
Eaton, Tenn., 112, 118–19, 127, 130, 280n.24
Edmondson's Sharpshooters, 272n.5
Edwards, Thomas,
"Egypt," 136, 165
Elk River, 174
Ellistown, Miss., 153–54, 161
Elyton, Ala., 225–26, 229
Estenaula, Tenn., 95–96, 109

Fakes, John, 232–34
Farley, Andrew, 243
Farris, Oliver B., 291n.28,
Faulkner, William Wallace, 82, 88, 96, 108, 220–23, 258, 307n.2, 308n.9
Fayette County, Tenn., 63
Fayetteville, Tenn., 14
Ferguson, Samuel W., 94, 105
Ferguson, William, 127
Fielder, Alfred T., 21–22, 24, 31–33, 39 36, 41, 43, 49–50, 55, 61, 64–65, 68, 72, 74–75, 83, 276n.5, 277n.20, 290n.8, 307n.1
First Seminole War, 3
Fitch, Charles, 117, 124–25
Fitzgerald, Edward, 57–59, 63
Florence, Ala., 88, 172, 176, 189–90
Forked Deer River, 80, 89, 118, 231
"Forrest Country," 115
Forrest, Jeffrey E., 93, 100, 106, 108, 284n.4
Forrest, Nathan Bedford, ix, xi, 13, 43–44, 75, 79–81, 86–87, 90–108, 110–12, 115–18, 122–24, 128–29, 131–37, 139–45, 147, 149, 151, 153–57, 160–63, 165–70, 172–77, 179–80, 182, 185–89, 195, 197–203, 205–7, 210, 213, 215, 219–21, 223–25, 228–29, 250, 258–59, 290n.3
Forrest's Veterans Cavalry, 249
Forrest, William H. "Bill," 167
Fort, DeWitt Clinton, 128, 288n.35
Fort Anderson, Ky., 111, 117, 286n.8
Fort Donelson, 32, 135
Fort Granger, 202
Fort Heiman, 179, 182–84
Fort Henry, 32, 182
Fort Pillow, 81, 88, 94, 118, 285n.2

Fort Pillow, battle of, xi, 115–30
Fort Randolph, Tenn., 16
Fortress Rosecrans, 209
Fort Towson, Indian Terr., 15
Fowlks, W. L., 272n.44
Fowlks, W. P., 272n.44
Frankfort, Ky., 66–68, 274n.30
Franklin, Tenn., 195, 197, 200–202, 211–12
Franklin, battle of, 200–203
Freeman, Thomas J., 13, 27, 31
Fresno City, Calif., 240–45, 247, 257
Fresno Blue and Gray Veterans, 244, 246–47
Fresno City Band, 244
Fresno County, Calif., 243, 246
Fresno *Morning Republican*, 257
Friendship Volunteers, 21
Fry, Jacob, 44
Fulcher, Richard Carlton, 304n.40
Fuller, Mr., 271n.44
Fulton, Miss., 170

Gadsden, Ala., 90–91
Gainesville, Ala., 229–31, 233
Gallatin, Tenn., 205, 250, 252, 254–57
Gallatin Union, 2
Gano, Richard M., 65
Garrard County, Ky., 2, 5–6, 276n.20
Gayoso Hotel, Memphis, 167
Georgetown, Ky., 54, 66–68
Gibson County, Tenn., 13–14, 29, 33, 43, 63, 81, 89, 112, 116, 131
Glenn, William, 241–42
Goodwin, John, 288n.36
Gordon, George W., 199–200
Gordon, John B., 247, 252–54
Grand Army of the Republic, 245, 247
Grand Junction, Tenn., 44, 166
Grant, Ulysses S., 19–22, 24, 32, 36, 46, 85, 94–95, 132, 137, 194, 236
Green County, Ala., 225
Green, John Uriah, 88
Green River line, 32
Greensboro, Ala., 229
Greenville, Ala., 49
Greenwood, Miss., 104
Greer, Henry C., 86–88, 92, 282n.5
Grenada, Miss., 44, 105, 167
Grierson, Benjamin H., 96, 139–40, 147, 151, 156–60
Guntown, Miss., 148

Hall, S. S., 265n.9
Halleck, Henry W., 32
Hammons, James, 40–41
Hancock, R. R.,
Hardee's Tactics, 16
Hardee, William J., 36, 47, 68
Hardee's Corps, 37, 70
Hardeman County, Tenn., 63
Harding, William G., 284n.10
Hardison, W. T., 250
Hardison's Ford, 175
Hardison's Mill, 196, 203
Harpeth River, 201–2, 211
Harrel, Mr., 271n.44
Harrell, James, 234
Harrell, Margaret "Maggie," 234, 247
Harrell, Reuben Green, 14, 233–34, 239, 241–44, 247, 282n.9
Harrell, Robert, 239, 241
Harrell, Susan Bell, (Mrs. R. G.), 14, 233, 239, 247, 256
Harrell, William M., 14, 234
Harrell, Willie Maud, 239, 245
Harris Family, 2, 4–5, 70
Harris, Miller and Company, 232
Harris, Albert Gallatin, 1, 8–9, 11, 14, 24, 101, 221, 232, 265n.7, 282n.9, 312n.22
Harris, Allen, 8–9, 44, 232–34, 236, 271n.43
Harris, Brightberry, 4, 271n.43
Harris, Conquest Cross, 14, 101, 208, 243
Harris, George W. D., 110
Harris, Greenberry, 5,
Harris, Isham G., 1, 12, 15, 41, 79, 102, 110, 230, 265n.9
Harris, John Wesley, 5,
Harris, Mary Ann "Aunt Sallie" Walton (Mrs. Brightberry), 4–5, 271n.43
Harris, Milus King "M. K.," 243, 249, 254
Harris, Robert, 3–4
Harris, Russell A., 2, 6–7, 71
Harris, Sally Walton, 271n.43
Harris, Tyree Rodes, 2, 5–6, 262n.3, 265n.9
Harrisburg, Miss., battle of, 156–63
Harrison, Benjamin, 247
Harrodsburg, Ky., 68–69
Hartsville Academy, 105
Harwood, Charlie B.,
Haskins, Edward, 9, 11, 236, 265n.9
Haskins, Harriet (Mrs. Edward), 9, 222
Hatch, Edward, 194

Hatchie River, 95–97, 100, 132, 137
Hawkins, Isaac R., 82
Haywood County, Tenn., 236
Heard, John, 263n.13
Henderson County, Tenn., 240, 245
Henderson, Tom, 142, 291n.28
Henderson Station, Tenn., 35, 88, 180
Henry, Robert Selph, 162
Henry County, Tenn., 58, 86–87
Hernando, Miss., 167–68
Herron, Robert, 233
Heth, Henry, 67
Heth's Division, 67
Hibbitt, Joe, 143
Hickahala Creek, 167
Hickman, Ky., 31
Hicks, Stephen G., 111
Hill, Benjamin J., 55–58, 60
(B. J.) Hill's Brigade, 59, 61
Hill, Charley, 14
Hill, Munson R., 274n.27
Hindman, Thomas C., 39, 42
Hindman's Brigade, 39
Hodge, George B., 132
Holland, Jake, 210
Hollis, Elisha T., 102, 134
Hollow Tree Gap, engagement at, 210–11
Holly Springs, Miss., 131, 166
Hood, John Bell, 165, 177, 189–90, 195, 198, 200–201, 205–6, 208–10, 211
Hood's Tennessee Campaign, xi
Hoover's Gap, 74
Hord, Henry E.,
The Hornet's Nest, 40
House, William W., 17
Hubbard, Asa, 263n.13
Hudson, Alfred, 286n.14
Hudson Battery, 157, 173
Hudsonville, Miss., 131, 146
Huey, James K., 194
Humboldt, Tenn., 33, 35, 269n.2
Hunsaker, Rev. A. W., 238–39
Huntington, Tenn., 131, 180, 182
Huntsville, Ala., 95, 174–75
Hurlbut, Stephen A., 94–95, 115–16, 167, 225
Hurricane Creek, 166
Hurst, Fielding, 82, 110, 115–16
Hurt, Absalom DeBerry, 282n.9
Hurt's Crossroads, 197

Hutcherson, Tom M., 24, 38
Hyde, J. T., 245

Illinois troops: Waterhouse's Btry. E, 1st Illinois Light, 37–38, 42–43; 2nd Cav., 82; 3rd Cav., 167; 4th Cav., 82; 7th Cav., 82, 88, 96–97; 11th Cav., 38, 82; 15th Cav., 82; 11th Infantry, 41; 22nd Infantry, 25; 31st Infantry, 21; 62nd Infantry, 82
Iowa troops: 7th Infantry, 25; 8th Infantry, 296n.10; 66th Infantry, 112; 120th Infantry, 147
"Iron Banks," Ky., 267n.27
The Irving Block, Memphis, 167
Island No. 10, 220
Iuka, Miss., 170, 181, 190

Jack's Creek, 96
Jackson College, 45, 100
Jackson Purchase, 108, 220, 279n.2, 284n.6
Jackson, Tenn., 13, 33, 35, 44, 75, 82, 85, 87–88, 91–92, 94–95, 110, 115, 127, 179–80, 269n.2
Jackson, Andrew, 3, 5, 11, 264n.3, 284n.6
Jackson, William H. "Red," ix, 24, 79, 136, 190, 192, 194, 196, 200–201, 223–29, 254, 258–59, 277n.19, 284n.10
Jackson's Division, 192, 194–97, 202, 206–7, 214, 225–26
Jasper, Tenn., 73
Johnson, Andrew, 232
Johnson's (Bushrod) Brigade, 36–37, 43, 46
Johnson, William A., 137, 139, 141–42, 170
Johnson's (William A.) Brigade, 140, 144, 174
Johnson's Spring, Ky., 66
Johnsonville Raid, 179–88, 192
Johnston, Albert Sidney, 18, 29, 32, 36
Johnston, John, 91, 190, 211
Johnston, Joseph E., 86, 92–93, 99–100, 135–36, 151, 165, 169. 177
Johnston, William Preston, 47
Jolliet, Louis, 267n.27

Kargé, Joseph, 138
Kelley, David C., 174, 184, 230, 252, 254–55, 298n.4
Kelly's Mill, 153
Kenney, J. J. N., 257
Kentucky and Central Railroad, 54, 66

Kentucky Brigade (Lyon's, Crossland's), 134, 140, 154–55, 158, 168, 170, 173, 180, 182, 192, 201, 208, 214, 222, 228
Kentucky General Assembly, 2,
Kentucky Neutrality Laws, 17
Kentucky River, 67
Kentucky troops (CSA): Cobb's Btry., 182; Huey's Cav. Battalion, 194; 2nd Cav., 65; 12th Mounted Infantry, 82, 96, 108, 110, 142, 220–21; 2nd Infantry, 5; 3rd Infantry, 44, 108, 112; 7th Infantry, 112; 8th Infantry, 134, 214
Kentucky troops (USA): 1st Cav., 276n.20; 1st Heavy Artillery (Colored), 286n.8
King's [Anthony's] Hill, battle of, 191, 215
King's River, Calif., 241
Kingston, Ky., 54–55, 57
Kingston, Tenn., 73
Kirby Smith, Edmund, 47, 51–53, 55, 57–61, 64–65, 69, 259, 272nn.4, 5, 273n.9
Kirk, Elijah P., 265n.9
Kizer, Thomas N., 86–87
Kizer's Scouts, 87, 132
Knoxville, Tenn., 3, 51–52, 70, 72–73

"Lady Polk," 18, 29
LaFayette, Ga., battle of, 167
Lafayette, Tenn., 97–98, 109
LaGrange, Ga., 49
LaGrange, Tenn., 88, 94, 131, 147, 151, 153
Lake County, Tenn., 87
Lambert, D. Warren, 275n.32
Lancaster, Ky., 2, 5, 70–71
Lannom, William D., 96
Latham, Mr. and Mrs. J. T., 253
Lavender, John, 59
LaVergne, Tenn., 74
Lavinia, Tenn., 180–81
Lauderdale, John W., 25
Law, Sallie, 25
Lawrenceburg, Tenn., 176, 192, 194
Lea, James L. "Jo," 24, 41, 90–91, 96, 101, 282n.9
Leaming, Mack J., 121
Ledsinger, Cynthia (Mrs. John P.), 240, 243
Ledsinger, John P., 240, 243
Lee, Fitzhugh, 253
Lee, Stephen D., 91–94, 99, 118, 133, 136–37, 139–40, 152–53, 157–60, 162, 165–66, 211, 292n.34

Leesburg, Ky., 54, 67
Lemming, Mack J., 124
Lewisburg, Tenn., 175
Lexington, Ky., 51, 60, 64–65, 182
Lexington, Tenn., 75, 180, 224, 234
Lillard's Mills,
Lincoln, Abraham, 12
Logan, John A., 21
Logwood, Thomas H., 97, 173–74
London, Ky., 53–54, 72
Lookout Mountain, 50–51
Loring, William W., 201
Louisiana troops: Watson Btry., 19, 25; Scott's Cavalry Brigade, 53, 55; 11th Infantry, 24, 36, 38, 40
Louisville and Nashville Railroad, 180
Louisville, Ky., 68
Lusk, Samuel, 6–7
Lynnsville, Tenn., 194
Lyon, Hylan B., 134–35, 139–40, 142, 149, 155–56, 165, 182, 230, 258, 294nn.54, 12, 296n.3
Lyon's Brigade, 144
Lyon's Division, 155–57, 160, 162

Mabry, Hinchie P., 153–54, 157–59
Mabry's Brigade, 153–55, 168–69, 180
Macon, Ga., 229
Macon, Miss., 148
Madison County, Tenn., 82, 235–36
Maths, Bro, 256
Maury, Dabney H., 165, 169
Mayhew Station, Miss., 108
Mahon Family, 240
Mahon, Rev. R. H., 101
Mahon, Rev. William Jackson, "Jack," 42, 47, 51, 57, 67–68, 75, 101, 233, 238–40, 245, 252, 271n.34, 286n.14
Mainfort, Robert C., Jr., 288n.38
Manchester, Ky., 52–53, 61
Manchester, Tenn., 74
Mandeville, La., 256
Mansker's Station, 3,
Manson, Mahlon D., 57, 60–61
Marion, Ala., 229
"Marion," (newspaper correspondent), 128
Marks, Samuel F., 22, 24, 36
Marquette, Fr. Jacques, 267n.27
Mason, Joe, 182
Martin, Tom, 215

Mason County, Ky., 5,
Maury County, Tenn., 79
Maury, Dabney H., 165–66
Mayfield, Ky., 112
Mays, William F., 40–41
Mazeppa (steamer), 183–84
McAdoo, J. C., 124, 288n.34
McCaig, George W., 147
McCook, Edward M., 227–29
McCorkle, H. R. A., 167
McCown, John P., 51
McCray, T. H., 59
McCray's Brigade, 59
McCulloch, Robert C. "Black Bob," 94, 100–102, 105, 118, 120–23, 128, 130–31, 139, 165, 238, 258, 308n.12
McCullough's Brigade, 127, 134, 153–54, 161, 166, 168–69, 288n.35
McConnel, Oscar, 243
McDonald, Charles, 96
McDougal brothers, 222
McDowell, William W., 89
McGavock, John and Carolin Winder, 201
McGee, G. K., 32, 265n.9
McGee, J. P., 24, 215
McLagan, W. R., 128
McMurry, Lipscomb P., 44, 47, 61, 75–76
McNairy County, Tenn., 82
McNeil, T. C., 209
McRae, Francis M., 291n.28
Meetinghouse Ridge, 42
Memphis, Tenn., 12, 16, 45, 81–82, 85, 88, 98, 105, 110, 115–17, 136, 151, 153, 160–62, 166–69, 233–34, 249, 250, 254–55
"Memphis," (newspaper correspondent), 128
Memphis and Charleston Railroad, 44, 89, 91, 93–94, 97–98, 108, 132, 136–37, 151, 170, 174, 190, 216
Memphis and Ohio Railroad, 33
Memphis and Tennessee Railroad, 98
Memphis Appeal, 126, 128
Memphis *Commercial Appeal*, 257
Mendocino District, Calif., 244
Mercer County, Ky., 68
Meridian, Miss., 44, 92, 99, 104–5, 137, 169
Methodist Episcopal Church, South, 240, 246
Methodist Episcopal Church, South (Kingsburg Circuit), 243

Methodist Episcopal Church, South (Memphis Conference), 238
Methodist Episcopal Church, South (Wildflower Circuit), 243
Meux, Thomas R., 249
Michigan troops: 3rd Cav., 82
Mifflin, Tenn., 180–81
Military Division of the West, 189
Mill Springs, battle of, 32
Miller, George, 232, 234, 236
Milroy, Robert H., 206, 305n.6
Milus (Bell's servant), 231–32
Mineral King, Calif., 246
Missionary Ridge, 89, 92
Mississippi and Ohio Railroad, 15
Mississippi Central Railroad, 131
Mississippi River, 8, 17–19, 22, 24, 29, 81, 85, 115, 119, 123–24
Mississippi troops: Pettus Flying Artillery, 286n.14; Sanford's Btry., 39; 18th Cav. Battalion, 142; 8th Cav., 142; 2nd Partisan Rangers, 89; 2nd Infantry, 35
Mobile, Ala., 47–49, 139, 160, 165, 169, 222, 224, 229
Mobile and Great Northern Railroad, 49
Mobile and Ohio Railroad, 30–31, 33, 43, 105, 108, 132, 138, 156, 170, 223, 231, 269n.2
Montevallo, Ala., 139, 224–25, 228
Montgomery, Ala., 49, 229
Montgomery County, Md., 5,
Moody Landing, 182
Moorman, George, 256
Morgan, George W., 51–53
Morgan, James Dada, 176
Morgan, John Hunt, 65, 234
Morgan, Mrs. Henrietta Hunt (John H.'s mother), 64–65
Morris, William, 271n.44
Morton, George H., 306n.19
Morton, John W., 94, 98, 107, 139, 141, 149, 160, 163, 173, 176, 182–83, 185–86, 187–89, 202–3, 208, 226, 258–59
Moscow, Ky., 31, 34
Moscow, Tenn., 88, 94
Moulton, Ala., 280n.18
Mount Carmel, Tenn., 197
Mount Pleasant, Tenn., 171, 175
Mount Vernon, Ky., 70, 72
Mount Zion Church, battle of, 57–58, 61

Mower, Joseph A., 153, 156, 159–61, 193
Mulberry, Tenn., 171, 174
Murfreesboro, Tenn., 73–74, 205
Murfreesboro (Stones River), 1862 battle of, 75–76
Murfreesboro, 1864 battle of, 107, 206–8

Nashville *American*, 250
Nashville, Tenn., 4, 8, 16, 32, 36, 47, 51, 74, 136, 151, 180, 193, 195, 202–3, 205, 219, 249, 254–55
Nashville, battle of, 210
Nashville & Chattanooga Railroad, 174, 205
Nashville and Decatur Railroad, 173
Nashville and Northwestern Railroad, 179–80
Neely, James J., 115, 132, 167–68
Neely's Brigade, 134, 166–68
Nelson, William "Bull," 60–61, 274n.30
New Albany, Miss., 94, 154, 161
New Era (gunboat), 120, 123
New York *Sun*, 257
Newbern, Tenn., 1, 8–9, 12–13, 34, 44, 46, 92, 112, 221–22, 231–32, 237, 269n.6, 271n.43, 280n.24
Newbern Blues, 12–13, 15, 233–34
New Orleans, La., 232–34, 254–57
New Orleans, battle of, 264n.3
New Orleans *Daily Picayune*, 257–58
New Orleans Police Department, 258
New Orleans Sanitarium, 256
New Orleans *Times-Democrat*, 257
Newport, Ala., 172, 177
Newsom, John F., 86–88, 96–97, 100, 136, 162, 183, 223, 284n.4
Nixon, George H., 172–74, 186, 192, 199, 203, 206, 258, 297n.23, 300n.24
Northern Cavalry Department (Forrest's Cavalry Department), 99
Nunn, David A., 235–36
Nutt, Leroy M., 87–89

Obion County, Tenn., 13, 81, 89, 116
Obion River, 80, 112
O'Brien, Larry, 210
Odom, Joseph T. E., 211
Ohio River, 55, 67, 275n.8
Ohio troops: 22nd Cav., 82; 53rd Infantry, 38
Okolona, Miss., 92–95, 105, 108, 137, 154–55, 165–66

Okolona, battle of, 105–6, 139
Old Carrollville, Miss., 140
Old Town Creek, engagement at, 160–62
Olive Branch (steamer), 125
Olmstead, Charles H., 213
Otey, William Mercer, 108, 145
Outlaw, Drew A., 14, 36, 43, 97
Overall's Creek, engagement at, 206
Owens, Mr., 25
Owen's Crossroads, battle of, 203
Oxford, Miss., 44, 79, 93, 98, 102, 104–5, 166, 168, 170, 297n.11

Pacific Methodist Conference, 3, 238
Paducah, Ky., 18, 26, 81, 85, 108, 111–12, 116–17, 184
Paine, Eleazer A., 205–6, 304n.3
Panic of 1873, 237
Panola, Miss., 102, 105, 109, 166, 168
Paris, Ky., 65
Paris, Tenn., 57, 179–82, 185
Paris Landing, 182–83, 185
Parker's Crossroads, battle of, 75
Parker, Daniel E., 265n.9
Parks, Andrew S., 14
Parks, Hamilton, Jr., 249, 254, 257
Parrish, William, 22
PeeDee Creek, 4,
Pelham, Tenn., 73
Pemberton, John C., 81, 86
Pensacola, Fla., 169
Perryville, Ky., 69
Perryville, Tenn., 75, 109, 190
Peters, George B. (home), 200
Petersburg, Tenn., 203
Pickett, Edward, 31
Pikeville, Miss., 165
Pillow, Gideon J., 12–13, 15–20, 22–24, 26–27, 29–32, 38, 44, 46, 79, 82–83, 85–87, 102, 167, 224, 259, 265n.8, 267n.33, 277n.20
Pinson's Hill, 154
Pittsburg Landing, 36–37, 190
Platte Valley (steamer), 127
Pocahontas, Miss., 94, 153
Polk, Eva B. (Mrs. Marshall T.), 267n.33
Polk, James K., 7
Polk, Leonidas, 17–19, 22, 25–26, 29–30, 32–33, 36, 40, 42–44, 46–48, 50–51, 69, 73, 75, 77–79, 81, 86, 99, 105, 107, 116, 133–35, 224, 259, 267n.33
Polk's Corps (Wing), 36–37, 68, 70, 73, 76, 79
Polk, Marshall Tate, 267n.33
Polk, Sarah Childress, 7
Pollard, Ala., 49
Pond, Edward B., 247, 312n.24
Pontotoc, Miss., 146, 154–55, 166, 170
Port Hudson, Miss., 107
Porter, Judith Clark,
Porter, William H., 101, 147
Prairie Mound, Miss., 154
Prentiss, Benjamin M., 40
Price, Sterling, 101
Prince, Tom, 148
Proclamation of Pardon and Amnesty, 232
Provisional Army of Tennessee, 12, 16, 79, 265n.8
Pulaski, Tenn., 172, 174–75, 177, 192, 194, 213, 215
Purdy, Tenn., 82, 91, 132, 138, 180
Puryear, G. J., 155

Reivers, Scottish Border, 4, 116
Reynoldsburg Island, 187
Rice, George, 40
Richardson, Dr., 44
Richardson, Robert V., 82, 87, 93, 96, 100, 282n.4
Richardson, Thomas E., 77, 101, 277n.11, 279n.12
Richland Creek, 174, 214–15
Richmond, Ky., 53–55, 59–64
Richmond, Ky., battle of, 56–61
Rienzi, Miss., 132, 137–39
Ripley, Miss., 147–48, 153
Rockcastle Creek, 53–55
Roddey, Philip D., 93, 136–37, 139, 158, 162, 170, 224–25, 228
Roddey's Division, 153, 157
Rogers' Gap, 52, 54, 273n.9
Rome, Ga., 90, 92
Rosecrans, William S., 89
Ross, Lawrence S. "Sul," 94, 192, 223
Rosser, James N., 22
Rousseau, Lovell H., 206–9
Rucker, Edmund W., 131, 139, 165, 180, 185, 190, 253–54, 258, 298n.4

Rucker's Brigade, 134, 140, 142, 147, 161, 168, 170, 190
Rudder, J. W., 265n.9
Ruddles Mills, Ky., 54, 66
Ruggles, Daniel, 37
Russell, A. A., 279n.17
Russell, Fannie I. January (Mrs. R. M.), 15
Russell, James,
Russell, John Cowan, 15, 237, 266n.17
Russell, Mary Cowan (Mrs. James), 266n.17
Russell, Milton, 279n.17
Russell, Robert Milton, x, 14–16, 19, 26, 30, 38, 40, 42, 45, 75, 88–89, 94–95, 99–101, 106, 118, 124, 136, 143, 162, 183, 192, 198, 223, 227, 237, 242, 245, 247, 249, 259, 266n.17, 279n.17
Russell's Brigade, 16, 19, 24, 31, 36–38, 40–42, 44
Russell, William, 242, 245
Russellville (Russell's Valley), Ala., 89–91, 136–37, 280n.18
Rutherford Creek, 212
Ryan, Frank T., 61

Sacramento, Calif., 240
St. Louis, Mo., 232–33
St. Paul's Methodist Church, 249
Sale, T. Sanders, 159, 167–68
Salem, Miss., 137, 146–47, 161
Saltillo, Miss., 148, 154
Sampson, Franc "Frank," 77
Sampson, Isaac, 232
San Francisco, Calif., 240, 245
San Francisco *Chronicle*, 257
San Joachin Valley, 245
Sanger Cemetery District, 243
Saulsbury, Tenn., 151
Schofield, John McA., 192, 194–95, 198, 200, 202–3, 276n.20
Scott, John S., 53, 60–61
Scott, Winfield, 26
Scott, William L., 272n.5
Scottsville, Ala., 227
Seay, George E., 162
Selma, Ala., 92, 224–26, 228–29
Senatobia Creek, 98
Senatobia, Miss., 167
Sequatchie Valley, 73
Shacklett, Absalom R., 214

Shane, James, 233
Shane, Bell and Company, 233
Shaw, William J., 119
Shearon, Thomas R., 76
Shelby County, Tenn., 63, 80
Shelby, Isaac, 284n.6
Shelbyville, Ky., 54, 68
Shelbyville, Tenn., 76–83, 86, 277n.20
Sherman, William T., 42, 81, 94, 104, 107, 115, 132, 135–37, 151–52, 162, 169, 174, 176–77, 179, 245–46
Shiloh, battle of, 36–43, 46
Shoal Creek, 172, 176, 190, 192
Silver Cloud (steamer), 127
Sinclair, R. G., 265n.9
Skeffington (Skifington), John, 96, 233, 281n.33
Smiley, Mrs., 205, 304n.1
Smith, Andrew J., 136, 151–57, 160–62, 166–68, 193, 297n.11
Smith, Pleasant A., 282n.9
Smith, Preston "Pres," 24, 43, 45–46, 49–50, 56–62, 69–70, 81, 90, 259, 272n.5, 273n.10
(Preston) Smith's Brigade, 44, 46, 52, 58, 61, 67–68, 72–74, 81, 90
Smith, William Sooy, 104–6, 225
Southern Cavalry Department, 99
Southern Cross Drill, 253
Southern Methodist Ladies Aid Society, 245
Spanish Fort, 222
Spring Hill, Tenn., 45, 80, 175, 195, 197–99, 204, 212, 277n.19
Spring Hill, battle of, 198–200
Springdale, Miss., 168
Stainback, G. T., 252
Stanford, Thomas J., 39
Starkville, Miss., 105, 107
Stark, Mrs., 105
Starke, Peter Burwell, 229
State (Tenn.) Female College, 167
Station Camp Creek Valley, Tenn., 2–3, 6
Steenburn, Donald H., 183
Stephens's Brigade, 36
Stevenson, Ala., 151
Stevenson, Carter L., 52, 211
Stewart, Alexander P., 38–39, 42
Stewart's Brigade, 36–37
Stewart's Corps, 201

Stewart, Francis M., 281n.33, 297n.26
Stewart's Creek, 74
Stinnett, James, 122
Stones River,
Stones River (Murfreesboro, 1862 battle of, 75–76
Strother's Meeting House, 3,
Streight, Abel D., 80, 279n.17
Strahl, Otho F., 83
Sturgis, Samuel D., 136–37, 139–40, 142, 145, 153
Sugar Creek, engagement at, 215–16
Sulphur Springs Trestle, 173
Sumner County, Tenn., 2–3, 5–8, 11, 70, 100, 105, 206, 233, 237, 240–41, 243, 250, 252, 254–55
Sumterville, Ala., 230

Tallahatchie River, 94, 153, 166, 168
Tansil, Egbert E., 98
Tappan, James C., 19, 21–22, 27
Taylor, Richard, 169, 179–80, 189, 219, 223, 229
Taylor, William F., 214
Tennessee and Alabama Railroad, 173, 175, 177
Tennessee Methodist Conference, 3
Tennessee River, 8, 18, 32, 39, 50, 73, 75, 81, 85–86, 88–89, 108, 111–12, 115–16, 136, 170–72, 176–77, 179, 182–83, 189–90, 192, 216, 224
Tennessee State Militia, 265n.9
Tennessee troops (CSA): Bankhead's Btry., 36, 272n.5; Hudson's Btry., 157, 168, 173, 182; Morton's Btry., 98, 136–37, 144–45, 159, 166, 168, 182, 206, 208, 216; Rice's Btry., 134, 136–37, 145, 159, 161, 168, 186, 223; Thrall's Btry., 134, 168, 186–87; Walton's Btry., 118, 123, 182; McDonald's Cav. Battalion, 96, 108, 110; 2nd (22nd) Cav., 124, 153, 158–59, 168, 176, 196, 210, 287n.28; 7th Cav., 93, 108, 110, 214; 9th Cav., 234; 14th Cav., 91; 10th Cav., 223; 11th Cav., 223; 15th Cav., 92, 100, 173, 281n.33; 16th Cav.(Wilson's), 126, 142, 153, 161, 173, 176, 227, 255; 19th (18th) Cav. (Newsom's), 100, 132, 136, 138, 142–43, 149, 154, 167–68, 194, 210, 230, 284n.4; 20th (Russell's) Cav., 89, 92, 100, 102, 106, 118, 120, 124, 134, 142, 154–55, 167, 271n.43, 282n.5; 21st (16th) Cav. (Wilson's), 87, 100, 120, 122, 167–68; 22d (2d) Cav., 100, 105, 120; 22nd (Nixon's) Cav., 172–73, 186, 210; 2d Infantry, 55; 4th Infantry, 13, 25, 39; 5th Infantry, 86; 6th Infantry, 87; 7th Infantry, 100; 9th Infantry, 87; 12th Infantry, x, 13–17, 19–22, 24, 26, 29–33, 36–44, 46, 48–49, 90, 142, 266n.21; 12/22d (Cons.) Infantry, 44, 46, 47, 48, 50–52, 55, 58, 60–61, 63–65, 67, 70, 72–74, 101, 134; 12/47th (Cons.) Infantry, 74–78, 80, 83, 89, 101; 13th Infantry, 13, 16, 36, 38–39, 42, 46, 51, 59–61, 63, 72, 138; 20th Infantry, 31; 21st Infantry, 16; 22nd Infantry, 13, 31, 36, 38, 40, 81, 101, 134, 271n.34; 31st Infantry, 98; 33rd Infantry, 38, 224; 35th Infantry, 297n.23; 47th Infantry, 32, 46, 51, 60, 63, 74, 77, 134, 265n.11, 274n.27; 48th Infantry, 297n.23; 52nd Infantry, 87; 154th Sr. Infantry, 45–46, 51, 57–58, 60, 63, 78, 272n.5
Tennessee troops (USA): 2nd U.S. Heavy Artillery, (Colored), 117; 2nd U.S. Light Artillery (Colored), 117; 6th Cav., 82; 7th Cav., 82; 13th Cav., 285n.7; 14th Cav. Battalion, 82, 117
Tensas River, 49
Tensas Station, 49
Terry, F. G., 140–41
Texas troops: 9th Infantry, 69
Thomas, George H., 32, 174, 177, 209–10, 216
Thomas, William Price, 2,
Thompson, Albert P., 108, 111, 156, 284n.4
Thompson Station, Tenn., 191, 200
Tibbee Station, Miss., 107–8
Tishomingo Creek, 140, 145, 291n.28
Todd, William H., 265n.9
Traver, Calif., 247
Treaty of Tecumseh, 284n.6
Trenton, Tenn., 13, 15, 33, 44, 75, 88, 91, 95, 112, 221–22, 231, 237, 269n.2, 280n.24
Trigg, Sam, 74
Trion, Ala., 226
Tulare County, Calif., 244–46
Tullahoma, Tenn., 73, 75, 86, 175

Tupelo, Miss., 26, 44, 46–48, 91, 108, 132, 136–39, 141, 148, 151, 153, 155–56, 160–61, 169, 220
Tuscaloosa, Ala, 225–27, 229
Tuscumbia, Ala., 86, 89, 170, 217
Tuscumbia River, 138
Twenty-Mile Creek, 137
Tyler, H. A., 142, 144, 223

Undine (gunboat), 184–87, 299n.19,
Union City, Tenn., 15–17, 32, 81, 85, 88, 110, 117, 269n.2, 285n.7
United Confederate Veterans (UCV), 247, 249
United Confederate Veterans (California Brigade), 247
United Confederate Veterans (Fresno Camp), 250
United Confederate Veterans (Pacific Division), 247, 255
United Confederate Veterans (Sterling Price Camp), 247
United States Military Academy, 14
United States troops: 2nd West Tennessee Infantry (African Descent), 88; 5th Infantry, 15; 6th U. S. Colored Heavy Artillery, 117; First Brigade, U.S. Colored Troops, 157; XVI Corps, 151; XVII Corps, 151

Van Dorn, Earl, 79–80
Vaughan, Alfred J., 30, 38, 59, 61, 72
Venus (transport), 184–85, 300n.27
Verona, Miss., 146, 153, 155, 160, 169–70, 223
Versailles, Ky., 54, 66
Vicksburg, Miss., 46, 85, 86, 101, 107, 135, 286n.14
Visalia, Calif., 244–48
Visalia Times Delta, 248
Volunteer and Conscript Bureau (Army of Tennessee), 79, 82, 85
Volunteer and Conscript Bureau (CSA), 86, 102

Wade, William B., 168
Walden's Ridge, 73
Walker, Lawrence, 293n.51
Walton, Isaac Henry, 310n.10
Walton, John B., 310n.10
Walton, Lorana Spears, 310n.10

Walton, Minerva W. C. (Mrs. John B.), 310n.10
Walton, Sarah Walker, 293n.51
Walton, Tyree Harris "Tack," 310n.10
Ward, Mr., 66
Waynesboro, Tenn., 45
Walker, J. Knox, 18
Walker, W. M., 26
Walthall, Edward Cary, 213, 215–16
Walton Family, 6
Walton, Edgar, 239, 244
Walton, Edwin S., 118, 173, 182, 184
Walton, Isaac Alexander, 243
Walton, Isaac Henry "Ike," 234, 239, 241–42
Walton, John, 237
Walton, Josiah, 3–5, 7–8, 11, 264n.3
Walton, Josiah, 243
Walton, Sallie Bell (Mrs. Isaac H.), 234, 239, 241
Walton, Tyree Harris, 14, 234
Walton's Campground, 3,
Walton Road, 3
Washburn, Cadwallader C., 167–68
Watkins, William M., 274n.27
Weakley County, Tenn., 89
West Point, Ga., 49
West Point, Miss., 223
Westbrook, John R., 44, 271n.43
Wheeler, Joseph, 74, 170, 173, 253, 271n.4
Whitney, Josian D., 15
White's Farm (Rogersville), battle of, 59
White, Raleigh R., 198
Willard, D. B., 195, 203
William Glenn & Sons, 234–35
Williams, Sue, 13
Williamson, James A., 273n.10
Williamson, John A., 97
Wilson's Pike, Wilson's Cross (Owen's Crossroads), 304n.40
Wilson (slave), 212
Wilson, Andrew N., 86–88, 96, 100, 110, 120, 137, 143–44, 149, 155, 161–62, 177, 183, 198, 202, 216, 227, 258
Wilson, James H., 193–94, 196–97, 206, 211, 219–20, 224–26, 229
Winchester, Tenn., 83
Wingo, Thomas R., 282n.9
Winstead Hill, 201
Wisdom, Dew W., 96, 108, 138, 144, 149, 154–55, 162

Withers, Jones M., 76–77
Witherspoon, J. G., 230
Wolf Creek, 137
Wolf River, 97–98, 131, 147, 151
Wolford, Frank, 71–72, 276n.20
Womack, D. M., 282n.9
Wood, J. W., 265n.9
Wyatt, Josiah N. "Nick," 14, 43–44, 47, 76, 101, 237

Wyatt, Miss., encounter at, 105, 109
Wyeth, Dr. John A., 80, 90, 128–29, 161, 288n.35
Wyse, T. B., 265n.9

Yazoo River, 104

Zacona River, 168
Zarring, Lemuel, 182, 184
Zollicoffer, Felix, 32

www.ingramcontent.com/pod-product-compliance
Lightning Source LLC
Chambersburg PA
CBHW030302080526
44584CB00012B/407